Europe, Globalization and the Lisbon Agenda

Europe, Globalization and the Lisbon Agenda

Edited by

Maria João Rodrigues

Professor, IEE-ULB – Institute for European Studies, Université Libre de Bruxelles and Special Advisor to the European Commission

Sponsored by the Calouste Gulbenkian Foundation

Edward Elgar

Cheltenham, UK • Northampton, MA, USA

Published by
Edward Elgar Publishing Limited
The Lypiatts
15 Lansdown Road
Cheltenham
Glos GL50 2JA
UK

Edward Elgar Publishing, Inc.
William Pratt House
9 Dewey Court
Northampton
Massachusetts 01060
USA

A catalogue record for this book
is available from the British Library

Library of Congress Control Number: 2008939768

PEFC
PEFC/16-33-111
CATG-PEFC-052
www.pefc.org

ISBN   978 1 84844 196 5 (cased)
        978 1 84844 199 6 (paperback)

Printed and bound in Great Britain by MPG Books Ltd, Bodmin, Cornwall

Contents

PART II THE EUROPEAN LISBON AGENDA AND NATIONAL DIVERSITY

PART III THE EXTERNAL DIMENSION OF THE LISBON AGENDA

Contributors

Iain Begg
Professorial Research Fellow at the European Institute of the London School of Economics and Political Science (LSE), UK and Visiting Professor at the University of Paris I, France.

Jos Berghman
Professor of Social Policy at the Faculty of Social Sciences, Catholic University of Leuven, Belgium; Director of the International Master Programme in Social Policy Analysis (IMPALLA); President of the European Institute of Social Security and Chairman of the Supervisory Board of the Belgian social security system.

Robert Boyer
Economist at the Centre for Economic Research and its Applications (CEBREMAP), Paris; Senior Researcher at the French National Centre for Scientific Research (CNRS) and Professor at the School for Advanced Studies in Social Sciences (EHESS), Paris.

Benjamin Coriat
Professor of Economics at the University of Paris XIII and at CEPN (Centre de Recherche de l'Université Paris Nord), a Research Unit associated with the French National Centre for Scientific Research (CNRS) and Director of the research team on Institutions, Innovations and Economic Development.

Wolfgang Drechsler
Professor and Chair of Governance, Tallinn University of Technology, Estonia, and co-director of the Technology Governance graduate programme; former Advisor for Administrative Organization to the President of Estonia; former Executive Secretary for the German Council of Science and Humanities; American Political Science Association (APSA) Congressional Fellow and Senior Legislative Analyst in the United States Congress.

Janine Goetschy
Senior Research Fellow at the French National Centre for Scientific Research (CNRS); Member of the Institutional and Historical Dynamics of Economics (IDHE), associated with the University of Paris X Nanterre

and Lecturer at the Institute of European Studies, Université Libre de Bruxelles (IEE-ULB).

Bengt-Åke Lundvall
Professor of Economics, Aalborg University, Denmark; Special Invited Professor at Sciences Po, Paris and former Deputy Director of the OECD Directorate for Science, Technology and Industry.

Pier Carlo Padoan
Deputy Secretary-General of the Organisation for Economic Co-operation and Development (OECD); Professor of Economics at University of Rome La Sapienza (on leave); former Director of the Fondazione Italianieuropei and former Executive Director for Italy at the International Monetary Fund (IMF).

Maria João Rodrigues
Special Advisor to the European Commission; involved in the development of the Lisbon Agenda since the beginning; Professor of European Economic Policies at the Institute of European Studies, Université Libre de Bruxelles (IEE-ULB) and at the Lisbon University Institute (ISCTE); former Minister of Employment in Portugal and former President of the European Commission's Advisory Group for Social Sciences.

Luc Soete
Professor of International Economic Relations, Faculty of Economics and Business Administration, University of Maastricht and Director of Maastricht Economic and Social Research and Training Centre on Innovation and Technology (UNU-MERIT).

Mario Telò
President of the IEE-ULB; Jean Monnet Professor of International Relations, IEE-ULB and Member of the Royal Academy of Sciences, Belgium.

Ádám Török
Professor of Economics at the University of Pannonia, Veszprém; Director of the Network Research Group on Regional Innovation and Development Studies, Hungarian Academy of Sciences and former Chairman of the National Committee on Technological Development of the Hungarian Government.

Preface

The Lisbon Agenda is Europe's attempt to address the challenges posed by an evolving global economy. An ambitious choice was made in 2000 to promote a highly competitive knowledge and innovation-based economy to ensure sustainable growth, more and better jobs, social cohesion and respect for the environment. What is specific to the path adopted by Europe is not the prioritization of a knowledge-intensive economy – which is now found in many other regions of the world; it is, rather, the ambition to combine that pursuit with other features, to encourage balanced and sustainable development in accordance with European values. It is this particular combination of goals that is Europe's contribution to bringing about a richer experience of prosperity.

The Lisbon Agenda, however, involves deep transformations of Europe's economies and societies. What is at stake is not just the shift towards a high-knowledge and low-carbon economy, but the reform of a broad range of institutions, from universities, social protection and employment services, to public administration, financial systems and businesses as well. Since its inception, the Lisbon Agenda has redirected priorities in a wide range of policies, including information society, research, innovation, education, employment, social protection, environmental, single market, competition and fiscal policies. New initiatives have been launched at the European level, and several reforms are under way at the national level, albeit with great variations across Member States. More recently, the implications of the Lisbon Agenda for the financial and institutional instruments of the Union and for European Union (EU) external action have been recognized. Furthermore, the recently adopted Lisbon Treaty can provide a new framework for the implementation of the Lisbon Agenda. However, at the time of writing its ratification was still not completed.

A permanent interaction between the European agenda and the research agenda underpins these policy developments. This book is designed to illustrate how that interaction works. It presents the outcome of a dialogue between policy-making and academic perspectives, which was organized around four thematic workshops held between 2006 and 2008, in Brussels and in Lisbon. The book is organized according to the four major themes and the structure of discussions at these workshops. Thus, each section begins with a key issues chapter which adopts a policy-making perspective, is followed by 'reply' chapters prepared by renowned academics, and concludes with a chapter building on the debates held at each workshop. The four themes focus on strategic issues for the design and implementation of the Lisbon Agenda. They are: the development of the Lisbon Agenda at the European level; the Lisbon Agenda and national diversity; the external dimension of the Lisbon Agenda; and the Lisbon Agenda and European governance.

The Introduction (and Conclusion) to the book offer a narrative history of and examine the future prospects of the Lisbon Agenda. Relevant official documents are provided in the Appendices. These choices reflect my personal experience as a policy advisor for the Lisbon Agenda throughout its existence, in the European Commission and, more particularly, during the three presidencies of the European Union charged with defining the Lisbon Agenda (2000), undertaking its mid-term review (2005), and preparing the new cycle for 2008–10 (2007). Between 2002 and 2006, when I chaired the advisory group for the social sciences of the European Commission, there was also a broad exchange of views with the European academic community about the Lisbon Agenda.

The authors of this book have been major sources of inspiration for the Lisbon Agenda and have been very active in providing new contributions for its development, most of them since the launch of the Agenda. This 'Lisbon Agenda group', then, is one of the manifestations of the broader intellectual movement that extends throughout Europe and beyond, that has searched for new development models and explored paradigm shifts, maintaining an interdisciplinary, global and long-term approach in the analysis of the institutional framework of economies, combining new key concepts such as growth regime, knowledge economy, learning and innovation, welfare regime, sustainable development, multilevel governance and global order.

This book is also the outcome of many debates and conferences held across Europe and beyond, and of institutional meetings held within governments, the European Commission, the EU Council of Ministers, the European Parliament, the European Economic and Social Committee, the Committee of Regions and the European Council. As I was involved in this process from the start, it is impossible to acknowledge here the thousands of people I have met to discuss different aspects of this Agenda. Policymakers, scholars and different civil society actors have contributed to implement and develop this Agenda in what was a very creative process. It is to them that I want to express all my gratitude, even if the views expressed here can only be attributed to the authors of these chapters.

A final word of gratitude is due to Patrícia Cadeiras, Isabel Cernich, Sílvia José, Carina Ferreira, Bruno Martins and Carla Sorneta for all the work they did to develop this project, and to Alexandra Barahona de Brito for her work revising and preparing this book for publication; to Mario Telò as President of the Institute of European Studies of the Université Libre de Bruxelles (IEE-ULB), João Ferreira de Almeida, President the Lisbon University Institute (ISCTE), Álvaro de Vasconcelos, President of the Institute for International and Strategic Studies (IEEI), the institute that provided direct support for this undertaking. My final word of gratitude goes to João Caraça, as Director of the Science Department of the Calouste Gulbenkian Foundation, which has sponsored all the workshops of this project.

Maria João Rodrigues

Abbreviations

ACP	Africa, Caribbean and Pacific
APEC	Asia-Pacific Economic Cooperation
ASEAN	Association of South East Asian Nations
ASEM	Asia–Europe Meeting
BEPA	Bureau of European Policy Advisors
BEPGs	broad economic policy guidelines
BERD	business expenditure on research and development
BRIC	Brazil, Russia, India, China
BRs	Baltic republics
CAP	Common Agricultural Policy
CEECs	Central and Eastern European countries
CEPII	Centre d`études Prospectives et d`informations internationales
CFSP	Common Foreign and Security Policy
CIP	Competitiveness and Innovation Programme
CLP	Community Lisbon Programme
CLS	Core Labour Standards
COMESA	Common Market for Eastern and Southern Africa
CSR	corporate social responsibility
CT	Constitutional Treaty
DAC	Development Assistance Committee (of the OECD)
DG	directorate-general
DYNACOM	Dynamic Competences and Long-Term Growth of the Firms
EAC	Euro Area Council
EC	European Community
ECB	European Central Bank
DG ECFIN	Directorate-General for Economic and Financial Affairs
Ecofin	Economic and Financial Affairs Council
ECOSOC	Economic and Social Council (of the United Nations)
ECOWAS	Economic Community of West African States
EES	European Employment Strategy
EIB	European Investment Bank
EIF	European Investment Fund
EIT	European Institute of Technology

EMSU	Economic and Monetary Social Union
EMU	Economic and Monetary Union
EP	European Parliament
EPE	Energy Policy for Europe
EQF	European Qualifications Framework
EQVET	European Qualifications for Vocational Education and Training
ERA-Net	European Research Area Net
ERC	European Research Council
ERDF	European Regional Development Fund
ESF	European Social Fund
ESM	European Social Model
ESP	European Stability Programme
ESSY	European Sectoral Systems of Innovation
ETUC	European Trade Union Confederation
EU	European Union
FDI	foreign direct investment
FP	framework programme
FMN	foreign multinational
FTAA	Free Trade Area of the Americas
GAC	General Affairs Council
GDP	gross domestic product
GERD	gross expenditure on research and development
GNP	gross national product
GQFR	Good Quality Finance Rule
GSP	generalized system of preferences
IBSA	India, Brazil, South Africa
ICT	information and communication technologies
IFI	international finance institution
IGC	intergovernmental conference
ILO	International Labour Organization
IMF	International Monetary Fund
IP	intellectual property
IPR	intellectual property rights
IT	information technology
M&A	mergers and acquisitions
Mercosur	Southern Common Market
MNC	multinational corporation
NAIRU	non-accelerating inflation rate of unemployment
NAMA	non-agriculture manufacturing
NAP	national action programmes
NGO	non-governmental organization

NMCs	New Member Countries
NPM	new public management
NRP	national reform programmes
NSRF	national strategic reference frameworks
NWS	neo-Weberian state
OECD	Organisation for Economic Co-operation and Development
OMC	open method of coordination
PISA	Programme for International Student Assessment
PPP	public–private partnerships
PROGRESS	Community Programme for Employment and Social Solidarity
QMV	qualified majority voting
R&D	research and development
RG	European Regional Policy
RTD	research and technological development
SAARC	South Asian Association for Regional Cooperation
SADC	South African Development Community
SCP	stability and convergence programmes
SDS	Sustainable Development Strategy
SEZ	special economic zone
SGP	Stability and Growth Pact
SMEs	small and medium-sized enterprises
SOE	state-owned enterprise
SPSI	social protection and social inclusion
TEC	Treaty of the European Community
TENS	trans-European networks
TEU	Treaty of European Union
TFEU	Treaty on Functioning of the European Union
TFP	total factor productivity
TRIPS	Trade Related Aspects of Intellectual Property Rights
TSER	Targeted Socio-Economic Research
TVEs	township and village enterprises
UN	United Nations
UNDP	United Nations Development Programme
VAT	value added tax
VET	vocational education and training
WB	World Bank
WMD	weapons of mass destruction
WTO	World Trade Organization

Europe, globalization and the Lisbon Agenda: an introduction

Maria João Rodrigues

I.1 THE POINT OF DEPARTURE OF THE LISBON STRATEGY

The Lisbon Strategy adopted by the European Council in 2000 was designed to address the following main question: is it possible to update Europe's development strategy so that we can rise to the new challenges resulting from globalization, technological change and population ageing, while preserving European values? In the new emerging paradigm, knowledge and innovation are the main sources both of wealth and divergence between nations, companies and individuals. Europe has been losing ground to the United States, but this does not mean that Europe must follow that model.

The purpose was to define a European path towards the new innovation and knowledge-based economy, taking advantage of distinctive attributes, including the preservation of social cohesion and cultural diversity as well as technological options. A critical step was the establishment of a competitive platform to sustain the European social model, which also had to be renewed.

In order to fulfil this goal, institutional reforms were necessary to tap into the potential of this new paradigm while avoiding the risks of widening the social divide. These reforms included innovation of norms regulating international trade and competition, of social models, and of education systems. Moreover, institutional reforms had to internalize the level of integration in each Member State which had been accomplished through the single market and the single currency. This means that some level of European coordination was required to carry out institutional reforms, while respecting national specificity. A multilevel governance system was needed to permit an interaction between the various levels (namely, the European, national and local).

In order to find an answer to the initial question, an extensive intellectual and political review was undertaken of Europe's political agenda and the

1

main Community policy documents in light of the most up-to-date social science findings. European politicians, top officials, and experts with a broad experience in these fields were involved in this task (Rodrigues, 2002). Their purpose was to ascertain which institutional reforms could change how European societies are currently regulated, so as to pave the way for a new development trajectory geared towards the creation of a knowledge-based economy. But it was necessary for key ideas to result in political decisions and action. The entire Portuguese EU presidency in 2000 was tailored to achieve this goal, throughout its two European councils, 14 councils of ministers, seven ministerial conferences, several sessions of the European Parliament, and a high-level forum grouping the major stakeholders in Europe and the Member States.

It is relevant to recall the exact terms of the new strategic goal and overall strategy defined by the Lisbon European Council on 23–24 March 2000. To quote its Conclusions: 'The Union has today set itself a new strategic goal for the next decade: to become the most competitive and dynamic knowledge-based economy in the world capable of sustainable economic growth with more and better jobs and greater social cohesion.' This quote is important because it clarifies that, contrary to some vulgarizations, the strategic goal defined in Lisbon was not for Europe 'to become the most competitive' (although this was a central objective) but rather to achieve this particular combination of strong competitiveness with the other features mentioned above. So it is by reference to this combination that the European path must be defined, and that Europe can do better than its counterparts, notably the USA. This should have methodological implications for the indicators selected to compare relative performances.

Such a complex goal required a particular strategy, which was defined in the following terms:

> Achieving this goal requires an overall strategy aimed at: preparing the transition to a knowledge-based economy and society by better policies for the information society and R&D [research and development], as well as by stepping up the process of structural reform for competitiveness and innovation and by completing the internal market; modernizing the European social model, investing in people and combating social exclusion; sustaining the healthy economic outlook and favourable growth prospects by applying an appropriate macroeconomic policy mix.

Later on, the Spring European Council of Stockholm in 2001 emphasized the concern with the environment and sustainable development.

The implementation of the Lisbon Strategy should therefore be comprehensive, balanced, based on the synergies, but also focused on clear priorities, and adaptable to the diversity of national situations. One can argue that this seems to be about 'squaring the circle', because there are too many trade-offs between these different objectives. There certainly are difficult trade-offs requiring difficult political choices in the short run, but it is important to learn from some successful cases.

Success often depends on the capacity to overcome a specific trade-off by developing a specific synergy. For instance, it is possible to overcome the trade-offs between macroeconomic stability and growth, by creating some fiscal room for manoeuvre for key public investments to enhance growth potential; between productivity and employment, by fostering innovation in products and services and not just in technological process; between growth and cohesion, by shifting cohesion policies to equip the least favoured individuals and regions with more capabilities; between flexibility and security in the labour market, by negotiating new kinds of 'flexicurity' arrangements; and between growth and environment, by turning sustainable development into new opportunities for investment and growth. These examples show that the successful implementation of the Lisbon Strategy requires a comprehensive approach, with implications for both policies and governance.

I.2   THE LISBON AGENDA

The Lisbon Strategy was also translated into new general orientations for the following policies: information society, research and development, innovation, enterprise, single market, education, employment, social protection, social inclusion, the environment, and transport and telecommunications (see Box I.1).

It is important to keep in mind this list of policies because each has a specific institutional basis in the European Union (EU), as well as a network of specialized people involved in public administration and civil society across all Member States. Over the years that followed, these general orientations were transformed by these key actors into operational instruments, directives, regulations, Community programmes and action plans (see Table I.1) which are often designated as the 'Lisbon Agenda'.

I.3   A SHORT HISTORY OF THE LISBON AGENDA

The Lisbon Agenda was developed to address the evolving challenges posed by a global economy, by progressively adapting several existing policies, institutional and financial instruments to its strategic priorities. The

BOX I.1   THE LISBON AGENDA

A. Elaborating a policy for the information society aimed at improving citizens' standards of living, with concrete applications in the fields of education, public services, electronic commerce, health and urban management. Giving renewed impetus to the spread of information technologies in companies (namely e-commerce and knowledge management tools); establishing the goal of deploying advanced telecommunications networks, and democratizing access to the Internet, on the one hand, and producing content that adds value to Europe's cultural and scientific heritage, on the other.

B. Creating an R&D policy whereby the existing Community programme and national policies converge to create a European research area by networking R&D programmes and institutions.

C. Strongly prioritizing an innovation policy and the creation of a Community patent.

D. Designing an enterprise policy that transcends the existing Community programme, combining it with the coordination of national policies to create better conditions for entrepreneurship – namely administrative simplification, better regulation, access to venture capital or manager training.

E. Promoting economic reforms that target the creation of growth and innovation potential, improve financial markets to support new investments, and complete Europe's internal market by liberalizing the basic sectors while respecting the public service inherent to the European model.

F. Defining new priorities for national education policies (turning schools into open learning centres, providing support for each and every population group, and using the Internet and multimedia; in addition, Europe should adopt a framework of new basic skills and create a European diploma to combat computer illiteracy).

G. Intensifying active employment policies to make lifelong training generally available and expanding employment in services as a significant source of job creation, and improving adaptability and promoting equal opportunities for women and men. The key target of raising Europe's employment rate was adopted to reduce the unemployment rate and to consolidate the sustainability of the social protection systems.

H. Organizing cooperation between Member States to modernize social protection, identifying reforms to address common problems such as matching pension systems with population ageing.

I. Elaborating national plans to take action against all dimensions of social exclusion (including education, health and housing) and meeting the requirements of target groups specific to each national situation.

J. The environmental dimension was added to the economic and social dimensions of the Lisbon Agenda by the European Council of Stockholm in 2001, establishing a comprehensive strategy for sustainable development.

implementation of the Lisbon Strategy went through different phases, its time horizon being 2010.

The first phase focused on: translating the Lisbon European Council conclusions into policy instruments of the European Union, adding the environmental dimension and building on the sustainable development approach; preliminary implementation in the Member States (still very imbalanced from area to area, and from Member State to Member State); introducing the basic mechanisms for implementation (Spring European Council, reorganization of the Council formations and schedules, involvement of the European Parliament and the other European institutions, the social partners and organized civil society at the European level, development of the open method of coordination – OMC – tools); and introducing stronger mechanisms in the new European Constitutional Treaty, which were later retained in the Lisbon Treaty.

The second phase began with the mid-term review in 2005, putting the focus on implementation at the national level, including in the new Member States. This new focus called for stronger interface between the European and the national levels of governance, with implications for the behaviour of the main actors. This phase also served to clarify the financial basis of the implementation of the Lisbon Strategy.

A third phase began after 2007, and has consisted of fine-tuning implementation on the ground, to take into account the final outcome of the new European Treaty, and thus adapt to the new context and to prepare for the period after 2010.

Table I.1   Modes of governance by policy

Policies \ Instruments	Monetary (euro area)	Budget	Internal market	Competitiveness	Industrial
Exclusive EU competence	X			X	
Directives, regulations	X	X	X	X	X
Guidelines	X				X
Common objectives					
EU programmes					X
Reinforced cooperation					
Intergovernmental cooperation					
National reform programmes	X				X
National sectoral programmes					
National budgets	X				
Structural funds					X
European frameworks					

In fact, in 2001 and 2002, the Lisbon Strategy was transformed into an operational agenda by the Commission and the Council, which mobilized several available instruments and developed the OMC in 11 policy fields: from information society, research, innovation and enterprise policy, to education, employment, social protection and environmental policy. This process of policy-making and implementation also involved the other European institutions and stakeholders and their national counterparts. The new Member States were also involved from 2002 onwards. Nevertheless, from the beginning, the implementation has been very unequal in the various Member States and policy fields from the outset.

Innovation	Environment, energy	Research	Education, learning	Employment	Social protection
	X	X		X	X
X	X	X	X	X	
			X		X
X	X	X	X	X	X
X		X			
		X			
X	X	X	X	X	X
	X				X
X		X	X	X	X
X	X	X	X	X	X
			X		

The year 2003 was particularly marked by the debate on the possible connections between the Lisbon Agenda and the new Treaty being prepared by the Convention on the Future of Europe namely: the General Affairs Council, coordination between economic, employment and social policies, the instrument mix in each policy, and the basic tools of the OMC.

In parallel, some cooperation initiatives with partner countries, such as China and Brazil, initiated an exchange of experiences with development agendas, in which the Lisbon Strategy served as a point of reference.

In 2004, since implementation seemed to be hindered by inadequate financial means, there was another debate about the implications of the

Lisbon Strategy for the future Community budget, the priorities for the following generation of Community programmes and structural funds, state aid reform and, last but not least, the reform of the Stability and Growth Pact. In the meantime, the planned mid-term review of the Lisbon Agenda was also prepared.

In 2005, with the mid-term review conducted by the Luxembourg presidency, major decisions were taken to foster the implementation of the Agenda, notably to clarify priorities and launch new political and financial instruments. More specifically, new integrated guidelines were adopted for economic and employment policies, and Member States were invited to turn them into national reform programmes, adapting the Lisbon Strategy to national specificities. A new set of financial instruments was also adopted, comprising the Community budget, the guidelines for structural funds, the rules for state aid and a revised Stability and Growth Pact (the renewed content of the Lisbon Agenda is presented in section I.4 below).

During 2006, the focus was on implementation, involving the creation of new government structures for the Lisbon coordinators, the involvement of more stakeholders at the national level, the mobilization of new financial means, and the development of new policy measures. There was also a stronger political focus on energy and the environment because of increased evidence of climate change.

In 2007, there was a positive trend in terms of growth and net employment creation, but its sustainability depended on more growth potential generated by structural reforms, and on the broader trends in the global economy. In 2008, within the framework of the trio of presidencies (the German, Portuguese and Slovenian), a new cycle of the Lisbon Agenda was launched for the period 2008–10, with a stronger emphasis on the environment and energy, and social cohesion as well as on the external dimension of the Lisbon Strategy. The European Council of March 2008 (see its conclusions in Appendix 2) also defined a mandate to initiate a reflection on the future of the Lisbon Strategy in the post-2010 period.

Several structural reforms are now addressing social protection, health systems, public administration, financial systems, research and education, and labour markets but they are still insufficient and, above all, imbalanced when comparing policy fields and countries. Nevertheless, it is already possible to conclude that the Member States that have been most effective in implementing the kind of reforms outlined in the Lisbon Agenda are also those reaping the most benefits in terms of growth, job creation and sustainable development.

I.4 THE LISBON AGENDA AFTER THE MID-TERM REVIEW

The Lisbon Agenda was reshaped by the mid-term review in 2004–05, under the Luxembourg presidency, in order to provide answers to the main problems which had been identified (Kok, 2004; Sapir, 2004): blurring of the strategic objectives; inflation of priorities and measures; lack of implementation, coordination and participation mechanisms; and lack of financial incentives.

Clarifying Strategic Objectives

The first question related to the relevance of the Strategy itself. Was the Lisbon Strategy still relevant in light of new emerging challenges? Clearly, the global landscape was changing, and the Lisbon Strategy has had to take on board the emergence of new competitive players, as well as more evident population ageing trends. But the Spring European Council under the presidency of Luxembourg concluded that the general approach remained valid and was, indeed, becoming more urgent than before: 'Europe must renew the basis of its competitiveness, increase its growth potential and its productivity and strengthen social cohesion, placing the main emphasis on knowledge, innovation and the optimization of the human capital' (Council 7619/05, § 5). So stepping up the transition to a knowledge-intensive society remained the central priority. Within the more general context of sustainable development principles, there was also an emphasis on the need to improve the synergies between the economic, social and environmental dimensions of the strategy (Council 7619/05). It was concluded that the Strategy should refocus on growth and employment, however, with some implications for the definition of political priorities, as shown below.

Defining Political Priorities

After the mid-term review, the major political priorities of the Lisbon Strategy for growth and jobs were: generating knowledge and innovation as engines of sustainable growth; turning Europe into a more attractive place to invest and work; and creating more and better jobs. To these goals, a further macroeconomic policy strand was added, under the label 'Macroeconomic policies for growth and jobs'. A list of 24 guidelines, the so-called 'broad economic policy guidelines' and the 'employment guidelines', were elaborated to promote these four political priorities based on Treaty-based instruments (see Box I.2, and Council 10667/05 and 10205/05).

BOX I.2   THE LISBON STRATEGY: INTEGRATED GUIDELINES FOR GROWTH AND JOBS

Macroeconomic Policies for Growth and Jobs

1. To secure economic stability for sustainable growth.
2. To safeguard economic and fiscal sustainability as a basis for increased employment.
3. To promote a growth- and employment-orientated and efficient allocation of resources.
4. To ensure that wage developments contribute to macroeconomic stability and growth.
5. To promote greater coherence between macroeconomic, structural and employment policies.
6. To contribute to a dynamic and well-functioning EMU.

Knowledge and Innovation: Engines of Sustainable Growth

7. To increase and improve investment in R&D, in particular by private business.
8. To facilitate all forms of innovation.
9. To facilitate the spread and effective use of ICT, and build a fully inclusive information society.
10. To strengthen the competitive advantages of its industrial base.
11. To encourage the sustainable use of resources, and strengthen the synergies between environmental protection and growth.

Making Europe a More Attractive Place to Invest and Work

12. To extend and deepen the internal market.
13. To ensure open and competitive markets inside and outside Europe, and to reap the benefits of globalization.
14. To create a more competitive business environment and encourage private initiative through better regulation.
15. To promote a more entrepreneurial culture, and create a supportive environment for SMEs.
16. To expand and improve European infrastructure, and complete priority cross-border projects.

More and Better Jobs

17. To implement employment policies aimed at achieving full employment, improving quality and productivity at work, and strengthening social and territorial cohesion.
18. To promote a life-cycle approach to work.
19. To ensure inclusive labour markets, enhance work attractiveness, and make work pay for job-seekers, including disadvantaged people, and the inactive.
20. To improve matching of labour market needs.
21. To promote flexibility combined with employment security, and reduce labour market segmentation, having due regard to the role of the social partners.
22. To ensure employment-friendly labour cost developments and wage-setting mechanisms.
23. To expand and improve investment in human capital.
24. To adapt education and training systems in response to new competence requirements.

Source: Council of the European Union, 10667/05.

Thus, for the first time, the EU had an integrated package of guidelines governing its economic and social policies based on Treaty-based instruments. There was a long process of maturation that made this major political development possible, the latter then advancing because of recognition that better levels of implementation were necessary.

Fostering Implementation

It was in the 1990s that the aim of defining coordinated guidelines for economic and social policies emerged in the EU, with the preparation of economic and monetary union. During the Lisbon European Council in 2000, political conditions were still not ripe for the adoption of an economic and social strategy based on more compulsory instruments such as Treaty-based guidelines. This is what led to the creation of the new open method of coordination (OMC) (Council SN 100/00 and Presidency 9088/00), which is based on: the identification of common objectives or guidelines; their translation into national policies, adapted to national specificities; and the creation of a monitoring process based on common indicators, the identification of best practices, and peer review. Despite some, shortcomings, including bureaucratization and simplistic benchmarking, the development of this method in 11 policy fields after 2000 was instrumental in building the necessary consensus about the strategic challenges that Europe faced, and the key reforms that it had to undertake. In 2005, debate about the implementation and coordination gap had advanced sufficiently to turn some of the most important 'soft' guidelines into 'hard' Treaty-based guidelines (Council, 10667/05 and 10205/05).

In this way, the OMC has played a role in building a European dimension, instituting a learning process, and promoting some convergence, albeit with consideration for national differences. Has the OMC run its course now? The answer is no (Council 7619/05 § 39 d/ and Commission). The OMC can be used when necessary, allowing the policy-making process to operate on two levels, one more formal and precise than the other, ensuring that there is a necessary political refocusing with implementation.

A second important development regarding instruments for implementation concerns the national reform programmes prepared by the Member States in the autumn of 2005. These programmes set out a comprehensive strategy for the implementation of the integrated guidelines, adapting them to the national context. In addition to outlining political priorities and measures, they also outline the roles that the various stakeholders are to play, the budgetary resources that are needed, including structural funds linked to stability and convergence programmes. It is stipulated that the preparation, implementation and monitoring of national programmes should involve all key political institutions and civil society and, when appropriate, a national coordinator should be appointed. All Member States must present annual follow-up reports, which provide a basis for a general report that the European Commission must present to each Spring European Council.[1]

The Community Lisbon Programme is the final building block for implementation. It brings together for the first time all the regulatory and financing actions and policy developments to be launched at the European level, to ensure the implementation of the Lisbon Strategy for growth and jobs, and organizing them according to the three main above-mentioned priorities (Commission, COM(2005) 330). Some of the key actions it recommends are: support for knowledge and innovation in Europe; reform of state aid policies; better business regulation; the completion of the internal market for services; the completion of an ambitious agreement in the Doha Round; the removal of obstacles to physical, labour and academic mobility; the development of a common approach to economic migration; and support to manage the social consequences of economic restructuring.

While the implementation of the national programmes for growth and jobs requires stronger coordination among government bodies, the

Community Lisbon Programme requires similarly higher levels of coordination by the European Commission and the relevant formations of the Council of Ministers, namely: the Economic and Financial Affairs Council (Ecofin), Employment and Social Affairs, Competitiveness, Education and Environment. As regards the European Parliament (EP), there exists an internal coordination procedure involving the various EP commissions; and national parliaments should consider instituting mechanisms to coordinate their relevant commissions.

Developing Financial Incentives

Financial instruments are also the object of various reforms to align them with the political priorities of the Lisbon Strategy. The Community framework for state aid is being reviewed to promote a more horizontal approach, focusing on research and development (R&D), innovation and human capital; the European Investment Bank (EIB) and the European Investment Fund (EIF) are also deploying new instruments to the strategy for growth and jobs, and were asked to focus specially on the needs of innovative small and medium-sized enterprises (SMEs) in Europe; the Community programmes can also play an important role as catalysts for national programmes for growth and jobs. The Seventh Framework Programme for Research and Technological Development, the Community Programme for Competitiveness and Innovation, and the Community Programme for Lifelong Learning are particularly relevant here. However, the scope of these programmes was limited severely with the final agreement on the Community budget in December 2005, a major debate about this budget being scheduled for 2008. Finally, the Community Strategic Guidelines for the Cohesion Policy proposed by the European Commission were closely aligned with the integrated guidelines for the Lisbon Strategy, covering the three main goals of making Europe and its regions more attractive places to invest and work, of promoting knowledge and innovation for growth, and of creating more and better jobs (Commission, COM(2005) 299).

Beyond this, the Stability and Growth Pact underwent reforms that may be very relevant for the Lisbon Strategy (Council 7619/05). Macroeconomic stability remains a central concern, the limit on public deficits and public debt remains at 3 per cent and 60 per cent as a ratio of gross domestic product (GDP), and procyclical fiscal policies are discouraged, but there is a new emphasis on fostering economic growth and on the sustainability of the public debt in order to deal with demographic trends. Further, the Lisbon goals of reforming social protection systems, and redirecting public expenditure to key investments with growth potential (in

R&D, innovation and human capital), are among the relevant factors to be taken into account when assessing public deficits (either below or above 3 per cent), or when defining adjustment trajectories in the case of the excessive deficit procedure.

I.5   THE INSTITUTIONAL INSTRUMENTS OF THE LISBON PROCESS

The implementation of the Lisbon Agenda has given rise to a political and social process involving, in a progressively organized way, the following institutions and actors: the European Council, in its several annual meetings with a particular relevance for its spring meeting; the Council, in seven of its formations: General Affairs, Ecofin, Competitiveness, Employment, Education, Environment, Energy and Telecommunications; their Council committees and groups, which are also involved; the European Commission, involving 15 out of 27 commissioners and 17 directorates-general, with a smaller group of 'Lisbon' commissioners meeting on a more regular basis; the European Parliament, involving six of its committees; national parliaments, involving at least their European affairs committees, which organize a yearly Lisbon conference with the European Parliament; the European Economic and Social Committee and its Lisbon network of economic and social councils in the Member States that they exist in; the Committee of Regions and its Lisbon platform involving more than a hundred regions; the European confederations of social partners, representing their counterparts at the national level and meeting regularly with the other European institutions in the Tripartite Social Summit; and last but not least, the national governments with the involvement of several ministers and ministries as well as the prime ministers. A horizontal network of top officials is also emerging in all Member States due the role of a Lisbon coordinator, a minister or a top official reporting to a minister or the prime minister.

Beyond this institutional setting, there is a diversified network of civil society organizations in various areas, which in various ways follow and feed into the development of the Lisbon Agenda. Most of them are probably not aware of the European agenda, but only of its translation into concrete measures at the national level. The same happens with many political and media actors at the national level. This explains why the level of 'ownership' remains quite low, albeit with many differences across Member States. Still, quite a large network of civil society leaders across Europe is explicitly connecting the Lisbon Agenda with their regular work.

The Lisbon Treaty can create the institutional conditions for better governance of the Lisbon process, by clarifying Union competences, improving horizontal coordination, and fostering the decision-making process and strengthening its democratic legitimacy. It remains to be seen to what extent this potential will be taken advantage of.

I.6   POLICY ACHIEVEMENTS AND KEY ISSUES

The relaunching of the Lisbon Strategy focused more on national level implementation. Within the institutional framework defined in 2005, the EU Member States have prepared and implemented their national reform programmes. This has been the largest coordinated process of economic reform ever attempted in Europe. The purpose was to adapt a set of common priorities to foster growth and employment to each national context, and to prepare Europe for globalization. As these national programmes show, there are many reforms under way throughout Europe (see Table I.2). But are they heading in the right direction, and do they have the necessary scope?

The central question seems clear: how can Europe develop a knowledge-intensive and low-carbon economy and grow faster, creating more and better jobs and sustaining social inclusion, in today's globalized economy? We should acknowledge that there is a real problem here, because Europe is currently the economic bloc with the lowest potential growth. The answer also seems simple: Europe needs to explore new markets, increase competitiveness by investing in knowledge, as well as expand and train the employed population. From this viewpoint, what conclusions can we draw from the national reform programmes?

As regards new markets, there is the progress resulting from the enlargement and globalization strategies adopted by some European countries and companies. One example is the current race to invest in China or India. However, many other steps need to be taken to reach an agreement in the World Trade Organization (WTO) Doha Round; to develop long-term strategic partnerships with Europe's key external partners; to implement the reached agreement in the services directive; to turn the next generation of structural funds into more powerful tools to enable the less-developed regions to catch up; and to use the eurozone to coordinate more strongly macroeconomic policies for investment and growth.

In terms of competitiveness, what is at stake is the redeployment of European economies to engage in higher added-value activities, whatever the sector, be it biotech, information technologies, business services, automotive, textile or tourism industries. More public and private investment in

Table I.2   The Lisbon Agenda: relative achievements and failures as of 2007

Policy field	(Relative) achievements	(Relative) failures
Information society	• Schools connected with Internet • Public services: access via Internet • Extension of broadband	• Scale in content industries
Research	• European research networks • European research infrastructure • Technology platforms • European Institute of Technology	• Community patent • Mobility of researchers
Innovation	• Joint technology initiatives • Clusters • One stop-shop for start-ups • Galileo	• Interface business-universities • Venture capital
Lifelong learning	• Extension of early-school education • Extension of vocational and technological education	• Modernization of universities • Extension of training for adults
Single market	• Telecommunications • Single sky • Financial services • Services directive • Reducing red tape	• Energy • Portability of pensions • Better regulation
Trade	• Bilateral agreements	• Doha Round
Employment	• Net jobs creation (15 million) • Modernization of employment services • Women employment rate • Restructuring management	• Flexicurity • Employment of young people • Immigration management
Social protection	• Pensions reform	• Active ageing
Social inclusion	• Childcare services	• Poverty rate reduction
Environment	• Environmental awareness • Emissions trade scheme	• Renewable energies

R&D is crucial to step up this transition to a knowledge-intensive economy. This can be achieved with better infrastructure, more training and mobility of researchers, and more fiscal incentives. But this is not enough to turn knowledge into value. What is also missing in many European countries is a more ambitious development of their innovation systems, connecting companies and universities to create promising clusters and partnerships.

European employment policy has another focus now: not only to reduce unemployment, but also to increase the number of employed people, who can thereby contribute to sustaining social protection systems. For this reason, many countries are activating their employment services to make jobs or training proposals, expanding childcare and testing the first measures for active ageing. Nevertheless, something deeper is at stake: the reorganization and coordination of employment, training and social protection policies to support people during their life cycle, at a time when people are making increasingly diverse choices. This will make it easier to introduce more flexibility to the labour market, according to the so-called flexicurity models.

In the meantime, the original stamp of the Lisbon Strategy on the social dimension should remain clear. The best tool to adapt to change is lifelong learning. There is improvement in terms of the rate of workers who can access lifelong learning, or in terms of the share of young people completing secondary education. But, again, there is something broader at stake: building a lifelong learning system with access points in schools, companies and households, providing more tailor-made education and training services. Universities have a particular responsibility to respond to much more diversified demands.

A reorientation of national and European policies seems to be under way, but this needs to go much further and pass another crucial test: redirecting financial means. The recent review of the Stability and Growth Pact will be under scrutiny. Certainly, fiscal consolidation and improved sustainability of social protection systems is at stake; but redirecting public expenditure, tax systems and Structural Funds to the future-oriented priorities of investing in research, innovation and human capital are also crucial issues.

We can draw another conclusion from the review of the national reform programmes: differences in implementation are now very clear when we compare policy fields or Member States. The best general performance in growth, jobs, innovation, social inclusion and the environment seems to be happening in the countries that have implemented this Agenda more consistently. This is something that needs to be debated in each country.

NOTE

1. These programmes were prepared as of November 2005 and are available, together with the European Commission assessment, at: http://europa.eu.int/growthandjobs/index_en. htm.

BIBLIOGRAPHY

Boyer, R. (1998), *The Search for Labour Market Flexibility*, Oxford: Oxford University Press.

Council of the European Union (2000a), *Conclusions of the Lisbon European Council*, SN 100/00, 23–24 March 2000.

Council of the European Union (2000b), *The Ongoing Experience of the Open Method of Co-ordination*, Note of the Portuguese Presidency of the Union, 9088/00, 14 June 2000.

Council of the European Union (2005a), *Conclusions of the Brussels European Council*, 7619/05, 22–23 March 2005.

Council of the European Union (2005b), *Conclusions of the Brussels European Council*, 10255/05, 16–17 June 2005.

Council of the European Union (2005c), *Integrated Guidelines: Broad Economic Policy Guidelines*, 10667/05, 28 June 2005.

Council of the European Union (2005d), *Council Decision on Guidelines for the employment policies of the Member States*, 10205/05, 5 July 2005.

Council of the European Union (2008), *Conclusions of the Brussels European Council*, 7652/08, 13–14 March 2008.

European Commission (2005a), *Cohesion Policy in Support of Growth and Jobs: Community Strategic Guidelines, 2007–2013*, COM(2005) 299 final, 05.07.2005.

European Commission (2005b), *Common Actions for Growth and Employment: The Community Lisbon Programme*, COM(2005) 330 final, 20.07.2005.

Kok, W. (ed.) (2004), *Facing the Challenge: The Lisbon Strategy for Growth and Employment*, Report of the High Level Group, Brussels: European Commission.

Rodrigues, M.J. (ed.) (2000), *International Hearing for the Portuguese Presidency of the European Union*, Centro Cultural de Belém, 3–4 December 1999, Lisbon: Gabinete do Primeiro Ministro.

Rodrigues, M.J. (ed.) (2002), *The New Knowledge Economy in Europe: A Strategy for International Competitiveness and Social Cohesion*, with the collaboration of R. Boyer, M. Castells, G. Esping-Andersen, R. Lindley, B.A. Lundvall, L. Soete, M. Telò and M. Tomlinson, Cheltenham, UK and Northampton, MA, USA: Edward Elgar.

Rodrigues, M.J. (2003), *European Policies for a Knowledge Economy*, Cheltenham, UK and Northampton, MA, USA: Edward Elgar.

Rodrigues, M.J. (ed.) (2004a), *The Lisbon Strategy: A Follow-up for Researchers*, SSHERA Project Final Report, European Commission's Advisory Group on Social Sciences, SSHERA Project, EU 6th Framework Programme RTD.

Rodrigues, M.J. (2004b), 'For the Mid-Term Review of the Lisbon Strategy', Background Paper 4, in M.J. Rodrigues (ed.), *The Lisbon Strategy – a Follow-up for Researchers*, SSHERA Project Final Report, European Commission's Advisory Group on Social Sciences, SSHERA Project, EU 6th Framework Programme RTD.

Rodrigues, M.J., G. Arbix, J.C. Ferraz, S. Fisher, F. Godement, G. Grevi, C. Huang, L. Soete, M. Telò, A. Valladão, A. Vasconcelos, C. Wagner and H. Zhou (eds) (2007), *Developing the External Action of the European Union. New Instruments and New Global Players*, Portuguese Presidency of the European Union, Lisbon: Gabinete do Primeiro Ministro.

Sapir, A. (2004), *An Agenda for a Growing Europe: The Sapir Report*, Oxford: Oxford University Press.

http://www.europa.eu/growthandjobs/.
http://www.mariajoaorodrigues.eu.

See further bibliography in Appendix 4 of this book.

PART I

Developing the Lisbon Agenda at the
European Level

1. On the European innovation policy: key issues for policy-making

Maria João Rodrigues

The aim of the Lisbon Agenda is to prepare Europe for globalization. The knowledge 'triangle', which connects research, innovation and education, is at the heart of this agenda. Its goal is to generate new competitive advantages, which are crucial to sustain the European social model. Innovation gives added value to knowledge, leads to the creation of new products and services, and should become the main engine for smarter growth with more and better jobs. In recent times, innovation policy has undergone important changes, but new momentum is necessary to strengthen it as an engine of growth.

1.1 PREPARING EUROPE FOR GLOBALIZATION

The Community Lisbon Programme is now under way, together with the national reform programmes (NRP), developing the following instruments to prepare Europe for globalization (see Table 1.1): as regards European Union external action, it focuses on developing trade policy, cooperation policy, the external representation of the eurozone and the external dimension of Community policies such as research, transport and environment. As regards the single market, it is promoting the opening of markets in energy and services, the integration of financial services, the construction of trans-European networks and national enforcement of the relevant directives. Where competition policy is concerned, it is enforcing competition rules and reducing and redirecting state aid; as regards research policy, it is supporting the European Research Council (ERC), networks of excellence, infrastructures, human resources and opening up the national programmes; as for innovation policy, it is supporting innovative companies with technical and financial incentives, providing risk capital and developing innovation networks; regarding education, it is promoting a convergence of standards in higher education and vocational education, supporting European mobility and developing lifelong learning strategies.

Table 1.1 Preparing Europe for globalization: the toolbox

Policy areas / Governance levels	External action	Single market	Competition policy	Research policy
International	• WTO • International Monetary Fund (IMF), World Bank (WB) • United Nations Development Programme (UNDP)	• Relationship with third countries		• International cooperation
European	• Trade policy • Cooperation policy • External dimension of community policies	• Products • Network industries • Services • Financial markets • Public procurement • Labour • Trans-European Networks (TENS) • European Regional Development Fund (ERDF)	• State aid • Mergers and acquisitions	• European Research Council • Networks of excellence and integrated projects • Technology platforms • ERA-nets • Infrastructure • Human resources • Coordination of national research policies • ERDF
National	• Bilateral agreements • Cooperation policy	• Enforcement of directives to open the markets • Building trans-European networks	• Enforcing competition policy	• National research programmes • Reforming research institutions
Regional				• Developing research institutions and networks

Policy areas/ Governance levels	Innovation policy (environment, ICTs)	Education and training policies	Employment and social protection
International European	• International cooperation • European networks of innovation support services • European networks of clusters • European networks of innovative regions • Coordination of national innovation policies • Community patent • ERDF	• International cooperation • European mobility and cooperation in high-level education, secondary and basic training and adult education • Convergence process in high-level education and Vocational education and training (VET) • Coordination of national education policies • European Social Fund	• Common labour standards • Labour directives • Coordination of national employment policies • Coordination of national social protection policies • European Social Fund • Globalisation Adjustment Fund
National	• Supporting innovative companies • Developing innovation networks • Providing risk capital • Expending broadband and e-services • Spreading environmental technologies	• National strategies for lifelong learning • Reducing drop-outs • Improving quality standards • Increasing graduates for scientific and technological careers	• Raising employment rates • Adopting employment policies to the life cycle • Promoting flexicurity • Inclusive labour market • Investing in human capital • Ensuring adequate adaptable and sustainable social protection
Regional	• Supporting innovative companies • Developing innovation networks • Providing infrastructure	• Regional strategies for lifelong learning • Reducing drop-outs	• Raising employment rates • Adapting employment policies to the life cycle • Inclusive labour market • Investing in human capital

Finally, as regards employment and social protection policies, it is enforcing basic standards, raising employment levels, improving adaptability, managing industrial restructuring and ensuring that there is adequate, adaptable and sustainable social protection.

This is a quite ambitious agenda, but it is important to underline that there are key uncertainties that continue to hinder full implementation, notably the World Trade Organization (WTO) agreement, the final shape of the services directive, new resources for research, the Community patent and the mix of labour market reforms. In the meantime, the knowledge triangle is becoming stronger as a result of key measures (see Figure 1.1) covering research (the ERC, the technology platforms and Era-nets – European Research Area Nets), innovation (European networks of innovation clusters and the reorganization of innovation-supporting services), and education (the European Institute of Technology – EIT, recent developments with the Bologna process and new proposals to reform European universities).

1.2 DESIGNING A EUROPEAN INNOVATION POLICY

More specifically, innovation policy has undergone significant changes within the European Union (EU) with the 2005 mid-term review of the Lisbon Strategy, which placed greater emphasis on the central role of innovation policy within this general strategy. Thus, the Lisbon Community Programme, which encompasses all the actions taken at European level, includes not only a more ambitious Framework Programme for Research and Technological Development (RTD) but also a Community Programme for Competitiveness and Innovation; the European Investment Bank (EIB) and the European Investment Fund (EIF) were invited to deploy new instruments to support innovation within the framework of their initiative, 'Innovation 2010'; the Community Strategic Guidelines for the Cohesion Policy that addresses regional policy and the next generation of structural funds, are also strongly prioritizing innovation policy; with the recent reform of the Stability and Growth Pact (SGP), the quality of public expenditure is now a greater concern, and Member States are encouraged to redirect state budgets to foster public and private investments in key areas such as research and development (R&D), innovation, education and training; the Community framework for state aid is under review to ensure that it adopts a more horizontal approach, focusing on R&D, innovation and human capital; and, last but not least, there is a similar reform under way of the integrated guidelines for the Lisbon Strategy, which were discussed by various

RESEARCH ←			**EDUCATION AND TRAINING**			**→ INNOVATION**	**LEVELS**
European research agencies	European Research Council	Commission's advisory groups FP7		Technology platforms	European Institute of Technology	European Foresight on Innovation and Skills	**STRATEGIC DIRECTION**
Basic research projects	Networks of excellence	Integrated projects	Marie Curie Fellowships	University advanced projects	Vocational education and training advanced projects	Innovation clusters	**EXCELLENCE PROJECTS**
			MOBILITY INSTRUMENTS				
←			**STRUCTURAL FUNDS PROJECTS**			**→**	**CAPACITY BUILDING PROJECTS**
Research systems reform			Lifelong learning systems reform			Innovation systems reform	**NATIONAL REFORM PROGRAMMES**

Figure 1.1 European instruments to build a knowledge society

formations of the Council of Ministers, and finally endorsed by the June 2005 European Council in order to provide the framework for the implementation of national reform programmes over the following three years.

Taking into account these building blocks, Table 1.2 summarizes the state of the art in the process of creating the European innovation policy. The need to strengthen this process is confirmed by the common approach on innovation recently adopted by the European Commission (COM(2005) 488), as well as by the Spring European Council of March 2006 and its requirement that a comprehensive approach on innovation policy be developed. This only happened in the European Council meetings of October and December 2006, under the Finnish presidency.

1.3　NEW MOMENTUM FOR EUROPE'S INNOVATION POLICY

There is value added to knowledge through innovation, which also generates new products and services, and should become the main engine for smarter growth with more and better jobs. Recently, innovation policy has undergone important changes, but new momentum is necessary to strengthen it as an engine of growth.

New momentum can emerge from a stronger focus on demand and market opportunities, and a more effective linkage between innovation, research, education and job creation. As the Aho Report suggests and as the European Council of March 2006 has pointed out, we need a more comprehensive approach to innovation.

It is necessary to explore and exploit new market opportunities more effectively. Regarding the European internal market, promising areas can be found in health services, pharmaceuticals, tourism, cultural industries, urban renovation, environmental technologies, food safety, fashion, transport, telecommunications, software and manufacturing systems. Opportunities in external markets are even more diverse. The comparative advantages of the European economy suggest that transport, telecommunications, manufacturing systems, pharmaceuticals, environmental technologies, tourism, cultural activities, education and health are particularly relevant.

It is up to business to identify and take advantage of these opportunities, but greater cooperation in trade, public procurement and standardization policies is essential, as research, innovation and education can generate new markets and opportunities for their fuller exploitation. It is possible to turn new market opportunities into new products and services with greater speed if there are more effective innovation mechanisms and more abundant knowledge resources, including research capabilities, a skilled

Table 1.2 Building a European innovation policy

Innovation policy components	National level	European level
Fostering innovation in companies	• Training for innovation management • Business support services for innovation, including support for the modernization of work organization at enterprise level • Promoting learning organizations • Support to innovative start-ups	• Training for innovation management (RG, CIP) • Business support services for innovation (RG, CIP, EIB) • Support to innovative SMEs (EIB, EIF) • Capacity-building is required at regional level to provide the organizational infrastructure capable of delivering business support services
Developing knowledge production	• Increasing the private and public investment in R&D • Training and mobility of more researchers • Education and training for innovation (specialized skills and qualifications) • National policies for lifelong learning	• 7th Framework Programme for RTD • Community Programme for Lifelong Learning • EIB actions for human capital • Support to R&D (RG)
Developing networking for innovation	• Developing clusters, poles of innovation and partnerships for innovation • Supporting joint research by companies and universities	• Supporting clusters, poles of innovation and partnerships for innovation (RG, CIP) • Supporting international transfer of knowledge and the international cooperation between companies (CIP)
Improving the framework conditions for innovation	• Broadband infrastructures • Access to venture and seed capital • Tax incentives for innovation • Intellectual property regime	• Reform of state aid • Public incentives for innovation (RG) • Venture capital schemes (EIF) • Community patent

Table 1.2 (continued)

Innovation policy components	National level	European level
	• Innovation in social dialogue. Some really creative thinking is needed at both national and European levels. A strong role exists for action research	• Innovation in social dialogue
Using demand as a leverage for innovation	• Encouraging public procurement of innovative products and services • Improving quality standards and certification	• European competition policy • European trade policy • Setting standards by single European market directives
Improving governance for innovation	• Council of Ministers for Innovation • Innovation council and board • Lisbon coordinator	• Council of Ministers for Competitiveness

Notes:
RG   European Regional Policy.
CIP Competitiveness and Innovation Programme.
EIB European Investment Bank.
EIF European Investment Fund.

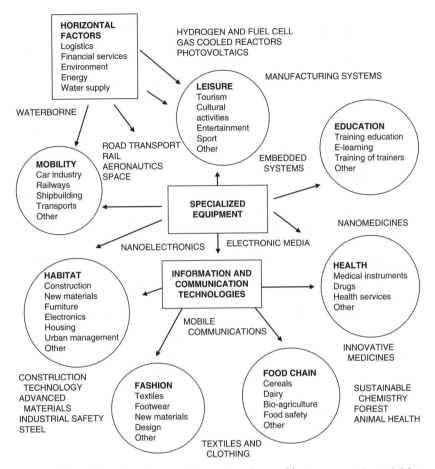

Figure 1.2   EU technology platforms: typology of basic economic activities

labour force, and specialized management expertise. It is necessary to encourage European networks for growth, innovation and jobs. Launching European policies on health, urban renovation or environmental technologies, for instance, would be useful. The Competitiveness Council of Ministers should follow up such initiatives, and more permanent strategic platforms in some sectors should become operational, in order to build a new competitive capacity of the European economy. Some existing mechanisms, such as technology platforms, the Innova clusters, and the sectoral high-level groups, already provide some relevant elements to this end (see Figures 1.2, 1.3 and 1.4). The so-called 'lead markets' initiative aims to go further.

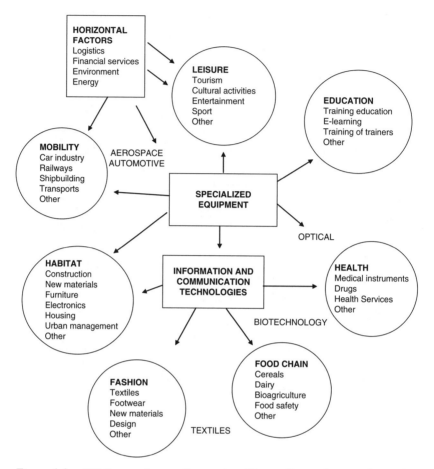

Figure 1.3   EU Europe Innova Innovation Cluster Networks: typology of basic economic activities

1.4   DEVELOPING CLUSTERS AND PARTNERSHIPS FOR INNOVATION

Apart from improving general conditions, European and national policies can also create special catalysts to speed up the innovation process. For example, clusters can develop partnerships for innovation, create jobs and build competence, involving all the relevant actors: companies, research institutions, education and training institutions, and financial bodies.

A cluster can be defined as a set of interconnected companies and knowledge-producing and disseminating institutions that aim to generate new

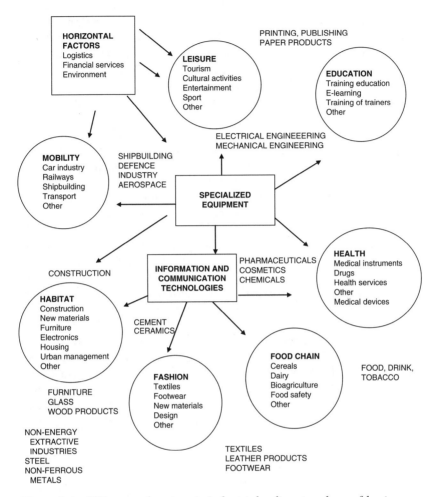

Figure 1.4   EU sectoral actions in industrial policy: typology of basic economic activities

competitive factors and competences, and increase added value. Depending on their main policy purpose, clusters can be identified and developed at different levels: they can be local or regional if the purpose is to strengthen concrete and personal relationships which underpin all clusters; they can be national if the purpose is to improve the framework conditions for clusters spread over a national territory; and they can be European if the purpose is to improve the framework conditions for clusters operating in various Member States.

The main policy objectives for supporting clusters development are to create a self-sustained process of cooperation for competition, bringing together companies and education, research, business support and financial institutions; to identify a critical path to develop a network and key connections to generate added value; to speed up the transition to a knowledge-intensive economy; and to increase comparative advantages in a globalized economy.

The main cluster activities to support as partnerships for innovation are: cooperation between enterprises working on areas of shared interest such as trade, e-business, the organization of the supply chain, and the diffusion of new technologies and certification; the development of joint research programmes; the development of joint training programmes; the development of joint business support services; and support for start-ups.

It is possible to identify a crucial path to develop a concrete cluster by asking how to add more value to already existing competences. For instance, if we take human needs as a broad point of reference to associate clusters of economic activity (see Figure 1.2): leisure can developed with a combination of competences in tourism, cultural activities, sport and entertainment; competences in construction, furniture, electronics and urban management can be combined in order to develop the area of habitat; competences in clothing, footwear, new materials and design can promote fashion; and car industry, transport and logistics competences combined can develop mobility. At the same time, other horizontal competences are required to develop all clusters of activities, such as those involving electro-mechanic equipment, information and communication technologies, and biotechnologies, which can be viewed as horizontal clusters.

1.5 FOSTERING NATIONAL INNOVATION CAPACITY-BUILDING

The crucial process of building innovation capacity begins at the national level. In the context of European-level policy developments, it is necessary to identify new possibilities for national innovation policies, taking the diversity of national settings into account.

The national reform programmes to implement the Lisbon Strategy in 2006–08, complemented by the national strategic reference frameworks for structural funds, offer a unique opportunity to determine national strategies of transition to knowledge-intensive economies, in which innovation policy should play a central role. The key question for each Member State is how to develop this process, adapting the European agenda and, more precisely, the guidelines for growth and jobs and for regional cohesion, to the specificities of the national innovation system. We should emphasize some of these specificities, which justify the need for diverse national strategies to promote a knowledge-intensive economy: one is industrial specialization patterns, the relationship with the global economy and the position in the international division of labour; another is the predominant types of companies and their need 'to climb the ladder of innovation'; and yet another is the institutional framework, particularly as it pertains to corporate organization, education and training systems, research systems, the financial system and labour market regulations. It is also necessary to take into account the quality of infrastructure; educational levels and specific labour force skills; the organization of civil society; and instruments to manage change.

Recent experiences suggest there is a critical path to develop an innovation policy that acts as a catalyst to ensure a transition to a knowledge-intensive economy. This path involves: using the European agenda as leverage to introduce this strategic goal into the national agenda; disseminating a richer concept of innovation, taking into account its different dimensions (technological and organizational innovation affecting processes or products and services, based on science, or in learning-by-doing, using or interacting); highlighting the implications of the innovation system approach for the coordination of policies; defining the areas of priority of an innovation policy and preparing a toolbox of operational measures; opening access to this toolbox in order to support innovative projects and companies, regardless of sector; focusing on some clusters to illustrate the advantages of developing partnerships for innovation, setting up a 'good practice' example that other clusters can emulate; introducing dynamism into national innovation systems, by focusing on the missions of and the interactions between institutions, including labour market flexibility; reforming aspects of public management that affect innovation; disseminating skills for innovation and training innovation managers; and, finally, improving governance for innovation, by improving the internal coordination within government and among relevant public departments, generating public awareness, and by developing specific consultation and participation mechanisms with the civil society.

There is an already rich repository of comparative analysis on innovation systems, which shows that these operate in quite different ways. At times, the main source of innovation is science and technology; in other cases, it is learning-by-doing, learning-by-using and learning-by-interacting, which lead to less codified kinds of knowledge. The purpose of policy-making should be to improve the mix of these different sources of innovation in each concrete situation, developing appropriate instruments to foster the development of each source. Innovation instruments can thus

---

BOX 1.1   INNOVATION POLICY: KEY QUESTIONS

What should be the key components of a comprehensive innovation policy approach?

How can we develop a European dimension in innovation policy?

What kinds of relationships between regional clusters and European global networks?

What should be the European approach to intellectual property rights?

What are the main conditions to develop venture capital?

What are the conditions for a win–win game between knowledge-intensive economies at international level?

How should we reform European and national innovation systems governance?

---

range from joint research projects between companies and universities to disseminating learning organizations within companies. The toolbox of innovation policy instruments should be rich enough to deal with different sources of innovation and to ensure the appropriate policy mix for each concrete situation.

Last, but certainly not least, we must underline the critical problems of improving governance for innovation. These are: coordination between the various relevant public policies (on enterprise, research, education, employment, regional and macroeconomic policies); different forms of networking with civil society; public–private partnerships; developing administrative capacities to foster innovation capacity; and the need to build coalitions for innovation.

BIBLIOGRAPHY

Conceição, P., D.V. Gibson, M.V. Heitor, G. Sirilli and F. Veloso (eds) (2002), *Knowledge for Inclusive Development*, International Series on Technology Policy and Innovation, Westport, CT and London: Quorum Books.

Delapierre, M., P. Moati and E.M. Mouhoud (eds) (2000), *Connaissance et mondialisation*, Paris: Economica.

European Commission (2005), *Implementing the Community Lisbon Programme: More Research and Innovation. Investing for Growth and Employment: A Common Approach*, COM(2005) 488 final, SEC(2005) 1253.

European Commission (2006), *European Innovation Progress Report 2006*,

Trendchart Initiative, Luxembourg: Office for Official Publications of the European Communities.

Fagerberg, F., D.C. Mowery and R.R. Nelson (eds) (2005), *The Oxford Handbook of Innovation*, New York: Oxford University Press.

Foray, D. (2000), *The Economics of Knowledge*, Cambridge, MA: Massachusetts Institute of Technology.

Lorenz, E. and B.A. Lundvall (eds) (2006), *How Europe's Economies Learn: Coordinating Competing Models*, New York: Oxford University Press.

Mundschenk, S., M.H. Stierle, U.S. Schütz and I. Traistaru (eds) (2006), *Competitiveness and Growth in Europe. Lessons and Policy Implications for the Lisbon Strategy*, Cheltenham, UK and Northampton, MA, USA: Edward Elgar.

Rodrigues, M.J. (ed.) (2002), *The New Knowledge Economy in Europe: A Strategy for International Competitiveness and Social Cohesion*, with the collaboration of R. Boyer, M. Castells, G. Esping-Andersen, R. Lindley, B.A. Lundvall, L. Soete, M. Telò and M. Tomlinson, Cheltenham, UK and Northampton, MA, USA: Edward Elgar.

Rodrigues, M.J. (2003), *European Policies for a Knowledge Economy*, Cheltenham, UK and Northampton, MA, USA: Edward Elgar.

Rodrigues, M.J. (2006), 'The European Way to a Knowledge-Intensive Economy: The Lisbon Strategy', in M. Castells and G. Cardoso (eds), *The Network Society: From Knowledge to Policy*, Washington, DC: Johns Hopkins Center for Transatlantic Relations, pp. 405–24.

http://www.europa.eu/growthandjobs/.
http://www.mariajoaorodrigues.eu.

See further bibliography in Appendix 4 of this book.

2. Some reflections on innovation policy

Luc Soete

In my view, the new Lisbon Strategy to prepare Europe for globalization must recognize, in much greater depth than suggested in the chapter by Maria João Rodrigues, that Europe is just one region in the world, and that it has various characteristics that make it particularly vulnerable to emerging global competition. There is increasing recognition of these characteristics, which include: demographic factors (an ageing population with low fertility rates); the failure to take full advantage of the scale offered by European integration; and national governance prerogatives in areas of research and development (R&D), innovation, education and employment, so that there are too many overlapping tools and too little subsidiarity.

The Lisbon initiative constituted a unique attempt to deal with what we can call an institutional failure in the formation of the European Union (EU). Up until that initiative, there were only two areas where Europe dominated national powers institutionally: competition policy and monetary policy (in the case of the eurozone countries). It is arguable that competition policy has an internal dynamic leading to a continuous broadening of its influence: an enlargement of the sphere of market forces, further harmonization of rules (such as the services directive or the European patent proposals). While this is likely to enhance efficiency in general, it has not contributed directly to knowledge accumulation or greater innovation within the EU. On the contrary, competition policy has generated growing legal uncertainty in Member States with respect to their R&D and innovation support policies, which explains the efforts and recent implementation by the Commission of a new State Aid Action Plan.

As regards monetary policy as implemented by the European Central Bank (ECB), the priority has been to address regional diversity in terms of growth and inflationary pressures. Here too, monetary policy has naturally influenced the fiscal policies of Member States. In principle the Stability and Growth Pact (SGP) provides Europe with an instrument to determine national fiscal policies in purely quantitative terms. But, again, there is no inherent incentive here to promote knowledge and innovation as engines of sustainable growth.

Not surprisingly, then, the new Lisbon Agenda on knowledge and innovation capacity-building in Europe is, by and large, dependent on the efforts of Member States, and on their willingness to give domestic priority to all aspects of knowledge accumulation, including innovation and knowledge diffusion, and education and training. In contrast with competition and monetary policy, there is no European knowledge and innovation policy that trumps national policies. Furthermore, the relevant policy areas involve a wide spectrum of fields ranging from research to education policy, with varying degrees of European involvement (as in the case of the proposed European Research Council, ERC). So it is hardly surprising that there has been little progress with the Lisbon Strategy.

Taking Table 1.1 in Chapter 1 as a starting point,[1] the international governance dimension appears to be the least developed, which is not surprising. Undoubtedly, this reflects the currently dominant perception that innovation governance remains primarily a national prerogative and that there are few policy instruments at the international level. But I tend to disagree with this impression. The international knowledge governance dimension has become increasingly important, and will have to become a more prominent part of the Lisbon Agenda. After all, the goal of the Lisbon Agenda is to prepare Europe for globalization.

The main force pushing the European international governance dimension forward is the European business community, particularly large European multinational corporations (MNCs), which have shifted their long-term business strategies from the European to the global arena. In what follows, I outline four areas that seem particularly relevant in this regard.

2.1 EUROPEAN DEPENDENCE ON A LEVEL PLAYING FIELD FOR INTERNATIONAL EXCHANGE

First, under the 'single market' and 'competition policy' columns (Table 1.1), there is the inclusion (and subsequent exclusion) in the Doha Round of the so-called 'new regulatory' Singapore issues: standards for public procurement, competition policy, investment policy and trade facilitation. The inclusion of these issues, which would have facilitated European MNC access to emerging markets in some of the world's most rapidly growing high-technology markets (telecom services, financial and insurance services, transport and logistics, business services, public utilities), prompted the European Commission to adopt a positive stance on trade liberalization, with the Commission prepared to lower agricultural tariffs in exchange for trade liberalization in more dynamic, innovative service sectors.[2]

In contrast with the US, for Europe, the central problem of innovation in each of those sectors is scale. The characteristic increasing-returns features associated with the delivery of such services (often of a network nature), cannot be fully realized in the European context, with its 27 Member States, each with its own regulatory regime, language, culture, tastes and habits. Slow progress with services in the internal market shows how Europe has failed to take advantage of scale. The international dimension, and the demands posed by the 'new regulatory issues' in particular, would have given European firms a much-needed boost to increase returns and take advantage of scale at the international level. The old colonial, language and cultural links of individual EU Member States with emerging and developing countries constituted a natural and more straightforward way to benefit from the global or international expansion of markets. It is all too easy to underestimate how historically developed international links based on old established trade and foreign investment relationships have served to build up cultural and business relations of trust (think of the presence of Ericsson or Saint-Gobain in China, which goes back to the nineteenth century; Belgian involvement in constructing Chinese railways; the activities of French firms in Francophone countries; or the merging of some British and Commonwealth banks).

The decision to exclude those 'Singapore issues' from the trade negotiations at Doha in 2004 did not simply place the Commission in a defensive position – trading tariff reductions for developing countries in non-agriculture manufacturing (NAMA) for tariff reductions in agriculture; it actually eliminated a crucial growth opportunity for sectors that are at the heart of the Lisbon Agenda. In my view, this is illustrative of the regressive international movement of the Lisbon Agenda since 2000, with agriculture returning to international trade negotiations as the central European bargaining topic in the Commission's trade liberalization negotiations.

2.2   BARCELONA AS A RESEARCH AND INNOVATION 'FORTRESS EUROPE'

The second area, falling under the research and innovation columns in Table 1.1, focuses on the geographical spillover of European national and regional R&D and innovation efforts. The national and European focus on investment in knowledge (R&D and innovation) accumulation in the EU and its various Member States as exemplified by the so-called Barcelona 3 per cent target is not just at odds with global decision-making about the knowledge investments of multinational firms; it also appears to ignore the increasingly global nature of long-term sustainability problems likely to affect the future welfare of developed countries directly.[3] In reality, the European framework programmes were designed at a time when the strengthening of the international competitiveness of specific European high-tech firms and sectors was considered essential for Europe's long-term welfare. This led to the strengthening of a number of industrial firms and sectors. Some became globally successful, others failed dramatically. Today, most EU research programmes benefit businesses of European or foreign origin alike, as long as they are located in Europe.

As argued elsewhere (Freeman and Soete, 2007) given the much higher risks involved in developing new products for global markets, firms often prefer to license such technologies today; or, alternatively, to outsource the most risky parts to small high-tech companies, which operate at arm's length but can be taken over after they succeed. Not surprisingly, large R&D-intensive firms in most EU countries currently seem to be less interested in increasing their R&D investments in Europe than in rationalizing them or, where possible, in reducing the risks involved in carrying out R&D by collaborating with other firms, sometimes through publicly sponsored or promoted programmes (micro- and, today, nano-electronics are cases in point), or through so-called open innovation collaboration.

Equally unsurprisingly, over the last few years many small, traditionally highly R&D-intensive EU Member States have witnessed a decline in the intensity of privately funded R&D with little or no relationship to their economic performance. The central question appears to be whether it is possible to appropriate domestically the benefits of knowledge investments or whether these will 'leak away' globally. In the catching-up growth literature (see Fagerberg, 1988 or Soete and Verspagen, 1993), it is emphasized that this phenomenon is characterized by lagging countries benefiting from the import and transfer of technology and knowledge, formally and informally in particular. As a logical extension, in today's globalized world economy it seems obvious that increasing R&D investment is unlikely to benefit domestic economies only. This holds especially for small countries, but is increasingly valid for a majority of countries regardless of size (with only a couple of exceptions). Thus, as Meister and Verspagen (2003) calculate, if the EU were to achieve the 3 per cent Barcelona target by 2010, this would ultimately not reduce the income gap between the EU and the US, because the benefits of increased R&D efforts would accrue not only to Europe but also to the US and the rest of the world. In a similar vein, Griffith et al. (2004) show how the British economy reaped the benefits of the US R&D boom of the 1990s, as did British businesses, which shifted their R&D to the US in particular. To give just one example, a British firm that shifted 10 per cent of its R&D activity to the US from the UK and kept its overall R&D expenditures at the same level could expect an additional 3 per cent increase in productivity, an effect which appeared to be of the same order of magnitude as 'that of a doubling in its R&D stock' (Griffith et al., 2004). In short, the link between the location of 'national' firms' private R&D activities, on the one hand, and national productivity gains on the other, appears increasingly tenuous today.

The same holds for universities and other public research institutes. Elsewhere, I have pointed to the inherent knowledge 'diversion' and European 'cocooning' implications of a European research networking strategy of this kind (Soete, 1997). The broadening of research priorities areas to include both local and global long-term issues increasingly raises questions about the territorial nature of framework programmes (FPs)-funded and implemented research. In the long run, for many research areas European welfare will be influenced directly not by the development of local knowledge through the FPs, their international commercial exploitation and intellectual appropriation, but by global access to such knowledge, the development of joint global standards, and by the rapid global diffusion of new technologies to other, non-EU countries. Examples of this include energy-saving technologies, research on sustainable development and climate change, health and epidemiology, food safety, security, as well as social sciences and humanities. In all these areas, limiting research funding to academic, public and private research institutes located in Europe appears to contradict the need for global solutions to safeguard European welfare in the long run.

2.3   THE DIRE EUROPEAN NEED FOR BRAINS

The third area (the last two columns of Table 1.1) covers education and training policies, and employment and social protection. Here, the international dimension is absolutely crucial for the Lisbon Agenda. Without a doubt, the most fundamental difference between the US and the EU is demographic. Europe has more to learn from countries such as Japan and Russia, which face similar demographic challenges.

The international dimension of education and employment policies must address growing competition for access to brains. Access to brains should be understood here in the broadest possible way: as access to talent, an essential ingredient in research, innovation and entrepreneurship; as access to particular technical skills as one element within a broader strategy to tackle growing labour shortages in particular skill categories; and as greater access to what is known in the literature as people skills, more personal communication and care-oriented qualifications, as Europe's population grows older and the demand for health and care support services consequently rises dramatically.

Clearly, access to brains has been an essential historical feature of European development and of knowledge diffusion within Europe, and between Europe and the rest of the world. Many European countries have changed over the last 50 years from being countries of emigration to countries of immigration (Ireland is probably the most notable example). At the same time, the migration of skilled labour from developing to developed countries has increased significantly.

This phenomenon has been called the 'brain drain' and 'brain exchange' or 'brain circulation'. 'Brain circulation' refers to the cycle of moving abroad to study, taking a job abroad, and later returning home to take advantage of the skills acquired abroad to enhance domestic job opportunities. 'Brain exchange' refers to a two-way flow of expertise between a sending and a receiving country. 'Brain drain' is used when the net flow is biased heavily in one direction.

There are various views of the brain drain issue, including the 'curse or boon' perspective (Commander et al., 2004) and the 'winners and losers' view (Beine et al., 2001). The earlier literature focused on how global welfare increased because of the rational choice of highly skilled emigrants seeking improved incomes abroad (Johnson, 1967; Berry and Soligo, 1969). Later studies present two main points of view on the effects of brain drain for the development of sending countries: on the one hand, from an endogenous growth perspective, economists argue that the brain drain reduces economic growth in sending countries (Miyagiwa, 1991; Haque and Kim, 1995; Reichlin and Rustichini, 1998; Haque and Aziz, 1999; Wong and Yip, 1999; Lowell, 2001). Furthermore, they argue that the drain is likely to reduce wages among unskilled workers, increase wages among skilled workers, and thereby increase inequality. According to this view, then, the brain drain increases inequality and slows down economic growth. The second perspective (Lucas, 1988) focuses on 'human capital accumulation' as an important source of economic growth, and suggests that the prospect of migration may actually foster human capital formation and growth in the sending countries (Mountford, 1997; Stark et al., 1998; Vidal, 1998; Beine et al., 2001). The opportunity to migrate to higher-wage countries may prompt people to pursue higher education in the hope of improving their expected wages abroad. Sending countries thus benefit from skilled emigration because it gives those staying at home an incentive to pursue higher education.

However, from the point of view of receiving countries, and the EU in particular, skilled migration is important not just for economic growth but also because of more general benefits like entrepreneurship, the contribution to increasing demand for goods and services, and attraction of new capital, among other factors. External markets offer new alternatives for initiatives and entrepreneurship. In short, immigration should be part of the Lisbon Agenda, as should be the challenges it raises in some of the sending countries (like the drain of nurses from South Africa).

2.4 GLOBALIZATION TRUMPS EUROPEAN HARMONIZATION

Global, multinational corporations successfully pressured the EU, Japan and the US to strengthen the intellectual property (IP) regime worldwide, so that knowledge can now be traded globally through various so-called bilaterally enforced Trade Related Aspects of Intellectual Property Rights (TRIPS+) trade agreements. This new international IP regime, which developed countries are imposing more or less globally, is likely to proceed much faster than the European harmonization process. The European patent is a case in point. The discussions on mutual automatic recognition of US, Japanese and European patents by the patent offices of each country and region will ultimately render obsolete the complex difficult discussions on the European patent.

CONCLUSIONS

In my view, the most appropriate approach for the new Lisbon Agenda is to address head on the global challenges Europe is likely to face. The Lisbon Agenda is the 'gateway' to the rest of the world and must therefore recognize that innovation and shifts in global demand play an increasingly central role in European and national debates about science and technology, and in the allocation of resources to those areas. Global growth and development over the last ten years is primarily a function of the accelerated diffusion of technological change and increased global access to codified information. In this, the role of information and communication technologies has been instrumental, as has been that of more capital-intensive and organizationally embedded forms of technology transfer such as foreign direct investment (which, as a percentage of gross domestic product is a decimal point greater than it was 50 years ago, and no longer limited to the old triad). By contrast, labour markets and, with them, knowledge embodied in skills and human capital, have hardly become globalized, with the exception of a mobile top rank of scientists, engineers, managers, actors, football players or other creative talent.

Thus, while information and communication technologies (ICT) permit easier diffusion of information, the global knowledge market and global access to knowledge (and knowledge creation in particular) remain highly unequal. The concentration of innovative activities in a small number of regions in the world is likely to continue, accompanied by persistent international differences in the share of resources devoted to science, technological development, and R&D in particular.

The triad countries of the Organisation for Economic Co-operation and Development (OECD) – the US, Japan and the EU – will remain leaders, with China likely to join them by 2020. But today, to some extent, it is no longer the concentration of efforts in one particular region of the world which provides the key to economic growth and international competitiveness; rather, it is the broader local organizational, economic and social embedding of new technologies and innovations, and the way these unleash or block particular specific development and growth opportunities, that matters.

As has become recognized in the endogenous growth literature,[4] the challenge of innovation policy, with its characteristic Schumpeter mark 1 features of 'creative destruction' on the one hand and Schumpeterian mark 2 features of incremental knowledge accumulation carried out primarily in large firms on the other, is closely associated with levels of development. In the high-income developed countries, the innovation policy challenge is increasingly about the sustainability of processes of 'creative destruction' in environments that reward insiders and produce aversion to risk, and focus on the maintenance of income and wealth. For emerging countries, by contrast, the challenge is the more traditional issue of 'backing winners', and promoting industrial science and technology policies, emphasizing the importance of engineering and design skills, and accumulating 'experience' in particular. Finally, as described by various development economics working on science and technology, in most developing countries which have 'disarticulated' knowledge systems, the endogenous innovation policy challenge is probably most complex of all.

In this context, there are four main challenges facing Europe and the Lisbon Agenda in particular. First, we need a 'Lisbonization' of international trade, of the community budget, macroeconomic policy, and Member State fiscal policy in particular (see Chapter 6 in this volume by Pier Carlo Padoan). None of the first six guidelines in Box I.2 refers to the need to restructure fiscal budgets at the national (or European level) to promote investment in knowledge and innovation. What is worse, the six macroeconomic policy headlines that are listed do not even recognize knowledge and innovation as engines of sustainable growth. Yet it is clear that if a Lisbonization were possible, if there were simultaneous alignment between member countries and of public funding, there could be significant growth externalities at the EU level.

Second, as regards the second headline in Box I.2, despite heroic Commission efforts, the Lisbon Strategy of 'knowledge and innovation as engines of sustainable growth'[5] is still a segmented policy, which primarily addresses the Member States that engage most in R&D and innovation.[6] From this perspective the proposed guidelines, and the detailed proposals from the Commission (EC, 2005), appear more reminiscent of the old national industrial R&D model than of the new, emerging international knowledge economy paradigm. The only European shift towards the new paradigm regards the focus on the potential regulatory barriers to research and innovation across Europe, reflecting the broader Commission's competition policy view that it is no longer enough to set a clear European level playing field for national support policies to R&D but it is also necessary to include innovation support policies in a more systematic way, which raises in itself new competition policy issues. However, there is nothing on Europe's social model, for example, while education policy is buried (as Guideline 23) under the 'more and better jobs' headline in Box I.2. The result of this relatively narrow focus is that the proposed integrated guidelines are anything but integrated, conveying an impression of 'overstructure' with target-setting for a multitude of particular knowledge and innovation areas which are ultimately mostly beyond the control of policymakers.

Third, given the increasingly global nature of Europe's social, economic, environmental and demographic problems, I would argue that the unilateral focus on the strengthening of knowledge and innovation activities within Europe with the aim of improving European competitiveness increasingly reflects a rather outdated 'Eurocentric' approach. It certainly does not do justice to the much broader societal and global impact that knowledge accumulation is having on the welfare of European citizens. As argued above, in a growing number of research fields, European welfare will be influenced in the long run not so much by the development of local knowledge, its international commercial exploitation and intellectual appropriation, but by global access to such knowledge, by the development of joint global standards, and by the rapid worldwide diffusion of such new technologies to other, non-EU countries. While the shift from the old to the new Lisbon Strategy sounds less Eurocentric, the question thus remains whether it is not time for a different EU approach to knowledge appropriation, with a more explicit recognition of the global nature of knowledge accumulation. This vision, I suggest, has also greater potential political appeal for European citizens than does the old Eurocentric view.

Fourth, we need to rethink fundamentally the principle of universality governing social security systems as developed in Europe over the last century in broad synergy with an emerging industrial society. We must recognize that there is an increasingly dual work force, divided between those who can only consider their work as 'labour' – undertaking physically or mentally taxing activity with little or no control about the time within which they have to carry out such work – and those who might consider their work much more as something positive, providing self-satisfaction from work in terms of recognition, realization and creativity. Workers involved in the former are likely to consider the European social achievements as reflected in European social security, limits in working hours and early retirement as intrinsically associated with their quality of life, and reject any change, considering it as deterioration in their quality of life. By contrast, workers involved in the latter, whom one may call knowledge workers, will not be so much in need of social security measures aimed at reducing some of the negative externalities of physical work. For them, large parts of their work might well involve positive externalities. Obviously, they will also appreciate social 'security' guarantees to their employment, but these will not amount to essential quality-of-life elements of their working life. In effect, most knowledge workers are currently 'free-riding' on the social 'security' guarantees designed for another, industrial age and aimed at a different category of workers. From this perspective, the automatic extension of social rights to knowledge workers appears largely unjustified; worse, they undermine the financial sustainability of the European social model, and may even explain the lack of dynamism among knowledge workers in Europe.

NOTES

1. This table clearly illustrates how broad are the policy areas that are relevant for innovation, and how necessary is a close interaction between levels of governance in this domain.
2. Under the reciprocity rule in multilateral trade negotiations, exporters' access to foreign markets depends on the openness of the home market. 'Under the reciprocity rule, trade policy formulation appears ultimately a political contest between import competitors and exporters. The central point of Multilateral Trade Negotiations is to create a domestic political constituency in favour of openness where none had existed before by giving exporters a reason to lobby governments in favour of home market liberalization. Hence, in the world of international trade negotiation exporters defend *offensive interests*, import competitors *defensive interests*' (Toro, 2006). At the Doha Round, initiated in 2001, the European Commission adopted an offensive stance during the agenda-setting phase, and then shifted to a more 'blocking' stance after the Geneva 2004 meeting.
3. By contrast, the national focus of developing countries on such investments questions the static, 'given' nature of their international production and trade specialization. It is interesting to observe that international trade specialists such as Samuelson (2004) have raised questions regarding the sustainability of trade gains for the US economy given the active, voluntary knowledge-accumulation process in emerging economies such as China.
4. The view that the philosophy and aims of innovation policy differ from country to country according to their level of development is reminiscent of old arguments about infant

industry, and has become popular in the endogenous growth literature. See Aghion and Howitt (2006).
5.　See the Communication from the Commission to the Council, the European Parliament, the European Economic and Social Committee, and the Committee of the Regions on *More Research and Innovation – Investing for Growth and Employment: A Common Approach* (EC, 2005).
6.　These range from the science, technology or research ministries and the various advisory committees, to the trade and industry, economic affairs or innovation ministries and their various advisory committees. Within the Commission, the Directorate-General for Research and Enterprise DG constituencies are crucial.

REFERENCES

Aghion, P. and P. Howitt (2005), 'Joseph Schumpeter Lecture: Appropriate Growth Policy: A Unifying Framework', *Journal of the European Economic Association*, **4** (2–3): 269–314.

Beine, M., F. Docquier and H. Rapoport (2001), 'Brain Drain and Economic Growth: Theory and Evidence', *Journal of Development Economics*, **64** (1): 275–89.

Berry, R.A. and R. Soligo (1969), 'Some Welfare Aspects of International Migration', *Journal of Political Economy*, **77** (5): 778–94.

Commander, S., M. Kangasniemi and L.A. Winters (2004), 'The Brain Drain: Curse or Boon?', in R.E. Baldwin and L.A. Winters (eds), *International Trade and Challenges to Globalization*, National Bureau of Economic Research Conference Report Series, Chicago, IL: University of Chicago Press, pp. 235–72.

European Commission (2005), *Implementing the Community Lisbon Programme, More Research and Innovation – Investing for Growth and Employment: A Common Approach*, SEC(2005), 1253.

Fagerberg, J. (1988), 'International Competitiveness', *Economic Journal*, **98** (391): 355–74.

Freeman, C. and L. Soete (2007), 'Developing Science Technology and Innovation Indicators: What Can We Learn from the Past?', in OECD, *Science, Technology and Innovation Indicators in a Changing World: Responding to Policy Needs*, Paris: OECD, pp. 193–212.

Griffith, R., R. Harrison, and J. Van Reenen (2004), 'How Special is the Special Relationship? Using the Impact of US R&D Spillovers on UK Firms as a Test of Technology Sourcing', CEP Discussion Paper 0659, Centre for Economic Performance, London School of Economics (LSE).

Haque, N.U. and J. Aziz (1999), 'The Quality of Governance: "Second-Generation" Civil Service Reform in Africa', *Journal of African Economies*, **8** (Supplement 1): 68–106.

Haque, N.U. and S.-J. Kim (1995), 'Human Capital Flight: Impact of Migration on Income and Growth', *IMF Staff Papers*, **42** (3): 577–607.

Johnson, G. (1967), 'Labour Quality in a General Equilibrium System: Some Initial Notes', Princeton Department of Economics, Industrial Relations Section Working Papers, No 379.

Krugman, P. (1994), 'Competitiveness: A Dangerous Obsession', *Foreign Affairs*, **73** (2) March–April: 28–44.

Lowell, B.L. (2001), 'Skilled Temporary and Permanent Immigrants in the United States', *Population Research and Policy Review*, **20** (1–2): 33–58.

Meister, H. and B. Verspagen (2003), 'European Productivity Gaps: Is R&D the solution?', ECIS Working Paper 04/03, Eindhoven: ECIS.

Miyagiwa, K. (1991), 'Scale Economies in Education and the Brain Drain Problem', *International Economic Review*, **32** (3): 743–59.

Mountford, A. (1997), 'Can a Brain Drain be Good for Growth in the Source Economy?', *Journal of Development Economics*, **53** (2): 287–303.

Mowery, D.C. (1983), 'Industrial Research and Firm Size, Survival and Growth in American Manufacturing, 1921–1946: An Assessment', *Journal of Economic History*, **43** (4): 953–80.

Reichlin, P. and A. Rustichini (1998), 'Diverging Patterns with Endogenous Labour Migration', *Journal of Economic Dynamics and Control*, **22** (5): 703–28.

Samuelson, P.A. (2004), 'Where Ricardo and Mill Rebut and Confirm Arguments of Mainstream Economists Supporting Globalization', *Journal of Economic Perspectives*, **18** (3): 135–46.

Soete, L. (1997), 'Technology Policy and the International Trading System: Where Do We Stand?', in H. Siebert (ed.), *Towards a New Global Framework for High Technology Competition*, Tübingen: J.C.B. Mohr, pp. 3–28.

Soete, L. and B. Verspagen (1993), 'Technology and Growth: The Complex Dynamics of Catching Up, Falling Behind and Taking Over', in A. Szirmai, B. Van Ark and D. Pilat (eds), *Explaining Economic Growth*, Asterdam: Elsevier Science Publishers, pp. 101–27.

Stark, O., C. Helmenstein and A. Prskawetz (1998), 'Human Capital Formation, Human Capital Depletion, and Migration: A Blessing or a "Curse"?', *Economics Letters*, **60** (3): 363–7.

Toro, F. (2006), Explaining the Doha Round's Collapse: The Quids and the Quos of Multilateral Liberalization', Mimeo, Maastricht: UNU-MERIT.

Vidal, J.P. (1998), 'The Effect of Emigration on Human Capital Formation', *Journal of Population Economics*, **11** (4): 589–600.

Wong, K.Y. and C.K. Yip (1999), 'Education, Economic Growth, and Brain Drain', *Journal of Economic Dynamics and Control*, **23** (5–6): 699–726.

3. Towards a sustainable European social model: key issues for policy-making

Maria João Rodrigues

The reform of the European social model is one of the most complex issues in the general debate about the future of Europe. The model is the product of a long and complex historical attempt to promote economic growth with social justice. Briefly, social policy is about social justice and contributing to growth and competitiveness. Conversely, growth and competitiveness are crucial for and should be designed to support social policy. Economic and social policies evolve over time and are therefore always part of the political debate and social dialogue. This is the European tradition, an achievement that is valued inside and outside Europe because of its contribution to prosperity and quality of life.

Many different models have emerged from this tradition. The most well-known typologies refer to the Scandinavian, Anglo-Saxon, Continental and South European models (Esping-Andersen in Rodrigues, 2002; Sakellaropoulos and Berghman, 2004). Despite the differences between them, they share certain features, so that one can speak of the European social model. These are: increased general access to education and training; regulated labour contracts; general access to social protection and healthcare; active policies for social inclusion; social dialogue procedures; and the predominance of public funding via taxes or social contributions, with a redistributive effect. These elements were shaped differently in each historical period, depending on existing institutional frameworks and actors, and on their responses to the strategic challenges of their time.

3.1 REFORMING THE EUROPEAN SOCIAL MODEL TO FACE NEW CHALLENGES

Clearly, the European social model faces new strategic challenges today, among them: globalization and new competitive pressures; the transition to a knowledge-intensive economy; population ageing trends; new family models; and the current stage of the process of European integration itself. The sustainability of the European social model depends on a renewal of its economic basis, and on the reform of its main components, so that it is ready to deal with key strategic challenges. This chapter identifies some of the priorities for structural reform in each of the components of the European social model regarding each of these challenges (see Table 3.1).

Education and Training

Lifelong learning systems should be adapted to meet these various challenges. Access to new skills is crucial for people to obtain new and better jobs. First, there are the challenges of globalization and the transition to a knowledge economy. These call for a more dynamic identification of skills needs, and the universalization of lifelong learning opportunities in schools, training centres, companies, public administrations and households, underpinned by universal preschool education and the reduction of early school leavers. New and more flexible ways to validate competences (such as the Europass) can also play an important role in this. Second, population ageing trends can be addressed by disseminating new methods to assess, enhance and use elderly-worker competences. Third, new family models can be dealt with by providing equal opportunities to career choices and more flexible access to lifelong learning over the life-course. Fourth, as regards European integration itself, we need to adopt a common framework on key competences and to facilitate recognition of qualifications and labour mobility.

Social Protection

Social protection systems also need structural reforms to cope with various challenges. As regards the transition to a knowledge economy, it is necessary to generate a more personalized approach with active labour market policies, by creating learning accounts with drawing rights, and providing for flexible personal choice when it comes to using the range of social benefits available. As regards globalization and new competitive pressures, more effective active labour market policies are a priority. We must carefully monitor benefits in order to make work pay, attract more people into the labour market, reduce unemployment and strengthen the financial basis of the social protection systems. There should also be careful monitoring of non-wage labour costs and a search for complementary (public and private) financial resources. Third, as regards population ageing trends, we must promote active ageing, reduce early retirement, provide incentives to

Table 3.1 Identifying reforms for the European social model

Main strategic challenges / Main components of the European social model	Transition to a dynamic knowledge-intensive economy	Globalization and new competitive pressures	Ageing	New family models	European integration
1. Access to education and training	• Anticipating skills needs • Generating access to lifelong learning in schools, companies and households • Personal competences portfolio (Europass) • Universal preschool education • Reduce school leavers	• Anticipating skills needs • Generating access to lifelong learning in schools, companies and households	• New methods of assessing and using competences	• Flexible access to lifelong learning • Equal opportunities for career choice	• European framework for lifelong learning opportunities

2. Social protection for all	• Activating social protection • Priority to active labour market policies • Drawing rights for lifelong learning	• Controlling non-wage labour costs • Mobilizing new kind of financial resources	• Active ageing • Incentives to work • Reducing early retirements • Delay/flexibility in retirement age • Three pillars and intergenerations balance	• Reconciling work with family life by working time flexibility and family care	• Coordinated reforms of social protection systems • European directives on social protection
3. Social inclusion	• More flexibility of choices in the life-course • Developing capabilities beyond income benefits	• To make work pay to increase the employment rates • Managing restructuring process • Targeted programme for social inclusion	• Active ageing • Larger measures for elderly poor people	• Target measures for single parents • Family care services	• European coordination for social inclusion • European programmes for social inclusion • European fund for social costs of restructuring
4. Labour regulations	• Learning organizations • Learning careers • Training leave • Learning accounts	• More internal labour flexibility (work organization, working time, wage)	• New forms of work organization • New working conditions	• Working time flexibility • Parental leave • Career break	• European directives on working conditions • Removing obstacles for

Table 3.1 (continued)

Main strategic challenges / Main components of the European social model	Transition to a dynamic knowledge-intensive economy	Globalization and new competitive pressures	Ageing	New family models	European integration
		• New forms of external flexibility with security • Managing restructuring			• mobility of workers at European level • European frame for economic migration
5. Social dialogue	• Learning agreements	• Innovation agreements • Social plans in restructuring	• Active ageing in collective agreements	• Equal opportunities in collective agreements	• European social dialogue on the strategy for growth and jobs

remain active and introduce a more flexible retirement age. Balancing the financial effort made by different generations may also require careful reconsideration of the balance between the three pillars of the social protection system. Fourth, as regards new family models, these call for the diffusion of family care services and working time flexibility as important ways to reconcile work and family life. Finally, as regards European integration, we need a common legal framework required by the single market on minimum standards and portability, complemented by the open coordination of the social protection system reforms.

Social Inclusion

Social inclusion policies must also be updated in order to cope with the challenges of: the transition to a knowledge economy (focusing more on developing new social and professional capabilities, and not just on simple income guarantees); globalization (calling for better targeting of social inclusion programmes and strengthening the management of industrial restructuring); ageing (which means the promotion of active ageing and designing target measures for the elderly poor); new family models (which means developing family care services and designing target measures for single parents); and finally, European integration (which means the open coordination of social inclusion policies, complemented by European programmes for social inclusion).

Labour Regulations

Labour regulations and human resources management should also evolve to meet the challenges of the knowledge economy, with the development of learning organizations in the workplace, the promotion of learning careers and 'learning first contracts' for young people, the organization of learning accounts, and improvements to working time flexibility for training. As regards the challenge of globalization, we need to generate more internal labour flexibility concerning work organization, working time and wage setting, and to combine new forms of external flexibility with security by strengthening the management of industrial restructuring. The active promotion of better labour standards at the international level can also play a crucial role. As regards the challenges posed by population ageing, we should encourage new forms of work organization, working time management and better working conditions. To address new family models, we must facilitate working time flexibility, parental leave and career breaks. And as regards European integration itself, it is necessary to update European directives regularly, removing the obstacles to worker mobility at the European level and defining a European framework for economic migration.

Social Dialogue

Finally, social dialogue should itself evolve to deal effectively with the same challenges, namely: the transition to a knowledge economy by negotiating learning agreements at company, sector and national levels; globalization, by negotiating innovation agreements and the social management of industrial restructuring at the company, sectoral and national levels; population ageing, by negotiating the conditions for active ageing in the collective agreements; new family models, by systematically introducing equal opportunities in the collective agreements; and European integration, by upgrading the social dialogue on the European strategy for growth and jobs.

All these changes are the outcome of intensive experimentation, debate and negotiation that is already under way in Europe. The integrated guidelines of the Lisbon Strategy for growth and jobs take into account most of these changes, after a very rich discussion which took place at the European level, involving all European institutions and committing prime ministers and ministers responsible for various different areas. These changes were subject to a broader debate within the Member States during the preparation of their national reform programmes for growth and jobs. But a lot remains to be done in order to implement them taking into account specific conditions in each Member State.

Reinterpreting the Basic Values

Specific debates in the Member States should take into account the general background of the European social model and the new strategic challenges it faces today. Moreover, there is also a reinterpretation of its underlying basic values. This is particularly clear when it is argued that security should be for change, and not against change; when the focus is not only on income guarantees but also on enabling and building capabilities; when the concern with equal opportunities is combined with a commitment to help the weakest members of society; when individual responsibility is complemented by the concept of equal opportunities, leading to more freedom of choice over lifetimes; and when the principles of sustainable development are taken into consideration when reconceptualizing social justice. Thus, there must be a balance in social protection contributions and benefits across generations.

BOX 3.1   TARGETS OF EUROPEAN EDUCATION POLICY

1. By 2010, there should be an EU average rate of no more than 10 per cent of early school leavers.
2. The total number of graduates in mathematics, science, technology in the EU should increase by at least 15 per cent by 2010, and the gender imbalance should decrease.
3. By 2010 at least 85 per cent of 22-year-olds in the EU should have completed upper secondary education.
4. By 2010, the percentage of low-achieving 15-year-olds in reading, mathematical and scientific literacy will be at least halved.
5. By 2010, EU average participation in lifelong learning should be at least 12.5 per cent of the adult working population (the 25 to 64 age group).

3.2   DEVELOPING LIFELONG LEARNING

The Goals of Lifelong Learning

The goals of lifelong learning should be defined in terms of education levels and educational attainments. The European Union recently adopted a short list of shared targets, based on the assumption that upper secondary schooling is now the minimal level necessary to provide a solid foundation for lifelong learning. The aim of these targets (see Box 3.1) is to concentrate investment in education and training in areas with clear value added in terms of economic growth and employability. This added effort should combine targeted public investments and higher private contributions.

Moreover, according to the above analysis, to this we should add two other targets, namely: a specific target concerning the education and training of the adult population that only has basic education; and a general target concerning preschool education for all children, as it has been shown that preschool plays a crucial role in cognitive development and subsequent educational and professional performance. This target can be linked with that on universal childcare services, which has already been adopted.

The EU also agreed on a short list of basic skills which, in addition to literacy and numeracy, includes information and communication technology (ICT) skills, foreign languages, entrepreneurship and social skills.

It is important to determine the goals of lifelong learning according to occupational profiles and their specific competences. The purpose is not to return to traditional forecasting models, establishing a mechanical and uni-directional relationship between industrial growth pattern, on the one hand, and skills needs, on the other; on the contrary, the purpose is to develop a permanent interaction between skills and the pattern of growth at the European, national, sectoral and local levels, involving the relevant actors, and taking into account both long- and short-term needs. The recently created SkillsNET should be enhanced as a basic point of reference for this process at the European level, building on the varied work that has already been done by Member States, and which combines very different techniques (enterprise and labour force surveys, case studies, expert inquiries, analyses of jobs advertisements, forecasting and scenarios, and observatories on skills development).

The Strategic Management of Human Resources

The strategic management of human resources is an important priority at a time when globalization and European integration are redeploying invest-ment and job creation to new sectors and areas; when the transition to a knowledge-intensive economy calls for new kinds of skills; when demo-graphic trends are leading to labour shortages; and when there is an expec-tation of increasing migration.

This is the situation in the European Union at present. That is why there are an increasing number of companies, regions and countries adopting ini-tiatives to enhance instruments to ensure a more strategic management of human resources. These instruments include identifying skills needs; defining job profiles; setting qualification standards; developing new train-ing programmes and curricula; improving vocational guidance; and vali-dating individual competences.

A regular forecast on skills needs is crucial for the proper development of all other instruments. It is only possible to identify specific skills needs at the company, sector and regional levels, but one can provide a general and strategic framework not only at the national but also at the European level, taking into account global trends in trade, technologies, investment and job creation.

In a knowledge-based society, lifelong learning can play a central role in paving the way for new areas of job creation. There is an increasingly close relationship between job creation and all dimensions of innovation: inno-vation not only in processes but also in products and services, and not just in technologies but also in organization, marketing and design. At the core of innovation lies the capacity to turn knowledge into more added value, and this requires skilled people with specific occupational profiles such as designers, engineers, different marketing specialists, management, logistics and telecommunications.

It is important to foster a permanent strategic exercise involving the relevant actors at each level, based on partnerships for innovation, job creation and competence-building. The question to ask is how it might be possible to add more value to already existing competence (see Chapter 1 and Figure 1.2) on associating clusters of economic activity.

Strategies for Lifelong Learning

The EU Member States are now committed to the development of national strategies for lifelong learning. The experience of the most successful cases shows that the following priorities must be addressed: to define the goals of lifelong learning not only in terms of educational levels but also in terms of new job profiles and competences; to develop a new infrastructure for lifelong learning; to create a diversified supply of learning opportunities that can provide more customized solutions (by developing new instruments of e-learning and exploring the potential of the digital TV; transforming schools and training centres into open learning centres; encouraging companies to adopt learning organizations; shaping the appropriate learning mode for each target group; spreading new learning solutions to low-skilled workers); fostering various existing demands for learning and creating a demand-led system (by developing a dynamic guidance system over the life-course; renewing the validation and recognition system; and creating compensations for the investment in learning); spreading financial arrangements in order to share the costs of lifelong learning; and improving governance for lifelong learning, involving all the stakeholders along the lines outlined below (see Table 3.2).

3.3   DEVELOPING FLEXICURITY

Having examined the reform of the European social model and the need to develop lifelong learning, we can now focus on another key issue of this reform: flexicurity. Flexicurity refers to the different ways that one can combine flexibility and security, through labour market regulations, active labour market policies, lifelong learning and social protection.

The way to deal with this issue is, first, to identify the main types of flexibility in the labour market; second, to specify the measures that can provide security for each kind of flexibility; third, to clarify the roles and instruments to be developed at the European level and/or at the national level; and fourth, to elaborate the general approach to labour market reform.

Table 3.2 *Sharing responsibilities for lifelong learning*

Main actors / Priorities for lifelong learning development	Public authorities	Companies	Individuals	Social partners	Public and private training suppliers
To define the goals for lifelong learning: new jobs profiles and competences	• Forecasting institutions • Partnerships for jobs creation	• Human resources management • Partnerships for jobs creation		• Innovation agreements • Partnerships for job creation	• Training development • Partnerships for job creation
To develop a new infrastructure for lifelong learning	• Telecommunications and TV regulation • Knowledge resource centres	• Digital equipment	• Digital equipment		• Broadband providers • Content providers
To develop e-learning activities					• e-learning products and services
To turn schools and training centres into open learning centres	• Education and training systems regulations	• New kinds of demand	• New kinds of demand		• Organizational development

To adopt learning organizations To shape the appropriate learning mode for each target group		• Organizational development	• New kinds of demand	• Innovation agreements • Negotiation of training in collective agreements	• Product development • Marketing
To spread new learning solutions for the low-skilled workers	• To support new solutions • To ensure basic education for all	• New kinds of demand • Organizational development	• Stronger personal commitment	• Special conditions for training	• Specialized courses • Focus on new basic skills
To improve the framework conditions for lifelong learning: time management, care services	• Family care services	• Family care services		• Negotiation of working time management • Time accounts and training leaves	
To develop a guidance system over the life-course	• To provide guidance services		• To develop a personal development plan		• To provide guidance services
To renew the validation and recognition system	• To create centres of competence validation	• Intellectual capital reports	• To get a personal portfolio • Europass	• To create centres of competence validation	

Table 3.2 (continued)

Main actors Priorities for lifelong learning development	Public authorities	Companies	Individuals	Social partners	Public and private training suppliers
To create compensations for investment in learning		• Productivity gains • Corporate assets	• Wage increases • Career improvements • Personal development	• Reciprocal compensation in the labour contracts and collective agreements	
To spread new financial arrangements to share the costs	• Basic education for all • Improving education of young people • Supporting target adult people by tax reliefs or direct incentives	• Funding job-related training	• Learning accounts or special entitlements for training	• Sharing costs in labour contracts or collective agreements	• Investment plans

The approach to flexibility in the labour market here is comprehensive, and it is assumed that the main types of flexibility are: the transition from education to employment; the transition from household to employment; the transition from unemployment to employment; functional flexibility inside companies; working time flexibility; wage flexibility; the transition between different types of labour contract; the transition from employment to unemployment; and the transition from employment to retirement.

Providing Security for Flexibility: Some Key Measures

In accordance with this framework, below are some measures which provide security and can be combined with the different types of flexibility identified in Table 3.3. As regards the transition from education to employment, the measures are: financial incentives for the recruitment of young people; regional development; support for geographical mobility; skills needs foresight; partnerships for innovation and job creation; vocational guidance; internships; and ensuring that workers are covered by the social protection system.

As regards the transition from household to employment, the measures include: parental leave, part-time parental leave, part-time care leave, catch-up training and the progressive individualization of social contributions and benefits.

As regards the transition from unemployment to employment, the suggested measures are: decreasing non-wage costs for lower-skilled jobs; non-discrimination measures; vocational and occupational guidance; education and training for unemployed people; enrolment of non-declared workers in social protection systems; universal minimum protection systems; the adaptation of social contributions and benefits in order to make work pay; and social inclusion measures.

As regards functional flexibility, these measures are recommended: organized internal mobility; career and job design; access to modular lifelong learning; learning organizations; multiskilling; and exchange of expertise between generations. As regards flexibility in working hours, measures include: negotiations on working time flexibility, time-saving accounts, job rotation, learning accounts, training leave and social drawing rights.

As regards wage flexibility, there need to be: agreements on wages, productivity and jobs; agreements on wages and competence-building; and innovation agreements.

Regarding the transition between different types of labour contract, measures include: ensuring membership of the social protection system; equalizing social benefits between different types of labour contracts; and equalizing access to lifelong learning.

Table 3.3 *Providing security for flexibility*

Forms of flexibility \ Levels of governance	European	National (to enforce European instruments plus)
Transition from education to employment	• European Employment Guidelines • European Youth Pact • Support to European mobility • Skills needs foresight • Vocational guidance • Partnership for innovation and jobs • European Social Fund • Labour law for young people	• Education planning • Internships • Financial incentives to recruitment of young people • Membership to social protection system
Transition from household to employment	• European Employment Guidelines • Labour law on anti-discrimination, equitable wage and parental leave	• Child and dependants' care services • Catch-up training • Progressive individualization of contributions and benefits
Transition from unemployment to employment	• European Employment Guidelines • Broad economic policy guidelines • Labour law on universal minimum protection system	• Strengthening employment services • Vocational and occupational guidance • Education and training • Decrease non-wage costs for lower-skilled jobs • Enrolment of non-declared workers in social protection systems • Social inclusion measures

Functional flexibility	• European Employment Guidelines • European law on health and safety, individual employment conditions, modernization of work organization, work councils, information and consultation	• Adapting social contributions and benefits in order to make work pay • Programmes to spread best practices in work organization and human resources management (learning organization, multiskilling, careers and job design, modular lifelong learning)
Working time flexibility	• European Employment Guidelines • Labour law on working time and part-time work	• Negotiations on working time • Time-saving accounts • Job rotation • Learning accounts • Training leave • Social drawing rights
Wage flexibility	• European Employment Guidelines • Broad economic policy guidelines • Macroeconomic dialogue	• Agreements on wages, productivity, competence building and jobs • Innovation agreements
Transition between different types of labour contract	• European Employment Guidelines • Labour law on fixed term work • Labour law on part-time work • Labour law on posting of workers • Labour law on temporary workers	• Membership to social protection system • Equalizing social benefits • Equalizing access to lifelong learning
Transition from employment to unemployment	• European Employment Guidelines • Labour law on collective redundancies • Labour law on corporate restructuring • Labour law on transfer of undertakings • Social fund • Globalization fund • Common objectives for social protection	• Raising unemployment insurance • Restructuring management • Regional development • Partnerships for innovation and jobs creation • Retraining during unemployment period • Active job search

Table 3.3 (continued)

Levels of governance / Forms of flexibility	European	National (to enforce European instruments plus)
Transition from employment to retirement	• European employment guidelines • Common objectives for social protection	• Adapting working conditions • New forms of work organization reducing early retirement • Flexible retirement age • Partial retirement • Pension calculation rules • Exchange of expertise between generations

Regarding the transition from employment to unemployment, we must ensure adequate unemployment insurance, retrain during unemployment, promote active job searching, restructure management, promote regional development and create partnerships for innovation and job creation.

Finally, as regards the transition from employment to retirement, the measures include: instituting a flexible retirement age, part-time jobs, adapting working conditions, new forms of work organization, an exchange of expertise between generations, the reduction of early retirement and the adjustment of pension calculation rules.

Reform Paths

As shown above, the instruments to develop flexicurity are quite diverse. Political instruments range from directives, common guidelines, the open method of coordination, and social dialogue at European level to law, programmes, partnerships and social dialogue at the national level. And financial instruments range from macroeconomic dialogue, Community programmes and structural funds at European level, to budgetary, tax and social protection policies at the national level.

Reform paths, priorities, trade-offs and synergies, sequencing and the packaging of concrete measures are to be defined at the national level. The same applies to the political method to design and implement these measures. However, a shared framework for reform and social dialogue can be enhanced, building on the principle of placing flexicurity mechanisms within the broader framework of the social model. These mechanisms will be easier to implement if they are complemented by reforms of other components of the social model, notably: social protection; active labour market policies and lifelong learning; designing flexicurity mechanisms with the transition to a knowledge-intensive economy and a framework of sustainable development in mind; and placing flexicurity mechanisms in the broader context of a strategy for growth in jobs, as it will be easier to implement them if the trend is towards more and better jobs. The synergy between flexicurity and growth should be deepened, making full use of social dialogue at the different levels, and strengthening conditions to develop a long-term partnership for change. We need a new social contract.

3.4 MANAGING THE RESTRUCTURING PROCESS AND JOB CREATION

We need to examine the restructuring processes under way in Europe in the broader context of the redeployment of the European economy towards new activities with more added value that provide new and better jobs. In order to succeed, this redeployment should be underpinned by a more strategic management of human resources, which encourages a more dynamic and future-oriented interaction between labour supply and demand. Otherwise, there is the risk that bigger shortages, gaps and mismatches of skills will coexist with structural unemployment.

Improving the Management of the Restructuring Process

Various elements have to be taken into account if the management of the restructuring process is to succeed (see Table 3.4) We must shift from the traditional passive approach, which puts the focus on reducing the social impact of the restructuring process, towards social plans in the restructuring companies. This is necessary, but not sufficient. We must also adopt an active approach, which involves various instruments to promote active labour market policies and regional development policies to move workers into new jobs. We also need to adopt a proactive approach which mobilizes the various instruments of the innovation policy, mixing trade, competition, employment and training policies to create stronger framework conditions for more and better investments and jobs. Given that the global economy is undergoing rapid change, it is urgent to develop this approach so as to prevent the tensions generated by a restructuring process that tends to be permanent.

New Opportunities for Growth and Job Creation in a Globalized Economy

Globalization is quickly changing specialization patterns of investment and job creation in each country, generating a new international division of labour. The European Union should reposition itself on this division of labour map to create more and better jobs. But it is necessary to develop a more proactive strategy to benefit from the opportunities of globalization.

The goal of the Lisbon Strategy is to create the conditions for the EU to respond positively to globalization by redeploying investment and job creation to new areas. So it is crucial to target these new areas, and the opportunities they offer, by enhancing the coordination of trade, competition, industry, innovation, education, training and employment policies.

First, we must take advantage of all the opportunities created by European integration, which include: enlargement (the catching-up process, managing real and nominal convergence, inter-sectoral and intra-sectoral specialization, foreign direct investment, capacity-building and using European policies and standards as a leverage); regional development (new priorities for economic and social cohesion policies); the internal

Table 3.4   *Managing industrial change: levels and stages*

Stages / Levels	Passive	Active	Proactive
Company	• Lay-off process • Unemployment insurance • Early retirements	• Corporate social plans for restructuring • Competence report (*bilan des competences*) and personal plan • Outplacement services • Training for new jobs in the region • Incentives to geographic and occupational mobility	• Strategic management of innovation • Strategic management of human resources • Competence-building • New models of work organization • Innovation agreements
Sector/regional	• Sectoral programmes of restructuring and downsizing • Social programmes with minimum income	• Rapid response system and change managers • Sectoral/regional programmes for labour force transfers between companies and sectors with specific training • Financial incentives for recruitment by new companies • Local employment initiatives • Incentives to new investments, both national and foreign • Local partnerships for growth and employment	• Clusters development • Networks and partnerships for innovation • Innovation poles • Plans for regional development • Learning regions

Table 3.4 (continued)

Stages Levels	Passive	Active	Proactive
National	• Labour law on lay-offs • Social protection regimes for unemployment and retirement	• Active labour market policies • Vocational guidance services • Training programmes to tackle labour market mismatches • Coordination of employment and industrial policies • Labour market regulations: flexibility with security • Social partners consultation • National employment observatories • Housing market and geographic mobility	• Coordination of employment, industrial, innovation, education and trade policies • Partnership for change involving social partners • Foresight system for new sources of job creation • Proactive programmes for education and training • Lifelong learning strategies • Labour market regulations: transitions and competence building
European	• Directives (lay-off, information and consultation) • Social protection guidelines	• Coordination of employment, competition and industrial policies • European Employment Strategy • European Social Fund (ESF) • Directive on works councils • Directive on portability of pensions	• Lisbon Strategy • Partnership for growth and jobs • European social dialogue (sectoral and cross-sectoral) • Community programmes for R&D, innovation, employment and lifelong learning • ESF and European Regional Development Fund (ERDF) • European Monitoring Centre on Change • European foresight system for new sources of job creation

---

BOX 3.2   THE EUROPEAN SOCIAL MODEL: KEY QUESTIONS

What critical reforms of the European social model should be introduced?
How can we analyse the different forms of flexicurity?
What are the main obstacles to disseminate opportunities for life-long learning?
How can we develop a more proactive approach to industrial restructuring?
Which key factors can ensure the sustainability of the social protection system?
How should the policy mix in social policies evolve at European level?

---

market (opening markets for goods and services, integrating financial markets, managing the restructuring process); economic and monetary union (coordinating macroeconomic policies to promote sustainable growth and enhance strategic priorities for public investment); and the existence of a European research area (networks for excellence, integrated projects and coordination of national initiatives, creating high-skilled jobs).

External markets can also provide a broad range of opportunities, including the current World Trade Organization (WTO) Round, which is set to create more opportunities for trade and foreign investment, not only among developed countries, but also with the developing countries (the so-called 'Development Round'). The reform of the international financial system can play a key role in underpinning this process, which will also be shaped by the European capacity to have a more coordinated voice in these arenas. In spite of the current difficulties, it remains very important to continue with negotiations within the multilateral framework, overcoming the bottlenecks by negotiating more 'win–win' trade-offs. A good combination of international trade, cooperation and development aid policies will make it possible to foster new investment and job creation opportunities in Europe, with the export of products and services to developing countries. This is already happening, for example, with European companies specialized in providing developing countries with tailor-made technologies, services and consultancy services for environment, and in the areas of health and telecommunications.

There are also opportunities emerging as a result of the new innovation-driven economic dynamism across all sectors in new products and services, process technologies, business concepts, and management and organization.

Finally, societal changes can also generate new opportunities, with a wide-ranging combination of private and public initiatives available. All the following sectors are labour-intensive and tend to be knowledge-intensive: adapting to environmental concerns; developing family care services; expanding preschool education; disseminating lifelong learning services; diversifying health services and social integration services; and developing business, regional development, urban management, cultural management and external cooperation services.

BIBLIOGRAPHY

Esping-Andersen, G. (ed.) (1996), *Welfare States in Transition: National Adaptations in Global Economies*, London, Thousand Oaks, CA and New Delhi: SAGE Publications.

Esping-Andersen, G. (2002), 'A New European Social Model for the Twenty-First Century?', in M.J. Rodrigues (ed.), *The New Knowledge Economy in Europe: A Strategy for International Competitiveness and Social Cohesion*, Cheltenham, UK and Northampton, MA, USA: Edward Elgar, pp. 54–94.

Gazier, B. (2003), *Tous 'Sublimes'. Vers un nouveau plein-emploi*, Paris: Éditions Flammarion.

Giddens, A. (2007), *Europe in the Global Age*, Cambridge, UK and Malden, MA, USA: Polity Press.

Gyllenhammar, P.G. (ed.) (1998), *Final Report of the High Level Group on Economic and Social Implications of Industrial Change*, Report of the High-Level Group composed by M. Beresford, B. Brunhes, J. Chereque, F.W. Huibregtsen, H. Klinkhammer, M.J. Rodrigues and B. Trentin, Brussels: European Commission.

Kok, W. (ed.) (2003), *Jobs, Jobs, Jobs – Creating More Employment in Europe*, Report of the Employment Taskforce composed by C.D. Aringa, A. Ekström, F.D. Lopez, C. Pissarides, M.J. Rodrigues, A. Roux and G. Schmid, Brussels: European Commission.

Lamothe, O.D. (ed.) (2004), *Report of the High-Level Group on the Future of Social Policy in an Enlarged European Union*, Report of the High-Level Group composed by T. Atkinson, F. Gerster, M.J. Rodrigues, L. Rychly and D. Schimanke, Brussels: European Commission.

Rodrigues, M.J. (ed.) (2002), *Report of the High Level Group on Industrial Relations and Change in the European Union*, Report of the High-Level Group composed by M. Biagi, J. Gandois, R. Hornung-Draus, M. Lado, P. O'Donovan, I. Ohlsson, D. Paraskevas, J. Visser and J.M. Zufiaur, Brussels: European Commission.

Rodrigues, M.J. (2005), 'Growth, Jobs and Lifelong Learning in a Knowledge Society', in *More People at Work*, Netherlands Presidency of the European Union, Ministry of Social Affairs and Employment, pp. 69–108.

Rodrigues, M.J. (ed.) (2007a), *Perspectives on Employment and Social Policy Coordination in the European Union*, with the collaboration of J. Berghman, C.

Erhel, B. Gazier, J. Goetschy, A. Hemerijck, E. Lorenz, R. O'Donnell, C. Porte, G. Schmid, P.A. Silva, R. Wilson and J. Zeitlin, Lisbon: Ministério do Trabalho e da Solidariedade Social.

Rodrigues, M.J. (ed.) (2007b), *Educação, Inovação e Desenvolvimento*, with the collaboration of L. Chisholm, J.P. Dionísio, K.B. Enghien, A. Fuente, E.M. Grilo, C. Jenner, M. Linna, M.C. Lopes, E. Lorenz, M.H. Nazaré, A. Oliveira, L. Oliveira, J. Pedrosa, J. Picoito, J. Rens, M.C. Rosa and A.C. Valente, Lisbon: Fundação Calouste Gulbenkian.

Sakellaropoulos, T. and J. Berghman (eds) (2004), *Connecting Welfare Diversity within the European Social Model*, Antwerp, Oxford and New York: Intersentia.

Schmid, G. and B. Gazier (eds) (2002), *The Dynamics of Full Employment: Social Integration Through Transitional Labour Markets*, Cheltenham, UK and Northampton, MA, USA: Edward Elgar.

http://www.europa.eu/growthandjobs/.
http://www.mariajoaorodrigues.eu.

See further bibliography in Appendix 4 of this book.

4. The Lisbon Strategy and social Europe: two closely linked destinies

Janine Goetschy

In reply to Rodrigues's key issues raised in Chapter 3, this chapter examines the extent to which the Lisbon Strategy has transformed the content and functioning of 'social Europe'. This calls for a 'contingent' and 'dynamic' analysis of the Lisbon Strategy: in 2000, the Lisbon Strategy was a 'contingent' answer to a specific European Union (EU) political, social and economic situation, but over the following eight years, the initial project has, on the basis of various EU-level assessments, transformed itself as a result of the increasing pressure of globalization and changing EU and Member State priorities (be it the preferences of the various EU presidencies, of the Commission or of the 27 Member States). The chapter is also a plea for the idea that the Lisbon Strategy and social Europe are two closely linked destinies for political and economic reasons.

4.1 A SOCIAL PERSPECTIVE ON THE GENESIS AND DEVELOPMENT OF THE LISBON STRATEGY

European Social Policy: Historical Evolution and Situation in 2000

In this section, I examine the genesis of the Lisbon Strategy, and the state of EU social policies in 2000, asking how a specific constellation of EU economic, social and education challenges produced a 'historical' strategy.

In 2000, after the establishment of the common market, the internal market, and the advent of economic and monetary union, the EU faced a new milestone: as an ever-evolving political project built progressively and on a piecemeal basis, it needed to gain renewed impetus by launching a new economic project.

From the outset, the hope was that the Lisbon Strategy would be much more than just another economic programme: the aim was to reform the labour market, social protection policies, and education and training to foster a new knowledge economy growth model. The Lisbon Strategy was to create a new and durable development umbrella. The aim was to open up new institutional and governance paths to ensure a tight fit between EU and national policies. By proposing a very broad EU economic and social agenda, and the coordination of these policy fields, the hope was that the Lisbon Strategy would help build 'the economic and social identity of the EU political economy' in a clearer and more holistic way.

The Strategy embodied the EU response to increasing globalization, and it sent out a twofold message: that the EU was reforming itself through accelerated economic and labour market structural reform, and the modernization of its social protection systems; and that these reforms aimed to achieve the right balance between regulation and deregulation, equity and efficiency, with the ultimate aim of safeguarding the European social model, and the diffusion of its intrinsic values and principles beyond the EU.

The Lisbon Strategy is an 'encompassing economic, social and political project', a new element for EU integration. However, as has been the case in the past, and in accordance with EU integration historically, economic issues were at the forefront of this project. In 2000 the internal market was seriously 'en panne' (Sapir, 2005; Sapir et al., 2004), stuck on the most difficult issues (sectoral liberalization policies). But the EU macroeconomic situation was still sufficiently positive for policy-makers to promote ambitious macroeconomic goals for the coming decade (including a 3 per cent annual growth rate). Various economic, social and political challenges apparent in 2000 shaped this project. In addition to the tough micro-, macro- and knowledge-economy issues, the EU also had to address a vast array of crucial challenges, particularly in the fields of employment and social policy, and education.

The 1990s witnessed the acceleration of EU economic integration (the constitution of the internal market and economic and monetary union, although the emphasis was on monetary policy rather than economic policy coordination). However, EU social and employment outputs lagged behind (Hyman, 2005; Goetschy, 2006). The impact of the correction mechanisms provided for by the Amsterdam Treaty (1997) and the European Employment Strategy (EES) had yet to make itself felt in 2000 (Ashigbor, 2005). The adoption of new and important EU social directives had slowed down compared to the early 1990s, and the social agreements expected from the Maastricht Treaty (1992) had been insufficient (few agreements had been reached by 2000, among other reasons because of reluctant employers). Notably, the themes they covered (parental leave, temporary work, fixed work contracts, telework and, more recently, stress and harassment at work) are closely linked with the European Employment

Strategy (EES) and the Lisbon Strategy. The agreements tackle matters related to employment creation, the quality of work, and legal employment rules. Indeed, they constitute 'flexicurity deals' although this paradigm was not as central then as it is today. Finally, the Nice Treaty (2000), which failed to bring about the shift from unanimity to qualified majority voting for social protection, showed that the classical method of broadening EU social competences (through the transfer of competence to the Community method for social matters) was going to become increasingly difficult. The transfer of social competences from the national to the EU level seemed to have reached a threshold, a trend broadly confirmed later with the Lisbon Treaty (2007).[1]

In sum, the EU social agenda had remained too narrow and its outputs had been insufficient throughout the 1990s, and feelings of 'social insecurity' and 'increasing inequality' gained ground in some Member States (as a result of the restructuring and relocation of companies; attempts to carry out national social protection reforms for more than a decade; unsuccessful labour market reform to overcome long-term unemployment and low employment rates; more visible situations of poverty and social exclusion; the segmentation of labour markets and access to social protection; and generational disparities in employment and social protection).

Given the stagnation of social initiatives at the EU level, and the increasing diversity of social security systems in the Member States (with enlargement to 25 and then 27 Member States), the proposed Lisbon Strategy social and employment agenda on the basis of a new regulatory model (the open method of coordination, or OMC), based on another EU reform paradigm of a non-compulsory nature, was a governance breakthrough, having the potential to renew the agenda and output of 'social Europe'.

Two further elements clarify the 2000 context: first, despite the increasing disparity between EU national social systems, labour market and social protection system challenges were increasingly similar for all countries; and second, most EU countries had long-term national experience with these areas (more than 20 years of labour market reforms and, in most cases, more than ten years of social protection reforms, including social inclusion policies, pensions and healthcare system reforms).

The expected benefits of the OMC in the employment and social fields were numerous: its non-compulsory dimension should enable enlargement of the agenda on 'national priorities' (which was not the case previously) without a classical transfer of competences. It established the means to deal with national priorities at EU level (that is, highly idiosyncratic issues) and to respect national diversity at the same time. Dealing with national priorities at the EU level could have led to stronger EU-level conflict, but this risk was contained by two elements: the fact that rules were non-compulsory, and the delegation of negotiations to expertise-driven political arenas such as the Employment Committee, the Social Protection Committee, and the Education Committee, among others, rather than exclusively to more classical politically oriented arenas of the EU polity. This is not to say that the OMC lacked political legitimacy: the fundamental political impetus of the various forms of the OMC was meant to emerge from the newly created 'Spring European Council' and the various specialized councils of ministers and whatever coordination processes emerged from there.

The flexibility and experimental nature of and possibilities generated by the revision of processes and outputs, and the regular assessments to be provided for by the OMCs, were supposed to help Member States to invent ad hoc and reversible solutions in their economic, employment and social policies in the face of 'uncertain' economic futures. Experimentalism was almost meant to soften conflict-prone issues. The longer 'durability' of a policy field on the agenda, on the one hand, and the step-by-step nature and 'iterativeness' of OMC processes between levels (EU, national and regional), on the other hand, were supposed to favour in-depth analysis, a finer tuning of outputs, and to foster learning and socialization between levels and actors over a more prolonged schedule. Compared with the community method (legislative and contractual), the OMC made it possible to take a whole policy field on board, a precondition for policy coordination. The aim of the OMC was to develop a culture of evaluation (benchmarking, a calendar, comparisons, assessment of results, and the development of statistical tools) at both EU and national levels, taking advantage of new public management tools and public policy developments already under way in many Member States. Finally, through its procedural and cognitive potentials, the OMC could serve to guide and bring to fruition an EU 'spearhead function' for difficult national labour market and social protection reforms. Moreover, it should foster convergent EU-level thinking and convergent EU-level outputs, while enabling some variation in national-level implementation.

The prior, albeit recent, experience of the Employment Strategy was encouraging, leading to the Lisbon Strategy adoption of various forms of the OMCs in a variety of other social fields (pensions, social inclusion, healthcare, education and training, and, later, on youth policy), although each functioned on very different premises.

To summarize, in 2000 there was a series of concomitant challenges facing the EU and its Member States, and affecting various economic, social, employment, and education and training fields, emerging at a specific moment in EU political history (a request for greater integration of EU and national-level policy-making; visible treaty reform limits as seen with Nice; and the projected enlargements), and at a specific moment in EU political economic history (the need for a new project after Economic and Monetory Union, EMU; also, the internal market was limping along), and in a world context of increasing globalization: all these factors facilitated potential trade-offs and made it possible for the Lisbon Strategy to emerge.

This is not to say that any EU presidency could have done the job given the contingencies. It was precisely the encompassing and broad prospective political economy insight and vision of the Portuguese presidency, as well as the fact that a political proposal of a smaller country could succeed where proposals from larger Member States (France, Germany or the UK) would have been likely to fail, which explain the result. Two further reasons explain why the political consensus necessary for such a high-level meta-deal was possible in 2000: a majority of Member States had a left-wing or centrist orientation; and growth and job creation were benefiting from some macroeconomic improvements at the time.

The Lisbon Strategy was structured around a triple compromise. First, it was a way to ensure that the social dimension caught up with the accelerated economic integration of the early 1990s. Second, the new steps taken with the Lisbon Strategy to deepen the still incomplete internal market (economic sector policy liberalization, for instance) were to become acceptable in exchange for a broadening of the social and employment agenda at the EU level. Third, in exchange for the latter (with broadly framed EU paradigms regarding social, employment and education policies, all of which thus became issues of 'high politics'), it was expected that it would be possible to make difficult reforms of several dimensions of the European social model (ESM), notably national-level employment, social protection, and education and training policy reforms.

Assessing the Lisbon Strategy and OMC: A Permanently Evolving Project

In line with the Lisbon Strategy governance philosophy, the Lisbon Strategy process as a whole and each individual OMC (I limit these to the social, employment and education spheres) have been subject to regular assessments, be it on behalf of EU political institutions or academic institutions. On the institutional side, each OMC has its own rhythm of procedural assessments and devices that have gradually become more coherent, the EES and broad economic policy guidelines (BEPGs) being better coordinated in terms of time, as well as all three social OMCs (social inclusion, pensions and healthcare) (for a comparison of OMC devices see Laffan and Shaw, 2005). The EES itself, in addition to its regular assessments, underwent deeper screening exercises in 2001, after five years of functioning, and again in 2003 with the first Kok Report (2004). The Lisbon Strategy as a whole was evaluated in 2004 (see the harsh conclusions of the Kok Report), which led to the major 2005 reform and the launching of the integrated guidelines – the aims of which are: fewer objectives focused on the macro- and microeconomy, research and development (R&D) and employment; reappropriation by Member States; the greater involvement of parliaments and governments with a 'Mr(s) Lisbon', the top official in change of the Lisbon Strategy at the national level; the streamlining of temporalities; and better policy coordination at the EU and national levels. The 2005 Lisbon Strategy reform was a subtle (and not tension-free) compromise between the conclusions of the second Kok Report, the Commission and the Luxembourg presidency (Mailand, 2006).

A study of March 2008 on the global outputs of the Lisbon Strategy carried out by Allianz SE (within the framework of a European think-tank close to the Commission, confusingly named the Lisbon Council Group), which covers the 14 largest economies of the EU (Austria, Belgium, Denmark, Finland, France, Greece, Germany, Ireland, Italy, the Netherlands, Poland, Spain, Sweden and the United Kingdom), and which ranks countries according to key criteria decisive for success in the twenty-first century (economic growth, productivity growth, employment, human capital, future-oriented investment and fiscal sustainability, and the economic impact of stronger environmental standards) reckons that 11 out of the 14 countries examined seem to be on course to meet the goals of the Lisbon Agenda. Further, only three of the countries surveyed – France, Austria and Italy – are currently not on track to meet their Lisbon targets. The five best-performing countries are Finland, Ireland, Denmark, Sweden and Poland. However, of the employment and education policy indicators presented in the study, only the employment rate (for employment) and the proportion of employees with tertiary education (for human capital) are retained, which provides a fairly restrictive picture of the social impact of the Lisbon Strategy.

There have been numerous academic research projects on the various OMCs and the Lisbon Strategy, some financed by the fifth and sixth EU framework programmes (such as Govecor, Connex, Newgov and Capright). Broadly speaking, most research results, which are particularly numerous for the EES, emphasize the following points (Zeitlin et al., 2005; Armstrong, 2006): each OMC has a life of its own; the EES is the most elaborate OMC; if the results of the OMCs have been disappointing at times in quantitative terms (although nearly 17 million more people have entered the workforce in the EU-15 since 2000, a rate of growth that outpaces the US), they have unleashed powerful qualitative EU-level reform paradigms for national reforms; the OMCs have tended to be elite-driven (through the key role played by specific committees, civil servants and the involvement of experts); social partners and non-governmental organizations (NGOs) have not been sufficiently engaged, although the latter have played an important role in the social exclusion process; the 2005 Lisbon Strategy reform, which condensed the integrated guidelines to address more limited objectives, has generated some turmoil for the stakeholders of the specific social OMCs (inclusion, pensions and healthcare); in many instances, the OMCs have led to changes in the work and coordination practices of national ministries; at the EU level, new collaboration practices between the Commission, the European Council and the rotating EU presidencies have also been devised, as well as within the Commission and among EU-level Council formations.

What has been the impact of the various rotating presidencies on the Lisbon Strategy? Although the Lisbon Strategy has been following a sort of rolling agenda from one presidency to another (even more formalized with the recent 18-month programme during the German, Portugal and Slovenian presidencies), it looks as though small countries have been more engaged in improving the initial Lisbon Agenda (Sweden has worked on employment and the environment, Belgium on pensions and quality of work, Austria on energy policy, Finland on information and communication technologies – ICTs – and innovation, Luxembourg on the balance between economic and social items of the Strategy; not to mention Portugal, which acted as an initiator and strategic actor of the Lisbon Strategy in both 2000 and 2007). Although the Lisbon Strategy is far from having been *un long fleuve tranquille* because of tensions inherent to different views on the appropriate dosage between neoliberal and social preferences, it has shown great stability in terms of objectives between 2000 and 2008 (and it has been protected from the heated debates on the Constitutional Treaty, particularly in France). Moreover, at the same time, it has evinced a significant capacity to adjust to evolving challenges at the global level (increasing globalization; and environment and energy issues under the durable development agenda), and it has attempted to reform itself and remedy governance and implementation failings.

From a more theoretical perspective, some researchers had invested much hope in the 'deliberative democracy' potential of the OMCs, while others see them essentially as a means to improve the efficiency of public policies and accelerate reforms, or as a way to put the theories of Europeanization to the test in specific policy fields, as their implementation means more closely intertwined national and EU-level policies (Featherstone and Radaelli, 2003; Schmidt, 2006). Compared to economists, political scientists have generally been less critical when assessing the national impact of the Lisbon Strategy; moreover, some influential macroeconomists have deplored the overly numerous policy fields of the Lisbon

Strategy, stating that only those with external (positive or negative) consequences across EU economies should be part of the Lisbon Strategy agenda, and that other fields (such as social and education policies) should be left to individual states. In addition to this somewhat functionalist outlook, this line of reasoning tends to ignore the legitimacy dimension and the protection function to be fulfilled by employment and social OMCs. The Lisbon Strategy has also been analysed from a sociology of law perspective, with lawyers discussing some of the potentially contentious aspects of the 'hard' versus 'soft' law debate: to what extent, and under which conditions, can one expect hybridization and complementarity between hard and soft law, and thus avoid rivalry between the two? (Scharpf, 2002; de la Rosa, 2007).

4.2   A SOCIAL EUROPE FOR THE TWENTY-FIRST CENTURY

The Lisbon Strategy and the Renewal of Traditional Social Europe

Compared to the past, the Lisbon Strategy and its OMCs have led to a substantial enlargement of the EU employment and social agenda on matters of national priority. Although two fairly stable governance principles had previously been set up (the sharing of competences in the social and employment field between the EU and Member States, and the principle of subsidiarity) in the Maastricht Treaty and its annexed social agreement (now confirmed with the Lisbon Treaty), the pressure for labour market and social protection reforms in a context of globalization (and the difficulty Member States have experienced implementing them), have led to a substantial broadening of the EU employment and social agenda. (The persistent strength of those two treaty principles was reflected during the discussions of the Constitutional Treaty, which proved to be quite contentious and disappointing on OMC matters, the latter seen by some as a threat to the two treaty principles.) Such a substantial broadening of the EU social agenda was not followed initially by a sufficient increase in budgetary means: however, indirectly it contributed to launching the debate on redesigning the qualitative content of the EU budget, taken up by the Sapir Report and especially by the UK, and to a direct reorientation of structural funds (2007–13) in support of the EES and the Lisbon Strategy.

The second discontinuity with the traditional pattern of social Europe is the fact that, with the Lisbon Strategy, the widening of the employment and social agenda has occurred on the basis of political commitments by European councils outside the intergovernmental conferences (IGCs); this is a break from the classical trend of social incrementalism through treaty reform. Indeed, only some OMC policies of the Lisbon Strategy can, for now, rely on existing treaty bases: for the internal market (hard law); for the BEPGs and employment guidelines (soft law with coordination processes); in the new Lisbon Treaty, OMCs are mentioned with regard to social policies, industry, R&D and the environment.

Third, probably the most crucial new path inaugurated with the Lisbon Strategy is the issue of policy coordination (at the EU and national levels) and the virtuous circles that are supposed to emerge from mutual policy effects. Moreover, a newly broadened social policy agenda is linked closely with other policy fields (economic, environmental, education and training, and R&D) so as to reap benefits from policy coordination at both the EU and national levels. This development takes place against the backdrop of a more traditional fragmented and piecemeal social Europe lacking a coherent project. Here, the Lisbon Strategy can be compared with another fairly encompassing social (and economic) project in terms of content, the Jacques Delors White Paper on *Growth, Competitiveness and Employment* (European Commission, 1993). But the subsequent institutional devices and actions adopted regarding the latter were clearly less important than those of the Lisbon Strategy, since the 1994 White Paper was the result of a Commission Communication (followed by some concrete measures) and not of European Council decisions.

Fourth, the new forms of governance and cooperation devices (the OMCs) introduced by the Lisbon Strategy and spread across numerous policy fields, inaugurated a new regulatory path for social Europe (Goetschy, 2003, 2004; Wendler, 2004; Wincott, 2006). Already in the past, this policy domain had involved a variety of policy regimes based on different institutional processes (the Community method, the contractual method and Structural Fund Procedures) to which was added the OMC. Is complementarity possible or do these different regulatory regimes compete with one another? In the future, is it likely that the traditionally dominant Community method will be slowly nibbled away at by more intergovernmental methods (the latter rendering ambitious Treaty reforms redundant)? Or will a subtle mechanism of hybridization between the various regulatory tools occur? Or, another possible scenario, will the variety of regulatory methods work alongside one another, without interfering much with each other? What is certain is that the variety of regulatory tools is already clearly at the heart of the new EU Social Agenda 2006–10. What remains highly uncertain is the type of institutional and strategic dynamics that such diversity may produce. For instance, how can the mutual learning outcomes of the EES, EU-level collective agreements on employment issues, EU directives relating to employment, the tough ongoing negotiations on the proposals of directives concerning working time and interim work, be viewed in a more congruent way in terms of content, when it is known that the polity and politics of each arena behind those outputs differ greatly?

Two Major Social Issues for the Future of Social Europe

Flexicurity debates at EU level: evolution and perspectives
The flexibility – security nexus has been playing a dominant role in the EU policy discourse and policies since 1993: with the Delors White Paper (European Commission, 1993); the Green Paper on a Partnership for a New Organization of Work (European Commission, 1997); the EES inaugurated at Essen (1994); the Amsterdam Treaty and the EES (1997); the Lisbon Strategy (2000); and, gaining new momentum from 2004 onwards in particular, the 2005 EU integrated guidelines. Its roots lie in the Organisation for Economic Co-operation and Development (OECD) of the 1980s and two successful national cases (the Netherlands and Denmark), which were heavily documented and divulged abroad. The great publicity received by these two national success stories certainly had an important cognitive and even political impact in the other EU Member States, and on EU-level policy paradigms, but has probably also contributed to increased feelings of 'social insecurity' in countries where unemployment problems (especially long-term unemployment) are particularly difficult. Faced with foreign success stories and some enduring issues such as long-term unemployment, citizens in the less successful countries could feel even more desperate.

At the policy level, the new directions taken by flexicurity in all countries include labour market 'activation' policies, the individualization of social protection policies (unemployment benefit system reforms, social assistance reforms and qualitative guidance for job-seekers), pension reforms, collective bargaining reforms and new legal provisions (new working time arrangements and time-saving accounts; parental leave and better formulae to reconcile work and family life; training schemes and lifelong learning; unemployment protection revisions; and reforms in labour contract laws). There is a much closer articulation between labour market and social protection reforms in all EU countries, albeit to different degrees and at different speeds. France and Germany, for example, have been slower (due to important veto points, the specificities of the 'Continental system', and their large size), but even there the speed of reforms has accelerated in the last few years.

At a research level, studies on flexibility from the 1980s (see the work by Brunhes or Boyer, for instance) were complemented in the 1990s with the notion of 'flexicurity trade-off issues over a life time', such as found in the 'transitional labour market approach' (Schmid, 2006; Auer and Gazier, 2006), or with the notion of 'professional status' and 'social drawing rights' (Supiot, 1999).

Though flexibility issues have been on the EU agenda for more than 15 years, they became more salient and gained momentum after 2004, particularly the transitional labour market approach. The latter now prefigures one of the essential components of a possible 'new social pact' at the EU and Member State levels.

Flexicurity touches essentially upon five types of policies: a generic, transversal and strategic transitional labour market policy; reformed social protection policies (social inclusion, health, pension schemes and family policies); reformed employment policies; revised collective bargaining patterns; and human resource policies and the promotion of strategies for anticipating change on behalf of enterprises.

Flexicurity analyses (especially the transitional labour market dimension) and the identification of the major challenges facing the EU (globalization, demographic shifts and an atonic internal market) clearly show that the three key horizontal issues which should be given priority in all five types of policies mentioned above are: lifelong learning arrangements; the conciliation of work and family life; less non-egalitarian developments among different generational groups; the regions; and qualified and unqualified employees (Wilthagen and Tros, 2004; Wilthagen et al., 2007).

The implementation of flexicurity approaches calls for recourse to a diversity of modes of regulation at the national and regional levels but also at the EU level. One is a procedural mode of regulation, a fairly flexible method to adapt needs for the market and the individual, based on 'non-binding' rules, which should make evaluation processes and correction mechanisms possible. Another is a substantive mode of regulation, based on a strong, 'active social state' which guarantees various forms of social protection and rights. The EU level could provide some useful framework laws and ad hoc directives in this regard. Then there is the contractual mode of regulation based on social partner agreements at all levels. The contractual mode means that collective bargaining content must be enriched to foster social pacts at the national level and also the decentralization of collective bargaining both at the enterprise and regional levels, to open negotiations to new actors (such as associations, municipalities, *bassins d'emploi* and training institutions) at the local level. Finally, appropriate financial resources are necessary.

The various roles the EU can play when it comes to flexicurity are as follows: it can provide an arena for debate on various flexicurity alternatives and institutional dynamics; it can outline the values and principles to govern the implementation of a lifetime perspective (the transitional labour market approach) such as fairness, partnership, decentralization, evaluation, the provision of social rights as a safety net, the promotion of lifelong learning, and the conciliation of work and family life; it can provide minimal social rights (and possibly incomes) through ad hoc directives in order to curb negative social developments; it can encourage Member States to carry out appropriate national reforms in the areas of employment, social protection and tax policy, and policy coordination; and it can encourage Member States to carry out impact and assessment studies. And in doing so, it can rely on the previous experience with ongoing OMC processes pertaining to the Lisbon Strategy in the various domains of social, employment and education policy.

Debates and policies on the EU's global role: the issue of labour standards

Faced with increased globalization, over the last ten years the EU has made ever greater efforts to link its foreign and domestic policies, an endeavour that became a key Lisbon Strategy priority in 2007, as witnessed by the Commission Communication (COM(2007) 581).

The EU has promoted core labour standards (CLS) both at home and abroad. In addition to the *acquis communautaire*, the EU adopted a Charter of Fundamental Rights in 2000 which is now part of the Lisbon Treaty. As regards the external dimension, it is important to stress that new steps have been taken in recent years to revive bilateral EU trade agreements, among other reasons because of the shortcomings of multilateralism. Such an approach calls for bilateral and regional agreements of a more encompassing nature, including trade, economic growth, energy, social and sustainable development elements. In general, it could promote much more intensively the effective application of core labour standards, through positive instruments and an incentive-based approach in trade policy. But the EU remains firmly opposed to any sanction-based approach, and refuses to use labour rights for protectionist purposes. In addition, the Commission is due to carry out sustainability impact assessments of bilateral agreements, which include, among other things, an assessment of the impact on social development (see European Commission COM(2006), 249).

While labour standards are not part of ongoing World Trade Organization (WTO) negotiations, the Doha development agenda and closer cooperation with International Labour Organization (ILO) has enabled the EU to promote these standards at the multilateral level. Finally, the EU encourages the private sector to get involved in the development of social standards through corporate social responsibility schemes.[2]

The Lisbon Strategy began to address the external social dimension after 2007, but it is worth recalling that in 2002 the Commission had already welcomed the creation of the World Commission on the social dimension of globalization established under the aegis of the ILO, as well as the relevant ILO report (ILO, 2004). This report was fairly critical, stressing the detrimental effects of globalization on labour standards. It reckoned that the establishment of core labour standards is the way to promote improvements, along with adequate macroeconomic policies, public investment, quality employment, durable social institutions, the involvement of social actors and engagement in social dialogue, relevant development policies, and revised trade policies to reduce developing countries' import tariffs and export subsidies. It also highlighted the importance of the social dimension of regional integration, which can help introduce a social dimension to the governance of globalization. The reaction of the European Commission to the ILO report (European Commission, 2004) was sympathetic to the position of the ILO, particularly as regards the importance of balanced regional integration schemes and their role in promoting a worldwide social dimension. The Commission document of 2004 is crucial because it matches the broader ILO and United Nations strategy.

CONCLUSION

Altogether, the extremely broad EU employment and social agenda (which permits a growing number of deals and trade-offs), the variety of existing EU regulatory modes covering the same area (legislative, contractual, the OMC and financial redistribution), the existence of a few stable reform paradigms (such as flexicurity, new skills, active inclusion and non-discrimination, gender equality, sustainable pensions and healthcare systems), the possibility of having committees of experts handling contentious issues, mutual learning, and the new possibilities opened up by the Lisbon Treaty, will help to improve the employment and social situation.

The Lisbon Agenda has proved to be flexible in terms of agenda and governance modalities in the face of a rapidly changing context, both within and outside the EU, but national implementation has varied greatly.

The Lisbon Strategy has introduced two new lasting elements that will shape the future of EU integration: first, a double overlap between EU and national-level economic, employment and social agendas (in other words, an overlap between polity levels and policy fields); second, through the OMC, it has led to quasi-permanent iterative policy action between the EU and national levels. These innovations have two advantages and one shortcoming. The advantages are that this 'encompassing political economy register' will constitute an open project of some convergent paradigms to move ahead alongside the very neat competence distribution of the Treaty; and they should also contribute to strengthen the EU as a regional bloc. The shortcoming is that evaluating the precise 'EU added value' of EU Lisbon Strategy policies in each Member State (particularly evaluating the impact of qualitative paradigms in the employment, social and education domains) becomes increasingly complicated and intricate (if at all possible). The difficulty of assessing EU output is a serious problem at a time when the EU is under increasing pressure 'to deliver'. The Cohen-Tanugi report (2008), which provides both a useful assessment of the quantitative impacts of the Lisbon Strategy and some ambitious guidelines for its post-2010 era supposed to inspire the French EU presidency during the second semester of 2008, could have provided more insights into the more qualitative and less easily measurable impacts of the Lisbon Strategy and its various OMCs.

Broadly speaking, the combined goals of the various policy spheres of the Lisbon Strategy (economic, employment, social, environment, education and energy) should increase efficiency and equity in Member State economies and societies in a context of increasing globalization (European Commission, 2007b). Trying to conciliate these goals has always been a difficult challenge (if one considers the diversity of capitalisms in the EU-15 and then the EU-27, and their varied modes of insertion into the global economy). Although employment and social policy has become EU 'high politics' with the Lisbon Strategy, the implicit tension has led unavoidably to a 'hierarchy' of policy fields. Of course, the narrative, and institutional and policy designs (on complementarity and mutual reinforcement between economic and social development) can be improved.

As of 2008, very different stakeholders have attempted to ensure that social policies are more broadly inserted (or reinserted) into the Lisbon Strategy (with a special emphasis on child poverty, employment targets for youth, the elderly, women and immigrants, as well as improved educational levels, skills and a reduction of the number of early school leavers). However, a balance needs to be struck between 'the administrative sustainability' of the Lisbon Strategy (as past experience shows, the operational aspects of the Lisbon Strategy in light of the breadth of the agenda must be monitored) and its 'EU legitimization power'.

The increasing importance of a 'more socially oriented narrative' for the Lisbon Strategy in 2008 is a result of five factors. First, from the mid-2000s onwards, thinking about social Europe and EU social realities and challenges changed, as shown by the European Commission Bureau of European Policy Advisors (BEPA) Report (2007a), which adopts a social 'well-being approach' (adopted by other international organizations), there was a more sociological and prospective view of employment and social problems than was the case in the past, and a more global view of the EU in the world, while noting the specificities of the European social model. Second, the Commission is preparing a renewed social agenda (the current agenda runs from 2006 to 2010) on the basis of a broad public consultation and a new perspective based on the BEPA Report, which is leading to reconsideration of the social dimension of the Lisbon Strategy (European Commission, COM (726)). Third, given that there are various political deadlines for 2009 (the European Parliament elections; the election of a new president for the Commission; the designation of a stable EU president of the Council and a High Representative for external affairs), we have entered a more political phase in which social democratic stakeholders will gain a higher profile (see, for example, the van Lancker EP report to the 2008 Spring Council on the Lisbon Strategy). The new institutions of the Lisbon Treaty will benefit the Lisbon Strategy in the future, providing the EU with more leadership and broadening its competences. At the same time, the groundwork for the post-2010 Lisbon era and the content of the agenda is being prepared (see the Conclusions of the December 2007 European Council). Fourth, political contingencies aside, the breadth of the Lisbon Strategy agenda will be subject to cyclical development, with broadening in some periods (as in 2000 and 2008) and narrowing in others (as in 2005). Finally, the Lisbon Treaty (2007), which spells out the social and economic values of the EU and integrates the Charter of Fundamental Rights, as well as heated debates about the Constitutional Treaty, remind us of the crucial importance of the social dimension for the development of the political economy of the European Union.

NOTES

1. Of course the fact that the latter now entails a core of legally binding fundamental rights – apart from the UK and Poland – is not to be neglected, though they can only be invoked regarding EU-level legislation; the few elements of progress concerning the OMC for social policies, and the official setting up of the tripartite summit, are not to be ignored but remain scarce.
2. See European Commission (COM(2002) 347 final); and European Commission (COM(2006) 136 final).

REFERENCES

Armstrong, K. (ed.) (2006), 'The Open Method of Coordination: Governance after Lisbon', Special Issue, *Journal of Contemporary European Research*, **2** (1): 1–104.
Ashigbor, D. (2005), *The European Employment Strategy: Labour Market Regulation and New Governance*, Oxford: Oxford University Press.
Auer, P. and B. Gazier (2006), *L'introuvable sécurité de l'emploi*, Paris: Flammarion.

Cohen-Tanugi, Laurent (2008), *Euroworld 2015: A European Strategy for Globalization*, Final Report of the Europe and Globalisation Mission, chaired by Laurent Cohen-Tanugi, Paris: Centre d'Analyse Strategique.

de la Rosa, S. (2007), *La méthode ouverte de coordination dans le système juridique communautaire*, Brussels: Bruylant.

European Commission (1993), White Paper on *Growth, Competitiveness, and Employment: The Challenges and Ways Forward into the 21st Century*, COM(1993) 700 final. Brussels: 05.12.1993 (also known as the Delors White Paper).

European Commission (1997), *Green Paper: Partnership for a New Organization of Work*, COM(1997) 128 final.

European Commission (2002), *Corporate Social Responsibility: A Business Contribution to Sustainable Development*, COM(2002), 347 final.

European Commission (2004), *The Social Dimension of Globalization: The EU's Policy Contribution on Extending Benefits to All*, Brussels, 18.5.2004.

European Commission (2006a), *Implementing the Partnership for Growth and Jobs: Making Europe a Pole of Excellence on Corporate Social Responsibility*, COM(2006), 136 final.

European Commission (2006b), *Promoting Decent Work for All: The EU Contribution to the Implementation of the Decent Work Agenda in the World*, COM(2006), 249 final.

European Commission (2007a), BEPA Report on *Social Reality Stock Taking*, 02/D09, B Brussels, edited by R. Liddle, F. Lerais and the Bureau of European Policy Advisors, http//ec.europa.eu.

European Commission (2007b), *The European Interest: Succeeding in the Age of Globalization*, COM(2007), 581 final.

European Commission (2007c), *Opportunities, Access and Solidarity: Towards a New Social Vision for 21st Century*, COM (726).

Featherstone, K. and C. Radaelli (eds) (2003), *The Politics of Europeanization*, Oxford: Oxford University Press.

Goetschy, J. (2003), 'The European Employment Strategy, Multi-Level Governance and Policy Coordination: Past, Present and Future', in J. Zeitlin and D. Trubek (eds), *Governing Work and Welfare in a New Economy: European and American Experiments*, London: Blackwell and Oxford University Press, pp. 59–87.

Goetschy, J. (2004) 'L'apport de la méthode ouverte de coordination à l'intégration européenne: des fondements au bilan', in P. Magnette (ed.), *La grande Europe*, Brussels: Presses Universitaires de Bruxelles, pp. 141–67.

Goetschy, J. (2005), 'The Open Method of Coordination and the Lisbon Strategy: The Difficult Road from Potentials to Results', *Transfer European Review of Labour and Research*, **11** (1): 64–81.

Goetschy, J. (2006), 'Taking Stock of Social Europe: Is There Such a Thing as a Community Social Model?', in Serrano and Jepsen (eds), *Unwrapping the European Social Model*, London: Polity Press, pp. 43–73.

Goetschy, J. (2007), 'The Implications of the Lisbon Strategy for the Future of Social Europe: "On the Road" or "New Age"?', *International Journal of Comparative Labour Law and Industrial Relations*, Winter 2007: 499–524.

Hyman, R. (2005), 'Trade Unions and the Politics of the European Social Model', *Economic and Industrial Democracy*, **26** (1): 9–40.

International Labour Organization (ILO) (2004), *A Fair Globalization: Creating Opportunities for All*, Geneva: International Labour Office.

Kok, W. (2004), *Facing the Challenge: The Lisbon Strategy for Growth and Employment*, Report from the High Level Group, November.

Laffan, B. and C. Shaw (2005), *Classifying and Mapping OMC in Different Policy Areas*, Report for NEWGOV New Modes of Governance (Integrated Project Priority 7: Citizens and Governance in the Knowledge-based Society), http://eucenter.wisc.edu/OMC/Papers/laffanShaw.pdf.

Mailand, M. (2006), *Coalitions and Policy Coordination: Revision and Impact of the European Employment Strategy*, Copenhagen: DJØF Forlagene.

Rodrigues, M.J. (2003), *The New Knowledge Economy in Europe: A Strategy for International Competitiveness and Social Cohesion*, Cheltenham, UK and Northampton, MA, USA: Edward Elgar.

Sapir, A. (2005), *Globalisation and the Reform of European Social Models*, Bruegel Policy Brief, no 1, Brussels.

Sapir, A., P. Aghion, G. Bertola, M. Hellwig, J. Pisani-Ferry, J. Vinals, D. Rosati, M. Buti and H. Wallace (2004), *An Agenda for a Growing Europe: The Sapir Report*, Oxford: Oxford University Press.

Scharpf, F. (2002), 'The European Social Model: Coping with the Challenges of Diversity', *Journal of Common Market Studies*, **40** (4): 665–70.

Schmid, G. (2006), 'Social Risk Management through Transitional Labour Markets', *Socio-Economic Review*, **4** (1): 1–33.

Schmidt, V. (2006), *Democracy in Europe: The EU and National Polities*, Oxford: Oxford University Press.

Supiot, A. (1999), *Au-delà de l'emploi: Transformations du travail et devenir du droit du travail en Europe*, Paris: Flammarion.

Telò, M. (2006), *Europe: A Civilian Power? European Union, Global Governance, World Order*, London: Palgrave Macmillan.

Wendler, F. (2004), 'The Paradoxical Effects of Institutional Change for the Legitimacy of European Governance: The Case of EU Social Policy', *European Integration Online Papers* (EIOP), **8** (7).

Wilthagen, T. and F. Tros (2004), 'The Concept of Flexicurity: A New Approach to Regulating Employment and Labour Markets', *Transfer, European Review of Labour and Research*, **10** (2) Summer: 166–86.

Wilthagen, T., Bekker and S. Klosse (2007), 'Making it Work: Introduction to the Special Issue on the Future of the European Employment Strategy', *International Journal of Comparative Labour Law and Industrial Relations*, Winter: 489–99.

Wincott, D. (2006), 'European Political Development, Regulatory Governance, and the European Social Model: the Challenge of Substantive Legitimacy', *European Law Journal*, **12** (6): 743–63.

Zeitlin, J., P. Pochet and L. Magnusson (eds) (2005), *The Open Method of Coordination in Action: The European Employment and Social Inclusion Strategies*, Brussels: Peter Lang.

5. The economic governance of the Union and the quality of public finances: key issues for policy-making

Maria João Rodrigues

5.1 IMPROVING EU ECONOMIC GOVERNANCE

EU economic governance faces several overlapping challenges in order to relaunch growth: globalization, fostering structural reforms, strengthening the eurozone, and supporting internal convergence. The EU can take steps to improve economic governance by developing the links between recently updated key instruments, namely: the renewed Lisbon Strategy and the integrated guidelines for growth and jobs; the revised Stability and Growth Pact (SGP); the guidelines for cohesion policy and the next generation of structural funds. For Member States, this means developing the links between the national reform programmes (NRP), the stability and convergence programmes (SCP) and the national strategic reference frameworks (NSRF).

The main links that must be developed are the following: structural reforms to ensure fiscal consolidation and sustainability; structural reforms to strengthen long-term growth potential and boost the growth rate, which will make it easier to improve fiscal consolidation and sustainability; macroeconomic policies supporting structural reforms and strengthening long-term growth potential, within a framework of fiscal consolidation; structural funds complementing macroeconomic policies to support structural reforms and growth potential.

The key issue, then, is how to exploit fully synergies by improving the consistency and mutual re-enforcement of these instruments. There are also difficulties and trade-offs, notably because some structural reforms can involve additional expense, at least in the short term, and also because spending of structural funds can be hindered by insufficient absorption capacity; furthermore, there is a structural problem for sustainability, stemming from ageing trends; and finally, the conflict between priorities for public spending increase in a framework of fiscal consolidation.

What solutions can we propose to overcome or limit the impact of these difficulties and trade-offs? So far, the following solutions can be identified: assessing the synergies between these three instruments in Member States on a intertemporal basis, within a framework to promote sustainable growth and fiscal consolidation; fostering the structural reforms needed to ensure the sustainability of social protection and health systems; and strengthening mechanisms to improve the quality of public finances, a concept for ensuring the most effective and efficient use of resources with a view to raising the long-term growth potential of the economy. This third solution is particularly important for the implementation of the Lisbon Agenda and deserves to be deepened.

5.2   IMPROVING THE QUALITY OF PUBLIC FINANCES

The countries that introduced national expenditure rules, within medium-term expenditure frameworks as well as performance budgeting, managed better to redirect their public expenditure towards their spending priorities (ECFINEOC, 2005). Effective budgetary institutions in Member States thus seem to be a key factor facilitating the implementation of medium-term economic policy objectives. How can Member States improve the quality of their public finances in practical terms, taking as a point of reference the integrated guidelines for growth and jobs? The argument proposed here is that the integrated guidelines for growth and jobs are a very useful instrument to identify how structural reforms can contribute to fiscal consolidation and sustainability, as well as to enhance long-term growth potential. However, if structural reforms are to interact with macroeconomic policies in both directions, we need some instruments to identify more clearly how macroeconomic policies support structural reforms, and to choose with this aim in mind, and within a framework of fiscal consolidation.

As a first exploratory response to this question, we elaborated a box based on the current integrated guidelines for growth and jobs (see Box 5.1). Box 5.1 presents the concrete measures with possible implications for public finances, and identifies what those implications might be (public expenditure, tax policy, Structural Funds, public–private partnerships, and public procurement criteria or modernization of public services). These implications may have a positive or a negative impact on public finances, according to national measures and financial choices as per national priorities. The purpose of this table, is to assist each Member State when answering the following question: how can a certain measure be supported? What

BOX 5.1 INTEGRATED GUIDELINES FOR GROWTH AND JOBS AND THEIR IMPLICATIONS FOR PUBLIC FINANCES

Microeconomic Reforms to Raise Europe's Growth Potential

B.1 Knowledge and innovation: engines of sustainable growth

Guideline No. 7: To increase and improve investment in R&D, in particular by private business, the overall objective for 2010 of 3% of GDP is confirmed with an adequate split between private and public investment, Member States will define specific intermediate levels. Member States should further develop a mix of measures appropriate to foster R&D, in particular business R&D, through:

- more effective and efficient public expenditure on research and development (R&D) and developing public–private partnerships (PPPs); *PE, PP, SF, PPP*
- developing and strengthening centres of excellence of educational and research institutions in Member States, as well as creating new ones where appropriate, and improving the cooperation and transfer of technologies between public research institute and private enterprises; *PE, PPP, SF*
- developing and making better use of incentives to leverage private R&D; *TI*
- modernizing the management of research institutions and universities; *M*
- ensuring a sufficient supply of qualified researchers by attracting more students into scientific, technical and engineering disciplines and enhancing the career development and the European, international as well as intersectoral mobility of researchers and development personnel. *PE, M, SF*

Guideline No. 8: To facilitate all forms of innovation, Member States should focus on:

- improvements in innovation support services, in particular for dissemination and technology transfer; *PE, SF*

- the creation and development of innovation poles, networks and incubators bringing together universities, research institutions and enterprises, including at regional and local level, helping to bridge the technology gap between regions; *PE, SF, M*
- the encouragement of cross-border knowledge transfer, including from foreign direct investment; *TI, SF*
- encouraging public procurement of innovative products and services; *PP*
- better access to domestic and international finance; *M*
- efficient and affordable means to enforce intellectual property rights. *M*

Guideline No. 9: To facilitate the spread and effective use of ICT and build a fully inclusive information society, Member States should:

- encourage the widespread use of ICT in public services, SMEs and households; *PE, TI, PP, SF, M*
- fix the necessary framework for the related changes in the organization of work in the economy; *M*
- promote a strong European industrial presence in the key segments of ICT; *TI, PP, SF*
- encourage the development of strong ICT and content industries, and well-functioning markets; *M, PP*
- ensure the security of networks and information, as well as convergence and interoperability in order to establish an information area without frontiers; *M*
- encourage the deployment of broadband networks, including for the poorly served regions, in order to develop the knowledge economy. *PE, PPP, SF*

Guideline No. 10: To strengthen the competitive advantages of its industrial base, Europe needs a solid industrial fabric throughout its territory. The necessary pursuit of a modern and active industrial policy means strengthening the competitive advantages of the industrial base, including by contributing to attractive framework conditions for both manufacturing and services, while ensuring the complementarity of the action at national, transnational and European level. Member States should:

- focus on the development of new technologies and markets:
  - This implies in particular commitment to promote new technological initiatives based on public–private partnerships and cooperation between Member States, that help tackle genuine market failures; *PP, PPP*
  - This also implies the creation and development of networks of regional or local clusters across the EU with greater involvement of SMEs. *SF*

Guideline No. 11: To encourage the sustainable use of resources and strengthen the synergies between environmental protection and growth, Member States should:

- give priority to energy efficiency and co-generation, the development of sustainable, including renewable, energies and the rapid spread of environmentally friendly and eco-efficient technologies:
  - inside the internal market on the one hand particularly in transport and energy, *inter alia* in order to reduce the vulnerability of the European economy to oil price variations; *PE, TI, PPP, PP, SF*
- promote the development of means of internalization of external environmental costs and decoupling of economic growth from environmental degradations. The implementation of these priorities should be in line with existing Community legislation and with the actions and instruments proposed in the Environmental Technologies Action Plan (ETAP), inter alia, through:
  - the use of market-based instruments;
  - risk funds and R&D funding; *PE*
  - the promotion of sustainable production and consumption patterns including the greening of public procurement; *TI, PP*
  - paying a particular attention to SME;
  - a reform of subsidies that have considerable negative effects on the environment and are incompatible with sustainable development, with a view to eliminating them gradually. *TI*

B.2   Making Europe a more attractive place to invest and work

Guideline No. 12: To extend and deepen the internal market, Member States should:

- apply EU public procurement rules effectively; *PP*
- promote a fully operational internal market of services, while preserving the European social model. *PE*

Guideline No. 13: To ensure open and competitive markets inside and outside Europe and to reap the benefits of globalization, Member States should give priority to:

- a reduction in state aid that distorts competition; *TI*
- in line with the upcoming Community framework, a redeployment of aid in favour of support for certain horizontal objectives such as research, innovation and the optimization of human capital and for well-identified market failures. *TI*

Guideline No. 14: To create a more competitive business environment and encourage private initiative through better regulation, Member States should:

- reduce the administrative burden that bears upon enterprises, particularly on SMEs and start-ups. *M*

Guideline No. 15: To promote a more entrepreneurial culture and create a supportive environment for SMEs, Member States should:

- improve access to finance, in order to favour their creation and growth, in particular micro-loans and other forms of risk capital; *TI, PP*
- strengthen economic incentives, including by simplifying tax systems and reducing non-wage labour costs; *TI*
- strengthen the innovative potential of SMEs; *M*
- provide relevant support services, like the creation of one-stop contact points and the stimulation of national support networks for enterprises, in order to favour their creation and growth in line with Small Firms Charter. In addition, Member States should reinforce entrepreneurship education and training for SMEs. They should also facilitate the

transfer of ownership, modernize where necessary their bankruptcy laws, and improve their rescue and restructuring proceedings. *M*

Guideline No. 16: To expand, improve and link up European infrastructure and complete priority cross-border projects with the particular aim of achieving a greater integration of national markets within the enlarged EU. Member States should:

- develop adequate conditions for resource-efficient transport, energy and ICT infrastructures – in priority, those included in the TEN networks – by complementing Community mechanisms, notably including in cross-border sections and peripherical regions, as an essential condition to achieve a successful opening up of the network industries to competition. *PE, PPP, SF*

The Employment Guidelines
(Integrated Guidelines Nos 17–24)

Guideline No. 17: Implement employment policies aiming at achieving full employment, improving quality and productivity at work, and strengthening social and territorial cohesion.

Policies should contribute to achieving an average employment rate for the European Union (EU) of 70% overall, of at least 60% for women and of 50% for older workers (55 to 64) by 2010, and to reduce unemployment and inactivity. Member States should consider setting national employment rate targets.

Guideline No. 18: Promote a life-cycle approach to work through:

- a renewed endeavour to build employment pathways for young people and reduce youth unemployment, as called for in the European Youth Pact; *PE*
- resolute action to increase female participation and reduce gender gaps in employment, unemployment and pay; *TI*
- better reconciliation of work and private life and the provision of accessible and affordable childcare facilities and care for other dependants; *PE, PPP, TI, SF*

- support for active ageing, including appropriate working conditions, improved (occupational) health status and adequate incentives to work and discouragement of early retirement; *TI*
- modern social protection systems, including pensions and healthcare, ensuring their social adequacy, financial sustainability and responsiveness to changing needs, so as to support participation and better retention in employment and longer working lives. *PE, TI*

Guideline No. 19: Ensure inclusive labour markets, enhance work attractiveness, and make work pay for job-seekers, including disadvantaged people, and the inactive through:

- active and preventive labour market measures including early identification of needs, job search assistance, guidance and training as part of personalized action plans, provision of necessary social services to support the inclusion of those furthest away from the labour market and contribute to the eradication of poverty; *PE, SF*
- continual review of the incentives and disincentives resulting from the tax and benefit systems, including the management and conditionality of benefits and a significant reduction of high marginal effective tax rates, notably for those with low incomes, whilst ensuring adequate levels of social protection; *TI*
- development of new sources of jobs in services for individuals and businesses, notably at local level. *SF*

Guideline No. 20: Improve matching of labour market needs through:

- the modernization and strengthening of labour market institutions, notably employment services, also with a view to ensuring greater transparency of employment and training opportunities at national and European level; *PE, SF, M*
- better anticipation of skills needs, labour market shortages and bottlenecks. *M*

Guideline No. 21: Promote flexibility combined with employment security and reduce labour market segmentation, having due regard to the role of the social partners, through:

- the adaptation of employment legislation, reviewing where necessary the different contractual and working time arrangements; *TI*
- addressing the issue of undeclared work; *TI*
- better anticipation and positive management of change, including economic restructuring, notably changes linked to trade opening, so as to minimize their social costs and facilitate adaptation; *SF*
- support for transitions in occupational status, including training, self-employment, business creation and geographic mobility. *TI*

Guideline No. 22: Ensure employment-friendly labour cost developments and wage-setting mechanisms by:

- reviewing the impact on employment of non-wage labour costs and where appropriate adjust their structure and level, especially to reduce the tax burden on the low-paid. *TI*

Guideline No. 23: Expand and improve investment in human capital through:

- inclusive education and training policies and action to facilitate significantly access to initial vocational, secondary and higher education, including apprenticeships and entrepreneurship training; *PE*
- significantly reducing the number of early school leavers; *PE, SF, M*
- efficient lifelong learning strategies open to all in schools, businesses, public authorities and households according to European agreements, including appropriate incentives and cost-sharing mechanisms, with a view to enhancing participation in continuous and workplace training throughout the life cycle, especially for the low-skilled and older workers. *PE, TI, PPP, SF*

Guideline No. 24: Adapt education and training systems in response to new competence requirements by:

- easing and diversifying access for all to education and training and to knowledge by means of working time organization, family support services, vocational guidance and, if appropriate, new forms of cost sharing; *PE, TI, PPP, SF*

- responding to new occupational needs, key competences and future skill requirements by improving the definition and transparency of qualifications, their effective recognition and the validation of non-formal and informal learning. *SF, M*

Note: *PE* = Public expenditure; *TI* = Tax policy; *SF* = Structural funds; *PPP* = Public–private partnerships; *PP* = Public procurement criteria; *M* = Modernization of public services.

Source: Based on Council of the European Union (2005).

BOX 5.2   MACROECONOMIC POLICY: KEY QUESTIONS

What should be the terms of a regular dialogue between the Eurogroup and the European Central Bank (ECB) on the interest rate and the exchange rate?

How can the macroeconomic dialogue improve the follow-up of unit labour costs and their implications for wages and productivity?

To what extent is it possible to converge on shared tax policy principles, notably corporate taxes, or on the financial basis of social protection?

How can we assess the recent review of the Stability and Growth Pact, particularly its refocusing on the long-term sustainability of social protection and its new margin of manoeuvre to reduce the public deficit, taking time and other relevant factors into account?

What are the main links between structural reforms and macro-economic policies? More specifically, how can we analyse the budgetary implications of the Lisbon Agenda?

How can we redirect expenditure and taxes to fulfil the Lisbon goals? How should we reform state aid?

What can we say about emerging proposals to make progress on the demand side, notably: the coordination of national public investments at the European level; a more active use of public procurement to implement the Lisbon goals; the need for a 'growth spurt' (growth above the growth potential); the advantage of setting an aggregate fiscal position at the European level, to be broken down by 'tradable deficits' between Member States?

How can we redesign the European budget (expenditure structure and new resources) to be more in line with the Lisbon goals?

are the necessary public finance choices and policy mix? These instruments can also be used to assess the internal consistency of national reform programmes.

BIBLIOGRAPHY

Aglietta, M. and L. Berrebi (2007), *Désordres dans le capitalisme mondial*, Paris: Éditions Odile Jacob.
Buti, M. and A. Sapir (eds) (2002), *EMU and Economic Policy in Europe: The Challenge of the Early Years*, Cheltenham, UK and Northampton, MA, USA: Edward Elgar.
Collignon, S. (2006), *Why Europe is Not Becoming the World's Most Dynamic Economy. The Lisbon Strategy, Macroeconomic Stability and the Dilemma of Governance with Governments*, Pisa: Scuola Superiore Sant'Anna.
Council of the European Union (2005), *Guidelines for the Employment Policies of the Member States*, 10205/05, Brussels, 5 July 2005.
ECFIN/EOC (2005), *Restructuring Public Expenditure: Challenges and Achievements Progress Report on the Quality of Public Finances*, REP/53776 rev2, September.
Padoan, P.C. and M.J. Rodrigues (2004), 'A Good Quality Finance Rule', EPC Issue Paper no 12, Brussels: European Policy Centre.
Sapir, A. (ed.) (2004), *An Agenda for a Growing Europe: The Sapir Report*, Oxford: Oxford University Press.
Tabellini, G., C. Wyplosz, J.P. Ferry and J.P. Vesperini (2004), *Réformes structurelles et coordination en Europe*, Conseil d'Analyse Économique, Paris: La Documentation Française.

http://www.europa.eu/growthandjobs/.
http://www.mariajoaorodrigues.eu.

See further bibliography in Appendix 4 of this book.

6. Some reflections on the macroeconomic dimension of the Lisbon Agenda

Pier Carlo Padoan

The interactions between the Lisbon Agenda and the macroeconomic dimension are many and complex to say the least. In this chapter, I reflect on what are, in my view, the crucial points to address when discussing the issue. I will touch upon the following points: first, the interaction between the macroeconomic environment and the Lisbon Agenda; second, institutional and operational modifications to strengthen the European Union (EU) macroeconomic framework; third, the Stability and Growth Pact (SGP) and the Lisbon Agenda; fourth, other policy instruments in support of the Lisbon Agenda; and fifth, the external dimension.

6.1 THE MACROECONOMIC ENVIRONMENT AND THE LISBON AGENDA

An appropriate macroeconomic environment is a necessary condition for the success of the Lisbon Agenda. But without a successful Lisbon Agenda, the European macroeconomic environment, and the euro area in particular, may face significant risks.

Greater Investment in Physical and Knowledge Capital

Knowledge-based growth requires a stable macroeconomic environment. This is a generally accepted point in discussions of the relationship between macroeconomic policy and growth. Low and stable inflation provide a pro-growth environment in the medium to long run. While some short-term costs to macroeconomic stabilization may materialize, they tend to be negligible. This common wisdom needs to be qualified, however.

Growth driven by the Lisbon Agenda requires greater investment in physical and knowledge capital. Above all, the macro-environment must

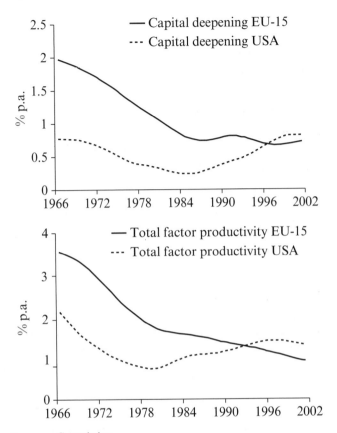

Source: European Commission.

Figure 6.1   *Breakdown of trend labour productivity into capital deepening and TFP*

provide incentives for investment. Figure 6.1 shows that both physical capital and total factor productivity (TFP) growth have been declining in the EU-15, while they have been on the rise in the US.

Figure 6.2 shows that, in the euro area, disappointing productivity is driven mainly by investment and TFP. Table 6.1 offers a more disaggregated analysis. Growth rates of capital deepening and TFP have been declining over time, contrary to what has happened in the US.

A Less Procyclical Macroeconomic Stance Supports Investment

In the EU, and in the euro area in particular, the success of the Lisbon Agenda, which requires more investment in physical and knowledge

Source: European Commission.

Figure 6.2   Investment and productivity growth in the euro area

capital, macroeconomic and financial market conditions, must be such as to prevent cyclical factors from inhibiting investment. Such a result is largely the consequence of the interaction between the policy stance and the degree of financial market development and integration. As Philippe Aghion (2006: 9) states:

> structural budget deficits and short-term interest rates fluctuate much less over the cycle in the EMU [Economic and Monetary Union] zone than in the US and UK, and . . . this in turn may inhibit growth in the euro area . . . This depends on whether firms can borrow enough funds to maintain their research and development (R&D) investments during bad times and, therefore, throughout the cycle. If they can, the best would be, at least from a growth perspective, to recommend that governments do not intervene over the business cycle, and instead let markets operate. However, the prescription might be quite different when credit market imperfections prevent firms from borrowing enough in recessions. For example, suppose that the borrowing capacity of firms is proportional to their current earnings. In a recession, current earnings decline, and so is the ability of firms to borrow in order to maintain R&D investments. In this case, a counter-cyclical policy will foster innovation and growth by reducing the negative consequences of a recession (or a bad aggregate shock) on firms' innovative investments.

In sum, if the EU macroeconomic policy stance were to become less procyclical, investment and growth could increase significantly.

Table 6.1   *Decomposition of US and EU 15-hourly labour productivity growth rates into capital deepening and TFP*

	1966–70	1971–80	1981–90	1991–95	1996–2000	1996–2003
US						
Labour productivity (hourly)	2.2	1.6	1.3	1.5	2.4	2.4
(TFP)	(1.4)	(1.1)	(1.0)	(1.0)	(1.7)	(1.5)
(Capital deepening)	(0.8)	(0.5)	(0.3)	(0.5)	(0.7)	(0.9)
EU-15						
Labour productivity (hourly)	5.4	3.7	2.3	2.5	1.8	1.5
(TFP)	(3.6)	(2.3)	(1.5)	(1.4)	(1.3)	(0.9)
(Capital deepening)	(1.8)	(1.4)	(0.8)	(1.1)	(0.5)	(0.6)

Source: EU Commission, own calculations.

Euro Area Divergence

Coping with increasing divergence in the euro area requires a more effective implementation of the Lisbon Agenda. During the first half of the first decade of the 2000s macroeconomic trends in the EU, and especially in the euro area, point at increasing divergences which, if unchallenged, may put the functioning of the eurozone at risk. We can identify divergences in a number of ways. One way is by looking at real exchange rates which show increasing divergences among the major EU economies (see Figure 6.3).

Real exchange rate divergences reflect the dynamics of wages and productivity. The evolution of the latter is particularly worrying. Not only has euro area productivity been rising less than US productivity, but productivity growth rates in the EU have diverged substantially between the euro and non-euro area, within the euro area between the large and small countries, as well as among the large euro area members (see Tables 6.2 and 6.3).

The differences in national labour productivity are mostly due to differences in TFP. Figure 6.4 (averages 1996–2003) shows that the EU and the euro area have a double problem: they need to increase aggregate productivity growth, and they also need to close the gap between national productivity trends. This, in turn, requires both EU aggregate and national

1995 = 100   1995 = 100

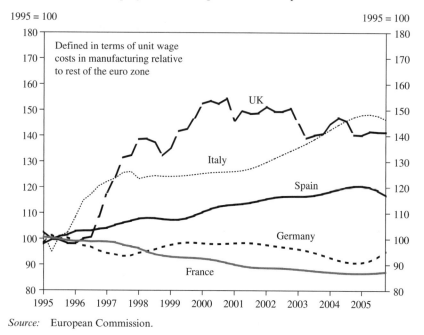

Source: European Commission.

Figure 6.3   Real effective exchange rates

Table 6.2   Labour productivity compared

	Labour productivity (period averages per person employed)			
	1981–90	1991–95	1996–2000	2001–03
World	5.0	3.3	3.1	1.0
China	10.1	13.0	8.0	7.3
India	7.6	5.4	4.4	3.8
Japan	2.7	0.8	1.4	1.5
US	1.3	1.4	2.2	1.3
EU-25	NA	NA	1.5	0.9
Further breakdown of EU-25				
New Member States (EU-10)	NA	NA	3.6	3.8
Existing Member States (EU15)	1.8	2.0	1.2	0.4
Non-euro area	1.8	2.4	1.7	1.1
Euro area	1.8	1.8	1.0	0.3
Further breakdown of euro area				
Big Four	1.9	2.0	0.8	0.2
Small Eight	1.4	1.3	2.0	0.7

Table 6.3   Labour productivity and cost compared

		1992–95	1996–99	2000–04
Unit labour cost	Italy	1.3	2.1	3.0
	France	−1.2	−1.4	−0.6
	Germany	2.9	0.6	−0.6
	Euro area		0.2	0.4
Labour cost per	Italy	5.1	2.7	2.9
employee	France	2.7	2.3	2.5
	Germany	6.7	2.0	2.3
	Euro area		2.2	2.7
	Italy	3.8	0.6	−0.1
Labour productivity	France	3.9	3.6	3.1
	Germany	3.7	1.4	2.8
	Euro area		2.0	2.3

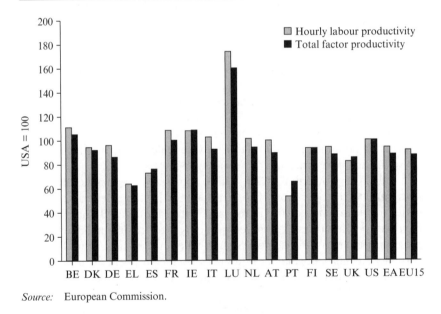

Source: European Commission.

Figure 6.4   TFP and labour productivity gap

efforts in the direction of a knowledge-based economy. In other words, the Lisbon Agenda is necessary to ensure macroeconomic sustainability. This evidence also suggests that a macroeconomic environment supportive of the Lisbon Agenda requires action at both the EU and euro area level and the national level.

6.2   INSTITUTIONAL AND OPERATIONAL REFORM

Macroeconomic Institutions: The European Dimension

There are ways, short of setting up a single EU fiscal authority, to improve the degree of fiscal coordination in Europe so as to obtain a less procyclical policy stance. There could be a decrease in the procyclicality of national fiscal policies by giving more room to automatic stabilizers and setting expenditure targets over the medium term (on the issue of the composition of spending see below). Given national fiscal policy programmes, macroeconomic coordination can be strengthened. There could be an alignment of national budgetary processes, which would allow national programmes to be based on consistent assumptions of other Member States' policies and eventual spillovers. As suggested in the Sapir Report (2004) the Commission could define the external framework to be used when preparing national stability and convergence programmes, taking into account both national and euro area conditions.

National programmes of the euro area Member States could be consolidated into an aggregate 'European Stability Programme', which would serve to assess the overall fiscal policy stance within the area, and help to determine whether adjustments to national programmes would be desirable. This step could also help to assess better the impact of structural reforms on potential growth on an EU-wide scale, and to assess the possible spillovers of reform from one country to another.

A Euro Area Council (EAC) should be entrusted with all policy decisions pertaining to the operation of the euro area (with the exception of issues under the jurisdiction of the European Central Bank, ECB), and be given the right to adapt rules that are relevant only for euro area members, while preserving the rights of Member States that do not participate in the single currency. Regular informal meetings between the president of the EAC, the relevant commissioner and the president of the ECB would reinforce the process.

Such a framework (the European Stability Programme and the EAC) would also help to formulate and implement a common external policy of the EU and euro area vis-à-vis other countries and in international institutions. This would strengthen the role of Europe in addressing global policy management.

Other measures include the possibility of tradable fiscal deficits. It is a good idea in principle, but in practice it should be accompanied by an assessment of the quality of the deficit in terms of structural versus cyclical components as well as the spending and taxation items. In order to strengthen the quality of public finances, tradable deficits could be limited to Lisbon Agenda-relevant items.

Strengthening the Macroeconomic Dialogue

Macroeconomic issues to be discussed jointly by the EAC and the ECB would be the appropriateness of the monetary and fiscal policy stance, which should include the degree of monetary tightness as determined jointly by interest rate and exchange rate developments. The assessment of the fiscal policy stance would be facilitated by the definition of an aggregate European Stability Programme. Dialogue with trade unions and social partners at the EU level should deal with general reform issues, including ways to use EU budget resources in the restructuring fund (see below). More ownership of the national reform programmes (NRP) at the national levels should include a systematic dialogue with social partners on the reform process. Given the wide dispersion of productivity trends at the national (and, possibly even more so, local) level it is difficult to envisage an EU-wide 'income policy' negotiation.

6.3   THE STABILITY AND GROWTH PACT (SGP)

The Pact and the Lisbon Agenda are the two pillars of the EU economic policy framework and should become more fully integrated. There are (at least) three reasons why the SGP and the Lisbon Agenda should be integrated better to form a unified EU and euro area economic strategy: first, incentives for policy action would be strengthened; second, the reform process would be accelerated; and third, the overall quality of public finances would improve.

Symmetrical Incentive Problems with the SGP and the Lisbon Agenda

The SGP is based on a clearly defined incentive set, which is itself underpinned by behavioural rules which have produced only a limited boost to growth, however. Conversely, the Lisbon Strategy would significantly boost growth if it could rely on stronger incentives. As a consequence, the overall EU strategy has been weakly oriented to growth, if at all. Eliminating or limiting such a bias is imperative. To do so, the SGP and the Lisbon Agenda, while clearly representing two separate pillars of the EU model, should be linked more strongly by allowing the full operation of the two channels through which public finances influence growth: factor accumulation and provision of the right incentives (in addition to setting an appropriate and stable macroeconomic environment).

A reformed SGP would also interact better with the NRP by lengthening the relevant policy time horizon. There was a recent reform to the SGP, but more change is necessary. It would also help to overcome the 'reform fatigue' which is present in several EU countries given the priority assigned to fiscal adjustment.

There was a reform of the SGP so as to avoid procyclicality, especially to encourage adjustment in good times. But the most important change is the possibility to consider deviations from the adjustment path to take into account the consequences of the implementation of structural reforms. In the reformed SGP, there is consideration of the impact of reforms on the budget, in accordance with various conditions: only major reforms that have a verifiable positive impact on the long-term sustainability of public finances are taken into account; only adopted reforms are considered; a safety margin to ensure respect for the 3 per cent of gross domestic product (GDP) reference value for the deficit needs to be guaranteed; it is expected that the budgetary position will reach medium-term objectives within four years, following the year of presentation of the programme; a detailed cost–benefit analysis of the reforms from the budgetary point of view must be provided in the stability and convergence programmes.

These modifications may increase incentives to undertake reform programmes. The above criteria remain subject to a high degree of uncertainty, however, particularly where the magnitude of the impact is concerned. Some initial evidence on the impact of reform on the budget does not lead to compelling results.

Reforms and the Budget: Mutual Impacts

There is evidence of the impact of reforms on the budget, and of the influence of the budget on propensity to undertake reforms. Servaas Deroose and Alessandro Turrini (2005) find that, in the aftermath of reforms, budgets do not worsen significantly compared with cases where no reforms occur. However, the evaluation of the short-term budgetary impact of reforms provides evidence that product and market reforms and pension reforms are associated with the deterioration of budgets. The impact appears to be rather weak (a primary balance reduced by few decimal points of GDP depending on the specific reform considered) and is not always statistically significant.

Overall, there is a strong indication that generalizations are not easy when it comes to the link between structural reforms and budgets in the short run. Results differ depending on the specific type of reforms considered. Also, within a given type of reforms (such as pension reforms) the fiscal implications are likely to differ considerably depending on the main elements of the reform and on the design of reforms. These results point to some lessons for policy. In the implementation of the EU fiscal framework, there are reasons for better taking into account the role of economic reforms, especially when there are strong *ex ante* expectations that reforms may have a positive impact on public finances in the long term, coupled with budgetary costs in the short term. However, we should avoid a mechanistic, one-size-fits-all judgement of all reforms, or all reforms belonging to some broad categories. We must judge on a case-by-case basis.

Friedrich Heinemann (2005) does not find a general short-run trade-off between Maastricht and Lisbon, since the link between budgetary outcomes and structural reforms is rather weak. While Maastricht and Lisbon tend to be mutually reinforcing for the liberalization of financial and product markets, there can be short-term conflicts for tax and labour market reforms. In addition, expectation effects may be a more important part of the link between reforms and the budget. The perception of reforms can be a crucial driver of any short-term consequences for employment, growth and the budget. The finding of negative expectation effects associated with labour market reforms is likely to be one of the explanations for why these reforms are particularly slow to materialize. Finally, Heinemann finds that an unfavourable deficit situation makes it very unlikely for certain reforms to be initiated in the first place.

Romain Duval (2005) finds that the descriptive evidence on reform patterns suggests that over the period between 1995 and 2005 EU (including euro area) countries typically have undertaken more comprehensive and far-reaching labour market reforms than other countries in the Organisation for Economic Co-operation and Development (OECD). However, he also finds different reform intensities between EU and non-EU countries, and within EU countries. Large EU countries have not shown a particular ability to carry out reforms in areas where political resistance is normally strong (with the exception of retirement schemes, where impending fiscal pressures are particularly large in EU countries). Furthermore, in the more specific case of the Economic and Monetary Union (EMU) countries, there appears to have been a slowdown in the reform process after the formal advent of the euro – although this could reflect the fatigue due to the prior race to qualify for EMU. There is some evidence that the top reformers (Denmark, Finland and the Netherlands) started their reform programmes with relatively favourable fiscal positions, and made only limited efforts to improve them during their reform years. Conversely, in a number of EU countries where few reforms have been implemented, the state of public finances was initially poor and major fiscal adjustment efforts were made, especially during the run-up to EMU (in Greece, Italy and Spain). The propensity to undertake reforms depends on a number of variables. An economic crisis and high unemployment provide a sense of urgency that favours the implementation of the reforms. Small countries appear to have a greater propensity to undertake reforms, possibly reflecting lower risks of short-run economic slack and/or lower product market rents, and thus lower public support for existing institutions aimed at capturing them. There is also evidence that a sound fiscal balance helps. Conversely, it appears that fiscal adjustment hinders the structural reform process. There is also more tentative evidence that the latter effect may be greater for countries that pursue fixed exchange rate regimes or participate in a monetary union such as EMU, and therefore have little or no monetary autonomy.

The above evidence highlights two important aspects: first, the impact of reforms on the budget is there, but it tends to disappear in the long run, so that there is no contradiction between reforms and fiscal adjustment, at least in the long run; however, second, countries with a bad fiscal position tend to postpone reforms or avoid them in order to pursue fiscal consolidation. A tentative conclusion is that the reform of the SGP, whether effectively implemented or not, does not provide sufficient incentives to carry out growth-enhancing reforms and, particularly for countries undergoing difficult public finance conditions, they do not provide sufficient incentives for a strong contribution of public finances to the Lisbon Agenda. Hence, it is necessary to consider further incentives to direct the budget towards Lisbon Agenda targets.

The Changing Composition of Public Finances and their Contribution to Growth[1]

Individual items on the government budget, be they expenditure or taxes, have different impacts on growth. For example, spending on education and research, by increasing factor accumulation and providing fiscal incentives to innovation, increases growth potential more than current spending on wages. Some of the Lisbon Agenda targets, such as devoting 3 per cent of GDP to research and development (R&D) have a direct impact on budget allocation measures.

On the other hand, one-off measures such as tax amnesties hinder growth by decreasing long-run tax certainty and depressing the propensity to invest, generating the wrong incentives for the private sector. In other words, for given size of the budget and of the deficit, composition of public spending between, say, capital and current account, and/or composition of receipts between, say, consumption taxes and tax on profits, will have a different impact on sustainable growth. It should be possible to use the discipline element of the SGP, its incentive structure, in order to redirect resources towards those items that are more conducive to sustained growth and to reinforce the implementation of the Lisbon Agenda. This would reinforce EU potential output growth, and strengthen the sustainability of growth by putting more emphasis on the intertemporal dimension of financial equilibrium. To this end, it would be helpful to introduce a Good Quality Finance Rule (GQFR) to complement the rules already underpinning the SGP. The basis of the GQFR is two pillars: a budget and a debt pillar.

The Budget Pillar

While maintaining the 3 per cent deficit limit and the commitment to reach a surplus budget position or one close to balance in the medium term according to the revised version of the SGP, the budget items would count differently in respect of such requirements, as in the case of the budget costs of structural reforms already included in the reformed SGP.

There should be a total or partial exclusion of factor accumulation measures in the computation of the SGP deficit definition. (For example, the increase in the deficit resulting from expenditure on research or education, or tax incentives for innovation, would be excluded or count only partially towards SGP requirements.) Conversely, measures that depress long-run growth, such as tax amnesties, the revenue from which reduces the deficit, would not count towards meeting the SGP requirements. Both sets of measures would enhance growth by supporting factor accumulation and suppressing negative incentives, respectively.

This requires careful identification of those budget items that should be considered as supporting factor accumulation (such as physical, human and knowledge capital). An accurate and independent assessment of the specific budget items by Eurostat and strengthened monitoring by the Commission can guarantee the transparency of the process. It remains a controversial issue whether an independent audit agency could increase the transparency and efficiency of the budget process in this respect.

The Debt Pillar

Reinforcing the role of public finances to support growth should not be detrimental to debt sustainability. Long-term sustainability requires a decline of the debt-to-GDP ratio, which should be as rapid as possible, particularly for high-debt countries. The measures suggested under the budget pillar should be implemented, subject to the conditions of a sufficiently rapid fall in the debt-to-GDP ratio (for countries whose debt–GDP ratio is above 60 per cent); or, in any case, that ratio should not go above 60 per cent (for countries whose debt–GDP ratio is below 60 per cent).

Both pillars would need an appropriate time frame, taking into account the intertemporal dimension and avoiding procyclical effects. Several proposals have already been put forward. (For example, setting aside resources for contingencies; the adoption of indicators to assess long-term debt sustainability, including the implications of implicit liabilities related to pension systems; and the adoption of an explicit minimum debt reduction requirement.)

6.4   FURTHER POLICY INSTRUMENTS IN SUPPORT OF THE LISBON AGENDA

Here, I discuss further instruments that can complement the implementation of the Lisbon Agenda at the EU level, specifically the EU budget, tax base harmonization, EU growth initiatives, and public–private partnerships (PPP).

The EU Budget

While complex in practice, we can summarize the issue of the reform of the EU budget in a few points. On the spending side, four main points: first, for a given size of the budget, resources should shift significantly from agriculture and traditional structural fund allocation towards knowledge-driven growth. One can think of several ways of achieving these targets. As an example, there are the suggestions included in the Sapir Report. The latter suggests the concentration of budget resources in three separate funds. The allocation of resources should respect the principle of 'one fund for one goal'. There can be a clear division of growth and solidarity goals across the different funds. Second, there could be a fund for economic growth within the EU area. It should cover three areas of spending: R&D and innovation, education and training, and infrastructure connecting national markets. With such a fund acting as a catalyst for national expenditure, the EU budget can also provide an incentive for governments to improve the quality of national public finances.

Third, there could be a convergence fund to help low-income countries in need of above-average growth in order to converge with the rest of the EU. It could fulfil two purposes: institution-building and investment in physical and human capital. Fourth, there could be a restructuring fund to facilitate the process of resource reallocation required as a result of deeper and wider economic integration. It should be available, with no restrictions, to all workers adversely affected by change, irrespective of their country of residence or their sector of activity. Affected workers could use the restructuring fund to cover three main needs: retraining, compensation for relocation costs, and setting up a new business. Eligibility for the restructuring fund should be limited in time with the possibility for renewal. This fund would cover persons occupied either in manufacturing and services or in the agricultural sector.

On the revenue side, changes should be significant too, moving away from the predominant role of national contributions towards a EU-wide tax base, and related to EU-wide projects or funds such as those mentioned above.

EU Networks

The macroeconomic benefits of knowledge-driven growth require not only more knowledge accumulation in terms of R&D and human capital, but also a greater emphasis on innovation diffusion to exploit fully the advantages of information and communication technologies (ICT). Among other things, this requires the development of Europe-wide infra-structure networks (see Guerrieri et al., 2005, for example). There arises the issue of how to finance and develop such networks. While clearly of EU interest, national (private and public) expenditure can finance them, with the renewed EU budget playing a catalytic role. A complementary way of addressing the financing needs of large infrastructure projects is through public–private partnerships. In cases of EU-wide infrastructure projects financed through national public funds, there might be consideration of whether to separate these items from the spending items that determine the definition of national deficits relevant for SGP procedures.

Should there be tax rate harmonization to enhance knowledge-driven growth in Europe while avoiding social and fiscal dumping? As financial markets become increasingly integrated, there is the risk that the coordination of tax rates will become ineffective, if not counterproductive, given the high risks of free-riding. A more effective way to proceed is to obtain an EU-wide set of accounting rules in order to establish a common tax base for firms operating in the EU. Also strong joint action against harmful tax practices would avoid the subtraction of resources for growth as well as other social purposes.

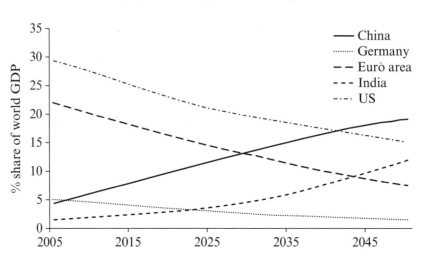

Source: IMF, European Commission, Goldman Sachs.

Figure 6.5   Shares of key emerging economies in world's GDP (in PPP)

6.5   THE EXTERNAL DIMENSION: SPEAKING WITH ONE VOICE

Europe needs to speak with one voice to manage the global system better. Increased coordination between the euro area and the ECB as suggested above is also relevant for the external dimension of macroeconomic policy. The key issue here is not so much agreeing on the exchange rate, but speaking with one European voice when managing the global economy. This is particularly relevant in the medium to long term, since if current trends are an indicator, the share of euro area and the EU in general in world GDP is set to decline (see Figure 6.5).

The issue of global exchange rate arrangements is becoming increasingly urgent since the quasi-fixed exchange rate regime between the dollar and several Asian currencies (first among them, the Chinese renmimbi) is generating an appreciation of the euro in real effective terms, which is damaging to euro area competitiveness. Given the tendency to establish regional monetary agreements in Asia, this pressure could increase in the future. It is in the interest of Europe, and in the interest of effective global governance, that Europe should identify a long-term strategy to deal with this issue, and speak with a single voice. This requires a strong European economy as well as appropriate institutional arrangements.

By generating stronger growth, the successful implementation of the

Lisbon Agenda would reinforce the voice of Europe in global issues and constitute a response to international calls for Europe to contribute to addressing global imbalances (to implement structural reforms to enhance the contribution of the EU to global growth). Conversely, a strong European voice in the global arena would allow for the establishment of a system of governance that would support EU interests while strengthening a multilateral approach to global governance.

An obvious step in the right direction is to move from national to euro area representation in international institutions such as the International Monetary Fund (IMF). Tables 6.4 and 6.5, taken from Bini Smaghi (2005), illustrate the implications in terms of the voting and blocking power of a single euro area chair. This would be clearly superior to that of any of the current national chairs. As regards long-term objectives, the guiding strategy should be one of reinforcing the formation of open regional monetary blocs that cooperate to manage global imbalances, strengthening multilateral institutions and the multilateral approach.

Table 6.4 Current voting shares and powers in the IMF

Constituencies[a]	Voting share	50% majority threshold		70% majority threshold		85% majority threshold	
		Voting power	Blocking power	Voting power	Blocking power	Voting power	Blocking power
United States	17.08	21.48	65.46	11.12	98.85	6.65	100.00
Japan	6.13	5.81	17.71	6.46	57.38	5.84	87.87
Germany	5.99	5.68	17.31	6.32	56.17	5.79	87.02
Belgium	5.14	4.87	14.84	5.47	48.64	5.36	80.67
France	4.95	4.69	14.29	5.28	46.92	5.25	78.97
United Kingdom	4.95	4.69	14.29	5.28	46.92	5.25	78.97
Netherlands	4.84	4.59	13.97	5.17	45.92	5.18	77.93
Mexico	4.27	4.04	12.32	4.58	40.68	4.78	71.92
Italy	4.18	3.96	12.06	4.49	39.88	4.65	69.93
Canada	3.73	3.53	10.76	4.01	35.67	4.30	64.60
Norway	3.51	3.32	10.12	3.78	33.60	4.10	61.72
Korea	3.32	3.14	9.57	3.58	31.81	3.93	59.10
Egypt	3.26	3.08	9.40	3.51	31.24	3.87	58.24
Saudi Arabia	3.22	3.05	9.28	3.47	30.86	3.83	57.67
Malaysia	3.17	3.00	9.14	3.42	30.39	3.79	56.94
Tanzania	2.99	2.83	8.62	3.23	28.69	3.61	54.27
China	2.94	2.78	8.47	3.17	28.21	3.56	53.50
Switzerland	2.85	2.70	8.21	3.08	27.36	3.47	52.12
Russia	2.74	2.59	7.89	2.96	26.31	3.35	50.39
Iran	2.47	2.34	7.12	2.67	23.74	3.06	46.01
Brazil	2.47	2.34	7.12	2.67	23.74	3.06	46.01
India	2.39	2.26	6.88	2.58	22.98	2.97	44.68
Argentina	1.98	1.87	5.70	2.14	19.06	2.50	37.61
Equatorial Guinea	1.44	1.36	4.15	1.56	13.88	1.85	27.81

Note: [a]Current executive director.

Source: Bini Smaghi (2005).

Table 6.5   A euro area countries' coalition

Constituencies[a]	Voting share	50% majority threshold		70% majority threshold		85% majority threshold	
		Voting power	Blocking power	Voting power	Blocking power	Voting power	Blocking power
Euro area (12)	22.91	25.36	88.06	18.06	99.86	8.04	100.00
United States	17.08	13.17	45.73	17.60	97.35	8.04	100.00
Japan	6.13	6.52	22.64	6.85	37.86	7.07	88.01
United Kingdom	4.95	5.15	17.88	5.39	29.79	6.32	78.61
Ex-Canada	3.33	3.40	11.81	3.56	19.68	4.70	58.49
Korea	3.32	3.39	11.78	3.55	19.62	4.69	58.34
Egypt	3.26	3.33	11.56	3.48	19.26	4.62	57.45
Saudi Arabia	3.22	3.29	11.41	3.44	19.00	4.57	56.91
Malaysia	3.16	3.22	11.19	3.37	18.64	4.50	55.99
Tanzania	2.99	3.05	10.58	3.19	17.62	4.29	53.35
China	2.94	2.99	10.40	3.13	17.32	4.22	52.57
Ex-Denmark	2.92	2.97	10.32	3.11	17.20	4.20	52.25
Ex-Mexico	2.86	2.91	10.11	3.05	16.84	4.12	51.29
Switzerland	2.85	2.90	10.07	3.03	16.78	4.11	51.13
Russia	2.74	2.79	9.68	2.92	16.13	3.97	49.36
Iran	2.47	2.51	8.71	2.62	14.52	3.61	44.91
Brazil	2.47	2.51	8.71	2.62	14.52	3.61	44.91
Ex-Netherlands	2.46	2.50	8.67	2.61	14.46	3.60	44.74
India	2.39	2.43	8.42	2.54	14.04	3.50	43.57
Ex-Belgium & Italy	2.13	2.16	7.50	2.26	12.50	3.14	39.12
Argentina	1.98	2.01	6.97	2.10	11.61	2.93	36.51
Equitorial Guinea	1.44	1.46	5.06	1.52	8.43	2.16	26.87

Source: Bini Smaghi (2005).

BOX 6.1   MEASURES ENHANCING GROWTH POTENTIAL AND WITH POSSIBLE BUDGETARY IMPLICATIONS

These examples are included in the common objectives or guidelines adopted by the Member States in the framework of the open method of coordination.

Information Society Policy

- Cheaper and faster Internet access.
- Faster Internet for researchers and students.
- Participation for all in the knowledge-based economy.
- Government online: electronic access to public services.
- Health online.

Research and Development Policy

- Networking of existing centres of excellence in Europe and the creation of virtual centres through new interactive communication tools.
- A common approach to creating and financing large research facilities.
- More abundant and more mobile human resources.
- Improving Europe's attraction for researchers from the rest of the world.
- Enhancing European cohesion in research by fostering the exchange and the transfer of knowledge among regions.
- Putting in place fiscal incentives to private investment in research and innovation as well as employment of researchers.

Innovation Policy

- Improve the environment for innovative enterprises.
- Developing support services including incubators and by spreading educational and training schemes in entrepreneurship and innovation.
- Improving the key interfaces in the innovation system, namely by:

- stimulating regional initiatives for networking the innovation system;
- developing education and training programmes addressing the skill gaps;
- encouraging universities to promote the diffusion of knowledge and technologies; and
- stimulating large public research facilities to improve their partnerships with enterprises.

Education Policy

- Improving the education and training for teachers and trainers; providing an adequate supply of qualified entrants in the profession and making it more attractive.
- Ensuring access to ICT for everyone. Widening the range of equipment and educational software so that ICT can be best applied in teaching and training practices.
- Increasing recruitment to scientific and technical studies, in particular research careers and scientific disciplines.
- Developing an open learning environment. Providing education and training so that adults can effectively participate and so that people can combine their participation in learning with other family and professional activities.
- Increasing mobility and exchanges. Ensuring that less privileged establishments and individuals take part in mobility programmes. Certifying the skills acquired through mobility.

Employment Policy

- Implementing active and preventive measures for the unemployed and the inactive.
- Fostering entrepreneurship to create more and better jobs.
- Promoting active ageing.
- Investing in human capital and strategies for lifelong learning.
- Promoting gender equality and combining working life and family life.
- Supporting integration and combating discrimination in the labour market.
- Preventing the risks of social exclusion.

Sustainable Development

- Address threats to public health.
- Manage natural resources more responsibly.

Source: Padoan and Rodrigues (2004).

NOTE

1. This section is based on Padoan and Rodrigues (2004).

REFERENCES

Aghion, P. (2006), *A Primer on Innovation and Growth*, Brussels: Bruegel.
Bini Smaghi, L. (2005), 'IMF Governance and the Political Economy of a Consolidated European Seat', paper presented at the Conference on IMF Reform, Institute for International Economics, Washington, DC, 23 September.
Deroose, S. and A. Turrini (2005), 'The Short-Term Budgetary Implications of Structural Reforms: Evidence from a Panel of EU Countries', paper prepared for the conference on Budgetary Implications of Structural Reforms, organized by the Directorate-General for Economic and Financial Affairs (DG ECFIN) of the Commission of the European Union, 2 December.
Duval, R. (2005), 'Fiscal Positions, Fiscal Adjustment and Structural Reforms in Labour and Product Markets', paper prepared for the conference on Budgetary Implications of Structural Reforms, organized by the Directorate-General for Economic and Financial Affairs (DG ECFIN) of the Commission of the European Union, 2 December.
Guerrieri, P., B. Maggi, V. Meliciani and P.C. Padoan (2005), 'Technology Diffusion, Services, and Endogenous Growth in Europe: Is the Lisbon Strategy Useful?', IMF Working Paper 105/05; also in M. Malgarini and G. Piga (eds), *Capital Accumulation, Productivity and Growth*, London: Palgrave Macmillan, pp. 115–39.
Heinemann, F. (2005), 'How Distant is Lisbon from Maastricht? The Short-Run Link Between Structural Reforms and Budgetary Performance', paper prepared for the conference on Budgetary Implications of Structural Reforms, organized by the Directorate-General for Economic and Financial Affairs (DG ECFIN) of the Commission of the European Union, 2 December.
Padoan, P.C. and M.J. Rodrigues (2004), 'A Good Quality Finance Rule', EPC Issue Paper no 12, Brussels: European Policy Centre.
Sapir, A., (ed.) (2004), *An Agenda for a Growing Europe; The Sapir Report*, Oxford: Oxford University Press.

7. Developing the Lisbon Agenda at the European level: conclusions of the debate

Maria João Rodrigues

7.1 EUROPE IN A GLOBALIZED KNOWLEDGE ECONOMY: THE WAY FORWARD

The point of departure for strategic thinking on Europe should always be the 'globalized' world. More particularly, when reconsidering the Lisbon Agenda, we should take into account that the global process of knowledge accumulation and diffusion is speeding up because of increasing investments in research, innovation and education, and because of the impact of information and communication technologies (ICT). The organization of the global production chains led by multinational companies, and competition among countries to attract international investment, are deeply restructuring this process. Silicon Valley may be unique, but innovation poles that are attempting to replicate that model are emerging all over the world. More specifically, the emergence of large-scale competitors, such as China and India, is dramatically changing the global landscape.

In this new context, the key questions for Europe seem to be the following. How can the multiplication of knowledge-intensive economies lead to a win–win game? How can European companies develop at the global level? And how can Europe remain attractive for worldwide investment?

Before addressing these questions, we should assess Europe's medium-term comparative advantages. Market size, research capabilities and education levels will remain important but no longer distinctive European features. Rather, Europe's distinctive advantages may be quality of life, consumer sophistication, the creativity of workers, the ability to offer sophisticated services and production systems, the quality of public services, the environmental balance, the single currency and political capability to manage diversity. With these elements in mind, let us now address the three above-mentioned questions.

A Win–Win Game

First, how can the multiplication of knowledge-intensive economies lead to a win–win game? We must develop common global social, environmental and economic standards, and intellectual property rights rules to create a level playing field. It is not possible for Europe to implement an ambitious agenda covering all three domains unless its main international partners move in the same direction. So the European Union (EU) must strengthen its external action to improve global governance, notably within the World Trade Organization (WTO), the Bretton Woods institutions, and by coordinating with UN development agencies to promote global standards. More specifically, the EU should shift within the WTO from a defensive approach on agriculture to a proactive stance on the 'Singapore issues', using trade as a form of leverage to promote a more forward-looking international division of labour. In addition to the broad multilateral negotiation, bilateral agreements under discussion also serve to encourage existing processes of regional integration.

The Global Development of European Companies

Second, how can European companies develop at the global level? European companies, both large and small, may continue to be based in Europe, but they should be encouraged to 'go global' in terms of markets and new productive factors. The first condition to ensure that this happens is to create scale, by making better use of the European single market, avoiding protectionism of national champions, and supporting dynamic small and medium-sized enterprises (SMEs) so that they reach a critical size. Competition policy, common standard-setting and public procurement can all help to increase the size of this market. The integration of financial markets can also play a very important role in the reorganization of business models on a European scale. Critical mass for global competition should also be developed by: organizing European-wide strategic platforms; mobilizing companies, research, education and financial institutions; coherently identifying priorities for research, innovation and education; and by aiming to build capacity to explore new markets. We can work in this direction using the concept of 'lead markets' and building on technology platforms and European clusters.

Attracting Investment to Europe

Third, how can Europe remain attractive for global investment? The first step to take is to enhance Europe's distinctive advantages in a sustainable way. The second step is to speed up the European knowledge accumulation and diffusion process. We must invest not only in research but also in innovation and in education, so it would be useful to complement the widely publicized indicator on research investment with a more comprehensive indicator on knowledge accumulation. Shortages of human resources broadly speaking deserve special attention, including highly skilled people as well as creative professionals, professional of technical routines, and personal service professionals. There needs to be a reconsideration of European immigration policy to establish new models, which can turn the brain drain into brain circulation and brain exchange. The ongoing restructuring of the labour market in terms of skills also has implications for the reform of social protection systems. We need a more personalized approach to support those who lose their jobs, as well as more dynamic careers among so-called knowledge workers. More fundamentally, what seems to be at stake is the establishment of a model of creative destruction, and speeding up the transition to a knowledge-intensive economy, which should be supported not only by financial markets but also by the European social model in accordance with its values. This leads us to the issue of the reform of the European social model and the role of European social policy.

7.2   EUROPEAN SOCIAL POLICY

Updating the Policy Mix

The goal of European social policy has been to maintain social cohesion and support change throughout the different stages of European integration: building the common and single market, creating a monetary zone, dealing with the shared challenges posed by globalization and addressing key demographic trends. The specificity of the Lisbon Agenda is that, after the 1997 shift promoted by the European Employment Strategy (EES), Member States agreed to the adoption of European measures for the coordination of national social policies (employment, social protection, social inclusion, education and, more recently, health). The main argument for this development is that Member States face common challenges and similar reform needs which, despite differences among social systems, are indicative of a shared European model.

The approach developed by the Lisbon Agenda has certain characteristics. It is based on the view that social policy has a value in itself and is also a productive factor; that social policy should be renewed to support the current transition to a knowledge-intensive economy. Here, the role of education, training, learning organizations, and of restructuring management is central. Concern with sustainability broadens the concept of social justice to take into account intergenerational relations. It also leads to a new emphasis not only on reducing unemployment but also on raising the employment rate, as a crucial factor to sustain social protection systems. There needs to be a more dynamic analysis of the labour market, one that takes into account life-cycle transitions, and should inspire the redesign of social policies.

What is the current policy and instrument mix of European social policy? The social dialogue at the European level built up and complemented the *acquis communautaire* in terms of labour, employment and social protection directives. Although it had the support of a bilateral work programme and was the subject of regular tripartite summits, this dialogue seems to have lost its capacity to generate reforms of the legal framework governing European social policy. Alongside this, a new phase of the European Social Fund (ESF) has been launched, covering the period of 2007–13. Now complemented by the new Globalization Fund, the new ESF is likely to be more in line with the Lisbon goals.

Finally, the employment guidelines, along with the broad economic policy guidelines, are now part of the integrated guidelines for growth and jobs, defining the current version of the Lisbon Agenda by using these Treaty-based instruments. While there are clearly fewer references to social protection and social inclusion in this version of the Lisbon Agenda compared to the previous one, a parallel process covering these policies has been established, governed by the open method of coordination, which should feed into the central Lisbon process.

A key question is whether current European social policy can support European citizens and companies in their efforts to adapt to globalization. There are some new developments in the policy mix and instruments of European social policy that may be introduced.

Improving the Policy Mix

A major step would be to include social protection and social inclusion issues in the Lisbon Agenda integrated guidelines, which also require streamlining. This would avoid a parallel process and allow the social dimension to be addressed more consistently. This will also make it easier to draw all the implications of the life-cycle approach, by designing a consistent combination of employment, lifelong learning and social protection measures for each phase: integration of young people into the labour market, conciliation of family and working life, active ageing, mobility and immigration. This framework will also facilitate the identification of the kind of security that must be provided to ensure flexibility of labour markets, and the design of more tailored flexicurity instruments.

Lifelong learning should become a more central policy within a policy mix, in accordance with the Lisbon Agenda. This calls for greater political efforts to address problems of demand and supply. On the demand side, generalized and updated vocational guidance, the validation and recognition of training, working hours flexibility, childcare and new financial facilities (such as learning accounts), are crucial to encourage citizens to participate in lifelong learning. On the supply side, the investment of companies in training can be fostered by ensuring that their human assets have a stronger influence on their financial value, and by new funding arrangements for training by companies, including labour contract arrangements in which training costs are taken into account when there is professional mobility. In the restructuring of management, traditional passive and cushioning instruments should be complemented increasingly by active approaches based on regional and industrial policy and, furthermore, by a proactive approach based on innovation policy.

As regards social protection policies, in addition to undertaking a general recalibration of benefits and contributions to take into account new social risks and intergenerational balance, we need a more personalized approach to make room for personal choice, precisely to account for the various stages of the life cycle and the need for widespread lifelong learning. As regards social inclusion, we need a better mix between minimum income and activation for a new social contract. A composite indicator of social inclusion should be considered in the political assessment of the Lisbon Agenda, in parallel with the composite indicator on knowledge accumulation, as mentioned above. It will not be possible to sustain European social standards without stronger international action by the European Union to improve social standards in other countries. Change can be promoted through international regulations, such as the International Labour Organization (ILO) conventions, and through trade negotiations or cooperation programmes.

Improving Instruments

This policy mix will have various implications for the mix of instruments to be used. The next generation of integrated guidelines to define the Lisbon Agenda should also include social protection and inclusion, and avoid parallel processes. Some open method of coordination (OMC) instruments should be used to be more specific in the implementation of these guidelines, notably as regards regular monitoring, peer learning and the participation of stakeholders. The scope of restructuring problems covered by the

Globalization Adjustment Fund should be broadened. In addition to stronger enforcement of current directives, new legislative initiatives could be considered, notably on retraining opportunities, and the general principle of minimum income with activation.

7.3   MACROECONOMIC POLICY AND THE LISBON AGENDA: PROMOTING STRONGER SYNERGIES[1]

The macroeconomic dimension of the Lisbon Agenda also needs to be worked on. There are many complex interactions between the Agenda and macroeconomic issues. Among the most important areas to be considered are: the interaction between the macroeconomic environment and the Lisbon Agenda; institutional and operational modifications to strengthen the EU macroeconomic framework; the links between the Stability and Growth Pact (SGP) and the Lisbon Agenda; other policy instruments to support the Lisbon Agenda; and the external dimension of the Lisbon Agenda.

Overall, an appropriate macroeconomic environment is a necessary condition for the success of the Lisbon Agenda. Conversely, if the Lisbon Agenda is not successful, Europe's macroeconomic environment, and the euro area in particular, could face significant risks.

The Symmetrical Incentive Problems of the SGP and the Lisbon Agenda

The SGP and the Lisbon Agenda are the two pillars of the EU economic policy framework and need to be better integrated. There are three reasons why the SGP and the Lisbon Agenda should be more closely integrated to form a unified single EU and euro area economic strategy: first, because incentives for policy action would be strengthened; second, because the reform process would be accelerated; and third, because the overall quality of public finances would be improved.

The SGP is based on a clearly defined incentive set, itself underpinned by behavioural rules. These, however, have provided only a limited boost to growth. With stronger incentives, though, the Lisbon Strategy could significantly boost growth.

A reformed SGP would also interact more effectively with the national reform programmes (NRP) by lengthening the relevant policy time horizon. The SGP was recently reformed, but further change is necessary. It has been reformed in the direction of avoiding procyclicality, especially to encourage adjustment in good times. But the most important change is the possibility to consider deviations from the adjustment path to take into account the consequences of the implementation of structural reforms. In the reformed SGP, the impact of reforms on the budget are taken into consideration according to a number of conditions.

However, independently of whether it is effectively implemented or not, this SPG reform does not provide sufficient incentives to carry out growth-enhancing reforms and, for countries with a difficult public finance condition in particular, they do not provide sufficient incentives for a strong contribution of public finances to the Lisbon Agenda. Hence, further incentives to direct the budget towards Lisbon Agenda targets should be considered.

It should be possible to use the discipline element and the incentive structure of the SGP to redirect resources towards more sustained growth, and to reinforce the implementation of the Lisbon Agenda. This would strengthen EU potential output growth and its sustainability by putting more emphasis on the intertemporal dimension of financial equilibrium. To this end, a Good Quality Finance Rule (GQFR) should be introduced to complement the rules already underpinning the SGP. The GQFR is based on two pillars: a budget pillar and a debt pillar.

The Budget Pillar

While maintaining the 3 per cent deficit limit and the commitment to reach a surplus or nearly balanced budget position in the medium term, in accordance with the revised SGP, the budget items would count differently in respect of such requirements, as in the case of the budget costs of structural reforms. This requires careful identification of those budget items that should be viewed as supporting factor accumulation (notably, physical, human and knowledge capital). The transparency of the process is to be guaranteed through an accurate and independent assessment of the specific budget items by Eurostat, and by strengthened monitoring by the Commission.

The Debt Pillar

Debt sustainability should not be negatively affected by a reinforcement of the role of public finances to support growth. Long-term sustainability requires a decline of the debt-to-GDP ratio as soon as possible, especially in high-debt countries. The measures suggested under the budget pillar should be implemented, subject to the conditions of a sufficiently rapid decline of the debt-to-GDP ratio (for countries whose debt–GDP ratio is above 60 per cent) or, in any case, that ratio should not go above 60 per cent (for countries whose debt–GDP ratio is below 60 per cent). Both pillars would have to be put in an appropriate time frame, taking into account the intertemporal dimension and avoiding procyclical effects.

The EU Budget

The reform of the EU budget, while complex in practice, can be summarized as follows: on the spending side, for a given size of the budget, resources should be significantly redirected from agriculture and traditional structural fund allocation towards knowledge-driven growth; on the revenue side, changes should also be significant, with move away from the predominance of national contributions towards an EU-wide tax base, and related to EU-wide projects and/or European structural funds.

EU Networks

For the macroeconomic benefits of knowledge-driven growth to emerge, it is necessary to have more knowledge accumulation in terms of research and development (R&D) and human capital, as well as greater emphasis on innovation diffusion to exploit fully the advantages of ICT. Among other things, this calls for the development of Europe-wide infrastructure networks. This raises the issue of the financing and development of such networks. While clearly of EU interest, the latter can be financed by national (private and public) expenditure, with the renewed EU budget playing a catalytic role. A complementary way of addressing the financing needs of large infrastructure projects is through public–private partnerships. In cases of EU-wide infrastructure projects financed through national public funds, there could be consideration of a separation of these items from the spending items that determine the definition of national deficits relevant for SGP procedures.

NOTE

1. Adapted from Chapter 6 and Padoan and Rodrigues (2004).

REFERENCE

Padoan, P.C. and M.J. Rodrigues (2004), 'A Good Quality Finance Rule', EPC Issue Paper no 12, Brussels: European Policy Centre.

PART II

The European Lisbon Agenda and National
Diversity

8. The European Lisbon Agenda and national diversity: key issues for policy-making

Maria João Rodrigues

After the 2005 mid-term review, the Lisbon Strategy was translated into national reform programmes by all the Member States of the European Union (EU). There are assessments of some of these programmes available (see European Commission, 2006, for instance), but more in-depth analysis is still lacking. When undertaking such an analysis, it is necessary to consider the variety of capitalist economies coexisting within the EU. Some of the questions we must answer are: to what extent can a common European agenda for structural reforms be implemented at the national level, and adapted to specific national conditions? Should the Lisbon Strategy be a 'meta-reference' for minimal convergence and cross-fertilization between different types of capitalism? If so, which are the critical points for a transition in each type of capitalism? Before addressing these intriguing issues, let us recall briefly the state of play with the Lisbon Strategy since the mid-term review of 2005.

8.1 THE LISBON STRATEGY AFTER THE MID-TERM REVIEW

The Lisbon Strategy launched by the European Council of March 2000 is a European development strategy to confront the new challenges posed by globalization, population ageing and the increasingly fast pace of technological change. At its core is the recognition that to sustain the European social model it is necessary to renew it as well as its economic foundations by focusing on knowledge and innovation. Indeed, this should be the main purpose of an agenda for structural reforms. The Strategy should also comply with the general principles of sustainable development, as emphasized from the 2001 Swedish presidency onwards.

Over the following years, the Strategy was turned into an agenda proposing common goals and concrete measures, making use not only of traditional instruments, such as directives and Community programmes, but also of a new open method of coordination (OMC), which had already been tested in the domain of employment policy, and later extended to many others, including information society, research, enterprise, innovation, education, and social protection and inclusion policies.

The results of implementation in 2004 were clearly very unequal across policy areas and from country to country. Very broadly, progress was evident in some areas (such as Internet connections, networks for excellence in research, one-stop shops for small business, the integration of financial markets, the modernization of employment services, and in some social inclusion plans), but there were important and obvious bottlenecks when it came to fostering innovation, adopting a Community patent, opening the services market, developing lifelong learning and reforming social protection. Further, in general terms, the performance of some Northern countries was better than that of some Southern states; and some smaller countries seemed to perform better than most of the larger ones.

At the same time, the implementation gap worsened because of a communications gap caused by the absence of a communication policy that could link progress on the ground with the European agenda. In the face of these shortcomings, the mid-term review of 2004–05 undertaken during the Luxembourg presidency proposed some solutions to address the main problems identified (Kok, 2004; Sapir, 2004), namely: unclear strategic objectives; the inflation of priorities and measures; the absence of implementation, coordination and participation mechanisms; and lack of financial incentives.

With the mid-term review, the Lisbon Agenda was defined by a set of integrated guidelines for growth and jobs (see Box 5.1) to be translated at the European level by the Community Lisbon Programme and, at national level, by the national reform programmes.

Each Member State should determine its particular mix of priorities, which is why the preparation and implementation of national reform programmes deserves more in-depth analysis. Different political choices inform each specific combination adopted; but, perhaps more fundamentally, they are a function of the different types of capitalism existing in the Member States.

8.2   THE LISBON STRATEGY AND VARIETIES OF CAPITALISM

Analysing Varieties of Capitalism

There is a rich tradition of analysing varieties of capitalism in social sciences (see the overview in Hall and Soskice, 2001). Here, I build on the approach adopted by Amable (2003), which is particularly appropriate in the context of this analysis. Amable (2003: 92) presents a comprehensive theoretical framework based on the following key institutional areas: product-market competition; labour market institutions and the wage–labour nexus; the financial intermediation sector and corporate governance; social protection; and the education sector.

These institutional areas provide a framework to identify different types of capitalism, which can also be validated by empirical research. Accordingly, Amable identifies the following types of capitalism (Amable, 2003: 104): market-based economies, social-democratic economies, Asian capitalism, Continental European capitalism and South European capitalism.

Amable argues that there is a particular complementarity between the above-mentioned institutional areas in each type of capitalism. Recalling the distinction that Hall and Soskice (2001) make between a liberal market and coordinated market economy, he states that in the latter: 'the existence of durable relationships, and of proximity between banks and firms, enhances the implementation of long-term investment projects, and this in return facilitates the establishment of stable compromises in the labour market' (Amable, 2003: 61). He posits that it is also possible to identify a particular institutional hierarchy when analysing these interactions: based on the extensive research led by Boyer (1988), it appears that the nature of the wage–labour nexus plays a central role in the dynamics shaping each type of capitalism, as it affects both production and consumption norms. Furthermore, Amable contends that the type of capitalism influences the type of competitive advantages:

> liberal market economies have a comparative advantage in industries where radical innovation leads to market-stealing benefits and where competitiveness stems from fast adaptation to changing market conditions. Coordinated market economies have the edge in industries where competitiveness is based on cumulative build-up of knowledge and company-specific skills and where incremental innovation matters. (Amable, 2003: 78–79)

For a more in-depth analysis of this issue, Amable presents another typology, which focuses particularly on social systems of innovation and production, building on the following criteria (these overlap partially with those mentioned above), to analyse the different types of capitalism: science, technology, competence and skills, labour markets, competition, finance, and products (Amable, 2003: 85).

A Typology of Capitalisms in the European Union

This theoretical framework can be used to produce a more refined typology of capitalisms in the EU at a time when Member State economies are undergoing a dual process of structural change: namely, speeding up the transition to a more knowledge-intensive economy, and adapting social protection systems to cope with ageing trends. In this context, it is proposed that we should consider innovation systems and social protection systems as playing a central role in the institutional hierarchy of the process of structural change; consequently, that the two different typologies presented by Amable (the general one on varieties of capitalism and the more specific one on varieties of social systems of innovation and production) should be merged; and, finally, that we should consider a wider range of types of capitalism within the European Union – the above-mentioned Anglo-Saxon variant, the Nordic and the Central European variants, as well as the Southern and Eastern types of capitalism. Regarding the latter, a special effort of elaboration is necessary in light of the recent transition process.

The Central European model of capitalism is roughly characterized by (adapted from Amable et al., 1997):

- High employment protection, limited external flexibility, job stability, conflicting industrial relations, active employment policy, moderately strong unions, coordination of wage bargaining.
- Strong institutionalization of employment rules, working hours and social protection.
- A high degree of social protection, employment-based social protection, involvement of the state, high importance of social protection in society, contribution-financed social insurance, pay-as-you-go pension systems.
- Moderate competition, because of public intervention or business associations, even if intensified within the single market.
- The importance of banks and relatively low sophistication of financial services.
- Public basic research disconnected from new-product development within firms, but there are large-scale programmes.
- The importance of public impetus for private research.

- Internal rather than external mobility of the labour force.
- A high level of public expenditure, high enrolment rates in secondary education, emphasis on secondary-education homogeneity, developed vocational training, emphasis on specific skills.

The Anglo-Saxon model of capitalism is characterized by:

- Low employment protection, external flexibility, easy use of temporary work and easy 'hire and fire', no active employment policy, defensive union strategies.
- Decentralization of wage bargaining, individualized wage and labour-market segmentation.
- Weak social protection, low involvement of the state, emphasis on poverty alleviation (social safety net), means-tested benefits, privately funded pension system.
- Limits to concentration through legal action, constant evolution of oligopolistic competition.
- Market-based finance and sophistication of financial services, financial innovation, strong influence of shareholders.
- The research system is based on competition between researchers and between research institutions.
- The importance of intellectual property rights protection incentives towards innovation.
- A highly segmented labour force, high skills and innovation on one side, low skills and production on the other.
- Low public expenditure, highly competitive higher-education system, non-homogenized secondary education, weak vocational training, emphasis on general skills, lifelong learning.

The South European model of capitalism is characterized by:

- High employment protection (large firms) but dualism: a 'flexible' fringe of employment in temporary and part-time work, possible conflicts in industrial relations, weaker active employment policy, centralization of wage bargaining.
- Moderate level of social protection, expenditure structure oriented towards poverty alleviation and pensions, high involvement of the state.
- Low public expenditure, low enrolment rates in tertiary education, weak higher-education system, weak vocational training, no lifelong learning, emphasis on general skills.

The Nordic model of capitalism is characterized by:

- Moderate employment protection, coordinated or centralized wage bargaining, active employment policy, strong unions, cooperative industrial relations.
- A high level of social protection, high involvement of the state, high importance of the welfare state in public policy and society.
- A small number of large internationalized firms and networks of small local suppliers.
- Moderate employment protection, coordinated or centralized wage bargaining, active employment policy, strong unions, cooperative industrial relations.
- A bank-based financial system, no sophistication of financial services.
- Social needs are important in the definition of research objectives.
- Gradual evolution towards advanced technologies and new sectors – from natural-resources exploitation to information technology.
- Egalitarian ideals in education and wage-setting, limits through public action to the adverse consequences of technical progress.
- A high level of public expenditure, high enrolment rates, emphasis on the quality of primary and secondary education, importance of vocational training, emphasis on specific skills, importance of retraining, lifelong learning.

Table 8.1 presents this framework. The questions to ask when analysing this table are: are these the key institutional areas that distinguish the different types of capitalism? Are these the main types of capitalism in the EU that we must take into consideration? Are these the main features that characterize these types of capitalism? How can we fill in the blank boxes in order to complete this characterization?

Characterizing the 'Meta-Type Capitalism' Underlying the Lisbon Agenda

The same framework was applied to the Lisbon Agenda as defined by the integrated guidelines for national reform programmes, and the Lisbon Community Programme at the European level. The question is whether it is possible to identify a meta-type of capitalism underlying the Lisbon Agenda. We use the term 'meta-type' because we are referring to a more abstract and hybrid type of capitalism, which can provide a general horizon for the various different types of capitalism that exist in Europe.

The analysis is presented in Table 8.2, distinguishing between national-level and European-level governance instruments. In practice, this distinction

Table 8.1   *Ideal types of capitalism*

Institutional area	Market-based economies	Central European capitalism	South European capitalism	Nordic European
Science	The research system is based on competition between researchers and between research institutions	Public basic research is disconnected from new-product development within firms, but there are large-scale programmes		Social needs are important in the definition of research objectives
Technology	Importance of intellectual property rights protection, patents, and copyrights as incentives towards and protection for innovation	Importance of public impetus for private research		Gradual evolution towards advanced technologies and new sectors – from natural resources exploitation to information technology
Competence and skills	Highly segmented labour force; high skills and innovation on one side, low skills and production on the other	Internal rather than external mobility of the labour force		Egalitarian ideals in education and wage-setting; limits through public action to the adverse consequences of technical progress
Education	Low public expenditures, highly competitive higher education system, non-homogenized secondary education,	High level of public expenditure, high enrolment rates in secondary education, emphasis on secondary education homogeneity,	Low public expenditure, low enrolment rates in tertiary education, weak higher education system, weak vocational training,	High level of public expenditures, high enrolment rates, emphasis on the quality of primary and secondary

Table 8.1 (continued)

Institutional area	Market-based economies	Central European capitalism	South European capitalism	Nordic European
	weak vocational training, emphasis on general skills, lifelong learning	developed vocational training, emphasis on specific skills	no lifelong learning, emphasis on general skills	education, importance of vocational training, emphasis on specific skills, importance of retraining, lifelong learning
Wage–labour nexus	Low employment protection, external flexibility: easy recourse to temporary work and easy hire and fire, no active employment policy, defensive union strategies, decentralization of wage bargaining	High employment protection, limited external flexibility, job stability, conflicting industrial relations, active employment policy, moderately strong unions, coordination of wage bargaining	High employment protection (large firms) but dualism: a 'flexible' fringe of employment in temporary and part-time work, possible conflicts in industrial relations, no active employment policy, centralization of wage bargaining	Moderate employment protection, coordinated or centralized wage bargaining, active employment policy, strong unions, cooperative industrial relations
Labour markets	Decentralization of wage bargaining; individualized wage and labour-market segmentation	Strong institutionalization of employment rules, working hours and social protection		Centralization of wage bargaining under the external competitiveness constraint

Social protection	Weak social protection, low involvement of the state, emphasis on poverty alleviation (social safety net), means-tested benefits, private-funded pension system	High degree of social protection, employment-based social protection, involvement of the state, high importance of social protection in society, contribution-financed social insurance, pay-as-you-go pension systems	Moderate level of social protection, expenditures structure oriented towards poverty alleviation and pensions, high involvement of the state	High level of social protection, high involvement of the state, high importance of the welfare state in public policy and society
Competition	Limits to concentration through legal action; constant evolution of oligopolistic competition	Once moderate competition, because of public intervention or business associations, has intensified within the single market; concentration of capital		Small number of large internationalized firms and networks of small local suppliers
Product-market competition	High importance of price competition, non-involvement of the state in product markets, coordination through market (price) signals, openness to foreign competition and investment	Moderate importance of price competition, relatively high importance of quality competition, involvement of public authorities, relatively high non-price 'coordination', low protection against foreign firms and investment	Price- rather than quality-based competition, involvement of the state, little 'non-price' coordination, moderate protection against foreign trade or investment, importance of small firms	High importance of quality competition, high involvement of the state in product markets, high degree of 'coordination' through channels other than market signals, openness to foreign competition and investment

Table 8.1 (continued)

Institutional area	Market-based economies	Central European capitalism	South European capitalism	Nordic European
Finance	Market-based finance and sophistication of financial services; financial innovation; strong influence of shareholders	Importance of banks; relatively low sophistication of financial services		Bank-based financial system; no sophistication of financial services
Financial sector	High protection of minority shareholders, low ownership concentration, high importance of institutional investors, active market for corporate control (takeovers, mergers and acquisitions), high sophistication of financial markets, development of venture capital	Low protection of external shareholders, high ownership concentration, no active market for corporate control (takeovers, mergers and acquisitions), low sophistication of financial markets, moderate development of venture capital, high banking concentration, importance of banks in firms' investment funding	Low protection of external shareholders, high ownership concentration, bank-based corporate governance, no active market for corporate control (takeovers, mergers and acquisitions), low sophistication of financial markets, limited development of venture capital, high banking concentration	High ownership concentration, high share of institutional investors, no market for corporate control (takeovers, mergers and acquisitions), no sophistication of financial markets, high degree of banking concentration

Source: Based on Amable et al. (1997), Amable (2003).

Table 8.2   *Unveiling the meta-type of capitalism implicit in the Lisbon Agenda*

	European level	National level
Research	• Broad economic policy guidelines • Cooperation of Member States in European agencies • Research in community institutions • Competition between European networks of excellence and integrated projects for European thematic programmes • Competition between teams in basic research (European Research Council) • Support to research by structural funds	• Increase private and public investment in research • Opening and connecting research institutions and creating centres of excellence • Attracting more people for research careers
Innovation	• Developing European networks of clusters for innovation • Launching European technological initiatives • Adopting a Community patent • Support for innovation by structural funds • Support by EIB and EIF instruments	• Improving innovation support services • Developing innovation clusters, poles and incubators • Better access to domestic and international finance • Efficient and affordable means for intellectual property • Public procurement for innovative products and services
ICT	• Completing a single European information space • Achieving an inclusive European information society • Strengthening innovation and research on ICT • Support for the information society by structural funds	• Encouraging widespread use of ICT in public services, SMEs and households and couple with organizational change • Improving access to broadband • Developing content industries
Environment	• European strategy for sustainable development • Action plan for environmental technologies • Implementing Kyoto protocol • Support for the environment by structural funds	• Encouraging the adoption of environmental technologies by regulation, tax incentives and public procurement

Table 8.2 (continued)

	European level	National level
Education	• Employment guidelines • Developing European mobility for education and training • Implementing the Bologna process for convergence in high level education • Adopting a European Qualifications Framework and a European list of key competences • Support by structural funds	• Inclusive education and training policies to facilitate access to vocational, secondary and higher education • Reducing the early school leavers • Lifelong learning open to all in schools, business, public services and households; support by working time organization • Responding to new skills needs by defining and validating new skills
Labour markets	• Directives on: – wealth and safety – individual employment conditions – modernization of work organization – information and consultation – working time – fixed term, part-time, temporary work – corporate restructuring – anti-discrimination – parental leave • European social dialogue • Support to regional development by structural funds • Globalisation Adjustment Fund	• Raising the employment level, attracting more people into the labour market • Developing a life-cycle approach adapting labour market and social protection policies to young, adult and old workers • Strengthening active labour market policies • Regular review of the contributions and benefits systems to make work pay • Appropriate management of economic immigration • Ensuring employment-friendly labour costs developments by social partners • Promoting innovative and adaptable forms of work organization • Improving the management of restructuring process • Developing better combinations of flexibility with security • Social partnership for change, social pacts

Social protection	• Community Programme for Employment and Social Solidarity (PROGRESS) • European Social Agenda	• Ensuring adequate accessible, financially sustainable, adaptable and efficient social protection systems and social inclusion policies • Target actions to fight poverty
Competition	• Common trade policy aiming at agreement on free trade with promotion of basic standards • Internal market directives on products, workers' mobility and services, aiming at opening the markets while preserving the European social model including the services of public interest • Building trans-European networks • Support to regional development by structural funds • State aid regulations aiming at reducing and redirecting them to research, innovation and human capital • Competition policy (European statute, takeover, etc.) • Improving the quality of regulations • Broad economic policy guidelines • New industrial policy to improve framework conditions and advanced competitive factors • Financial Services Action Plan aiming at faster financial market integration and large diversification and access in financial services	• Promoting external groups in a multilateral context • Speeding up the transportation and enforcement of internal market directives • Applying EU public procurement rules • Removing trade barriers • Developing infrastructures, if necessary by using public–private partnerships • Reducing and redirecting state aids • Reducing administrative burden on enterprises and improve the quality of regulations • Encouraging enterprises in developing their corporate social responsibility • Supporting entrepreneurship by providing support services, strengthen the economic incentives, improving access to finance and facilitating the transfer of ownership • Implementing the directives for financial market integration
Macroeconomic Policies	Stability: • Stability and Growth Pact • Multilateral surveillance • Broad economic policy guidelines	• Member States should respect their medium-term budgetary objectives and take the necessary corrective measures to achieve them

Table 8.2 (continued)

European level	National level
Sustainability: • Monetary policy defined by the European Central Bank Quality: • Eurozone Member States need to ensure better coordination of their economic and budgetary policies – Policy mix that supports economic recovery and is compatible with price stability – Structural reforms that increase euro area's long-term growth potential – Euro area's influence in the global economic system	• Undertake public debt reduction • Reform pension, social insurance and health care systems to ensure they are financially viable, socially adequate and accessible • Redirect the composition of public expenditure towards growth-enhancing categories in line with the Lisbon Strategy, adapt tax structures to strengthen growth potential Wage developments • To ensure that they contribute to macroeconomic stability and growth and to increase adaptability • Wage-bargaining systems, while fully respecting the role of the social partners, should promote nominal wage and labour cost developments consistent with price stability and the trend in productivity over the mid-term taking into account differences across skills and local labour market conditions

Source: Based on *Integrated Guidelines for Growth and Jobs* (2005) and *Community Lisbon Programme* (2005).

BOX 8.1   IDENTIFYING PATHS FOR TRANSITION: KEY QUESTIONS

The Lisbon process is based on the assumption that it is possible to adapt a common reform agenda to different types of capitalism. To what extent can we accept the assumption that a certain degree of convergence towards a meta-type is possible? It may be possible with the Europeanization of policy-making in various policy fields, which can foster cross-fertilization between different types of capitalism in the EU. So the main questions we need to answer here are: retrospectively, is there evidence to confirm the convergence hypothesis? In 'prospective' terms, what are the critical reforms to make in each type of capitalism in order to converge towards this meta-type? Can we identify some transition paths? A more systematic answer to the latter question will enable us to extract some national and European level policy recommendations.

Further Questions for Discussion

Beyond this systematic exercise, other more general questions to be addressed include: what are the possible impacts and limits of this reform agenda? Are there any other conditions to be met to foster economic growth? What are the implications of all this for governance reforms? And what should be the content of a new social contract underlying this reform agenda?

---

is often not that clear, since the different instruments listed translate into different degrees of Europeanization of the policy-making process.

When analysing Table 8.2 it is useful to ask the following questions: how can we classify the particular mix of features characterizing the meta-type of capitalism underlying the Lisbon Agenda? How do we assess its internal consistency? What kind of cross-fertilization occurs between different types of capitalism identified in this particular mix underlying the Lisbon Agenda?

BIBLIOGRAPHY

Amable, B. (2003), *The Diversity of Modern Capitalism*, Oxford: Oxford University Press.

Amable, B., R. Barre and R. Boyer (1997), *Les systèmes d'innovation à l'ère de la globalisation*, Paris: Economica.

Boyer, R. (1988), *The Search for Labour Market Flexibility*, Oxford: Oxford University Press.

Boyer, R. (2004), *Une théorie du capitalisme est-elle possible?*, Paris: Odile Jacob.

European Commission (2006), *Progress Report on the Lisbon Strategy: Time to Move a Gear*, http://europa.eu.int/growthandjobs/annual-report_en.htm.

Kok, W. (ed.) (2004), *Facing the Challenge: The Lisbon Strategy for Growth and Employment*, Report from the High Level Group, Brussels: European Commission.

Hall, P.A. and D. Soskice (eds) (2001), *Varieties of Capitalism: The Institutional Foundations of Comparative Advantage*, Oxford: Oxford University Press.

Rodrigues, M.J. (2004), 'For the National Strategies of Transition to a Knowledge Economy in the European Union', Background Paper 5, in M.J. Rodrigues (ed.), *The Lisbon Strategy: A Follow-up for Researchers*, European Commission's Advisory Group on Social Sciences, SSHERA Project, EU 6th Framework Programme RTD.

Sapir, A. (ed.) (2004), *An Agenda for a Growing Europe: The Sapir Report*, Oxford: Oxford University Press.

http://www.europa.eu/growthandjobs/.
http://www.mariajoaorodrigues.eu.

See further bibliography in Appendix 4 of this book.

9. The Lisbon Strategy: merits, difficulties and possible reforms

Robert Boyer

9.1 THE LISBON STRATEGY IN RETROSPECT

Although short, the history of the strategy launched in Lisbon by the European Council in March 2000 may be usefully and briefly revisited. The so-called Lisbon Strategy has three main components: first, the goal is to promote growth and employment by maintaining a highly competitive European economy; second, it proposes an input, namely a coupling innovation with the preservation of social cohesiveness, as a compromise between market liberalization and a social democratic approach under the umbrella of a Schumpeterian vision of innovation; and third, it is a method, that is, the so-called open method of coordination (OMC), that was devised to overcome the present distribution of competences between Member States and Brussels, and to promote the structural reforms required to fulfil the Lisbon objectives at the national level.

The origin of this institutional innovation was clearly associated with the tendency towards increasing divergence between the United States and Europe, and the emergence of new pressures on the European welfare state (ageing, obsolescence of worker competences and persisting mass unemployment). The collapse of the Internet bubble, the emergence of China and India as major players in the world economy, and recurring demands by citizens for more security and related pressure on the so-called 'European social model' suggest that the diagnosis of early 2000 is even more valid today than it was before. It is not surprising, then, that even the more severe critics of the Lisbon Strategy recognize that the diagnosis was, and still is, relevant and that the overall Strategy points in the right direction (Kok et al., 2004; Pisani-Ferry and Sapir, 2006; Aghion et al., 2006). But there is also the general feeling that the Strategy basically has failed, which for some critics is why it has been redesigned, or even downgraded (Pisani-Ferry and Sapir, 2006). The paradox is that the 2005 Spring European Council made the reformed Lisbon Strategy a key component of its policy (Rodrigues, 2006).

A brief survey of the literature suggests another paradox. Generally speaking, economists tend to diagnose a clear failure, whereas political scientists and sociologists have a far more positive assessment, probably because they are looking at different issues.

Economists tend to focus on outputs and inputs. They see that European growth has been sluggish and job creation disappointing, and the gap with the US has been widening. In terms of input, the picture is also unsatisfactory. The research and development (R&D) to gross national product (GNP) ratio objective of 3 per cent in 2010 is probably beyond the reach of Europe as a whole, and welfare reforms have been difficult and partial, particularly in France, Germany and Italy. These are also the countries that failed to increase their innovation efforts.

Other social scientists, by contrast (Zeitlin and Pochet, 2005) are more interested in the method, and they find that there has been a significant learning and experimenting process that could, for example, serve to overcome some veto points in the reform of national welfare states (Obinger et al., 2005). On the one hand, they recognize that the national employment action plans are frequently formal exercises in window-dressing; but on the other hand, they note that there has been a significant transformation in the cognitive maps and agenda of decision-makers, through national interactions at national and European levels. For the authors under review, the OMC is a very promising institutional innovation that, in the long term at least, could help to overcome some of the deadlocks, such as that which sealed the fate of the European Constitution. By contrast, economists tend to deplore the weak enforcement of the Lisbon Strategy, the lack of a clear methodology to assess the national reform programmes, and the generally limited involvement of national stakeholders (Pisani-Ferry and Sapir, 2006).

This raises a difficult issue: what is the relevant time horizon of the Lisbon Strategy? A decade is quite a long period for macroeconomists, whereas for analysts of technological and institutional change this may be seen simply as the starting point of a very uncertain process of trial and error.

9.2   A COMPARATIVE APPROACH: BETWEEN ECLECTIC BENCHMARKING AND 'ONE SIZE FITS ALL'

The OMC is not totally new. Various international organizations such as the Organisation for Economic Co-operation and Development (OECD), the International Monetary Fund (IMF) and the World Bank (WB), have established various decision-making forums, and the practice of international benchmarking for at least some of their activities, so as to promote the diffusion of the best practise. Of course, the details of the institutional settings are different, but the intellectual challenges are similar.

The OMC generates the following dilemma. One the one hand, there is a strong temptation to propose a rather extended list of objectives and performance indexes just to cope with the complexity of modern societies and to include the largest possible number of decision-makers. The 24 integrated guidelines for growth and jobs are a good example of this. The assumption seems to be that one can never have too much of a good thing; but this is not evident at all.

First, some objectives are complementary, but others might be contradictory. Second, the links between objectives and economic and social policy components are difficult to disentangle in the absence of quite detailed investigations, other than the simple *ex post* statistical measures provided by each Member State. At a practical level, the dispersion of goals is very convenient for the civil servants in charge of drafting the Country Reports that outline progress with the Lisbon Strategy. Sometimes they simply describe the present strategy of their government. Eclectic benchmarking seems to be self-defeating.

On the other hand (and the Washington Consensus is another good example) there is a symmetric strategy (that is, an attempt to spread the same model across the world). But given the path-dependency of economic specialization, the complexity of institutional arrangements, and significant differences in political and social preferences, the probability of the complete transposition of a single model is almost non-existent. All the more so since even productive models have proven difficult to transpose from one national context to another (Boyer et al., 1998). Adaptation and hybridization are the rule; imitation is the exception. It is not surprising, then, that emerging models that are supposedly to be emulated all over the world (the German, the Japanese, the Polder model, the Silicon Valley model and, more recently, the Danish flexicurity model) have yet to produce the expected diffusion process. Thus, the era of 'one size fits all' appears to be over. The IMF, for instance, was forced to recognize that the 1997 Asian crises were not mere reproductions of the Latin American crises of the 1980s. Similarly, other studies have pointed out that even countries in the same region (say, in Latin America) do not follow the same pattern, and produce different macroeconomic outcomes in spite of the rather widespread application of similar economic reforms (opening to the world economy, privatization and deregulation) in the search for macroeconomic stability.

Consequently, it is now clear that cross-national comparisons call for another strategy, since piecemeal benchmarking and the importation of complete systems and institutional regimes do not seem to work. Thus, some authors have proposed 'contextual benchmarking', or the adaptation of a given economic strategy to existing institutional and political domestic contexts (Zeitlin and Pochet, 2005).

In this context, then, the central question of how the Lisbon Strategy should cope with national diversity has become a central issue for many international organizations because they face similar challenges. Internationally, the problem for organizations like the OECD, the IMF and the World Bank, is how to benefit from the diversity of national experience and convince (frequently reluctant) governments to undertake the reforms they recommend. In a sense, the 'Job Study' launched by the OECD shares the spirit of the Lisbon Agenda, since it asks what leverage can be used to implement benchmarking in the absence of direct control by an international organization. In other words, can 'soft' law be a (partial) alternative to 'hard' law? Another question is what tools are available to take into account the crucial finding that different policies may be required to achieve the same goals, such as growth (Hausmann, et al., 2005), given that the same policy applied in different contexts can produce quite different results.

There is another analogy between current development theories and the debate about the future of Europe. Economists find that sound macroeconomic policy may be a necessary but insufficient condition for convergence towards a fast growth path. Monetary stability and the promotion of competition have not proved sufficient to launch a new wave of innovation and growth acceleration in Latin America or Europe. Of course, some countries have been quite successful (Finland, Ireland and Denmark) but they have implemented specific policies that are not limited to compliance with macroeconomic orthodoxy and the belief in the efficiency of market forces. As the above suggests, then, the Lisbon Agenda is in line with other initiatives in other parts of the world, since the latter also attempt to address similar issues. It follows that Europeans can learn from these international experiences.

9.3   LEARNING FROM CRITICISM OF THE LISBON AGENDA

Europeans can also learn from the difficulties encountered in the implementation of the Lisbon Strategy. The mid-term review in 2004–05 clearly outlined some limits of the current model, and it triggered a reform of the Lisbon Agenda (Rodrigues, 2006). It was recognized that strategic objectives were blurred, that the inflation of measures and priorities was detrimental, and that the implementation of the Agenda called for the institution of some basic mechanisms and financial incentives. But this is only a fraction of the criticism that has been directed at the OMC, the most fundamental being that it is a form of 'one size fits all' approach (see Table 9.1).

One criticism is that the integrated guidelines for growth and jobs, which are divided into four major objectives and, in turn, subdivided into 24 sub-objectives, may be too numerous. Of course, the list is the outcome of political bargaining and compromise and it is supposed to take into account the complexity of European issues. However, reducing them should be considered. Alternatively, the guidelines should be assembled into a coherent process or set of mechanisms to produce the expected outcome (growth and jobs).

A second criticism is that, in contrast with monetary stability and budgetary discipline, which are governed by explicit European treaty clauses and backed by instruments of compliance, there is no hard rule for the Lisbon Agenda. As noted above, this can be a plus, but the absence of a conventional instrument of enforcement has not helped to make the Lisbon process efficient. This can be dealt with in two ways: there could be peer review, with 'blame and shame' for the more reluctant Member States (Pisani-Ferry and Sapir, 2006); or there could be explicit hard rules instituted at the European Community level in order, in the long run, to promote a better balance between macroeconomic stability, growth and employment objectives.

A third problem is that the Lisbon process is perceived by most outsiders as a typical technocratic exercise that does not fully engage policy-makers, either at the national or the Community level. This may be simply a problem of communication between policy-makers and citizens, but it is likely to be deeply rooted in the very process of Europeanization of domestic policies. As such, the Lisbon process is part of the general disenchantment with the evolution of European institutions and polities.

This brings to the fore a fourth issue: that of the low democratic accountability of many European procedures. Citizens feel that some European regulations are distant, obscure, arbitrary and even threatening to national traditions, affecting welfare, public utilities organization and labour market institutions. One response to this criticism is to argue that some stakeholders have been involved in the Lisbon process much more significantly than in the case of monetary policy or the enforcement of competition in the Single Market. Some political scientists point out that modern democracy has to rely on new mechanisms of control and accountability, since it cannot be the outcome of direct citizen control and must be mediated by independent administrative agencies, non-governmental organizations (NGOs), forums of various kinds and groups of experts. In any case, the diversity and broadening of stakeholders involved at the national level should be welcomed.

Table 9.1 An assessment of the Lisbon Strategy

Criticism	Reply	Possible reforms
1. Too many guidelines	1. A response to the complexity of modern economies. The expression of political compromises	1a. Reduce the number of guidelines 1b. Replace by mechanisms combining items
2. Lack of policy instruments to implement the strategy	2. On the contrary a promising method for overcoming institutional and political deadlock	2a. Design explicit hard rules at the Community level 2b. 'Blame and shame' as incentive to reform
3. Lack of political will, a technocratic exercise	3. Unequal across countries, common to many European issues	3a. Better marketing, repackaging of the Lisbon Strategy 3b. Explain more clearly the political objectives
4. Low democratic accountability	4. More involvement of diverse stakeholders than for other European policies (the ECB, competition, . . .)	4a. Extend the diversity of stakeholders at the national level 4b. Develop another concept of democracy
5. Few justifications of a eurozone dimension of benchmarking	5. Benchmarking as a learning process, a method to overcome institutional deadlock	5a. Either an unambiguous re-nationalization of reforms 5b. Or taking into account the Lisbon Strategy in the redesign of European instruments (for example SGP reform)
6. Fuzzy criteria in the assessment of National Reform Plans	6. This is only the first stage of a learning process	6a. Use the employment/growth diagnostics 6b. Build a genuine methodology
7. The same reform might have different, sometimes opposite, effects in different countries	7. It might be an exceptional case	7a. Contextual benchmarking 7b. Take into account national diversity

154

9.4   HOW TO COORDINATE: ACROSS OR WITHIN MEMBER STATES?

The Lisbon Strategy raises another central issue regarding the appropriate level of governance to ensure the institutional reforms necessary to fulfil its key objectives. Underlying the OMC is the assumption that the coordination among Member States is an important factor in the redesign of economic institutions. Basically, the literature notes that there are two externalities at the core of the Lisbon process.

First, if it is assumed, for instance, that macroeconomic problems are partly related to a rather restrictive monetary policy that is based on the view that labour markets are too rigid, then a reform that successfully reduces structural employment in one country may induce a change in the European policy mix, especially if such a reform takes place in a large country. There are other types of cross-border externalities. Actually, the successful redesign of a national system of innovation is expected to benefit other economies, through conventional positive spillover effects associated with technical change. From a theoretical standpoint, this would mean that in the long run, the related competences should at least be shared between the national and European levels. On this view, the Lisbon process is a way to overcome the imperfections of the present distribution of competences as outlined by existing European treaties.

Second, the Lisbon process is nevertheless specific because it relies on benchmarking, learning and peer pressure to propitiate economic reform. As mentioned earlier, many social scientists think that this is its major innovation, one that has contributed to significant advances in European integration. Therefore, the systematic comparison of domestic policies would be as important as positive and negative externalities in promoting a specific process that subtly combines domestic and European concerns as part of an iterative and long-term process. In this process, national preferences, procedures and policy tools and, finally, economic outcomes change and are redefined, leading to the possible, if uncertain, emergence of a new style of economic policy-making that would spread throughout Europe.

The experience of recent years suggests that these externalities, even if they exist, are quite weak and cannot trigger the emergence of a virtuous circle, whereby laggard countries emulate successful ones, leading to the progressive acceleration of European growth and job creation. On the contrary, the abundant literature on capitalist diversity is now confirmed by research on the complementarities between labour market reforms and welfare, innovation policy and a specific policy mix. The problem is that these complementarities are mainly, if not exclusively, national. A possible difficulty for the Lisbon process is this: the will to cope with cross-border externalities neglects the fact that the crucial issue is frequently the coordination and the sequencing of domestic reforms (see Figure 9.1).

This remark suggests a possible direction in the reform of the Lisbon process: instead of benchmarking individual measures, why not promote a set of interrelated policies that generate a positive spillover in terms of growth and employment, according to a set of complementary mechanisms that would cross the frontiers of various policy domains (legislation, taxation, public spending, finance, labour market, competition)? Of course the task is made more difficult, but simultaneously far more relevant. Furthermore, there exists a literature on social mechanisms that could be mobilized in order to redesign the current policies. In some instances, the relevant mechanisms could cross the regional, domestic and European boundaries, thus providing a clear basis for a multilevel coordination.

9.5   GROWTH AND EMPLOYMENT DIAGNOSTICS: RECOGNIZING NATIONAL SPECIFICITIES

The search for mechanisms has another merit: instead of looking for one best way in terms of policy instruments and institutions, the Lisbon process should focus on finding a series of generic mechanisms existing in different countries, and then check if various configurations might produce the same mechanisms. This idea has also appeared in the development literature (Hausmann et al., 2005).

The diffusion of the so-called Washington Consensus over the past decade has not delivered the expected results. As mentioned earlier, sound macroeconomic policy and reliance on market price signals have been insufficient to promote the acceleration of growth, especially for Latin American countries. Other policies are required, such as innovation or industrial policies. These are more complex than the search for a good policy mix, since they call for sophisticated procedures of coordination in order to internalize externalities. The parallel with the European discussions is quite striking.

Even more importantly, the same measures can deliver quite positive results in one country and prove inefficient or even detrimental in another country facing different problems. Nowadays, the 'one size fits all' strategy is perceived as a clear failure, and there are calls for a more analytical approach that takes the diversity of national configurations into account. This diversity is not an expression of deviance from a canonical model, but is rather directly related to broad differences in productive structures, social values and political choices, as well as in economic policy preferences and styles.

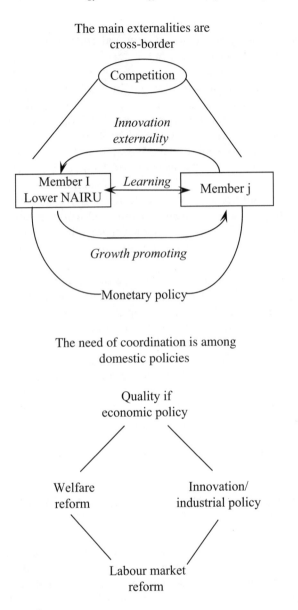

Figure 9.1   The need for coordination: across Member States or among domestic policies?

Consequently, conventional international comparisons need to be complemented by in-depth studies of national trajectories. For developing countries, a critical question is what factors limit growth. It turns out that a careful use of economic tools can help policy-makers to detect what the rate of return of various measures might be. The ranking of the corresponding reforms according to their impact on long-term growth differs significantly, even across countries that a priori look quite similar.

It would be fruitful to adopt this methodology to assess national reform plans, and respond to the frequent criticism that there are no policy instruments available to check the relevance of Member State proposals. One important consequence of this is that instead of enumerating the guidelines that have been fulfilled by a Member State, national reform plans should explain existing constraints on growth and employment creation and which policies have been adopted to overcome them. Thus, a kind of systemic, contextual benchmarking should replace the typical procedure of naive benchmarking.

As an example, Figure 9.2 describes how disequilibrium theory might be used to organize the Lisbon process so that it takes national differences into account more effectively. Some examples are useful. According to the employment diagnostic, the same action – wage flexibility – may increase employment in cases of classical unemployment, but it may be detrimental if unemployment is 'Keynesian'. Similarly, innovation is a priori a good thing, but it is not necessarily the most relevant and efficient measure if slow growth is a result of a lack of productive capacity, particularly if the country is far from the technological frontier. Imitation and adaptation may be more appropriate than the risky process of radical innovation. In most cases, increasing inputs that are not limiting production and growth misses the point that the benchmarking process is designed to target.

9.6 SOLVING DOMESTIC PROBLEMS WITH CONTEXTUAL BENCHMARKING

The section above suggests that European economies differ significantly in terms of growth and employment opportunities. Indeed, comparative research on the institutions and economic outcomes of different forms of capitalism confirms the existence of this diversity. Thus: the UK is a variant of market capitalism; Germany and France belong in another category, in which state intervention at the national or regional level plays a determining role in the coordination of individual strategies; countries such as Sweden, Denmark and Finland have yet another type of social democratic capitalism, where active and representative social partners are

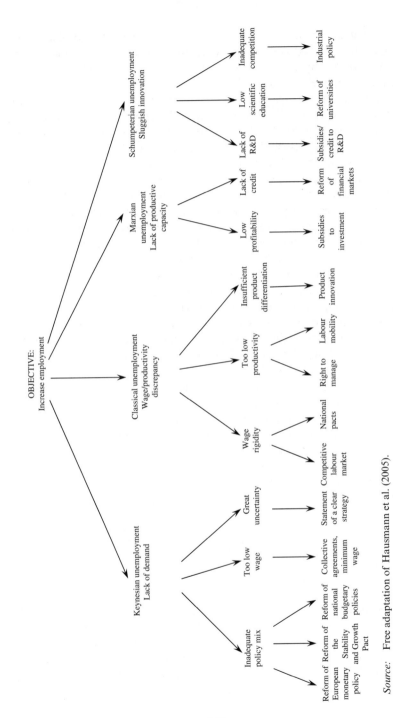

Source: Free adaptation of Hausmann et al. (2005).

Figure 9.2   Employment diagnostics applied to the Lisbon Strategy

able to negotiate new compromises in response to emerging problems and changes in the international environment; and Spain, Italy and Greece may well be examples of a fourth variety of capitalism, a variant of the Continental model (Amable, 2003).

Frequently, 'market capitalism' is the point of reference in terms of economic efficiency, particularly when systematic benchmarking is considered. But the global superiority of market-led capitalism is not confirmed by more careful analyses of the different indexes on efficiency. First, social democratic countries display rather satisfactory outcomes in terms of employment, innovation and growth. Furthermore, their dynamic efficiency has not been obtained with deepening social inequality, or pressure on the political principles that govern these countries. Second, each country has a specific set of values and possibly makes different kinds of trade-offs between efficiency and social justice. In this regard, the Lisbon Strategy is not sufficiently clear about the model that should govern Europe. On the one hand, many guidelines point in the direction of typical market-led flexibility; on the other, the Strategy as a whole is said to be necessary to rejuvenate the European 'social model'.

It is clear from public opinion polls that the citizens of most Continental European countries prefer the social democratic rather than the market-led type of capitalism. But the difficulty is precisely that the circumstances which generated this configuration in Scandinavian countries are not present in other medium-sized countries such as France, Italy and Germany.

This is why contextual benchmarking is to be preferred both to piecemeal and systemic benchmarking. Accordingly policy-makers in each country should try to understand which are the real factors hindering growth, and design institutional, social and economic reforms. In other words, their task should be to solve their own national problems rather than desperately importing distant models (Figure 9.3). But the danger here is that this will lead to an exclusively national strategy with no European dimension.

9.7   WHAT OF THE LISBON STRATEGY? THE NEED FOR A STRATEGIC VISION

The Lisbon Strategy could be designed according to the pattern at the European level; Member States should forge a common strategic vision. In fact, Europe does share common features when compared to North America or Asia. The initial diagnosis made in 2000 is correct. In essence, the common objective is to promote a series of innovations that can promote growth and employment while preserving the level of worker security that is typical of most European countries.

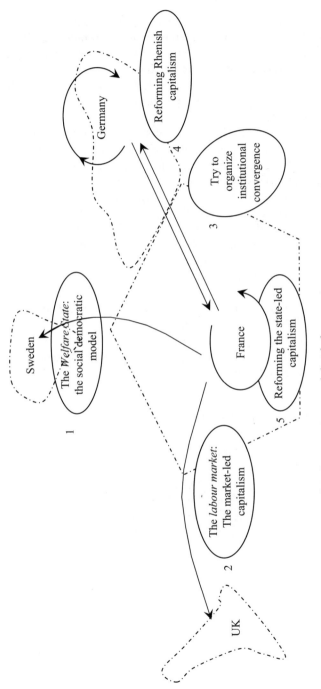

Figure 9.3   France, Germany and Italy: uncertain and divided strategies

At the national level, this common objective should trigger precise analyses about the factors that hinder growth and employment. The purpose is not to fulfil all the guidelines but to make the intensity of reforms proportional to the severity of constraints that are specific to each Member State. The outcome should be a series of coordinated measures at the national level that can generate positive spillover effects between innovation, welfare and the labour market.

The goal of having Brussels assess national reform plans would be to compare the various mechanisms elaborated by the Member States, to check whether policies converge – not necessarily in terms of institutional setting but in terms of processes and mechanisms. The basic idea is simple: positive spillover effects have to be organized in order to mobilize complementarities between a series of institutional reforms. Figure 9.4 illustrates this for the social democratic countries, highlighting the various complementarities that explain the dynamism of these economies. Each Member State should be challenged to find a functional equivalent, possibly with quite different institutions.

Once the ordering and synchronization of reforms at the domestic level have taken place, some cross-border externalities may make new coordinating mechanisms at the European level necessary These could be addressed either by the development of the OMC or by designing new European procedures. This is a long-term goal, of course, as it entails converting 'soft' law into 'hard' law.

SOME CONCLUSIONS

The Lisbon Agenda launched a new phase in European integration. For many analysts, the outcomes have not met expectations, but this is an incentive to prolong the experiment. Some recent methodological developments related to the complementarity hypothesis and growth diagnosis may help redesign the Agenda. The question is whether the political conditions are in place to permit such a process, at the domestic and European levels.

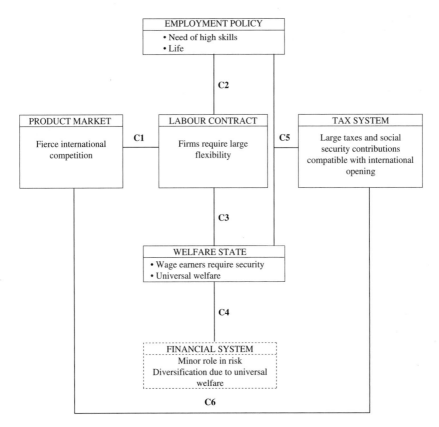

Source: Elaborated from Amable (2003), pp. 150, 139–40.

Figure 9.4 Organizing institutional complementarities: the social democratic strategy

REFERENCES

Aghion, P., E. Cohen and J. Pisani-Ferry (2006), 'Politique économique et croissance en Europe', *Rapport du Conseil d'Analyse Economique*, 59, Paris: La Documentation Française.

Amable, B. (2003), *The Diversity of Modern Capitalisms*, Oxford: Oxford University Press.

Boyer, R., E. Charron, J. Ulrich and S. Tolliday (1998), *Between Imitation and Innovation: Transfer and Hybridization of Productive Models in the International Automobile Industry*, Oxford: Oxford University Press.

Hausmann, R., D. Rodrik and A. Velasco (2005), 'Growth Diagnostic', Working Paper, Kennedy School of Government, March.

Kok, W., R. Bausch, N. FitzGerald, A. Gutiérrez Vegara, W. Hutton, A.M. Idrac, W. Lundby-Wedin, T. Mirow, B. Moldan, L. Paganetto, D. Rosati, V. Sundbäck and F. Verzetnitsch (2004), *Facing the Challenge: The Lisbon Strategy for Growth and Employment*, Report from the High Level Group, Luxembourg, November.

Obinger H., S. Leibfried and F. Castles (2005), 'Bypasses to a Social Europe? Lessons from Federal Experience', *Journal of European Public Policy*, **40** (3) June: 545–71.

Pisani-Ferry, J. and A. Sapir (2006), 'Last Exit to Lisbon', Bruegel Policy Brief, 2 (March), Brussels.

Rodrigues, M.J. (2006), 'The Lisbon Agenda and National Diversity', Mimeo 20.03.

Zeitlin, J. (2005), 'Social Europe and Experimentalist Governance: Towards a New Constitutional Compromise', European Governance Paper C05–04, http://www.connex-network.org/eurogov/pdf/egp-connex-C-05-04.pdf.

Zeitlin, J. and P. Pochet (eds) (2005), *The Open Method of Coordination in Action: The European Employment and Social Inclusion Strategies*, Brussels: Peter Lang.

10. The Lisbon Agenda on social policy: revitalizing the European social model

Jos Berghman

In a seminal policy paper written on the occasion of a conference on 'The European Identity in a Global Economy', held in Sintra, Portugal, in February 2000 in preparation for the Lisbon Summit under the Portuguese presidency, Manuel Castells argued that there is a need for 'a common European identity on whose behalf citizens around Europe could be ready to share problems and build common solutions' (Castells, 2002: 234). He wondered, though, how such an identity could either be found or built. Since religion, a common language, or a shared history are not obvious candidates for a quest of this kind, he explored other possibilities. It was only in the realm of values that Castells could identify a cluster of elements that looked promising. This cluster refers to the welfare state and explicitly embraces social protection. It consists of:

> shared feelings concerning the need for universal social protection of living conditions, social solidarity, stable employment, workers' rights, universal human rights, concern about poor people around the world, extension of democracy to regional and local levels, with a renewed emphasis in citizen participation, the defence of historically rooted cultures, often expressed in linguistic terms. If European institutions would be able to promote these values, and to accord life with these promises for all Europeans, probably the 'project identity' would grow (Castells, 2002: 234–5)

Castells is aware that some of these elements are being rethought, the welfare state among them. Yet, in identifying the latter as a common value carrier, he pointed to the possibly crucial role of social protection for the EU itself.

First, the need for a common European identity may be even greater now than it was in 2000. Second, given that social cohesion (including social policy and the fight against social exclusion) represented one of the angles of the Lisbon Agenda triangle, a critical assessment of the state of the art on this issue is very important. Third, as posited by M.J. Rodrigues in

Chapter 8 in this book, the central idea of the original Lisbon Strategy was 'the recognition that to sustain the European social model it is necessary to renew its economic foundations by focusing on knowledge and innovation'. But we have yet to clarify the specific nature of the European social model.

In this chapter, therefore, I deal first with the European social model, on the basis of which I then address three further points: the implementation of the Lisbon Strategy through the open method of coordination (OMC); and the actual shift of the social policy framework and the meta-type of the European welfare state in the Lisbon Agenda era. I conclude with some policy suggestions for the renewed Lisbon Strategy.

10.1   THE EUROPEAN SOCIAL MODEL

In my view, the European social model is not a monolithic reality, but rather a dynamic and possibly even dialectic process that combines two elements: on the one hand, diverse national welfare regimes that are nevertheless part of a shared heritage, and on the other hand, a shared EU social policy profile that is gradually gaining shape (Berghman and Sakellaropoulos, 2004: 242). The question then arises as to whether the shared social policy profile can become part of the shared heritage. Thus far, the common EU social policy profile refers mainly to initiatives that deal with the 'spillover' problems arising from European market integration. But one cannot deny the existence of the normative principles on promoting employment and social protection that figure in the Treaty, existing social regulations and directives, the recent practice of the OMC and its national action programmes (NAP), and even the relatively autonomous social policy network and institutions through which it is gaining shape (Hemerijck and Berghman, 2004: 24–5). But this shared profile remains fragile and needs support from the Member States and the principles they adhere to in EU decision-making by the Council. Let us see, then, if such a foundation can be provided by the common heritage underpinning the European social model.

Underlying the normative, cognitive and institutional commonalities among European welfare states, lie the crucial collective decisions on the labour–income nexus that underpin the welfare systems. Some basic indicators help to make this point, starting with a comparison between productivity in the European Union (EU-15) and the United States (Table 10.1). For the sake of clarity I take figures from the 1990s when the EU had had only 15 Member States, and a long-established approach.

Gross domestic product (GDP) per capita is 30 percentage points higher in the US than in the EU-15. Per employed person, however, this difference

Table 10.1   Productivity indicators – % differences (EU = 100)

	US	EU
GDP/capita	130	100
GDP/employed person	108	100
Number of hours worked/capita	144	100
GDP/hour worked	89	100
Remuneration/hour	101	100
Productivity/remuneration	87	100

Source: Cichon (1997).

is much smaller. The difference in the number of hours worked per capita provides the explanation: not because the hours worked by individual workers is higher in the US, but because more Americans are allowed to work, yielding a higher aggregate number of hours worked per capita. By contrast, GDP per hour worked in the US is lower than in the EU, suggesting that the lower-skilled workers that are nonetheless given access to the labour market are decreasing the average hourly productivity level. In fact, while average remuneration per hour is at a similar level, productivity per unit of remuneration is lower in the US than in the EU (Berghman, 1997). Implicitly, therefore, the EU has 'chosen' a strategy of high productivity by giving only the most productive workers access to the labour market.

Yet, while implicitly and collectively deciding to be very productive, the Member States of the EU also opted to guarantee adequate living conditions to those who cannot be productively inserted into the labour market because they do not yet, or no longer, have the required capacity to work. According to Adema (2001) and as shown in Figure 10.1, EU countries typically spend between 20 per cent and 26 per cent of their GDP on gross social expenditure, whereas the figure for Japan and the US is only 15 per cent. (In net terms, these figures are somewhat lower to the extent that part of this expenditure returns through direct taxes and social contributions. The latter have a considerable impact on social expenditure levels, in countries like the Netherlands and in the Nordic countries.)

When we add tax expenditure and private expenditure on the same 'social' contingencies, however, the picture changes fundamentally. It then appears that all countries spend at least a quarter of their GDP on social expenditure. Hence, the Member States of the EU and the US spend more or less the same share of GDP to provide various social services and benefits, the difference being that in the EU this is done more through obligatory and statutory schemes. In so doing, EU countries find it easier to

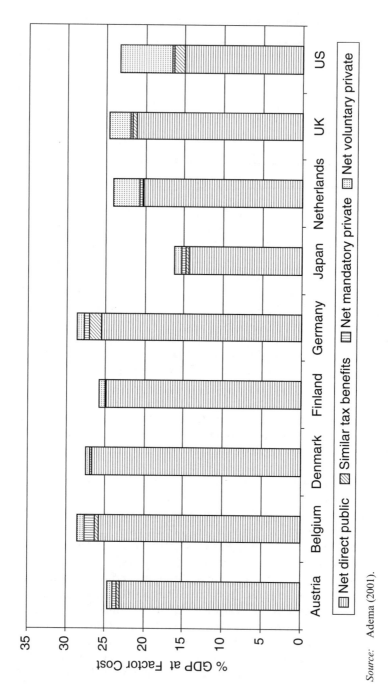

Source: Adema (2001).

Figure 10.1   Extended net social expenditure indicators, 1997

counter adverse selection mechanisms and thus to reduce poverty more effectively than the US. So, Europe's common patrimony seems to reside in the combination of productivity and solidarity, the latter leading to broad, obligatory, solidarity-oriented welfare institutions.

However, the institutions deployed by EU countries differ. This can be explained by reference to the basic social policy logic and to the relationship of the different European welfare state sub-models to that logic (Berghman, 1997). The social policy logic holds that we educate and train people to ensure that they are able to enter the (paid) labour market, and thereby have the opportunity to gain a primary income. Social protection, then, basically operates as a bypass mechanism in those cases where insertion in the labour force is no longer possible or desirable. In such cases, the aim is to resolve the problem by guaranteeing the availability of (replacement) income in order to safeguard social integration. But social protection policies cannot confine themselves to the mere provision of income protection, be it at a minimum or at an earnings-related level. Income schemes have to be complemented by reintegrative action like retraining, work mediation and rehabilitation schemes. Thus, the location of social protection within the broader socio-political context makes us aware of the intrinsic connections that exist between social protection, labour demand and labour supply. For society, social protection is a productive factor to the extent that it upholds the basic logic, and that it does so in an efficient way.

Social protection, and more broadly speaking the European welfare state, can then be seen as having three explicit objectives: guaranteeing minimum protection (the Beveridge legacy of the Anglo-Saxon sub-model), providing earnings-related income protection (the Bismarck legacy of the Continental sub-model), and to do so in ways that do not counteract reintegration (the Scandinavian legacy of the Nordic sub-model). In this context a fourth, Southern European sub-model can be viewed as a less elaborate variant of the Continental model, which still relies more on family solidarity.

It is very important to be aware that these four sub-models also refer to four different policy-making settings: in the Anglo-Saxon tradition, responsibility for policy-making on the fundamental income–labour nexus resides with the democratic political majority; in the Continental countries, it is the prime responsibility of the social partners whose commitments should be confirmed by the polity; the Nordic model has its tradition of close cooperation between social partners and polity; and the Southern sub-model also relies on social partners, albeit less starkly. This difference in policy-making traditions can largely explain the levels of difficulty that Member States encounter when trying to recalibrate their welfare states. The Continental and Southern European Member States in particular, which depend heavily on the social contract between autonomous social partners, need time to make fundamental policy shifts.

10.2 THE OMC IN SOCIAL POLICY

The Lisbon Summit was not only ground-breaking in terms of its conceptualization of the EU ambition to modernize itself by becoming a social knowledge-based society; it was also ground-breaking because it introduced a new method of decision-making, the so-called OMC. This points to the midway position that the EU had to adopt in the social policy field: confronted by the new challenges of globalization, population ageing and technological change, concerted action was thought to be necessary, but formal competences were to remain with the national authorities. As an intergovernmental device the OMC tried to reconcile both elements. Its success, then, should be assessed both in terms of its getting national authorities to deploy the needed policy initiatives, and in terms of its contribution to turn national initiatives into actions that safeguard, bolster or recalibrate the 'common heritage'.

In retrospect, it must be admitted that the original enthusiasm generated by the OMC in different social policy fields gradually lost its momentum. This is partly because of the heavy administrative and consultative process that was necessary to elaborate valid NAPs (National Action Programmes), and guarantee a reliable and feasible monitoring system. But social policy actors were more depressed by the overriding influence of the Economic and Financial Affairs Council (Ecofin), by the diminishing commitment of the Council to social objectives, and by the decision of the Commission to downplay the social angle of the Lisbon triangle.

Meanwhile, it was recently decided that the strategy for growth and jobs should be renewed within a mutually reinforcing economic, employment and social policy framework, to bring the social OMCs on social inclusion, pensions and health and long-term care together, and reinforce their mainstreaming at the EU level. But there are strong doubts among social policy actors about the awareness and commitment of the EU to social cohesion and the European social model and, above all, about the ability of the EU to promote a renewed and appealing vision of how to combine productivity and solidarity, and thus about the possibility of revitalizing the European social model.

It is by now clear that the operationalization of social policies should remain a national competence, to which the subsidiarity principle rightly applies. Building on this, there is a felt need to involve national competence levels explicitly in the preparation of the national action programmes.

Thus, there are pleas to submit the NAP explicitly to prior national governmental and parliamentary approval. At the same time, however, is is also clear that there needs to be a strong EU-level vision of how to safeguard the common social heritage of Europe. This calls for a clear commitment from the Commission and its administrators, as well as from the Council.

10.3 TOWARDS AN ADEQUATE SOCIAL POLICY FRAMEWORK

What should be the substance of the endeavour to revitalize the European social model in terms of the Lisbon Strategy, taking into account the challenges that triggered it, and to have the broader lines of this revitalization defined and voiced at the EU level? Tables 8.1 and 8.2 in Chapter 8 distinguish different institutional and policy areas that have a bearing on the revitalization. From the above, it is obvious that it is not only the social protection area but also the wage–labour nexus that are traditionally at stake when dealing with the European social model. From the actual discourse on social policy it becomes clear, however, that the education and the competence and skills areas must also be taken into account (Allmendinger and Leibfried, 2003).

The transition from an industrial to a post-industrial, reflexive, information society has produced important shifts in the conceptual and policy framework on social protection and the welfare state. The attention traditionally paid to curative transfer systems was challenged by the high unemployment rates of the late 1970 and 1980s. This has refocused attention on reintegrative policy initiatives. But the success of initiatives that focus on labour supply quickly reached its limits because of the lack of labour demand. So, the next policy phase has witnessed initiatives to enlarge labour demand. The latter may help to mitigate labour market problems in the short and medium term, but they are not a final solution. On the contrary, in the longer term, attention must shift to capabilities, capacity-building and transitional labour market, human resources and career management (Estevez-Abe et al., 2001). So, we need a convincing EU and national-level commitment to operationalize reliable flexicurity formulas.

In doing so, the scope of the redistribution which the social protection and welfare state systems are meant to generate is broadened. In fact, the horizontal redistribution that original social insurances hoped to ensure was later complemented by the vertical redistributive objectives of the social protection systems. But the high training and expertise needs of highly developed knowledge-based societies make investments in training of the younger cohorts and in retraining schemes for those of active age an additional priority. In the first place, this calls for much greater attention to and investment in children. Gösta Esping-Andersen comments that:

> current policy fashion advocates activation, retraining and life-long learning as a way to combat entrapment, but it is well documented that remedial pro- grammes are very ineffective unless participants come with strong and motiva- tional abilities to begin with. Mobility is a realistic possibility only for those who already possess skills from youth. (Esping-Andersen, 2005: 147)

So, both education and training programmes, as well as income protection during periods of retraining and parental leave and kindergarten, become crucial for a European social strategy.

All this leads to a more pronounced intergenerational redistribution, whereby the actual generation has to invest in the new cohorts, not only to make them fit for insertion into the production process and uphold eco- nomic growth in Europe, but also to guarantee that the coming generation of Europeans will be able to sustain the horizontal and vertical redistribu- tion devices that are part of their respective welfare state traditions, or at least to renew the operationalization of the productivity–solidarity nexus that represents their common heritage.

10.4   THE META-TYPE EUROPEAN SOCIAL MODEL IN THE LISBON ERA

Is there then a meta-type of capitalism that underpins, or should underlie, the Lisbon Agenda? From a social policy point of view, two elements come to the fore. The first relates to the European social model and the social policy framework it currently requires. Both call for a meta-type that liber- ates the welfare state from its traditional curative focus, but manages to incorporate reintegrating and activating policy initiatives. In this sense the Lisbon Agenda still holds. The weaker point, however, is that the social aspect of the Lisbon triangle must be more reliable, a fully recognized part of the triangle, and not just the 'runt' of the litter. If employment policies and the welfare state are the second and third elements of the Lisbon trip- tych, which allow the first to flourish and make it possible to revitalize the productivity–solidarity nexus of the European social model, then they should receive due attention and be materialized. We clearly need a longer- term, and clear and reliable vision that pays attention to intergenerational and flexicurity perspectives.

The second element that comes to the fore is the actual development of national welfare states. The meta-type envisaged in the Lisbon Strategy is most in line with the traditional Nordic welfare state sub-model, with its emphasis on universal coverage, reintegrative drive and high labour market participation (including of women with facilitated childcare facilities). This is not to say that all Member States should copy the Nordic sub-model, which is itself evolving. But many elements of the Lisbon Strategy are reminiscent of the Nordic tradition. Yet, what is promising is that many Member States are aware of this challenge and are fully engaged in adopting initiatives to meet it (Debels, 2008). As regards the conservative Continental sub-model which may be harder to reform, research by Koen Vleminckx on the conservative Northern welfare states could convincingly corroborate this trend (Vleminckx, 2006). Further, Johansson and Hvinden, who scrutinize social policy development in the Nordic, so-called social democratic welfare states, found some trends that converge with developments in other welfare state sub-models (Johansson and Hvinden, 2004).

10.5 SUGGESTIONS FOR THE RENEWED LISBON STRATEGY

Incremental convergence towards a common active welfare state regime appears to be under way. Of course, differences remain and further justify subsidiarity; but the common vision and commitment, the European social model, all that which unites Member States remains underdeveloped, undervoiced and lacks support. So Member States should deploy whatever resources they must to face the challenges ahead, respecting path-dependencies; but let there be full EU-level responsibility for the overall project. Manuel Castells may be right: there are not many things that Europeans can be proud of which also serve to bind them together, but the European social model may be one of them, and the Lisbon Agenda may be the opportunity to make it so. The EU president and rotating presidencies can promote varying initiatives, with quite differing scope in this regard.

Thus far, the European social model is the expression of a productivity drive combined with publicly organized solidarity. Following on from this, the introduction of a European minimum wage system could be decisive, especially for the Central and Eastern European countries (CEECs). This does not mean that there should be a single EU-wide minimum wage; on the contrary, one can look to poverty research for inspiration, and define country-specific poverty lines that are nonetheless based on a shared methodology.[1]

A second line of action might consist of shifting the focus of European social policy from social inclusion to an activating, capability-building approach. Almost by sheer accident, the EU had come to focus on poverty and, later, on social exclusion and inclusion. Competence and legitimacy constraints and political arguments may explain this (Marlier et al., 2007). Even so, until the 2000 Lisbon Summit this focus was only a minute part of the fight against poverty and social exclusion, and it hardly made sense in the light of the subsidiarity principle. Since then, the OMC on social inclusion may have had a more indirect impact through the monitoring of social inclusion via the National Action Programmes social inclusion (NAP-incls). It is astonishing, nonetheless, that the most outspoken discretionary, local and multifaceted part of social policy figures highest on the EU agenda. This is not to criticize the focus on social inclusion, but to advocate a EU-level complementary focus on the policy realm that is at the heart of the Lisbon Agenda, favouring activation, a capabilities approach and knowledge-building. Part of this field is covered by employment policy in a rather fragmented way, but substantial and crucial parts on the major social security schemes, on education and training, and on monitoring labour supply and organization are left out. In this way, the situation of the poor is addressed by the EU, but the bulk of citizens and of the working population are not. As regards the latter, the EU is not really providing for the major social correction devices that are necessary to address the dysfunctional effects of economic development and of the common market in a globalizing world. Yet, when the major institutions in the social field are taken care of, the lower end of these, which deal with social exclusion, will automatically be taken on board. The reverse is not automatically the case, however. The fight against social exclusion provides no guarantee that major social protection instruments will be safeguarded.

In line with the previous points, the EU could promote the Lisbon Agenda by launching a proper EU-initiative. A credit scheme to underpin lifelong learning would be an obvious move. It visualizes the productivity drive of the EU model, gives shape to the knowledge and innovation focus of the Lisbon Agenda, and could therefore convince European citizens that they are worth the investment. Part of the budget and most of the policy competence that is necessary may be found in existing European funds. However, restructuring them as a lifelong learning scheme may operationalize a timely new vision of social Europe.

Finally, there could be an integrated OMC for total social protection. Thus far, we have individual and separate OMCs for employment, social inclusion, pensions and parts of healthcare, which were later more or less integrated into more encompassing OMCs. However, they integrate only a selection of the relevant social policy sub-fields, so the call for an OMC that covers the totality of social protection makes sense. This may also generate a new vision of the European social model by showing that the EU is eager to complement its common market policy with a common social correction system. If social protection is an important mediator and productive factor that allows the economy to flourish, we should give it the opportunity to play its part in dealing with globalization, and in the Lisbon Agenda as well. Let the EU show, with an integrated social protection OMC, that its social dimension is not just some footnote to its common economic union policy, but rather a full social complement. We should not be afraid to discover how we can, once again, make social policy functional in the new economic context and to show this to the world.

NOTE

1. The starting point here is the country-specific amount of 60 per cent of median net disposable equivalized income, to which an equivalence scale of 1.0/0.5/0.3 is applied.

REFERENCES

Adema, W. (2001), *Net Social Expenditure: Second Edition*, Labour Market and Social Policy, Occasional Papers 20, Paris: OECD.

Allmendinger, J. and S. Leibfried (2003), 'Education and the Welfare State: The Four Worlds of Competence Production', *Journal of European Social Policy*, **13** (1): 63–81.

Berghman, J. (1997), 'Social Protection and Social Quality in Europe', in W. Beck, L. van der Maesen and A. Walker (eds), *The Social Quality of Europe*, The Hague, London and Boston, MA: Kluwer Law International, pp. 221–35.

Berghman, J. and T. Sakellaropoulos (2004), 'By Way of Conclusion', in T. Sakellaropoulos and J. Berghman (eds), *Connecting Welfare Diversity within the European Social Model*, Antwerp, Oxford and New York: Intersentia, pp. 241–50.

Castells, M. (2002), 'The Construction of European Identity', in M.J. Rodrigues (ed.), *The New Knowledge Economy in Europe: A Strategy for International Competitiveness and Social Cohesion*, Cheltenham, UK and Northampton, MA, USA: Edward Elgar, pp. 232–41.

Cichon, M. (1997), 'Can Europe Afford the Future Financing of the Welfare State?', in A. Bosco and M. Hutsebaut (eds) *Social Protection in Europe: Facing up to Changes and Challenges*, Brussels: ETUI, pp. 82–4.

Debels, A. (2008), 'Flexibility and Insecurity. The Impact of European Variants of Labour Market Flexibility on Employment, Income and Poverty Dynamics', Leuven: Centre for Sociological Research (CESO), New PhD Series 129, Mimeo.

Esping-Andersen, G. (2005), 'Education and Equal Life-Chances: Investing in Children', in O. Kangas and J. Palme (eds), *Social Policy and Economic Development in the Nordic Countries*, Basingstoke, UK, and New York: Palgrave Macmillan, pp. 147–63.

Estevez-Abe, M., T. Iversen, and D. Soskice (2001), 'Social Protection and the Formation of Skills: A Reinterpretation of the Welfare State', in P.A. Hall and

D. Soskice (eds), *Varieties of Capitalism*, Oxford: Oxford University Press, pp. 145–83.

Hemerijck, A. and J. Berghman (2004), 'The European Social Patrimony: Deepening Social Europe through Legitimate Diversity', in T. Sakellaropoulos and J. Berghman (eds), *Connecting Welfare Diversity within the European Social Model*, Antwerp, Oxford and New York: Intersentia, pp. 9–54.

Johansson, H. and B. Hvinden (2004), 'New Welfare States: New Forms of Citizenship? On the Implications for Social Protection Systems of the Turn to Active Citizenship', paper presented at the COST A 15 Conference on Reforming Social Protection Systems in Europe: Coordination and Diversity, Nantes, 21–22 May.

Marlier, E. and A.B. Atkinson (2007), *The EU and Social Inclusion: Facing the Challenges*, Bristol: Policy Press.

Vleminckx, K. (2006), 'Towards a New Certainty: A Study into the Recalibration of the Northern-Tier Conservative Welfare States from an Active Citizens Perspective', Leuven: Centre for Sociological Research (CESO), New PhD Series 99, Mimeo.

11. In-depth comment on the varieties of capitalism in the new Member States

Ádám Török

The varieties of capitalism in the old Member States of the EU can be described correctly using the Amable typology, with its Anglo-Saxon ('market-based economies'), Central European (the German-speaking part of Europe foremost), Southern European and Nordic types of capitalism. Maria João Rodrigues (see Chapter 8) rightly shows that the Eastern European transition countries are likely to embody a fifth type of capitalist development even though their recent experience in this respect is only a decade and a half old.

It is also true, however, that some of these countries, especially the Visegrad states (Poland, the Czech and Slovak republics and Hungary) as well as Slovenia had some experience with the Central European type of capitalist development prior to the Second World War. Due to more than 40 years of socialism in these countries, however, in most instances the reconstruction of market economy institutions had to start from scratch. Only the modestly liberal and more or less open Hungarian economy and the favourably located and also not centrally planned Slovenian economy were partial exceptions to this rule. By contrast, with them, most former Soviet republics (except for the three Baltic countries) did not have any real experience with capitalism, which is also reflected by their current economic and social models. In what follows, I focus on the Central European experience with 'Eastern European capitalism'.

The matrix-type scheme of types of capitalism makes it possible to define the social and economic models of the former transition countries, the recent new member countries (NMCs) of the EU, and compare them to other EU countries. In my view, the three Baltic republics (BRs) represent a sub-type of this model for several reasons. Without trying to be exhaustive, these include, first, the fact that the BRs were, with the limited exception of Estonia, extremely isolated from the West between 1945 and 1990. This made it possible for their post-1990 governments to launch the transition process without major concern about the social tensions arising from, or political reluctance to change. Not only were there no references to welfare state practices in Western Europe, but there was an unusually broad political consensus that the Soviet model should be left behind as quickly as possible. Second, the macroeconomic constraints on these economies were modest for at least one reason: the BRs did not inherit any foreign or internal debt. Third, the BRs were completely free to design their systems of economic and social regulation in the early 1990s. By contrast, the Visegrad countries had legislation in place (for instance, relatively inflexible labour market regulations), which it was difficult to discard. Furthermore, the less than unanimous political support for in-depth transition obliged most Visegrad countries to adopt transition-related elements of legislation that did not really help to accelerate the transition process, among them privatization and tax rules, labour market regulations and subsidy schemes for agriculture, among other areas, varying from country to country (see Csaba, 2005).

For the reasons listed above, the BRs cannot be considered entirely compatible with the model of Eastern European capitalism. Other former Soviet republics including Russia, Ukraine or Belarus are at even greater variance with the Eastern European capitalist sub-model.

Below are listed the main features of Eastern European capitalism, according to the structure outlined in Chapter 8 of this volume by Maria João Rodrigues.

11.1   SCIENCE

NMC research and development (R&D) systems are notoriously underfinanced – less than 1 per cent of gross domestic product (GDP), with the slight exceptions of Slovenia and the Czech Republic – but they are more productive than comparable systems among some old Member States, particularly in Southern Europe (Török et al., 2005). This is true for publications in particular, and patents to a lesser extent. Public money covers about two-thirds of gross expenditure on research and development (GERD) in these countries. Business expenditure on research and development (BERD) is low due to limited industrial interest in domestic R&D, the dominance of foreign ownership of high-tech output and export firms, and because only a minor sector of the corporate sphere is effectively interested in R&D. The R&D institutional system is fragmented in some countries, with government-financed basic research undertaken in both universities and research centres of the national academies of science. At the same time, research centres focusing on applied R&D are rare and, in many cases, have no direct links to the business community.

11.2 TECHNOLOGY

There is a sharp contrast between the considerably high average high-tech content of exports and the low level of domestic innovation. This is true especially for Hungary, the Czech Republic and Slovenia. Lack of clarity in regulations governing intellectual property rights (partly due to problems with applying the law) and scant legal provisions for venture capital-based financing of innovation mean that incentives for domestic innovation are also insufficient. In general, basic research performs much better than the entire domestic innovation system in these countries. In the small and medium-sized enterprise (SME) sector, innovation is sporadic and generally not very competitive.

11.3 COMPETENCE AND SKILLS

Generally speaking, labour markets are over-regulated, and formal job protection is quite strong. Mobility within these countries is hampered by very rigid housing markets and the insufficiency of infrastructural conditions of mobility (education, social and health services, among others). Skills structures are becoming increasingly counterproductive: the high percentage share of labour supply with higher education qualifications is not supported by an adequate supply of skilled workers. While these societies are ageing rapidly, the new age cohorts entering the labour market possess less of the skills required by business and industry, whilst too many within these cohorts are skilled for public sector jobs. The outcome of these biases is a shrinking supply of skilled workers. Some countries such as Hungary have high-tech manufacturing capacities based on foreign direct investment (FDI) and make significant use of immigrant employment as a result of the domestic shortage of skilled labour.

11.4 EDUCATION

As a rule, the pre-1990 governments emphasized and quite generously financed education. The emphasis on education served to promote both equal social opportunities and ideological indoctrination. Financial inputs did not dwindle in absolute terms after 1990, but shrinking human capital and soaring enrolment (first of all in higher education) brought some national education systems in the region close to crisis (Morgan, 2000). The Austro-Hungarian tradition of intensive and demanding high-school education remains in place, but the quality of high-school graduates is deteriorating as shown by the figures of the Programme for International Student Assessment (PISA) of the Organisation for Economic Co-operation and Development (OECD). Vocational training has also lost much ground. In general, the education sector of the Visegrad countries is suffering as a result of increasing international competitiveness. On the policy level, no appropriate solutions have been found as yet to address the dilemmas of theory versus business, and general knowledge versus techniques and methodologies-oriented middle and higher education. A further burden on these systems is the generally poor command of widely spoken foreign languages and widely used information technology (IT) techniques. Finally, systems of lifelong learning in these countries are also narrow in focus and underdeveloped.

11.5   THE WAGE–LABOUR NEXUS

Formerly strong systems of employment protection have been streamlined significantly since 1990. Trade unions have lost much of their political influence, their membership and social base. Labour legislation is still quite employee-friendly, but many instances of practices that are detrimental to the interests of workers fail to reach the courts. Some multinational firms, such as hypermarket chains, have a reputation for poor industrial relations. As a result of weak protections for workers, however, strikes are rare in the countries of the region, with the partial exception of Poland and Slovakia. Nationwide strikes in Slovakia in 2005 and 2006 were associated with aggressive reforms promoted by the government affecting parts of the public sector, such as the healthcare system. Wage bargaining is centralized, although many employers including SMEs and some foreign-owned firms do not always follow the recommendations arising from such bargaining processes.

11.6   LABOUR MARKETS

Labour markets are strongly regulated at least nominally, but both employers and workers are inventive when it comes to bypassing rules on minimal wages, job protection and social security. This is particularly the case in Hungary, but is also a problem elsewhere. One technique for bypassing regulations is to replace employment with subcontracting, so that people who technically work for a larger company are, in fact, employees of their own small firms and are subcontracted by their real employer. These kinds of practices decrease the level of social protection significantly, since a part of wage costs is transformed into payments to subcontracting firms. Labour markets are quite segmented in both sectoral and regional terms. In general, the underdeveloped eastern regions of these countries suffer from high structural unemployment.

11.7   SOCIAL PROTECTION

Healthcare and pension systems are far from efficient. Although they are financed by social security contributions which are comparatively high in European terms, and which add to wage costs significantly, quality healthcare is exceptional and pensions are low as compared to the cost of living. Reform proposals to increase self-financing of such services have been partially implemented (as with the Hungarian pension system reform of 1997, for instance), but major changes in the healthcare system have led to considerable social unrest (Slovakia was a case in point in 2006). As a rule, in the Visegrad countries, mortality rates and indicators of social health do not reflect relatively high current levels of public expenditure on healthcare. Healthcare-related social security spending is often badly structured. For example, hospital capacity is too large while outpatient clinics are underdeveloped, and governments are often unable to resist supplier pressures to increase the price of drugs and medical equipment.

11.8   COMPETITION

The strong presence of major multinational players makes a number of sectors highly concentrated. This reflects the fact that privatization has often been undertaken without attention to competition concerns. Concentration is usually very strong in network industries. Competition policies and legislation follow established EU models closely, but the implementation of competition law is sometimes slow and inefficient. Major competition policy problems include bid-rigging at government tenders, and mergers in highly concentrated industries dominated by the private successors of former state monopolies.

11.9   PRODUCT-MARKET COMPETITION

Price competition is still dominant owing to low average purchasing power levels as well as problems related to the state of competition and consumption cultures among the populations of the Eastern European countries.

Government involvement in market and price regulation is quite weak, which is reflected by the dominant position of a number of hypermarket chains vis-à-vis their suppliers, subcontractors and employees. The protection of domestic markets from overly aggressive import competition is usually weaker than in the EU-15. Non-price coordination exists in a number of sectors. The level of this kind of coordination depends on the sectoral and regional structures of FDI since most major market players are domestically owned. As a rule, many of their informal networks abroad are also present in the NMCs.

11.10   FINANCE

Financial institutions are technically well developed, and organized entirely according to Western European patterns. Banking and insurance markets are highly oligopolistic, and the suppliers of such services usually operate with considerable profit margins. This tends to make business credit unusually expensive and makes businesses reluctant to adopt overly high credit exposure. Banks are therefore increasingly oriented towards still considerably unexplored retail markets. A potential Achilles heel of the banking systems is soaring consumer debt, partly denominated in foreign currencies (in euros, US dollars and Swiss francs), and therefore strongly exposed to exchange rate fluctuations.

11.11   FINANCIAL SECTOR

Rules of corporate governance follow German patterns with some Anglo-Saxon influence (supervisory boards are less powerful than they are in Germany, for example). The protection of minority shareholders is formally well developed, but in practice there are a number of cases where such protection has been ineffective. Institutional investors play a major role in only a few firms, but these include the most important players in the energy, telecom and banking sectors, and are quoted on the national stock exchanges. In some countries, however, the ownership structure of many firms, including major exporters and employers, is still not transparent. The degree of sophistication of financial markets is rapidly increasing, and new instruments of investment are fast gaining ground, but conscious and strategic investor behaviour is somewhat rare among households.

11.12 SUMMARY

Eastern European capitalism has been described here as it exists in the NMCs of East-Central Europe (in the Visegrad countries). It can be summarized as a blend of the Central and the Southern European model, with formal (regulatory) elements borrowed from the German-speaking countries, and their economic and social systems functioning more along Southern European lines. While a few elements of the market-based model can be identified, elements of the Nordic model are completely absent.

REFERENCES

Csaba, L. (2005), *The New Political Economy of Emerging Europe*, Budapest: Akadémiai Kiadó.

Morgan, A. (2000), 'Reform in Hungarian Higher Education', *International Higher Education*, Spring, http://www.bc.edu/bc_org/avp/soe/cihe/newsletter/News 19/ text15.html.

Török, Á. with B. Borsi and A. Telcs (2005), *Competitiveness in Research and Development: Comparisons and Performance*, Cheltenham, UK and Northampton, MA, USA: Edward Elgar.

12. The Lisbon Agenda and the key reforms at national level: conclusions of the debate

Maria João Rodrigues

A cross-national analysis of some key indicators clearly shows that the implementation of the Lisbon Agenda varies a great deal. If we want to assess how performances can be improved, we must go beyond a comparison of output indicators, such as the growth rate, labour productivity or the employment rate, and analyse underlying structures and behaviour. To this end, we can use the available research on the varieties of capitalism.

12.1 DEVELOPING THE FRAMEWORK FOR COMPARATIVE ANALYSIS

In order to discuss the implications of the Lisbon Agenda, we must develop the above-mentioned available typologies on varieties of capitalism. First, we should take into account new institutional areas that are relevant for the Lisbon Agenda, notably regarding the environment and social inclusion within the broader context of sustainable development. Second, we should outline the characteristics of a new type of capitalism found in some new Member States, which can be called the 'Eastern type' (for a detailed analysis, see Chapter 11 in this volume). Third, we must highlight the factors shaping the various existing institutional settings. These, of course, reflect different historical backgrounds, but also current differences in terms of values, collective preferences, resources, general conditions and, last but not least, actors. Finally, we must emphasize that we are not comparing 'national models', but rather broader 'ideal types' of capitalism, which requires a higher level of abstraction to identify the internal institutional complementarities of each one.

12.2 UNCOVERING THE META-TYPE OF CAPITALISM UNDERLYING THE LISBON AGENDA

Taking into account the comparison of the different types of capitalism as well as the presentation of the Lisbon Agenda made in Table 8.2, it is possible to identify the contours of a new hybrid type of capitalism, which is proposed not as a model but as a broader point of reference for the evolution of the others. That is what we mean when we speak of a meta-type of capitalism underlying the Lisbon Agenda. What is the particular mix of this type?

On the one hand, it borrows a comprehensive education system from the Continental type; on the other hand, it evinces more openness to competition, which is typical of the Anglo-Saxon variant. The Nordic type seems to make a good synthesis of these two features, complemented by flexicurity in labour markets, which is supported by universal social protection. This specific combination seems particularly suited to promoting growth and social cohesion in a context of open markets and was, in fact, an important inspiration for the Lisbon Agenda.

But to what extent is the Nordic type transferable to other countries? The Scandinavian countries have sought the 'middle way' since the 1940s, although many of the current features of their variant of capitalism emerged more recently in response to the hard times some of these countries experienced. In spite of their differences, they seem to share a commitment to effectiveness, rather than efficiency, building on a concern with the environment and social cohesion and relying on their relatively smaller size to coordinate change. These are features that are not easily extended to other countries.

Moreover, others argue, if the spotlight is now on the Scandinavian countries, we should not forget that similar attention was paid quite recently to the 'polder model' in the Netherlands, or to the Japanese model in the 1980s. Thus, the 'reference model' seems to undergo a cycle of performance.

Others go even further, arguing that the Continental type has some of the strongest points: the 'Bismarck' system of social protection may be less vulnerable to tax competition than the universalistic tax-based one; moreover, the Scandinavian-style flexicurity mechanisms in the labour market can easily pave the way to flexibility alone, and this can be suboptimal in terms of growth and jobs. Thus, the Continental type is better equipped to avoid the risk of undermining social cohesion. But others argue the reverse, questioning the consistency of the Continental type, since in France and Germany there are remarkable differences in the role of social partners, in openness to financial markets, and the relative aptitude for manufacturing versus services.

An important conclusion in this debate is that the consistency of the meta-type suggested by the Lisbon Agenda should be tested against the main mechanisms to be developed. The central purpose of the Lisbon Agenda is to prepare Europe for globalization and new demographic trends. Its central goal is to foster growth and jobs with investment in knowledge and innovation, in a framework of sustainable development (meaning long-term balanced economic, social and environmental development).

Hence, the central mechanisms to be developed should be the following: in order to compete and create jobs in a globalized economy, companies should invest more in knowledge assets and rely on a more skilled and flexible labour force supported by more effective active labour market policies and social protection systems; patterns of production and consumption should become more environmentally friendly; in corporate governance, there needs to be a redefinition of the roles of stakeholders and shareholders in order to allow for a longer investment horizon combined with greater access to financial resources.

12.3   THREE KEY CRITERIA TO DEVELOP THE LISBON AGENDA

This suggests that when determining the political orientation of the Lisbon Agenda, three central economic and social processes (three main criteria) should be taken into account: first, that of moving towards a knowledge-intensive economy; second, that of fostering growth and jobs; and third, that of ensuring sustainable development (implying concern with social cohesion and the environment).

Table 12.1 illustrates how these three criteria should be taken into account and combined in all the different institutional areas already considered. This has different implications for different policy areas, as follows:

1. In research, this means taking the lead in some research areas, but also increasing their relevance for growth and jobs, and sustaining this long-term investment by attracting more people to research careers and by improving the mechanisms of intellectual property rights.
2. As regards innovation, this means developing innovation clusters as the main engine for the transition to a knowledge-intensive economy, but also turning them into partnerships to create more and better jobs, to

support innovation in all kinds of companies and sectors, and to sustain this movement by fostering and enlarging access to entrepreneurship.

3. For the environment, this means developing and spreading new environmental technologies as well as turning them into new opportunities for investment and job creation.

4. In education, this means not only raising educational levels, but also increasing their relevance for new economic activities, and sustaining this trend by widening the access to lifelong learning.

5. As regards labour markets, this involves the redeployment of jobs and people towards more knowledge-intensive activities, supporting this movement with more effective active labour market policies and better combinations between flexibility and security, as well as attracting more people to the labour market and reconsidering the role of immigration.

6. Where social protection is concerned, this means adjusting contributions and benefits to make work pay, but also improving the sustainability of the pensions system to address ageing trends, and adapting social protection to new social risks and needs, including regular lifelong learning.

7. As regards competition, this means opening markets and enforcing competition rules, as well as respecting the main features of the European social model and redirecting state aid to foster investment in research, innovation, education and training.

8. In financial markets, growth needs to be fostered by providing broader access to financial resources by integrating financial markets, as well as developing venture capital and reconsidering the role of stakeholders and shareholders in corporate governance models.

9. Finally, as regards macroeconomic policies, this means providing macroeconomic stability and improving the sustainability of public debt, as well as using automatic stabilizers and redirecting public expenditure to invest more in research, innovation and education in order to strengthen growth potential.

As shown above, the synergies between the knowledge economy, growth and sustainable development must increase in order to strengthen the internal consistency of the Lisbon Agenda. But it is also very clear that there are internal tensions and trade-offs, notably between competition on the one hand, and building a knowledge-intensive economy and ensuring a sustainable development on the other; and between economic growth on the one hand, and fiscal consolidation and strengthening monetary union on the other. In turn, this means that several scenarios are actually possible: there could be relative success with implementing the Lisbon Agenda by

Table 12.1   Three central processes in the Lisbon Agenda

Central process and criteria / Institutional area	Moving to a knowledge-intensive economy	Fostering growth and jobs	Ensuring sustainable development
Research	• Investing in leading research areas	• Increasing relevance of research for economic activity	• Attracting more people to research careers • Intellectual property rights
Innovation	• Developing innovation clusters	• Partnerships for innovation and jobs creation	• Promoting entrepreneurship
Environment	• More research and innovation on environmental technologies	• Producing environmental technologies and creating new jobs	• Changing patterns of consumption and production
Education	• Raising education levels • Learning organizations	• Foresight on skills needs	• Access to lifelong learning
Labour market	• Mobility of jobs and people for activities with more added value	• Stronger active labour market policies • Developing flexicurity	• Higher employment rates • Immigration policy
Social protection	• Adaptability of social protection schemes to lifelong learning needs	• Regular review of contributions and benefits to make work pay	• Sustainability of pension systems regarding ageing trends • Combating old and new forms of social exclusion

Competition	• Review of state aid rules to foster investment in research, education and innovation • Developing venture capital	• Opening the markets and fostering competition	• Respecting the main features of European Social Model
Financial markets		• Integrating financial markets and wider access to fund raising	• Corporate governance: new roles for stakeholders and shareholders
Macroeconomic policies	• Redirecting public expenditure to research, innovation and education	• Using the automatic stabilizers • Providing macroeconomic stability	• Improving the sustainability of public debt

instituting such synergies; or there could be a relative failure as a result of the trade-offs. Thus, we should move beyond a functionalist approach, and ask what we can expect to happen rather than focusing on what should happen. What, then, are the critical factors for success? Apart from those that depend on the European level (there are many), many depend on the national level as well, taking into account the varieties of capitalism in Europe. Enduring differences notwithstanding, to what extent can the different types of capitalism develop these new kinds of mechanisms and synergies? To what extent can they create a new 'virtuous circle'?

12.4   THE CRITICAL CHANGES TO CONVERGE TOWARDS THE LISBON GOALS

Performance in terms of the implementation of the Lisbon Agenda has varied significantly across Member States to date. This is the central conclusion of the main existing assessments. If we want to identify how performances can improve, we must go beyond a comparison of output indicators (such as the growth rate, labour productivity or the employment rate) and analyse underlying structures and behaviours.

The main assumption underlying this approach is that in order to improve overall performance, some kind of convergence is necessary: not in terms of patterns of sectoral specialization but rather a shift towards knowledge-intensive activities; not in terms of particular institutional settings but rather key institutional mechanisms and synergies that can deal with the new strategic problems outlined above. Nevertheless, taking into account the diversity of capitalism in Europe, convergence paths are quite different. Hence, in the Anglo-Saxon European type of capitalism, some of the critical changes to be introduced seem to be:

- in research, fostering cooperation of research institutions;
- in innovation, promoting public procurement for innovation and innovation networks;
- in environment policy, spreading environmental technologies and changing consumption and production patterns;
- in education, developing preschooling and secondary education for all, as well as vocational training and learning organizations;
- in the labour market, developing active employment policies, better combinations between flexibility and security, and the role of social partners;
- In social protection, increasing the adequacy of social protection systems and of the target actions to fight poverty;

- in competition, promoting competition with respect of the European social model and improving the restructuring of management;
- and in finance, strengthening the role of stakeholders in corporate governance.

For the Continental European type of capitalism, some of the critical changes to be introduced seem to be:

- in research, promoting openness, competition and relevance in research institutions;
- in innovation, developing innovation networks and competition policy;
- in environment policy, spreading environmental technologies and changing consumption and production patterns;
- in education, developing competitive and networking universities and competence by mobility, targeting new skills;
- in the labour market, raising employment levels, making a regular review of the contributions and benefit systems to make work pay, and achieving better combinations between flexibility and security;
- in social protection, ensuring the sustainability of social protection systems in the face of ageing trends;
- in competition, reducing the internal market barriers, promoting competition and supporting entrepreneurship;
- and in finance, developing more financial innovation and access to venture capital, and the role for shareholders in corporate governance.

In the South European type of capitalism, the critical changes to be introduced seem to be:

- in research, promoting openness, competition, relevance, capacity-building and internationalization;
- in innovation, developing technical and financial support to innovative companies, innovation networks, the role of public procurement and access to information and communication technologies (ICT);
- in environment policy, spreading environmental technologies and changing consumption and production patterns;
- in education, developing preschooling and secondary education for all, vocational training, lifelong learning, competitive and networking universities, and learning organizations;
- in the labour market, strengthening active labour market policies, promoting innovative and adaptable forms of work organizations and better combinations of flexibility and security;

- in social protection, increasing the adequacy and sustainability of social protection systems and promoting target actions to combat poverty;
- in competition, promoting better-quality competition and improving competition policy, and restructuring management;
- in finance, increasing financial innovation and access to venture capital, and the role for shareholders in corporate governance.

In the East European type of capitalism, some of the critical changes seem to be:

- in research, promoting openness, competition and relevance in research institutions;
- in innovation, developing technical and financial support to innovative companies, innovation networks, the role of public procurement as well as access to ICT;
- in environment policy, spreading environmental technologies and changing consumption and production patterns;
- in education, developing lifelong learning, and competitive and networking universities;
- in labour markets, strengthening active labour market policies, improving the management of restructuring processes, enforcing European directives, and developing better combinations of flexibility with security;
- in social protection, increasing the adequacy and sustainability of social protection systems and promoting target actions to fight poverty;
- in competition, developing better-quality competition, supporting entrepreneurship and improving the restructuring of management;
- and in finance, increasing financial innovation and access to venture capital, and developing the role of stakeholders in corporate governance.

12.5   ON THE REFORM STRATEGIES

The preparation of national reform programmes raised the issues of policy coordination and of how to get the relevant stakeholders involved. Today, the implementation of national reform programmes is raising the new issues of framework conditions and the reform method itself. We need to take into consideration the role that each level should play in the European multilevel system of governance.

Table 12.2   *European types of capitalism and convergence towards the Lisbon goals*

	Lisbon goals	Anglo-Saxon European	Continental European	South European	East European
Research	• Higher private and public investments research • More competition and cooperation between research institutions • More relevance • More internationalization	• Promoting cooperation of research institutions	• Promoting openness, competition and relevance in research institutions	• Promoting openness, competition and relevance in research institutions • Capacity-building and internationalization	• Promoting openness, competition and relevance in research institutions • Capacity-building and internationalization
Innovation	• More innovative companies • More innovation networks	• Public procurement for innovation • Innovation networks	• Innovation networks • Competition policy	• Technical and financial support to innovative companies • Innovation networks	• Technical and financial support to innovative companies • Innovation networks

Table 12.2 (continued)

	Lisbon goals	Anglo-Saxon European	Continental European	South European	East European
	• Public procurement for innovation • Community patent • Intensive use of ICT with social inclusion			• Public procurement • Access to ICT	• Public procurement • Access to ICT
Environment	• Environmentally friendly patterns of consumption and production	• Spreading environmental technologies • Changing consumption and production patterns	• Spreading environmental technologies • Changing consumption and production patterns	• Spreading environmental technologies • Changing consumption and production patterns	• Spreading environmental technologies • Changing consumption and production patterns
Education	• Higher education levels • Access to lifelong learning • Learning organization	• Preschooling and secondary education for all • Vocational training development • Learning organizations	• Competitive and networking universities • Developing new skills • Competence by mobility	• Preschooling and secondary education for all • Vocational training development • Lifelong learning • Competitive and networking	• Lifelong learning • Competitive and networking universities

Labour market				
• Competitive and networking universities • Higher employment rates • Life-cycle approach: adapting labour markets and social protection to young adults and old workers • Innovative forms of work organization • Better combination of flexibility and security • Stronger active labour market policies	• Better combinations between flexibility and security • Active employment policies • Developing the role of social partners	• Raising the employment levels • Better combinations between flexibility and security • Regular review of the contributions and benefit systems to make work pay	• universities • Learning organizations • Strengthening active labour market policies • Promoting innovative and adaptable forms of work organizations • Better combinations of flexibility and security	• Strengthening active labour market policies • Better combinations of flexibility with security • Improving management of restructuring processes • Enforcing European directives

Table 12.2 (continued)

	Lisbon goals	Anglo-Saxon European	Continental European	South European	East European
Social protection	• Social protection systems: – adequacy of levels – adaptability to new social risks – sustainability regarding ageing trends – social inclusion – combating old and new forms of social exclusion – reducing poverty	• Increasing the adequacy of social protection systems • Target actions to fight poverty	• Ensuring the sustainability of social protection systems in face of ageing trends	• Increasing the adequacy and sustainability of social protection systems • Target actions to fight poverty	• Increasing the adequacy and sustainability of social protection systems • Target actions to fight poverty

Competition	• More quality competition • Promoting trade respecting basic standards • Opening the markets • Competition policy with respect of social model • Restructuring management • Supporting entrepreneurship	• Competition with respect of European social model • Restructuring management	• Renewing internal market barriers • Competition policy • Supporting entrepreneurship	• Competition policy • Restructuring management • More quality competition	• Restructuring management • Supporting entrepreneurship • More quality management
Finance	• Corporate governance: new roles for stakeholders and shareholders • More financial innovation • Access to venture capital	• Corporate governance: more role for stakeholders • More financial innovation • Access to venture capital	• Corporate governance: more role for shareholders • More financial innovation • Access to venture capital	• Corporate governance: more role for stakeholders • More financial innovation • Access to venture capital	• Corporate governance: more role for stakeholders • More financial innovation • Access to venture capital

The European level provides an influential framework because it combines instruments for harmonization, coordination, cooperation, solidarity and capacity-building. By making use of all these, the Lisbon Agenda is certainly not providing a 'one size fits all' model but is rather creating an arena to compare reform strategies and, what is more, developing a 'centripetal process' with a new set of mechanisms created by Member States to address globalization and ageing.

Nevertheless, it seems that a precise reform strategy can only be elaborated at the national level because it requires a definition of how concrete measures are packaged and coordinated. These are important choices with implications not only for final outcomes and the performance, but also for the acceptability of reforms. For many Member States, one of the challenges seems to be to move from a 'patchwork' approach to reform, which is not able to create confidence and trust, towards a more comprehensive approach based on the collective creation of a virtuous circle for growth, employment, knowledge and sustainable development, which can overcome or offset the trade-offs. With this goal in mind, it is important to clarify the exact policy mix at stake. For instance, the debate on flexicurity or pensions reform can be more productive if it is linked up with the debate on innovation policy and the role of macroeconomic policies in fostering growth.

Several agreements and compromises in different institutional areas are necessary to support these reforms, but the so-called social contract is particularly important, since it affects overall life conditions of European citizens. The social contract should be renewed in order to create a sense of more social justice regarding life chances, not only across but also between generations.

Today, these life chances depend particularly on access to lifelong learning, adaptable social protection, effective labour market policies, and conditions for geographical mobility with portability of social benefits. National governance is particularly responsible and legitimate when dealing with these issues. Nevertheless, given increasing single market spillover effects, trade and Economic and Monetary Union (EMU), the EU level must also become more responsible for them, not least if it aims to gain greater legitimacy among European citizens.

PART III

The External Dimension of the Lisbon Agenda

13. On the external dimension of the Lisbon Agenda: key issues for policy-making

Maria João Rodrigues

13.1 KNOWLEDGE SOCIETIES IN A GLOBALIZED WORLD: KEY ISSUES FOR INTERNATIONAL CONVERGENCE

Knowledge Economies in the World: Race to the Bottom or the Top?

The aim of the Lisbon Agenda is to forge a European path to a knowledge society. Knowledge has become the main wealth of nations, companies and peoples, but it can also become a key factor of social divisions. Thus, investing in research, innovation and education, and developing a knowledge-intensive economy society are now the key means to develop competitiveness and prosperity.

Many other countries are making this choice. Not only the US and Japan, the first to work towards this goal, but also India, China, South Korea, Brazil and many others. There is now a clear international trend in this direction, as some examples from 2007 illustrate: Japan is preparing a very comprehensive Plan for Innovation focusing on citizens' needs; India has created a Knowledge Commission which is elaborating a broader development agenda for India; China has adopted a new Five-Year Plan introducing new concepts such as the role of knowledge and innovation, and including a new concern with social inclusion and the environment within the framework of the Chinese concept of a harmonious society, equivalent to the updated concept of sustainable development; after an ambitious foresight exercise called 'Brazil 3 Times', Brazil has adopted an ambitious agenda for development, emphasizing the role of knowledge, social inclusion and concern with the environment; and the USA is launching a new initiative to keep its lead in a more competitive knowledge economy.

However, a central question emerges, namely: under which conditions can this international trend lead to a win–win game? How can this lead to a race to the top rather than a race to the bottom where social and environmental issues in the transition to a knowledge intensive economy are concerned? It is now particularly relevant to identify the conditions which should be fulfilled. These are: the development of our relationships with global partners facing common challenges; transforming the strategy to create a knowledge-intensive economy into a more comprehensive development agenda; establishing global basic standards to define a level playing field; and developing international cooperation to promote capacity-building in order to disseminate new and better standards. A strategic dialogue should be developed with these purposes. Most particularly, EU external action should be updated so that it can undertake these new tasks.

The International Relevance of the Lisbon Agenda

The EU experience with the Lisbon Agenda can provide a relevant contribution to this strategic dialogue. In the year 2000, the European Union (EU) adopted a long-term strategy to develop a competitive knowledge economy, with sustainable growth, more and better jobs, and respect for the environment. Innovation, turning knowledge into added value, and growth and jobs were at the heart of this agenda, which called for more entrepreneurship and innovative companies; stronger networks between companies, research and education institutions; knowledge infrastructures; venture capital; and more people that are creative. To speed up redeployment towards a knowledge-intensive economy, exploit the scope of the European single market, reform the European social model in order to address the challenges posed by globalization, ageing and technological change, however, called for a broader agenda. Moreover, new political instruments were necessary to coordinate the development and implementation of this agenda at the different levels of governance: European, national and local. This was the purpose of the open method of coordination (OMC), combined with the other existing instruments such as directives, community programmes and structural funds.

Thus, in 2001, the so-called Lisbon Strategy was turned into a political agenda with many new measures introduced in various policy fields: information society, research, innovation, single market, education, employment, social protection, environmental and macroeconomic policies. In 2002, this agenda was extended to the ten new Member States, and in 2003 the agenda was connected with the upcoming Constitutional Treaty. In 2004, in both cases, this happened to an insufficient degree, given the upcoming Community budget. Recognizing the mixed results and slow and uneven implementation at national level, in 2005 the European Council adopted clearer political guidelines and launched the national reform programmes for Member States to use when adapting the Lisbon guidelines to national conditions.

As of 2007, we can say that a positive trend has been emerging in terms of growth and net job creation, but the sustainability of this trend depends on more growth potential to be created by structural reforms. Many structural reforms in social protection, health systems, public administration, financial systems, research and education, and labour markets are under way in Europe, but this is still insufficient and, above all, imbalanced when comparing policy fields and countries. Nevertheless, it is already possible to conclude that the Member States which have been most effective in implementing the Lisbon Agenda are also those reaping most benefits in terms of growth, job creation and sustainable development.

From this European experience, we can draw some conclusions, which can be used in a strategic dialogue with EU partner countries, within the framework of either the strategic partnerships or the partnerships for cooperation and development.

13.2 IMPLICATIONS FOR EU EXTERNAL ACTION

A New Phase in Union External Action

What can be the specific role of the European Union in this process of international convergence towards a more balanced and sustainable development? The European Union can play a very relevant role in disseminating new points of reference for a new development agenda, by different means. It can do so, first, by setting a positive example in implementing a new development agenda among its own Member States (see above); second, it can intertwine the new development agenda with its enlargement and neighbourhood policies; and finally, it can connect this new development agenda with the various components of its external action: cooperation policy, external projection of its internal policies, trade policy and foreign policy regarding countries, macro-regions and multilateral organizations.

This concern should be more systematically integrated in the new phase of EU external action for 2007–13, which is now being redesigned following proposals presented by the European Commission. These proposals include the development of a broader approach for the external action of the Union, combining Common Foreign and Security Policy (CFSP), trade and cooperation policies, and the external projection of the internal policies of the Union. This means that the external action of the EU should also integrate the external dimension of policies such as research, environmental, education and employment policies (see COM(2006) 278). Second, they include the preparation of a new generation of EU coopera-tion programmes, based on the new political orientations defined by the 'European Consensus' (see COM(2005) 311); and third, a new approach is being developed in trade policy in connection to the Lisbon Agenda, which aims to prepare Europe for globalization using trade combined with basic standards as well as internal markets as a major lever for growth and more and better jobs (see COM(2006) 278).

A New Development Agenda and EU Cooperation Policy

The next generation of the EU cooperation programmes can play a very relevant role in disseminating a new development agenda, but there is a central dilemma in this regard: should the strategy papers and the national programmes for partner countries cover all the priorities or address only some? And, in the latter case, how should priorities be selected?

There is a possible third approach to overcome this dilemma, consisting of two different steps: first, encouraging a preliminary step, by requiring a more comprehensive development strategy in each country and defining a strategic framework for development; second, supporting some concrete priorities, complementing other financial sources within this strategic framework. The other financial sources can have very diverse origins: mul-tilateral organizations, non-European countries, EU Member States, other EU policies, including the external projection of internal policies of the Union such as research, education, environment and employment.

More effective programming of cooperation should also combine core cooperation measures with this external dimension of EU internal policies, such as research, education, employment, environment, immigration or cultural policies, which should be better coordinated for this purpose.

Nevertheless, this third approach requires improvements in the method-ology for technical assistance in the programming phase regarding the discussion of a more comprehensive strategy for development in the frame-work of the strategic dialogue mentioned above; and measures to enhance the knowledge base and technical expertise to support the policy-making process.

Moreover, regarding the implementation phase, new governance mecha-nisms should also be developed in order to: strengthen ownership of all the relevant stakeholders; build coalitions for change; and monitor and evalu-ate the impact of public policies on economic and social change.

Further elaboration can lead to more policy coherence by formulating more comprehensive development strategies, beyond the traditional poverty reduction strategies or even the more recent decent work strategies.

The following principles built on the European experience can provide some useful inputs for the process of enriching the development agenda:

1. Employment policy is, by definition, a central bridge between social and economic policies because it combines the factors influencing labour supply with those influencing labour demand, such as trade, industrial and macroeconomic policies. Hence, a stronger focus on more and better jobs is necessary.
2. Social protection policy also provides a central bridge because it should be envisaged as a productive factor and also because it should take its financial sustainability into account.
3. The implications of trade cannot be dissociated from capacity-building policies for areas such as infrastructure, innovation, industry, education and health policies. The policies for promoting a transition to a knowledge society should always play a central role, whatever the level of development.
4. The aim of macroeconomic policy should be to combine macroeconomic stabilization with capacity-building to increase growth potential.

These are some of the central ideas underlying the Lisbon Strategy, or the European agenda for growth and jobs in a framework of sustainable development, which are also relevant for less developed countries. That said, many aspects of the European experience cannot be directly transposed due to the broad range of national specificities. Specificities concerning the weight of informal employment, the role of social entrepreneurship, or the level of basic social standard thresholds should be emphasized. This means that the general framework to be adopted should be flexible enough to take national diversity into account.

A New Development Agenda and EU Trade Policy

According to the above-mentioned European Commission Communication on trade policy (COM(2006) 278), the EU should develop a social dimension in trade policy. From this viewpoint, it is regrettable that basic labour standards were not included in the Generalized System of Preferences (GSP) and GSP Plus, with implications for the Doha Round.

Still, the European Union can introduce this issue in the negotiations of its bilateral agreements. The current perspective, of negotiating agreements with macro-regions undertaking processes of regional integration, can create important opportunities, although a special effort will be required to address new and specific problems regarding the social dimension of regional integration. The main underlying assumption should be that regional integration can become an important lever to promote trade with better social and environmental standards.

The EU approach should create an effective environment for these negotiations by combining incentives and sanctions. To improve this mix, it is particularly important to strengthen coordination between trade, cooperation and the other components of Union external action, including the external projection of internal EU policies. The role to be played by European companies investing abroad in promoting better labour and environmental standards can also be emphasized as a basic component of corporate social responsibility.

A New Development Agenda and the Need of more Consistent and Coherent EU External Action

The development and diffusion of a new development agenda depend crucially on multilateral institutions taking stronger initiatives. In this, the European Union has a special responsibility. Therefore, more effective action by the EU is required, notably: on the board of the World Bank and the International Monetary Fund (IMF); in the UN system, more specifically in the UN Economic and Social Council (ECOSOC) and in the UN Commission for Social Development; and in the interface between the International Labour Organization (ILO) and the World Trade Organization (WTO).

The debate on a new development agenda is also a debate about how to design rules so that globalization benefits populations throughout the world. In fact, these rules are crucial to support the implementation of new development agendas. These rules are emerging in different policy fields such as finance, the environment, intellectual property and labour. Nevertheless, they still need to be clarified, enforced and better coordinated. For instance, for labour and WTO rules to be coordinated, the following issues could be considered: how the WTO can take the role of the ILO into account; the creation of a Committee on Trade and Decent Work in the WTO; the definition of the role of specific indicators to introduce in the negotiation process; and how to advance further, by deciding that the ratification of ILO core labour standards should be a prerequisite for WTO membership.

In conclusion, the implementation of a new development agenda is challenging the coherence and the consistency of the external action of the European Union.

It is challenging its coherence because, if the Union wants to improve the success of its internal economic, social and environmental policies within

---

BOX 13.1   THE EXTERNAL DIMENSION OF THE LISBON STRATEGY: KEY QUESTIONS

1. What are the main international trends in the transition to a knowledge-intensive economy?
2. What are the specificities and the international implications of the Lisbon Agenda?
3. What should be the priorities for strategic dialogue on development agendas between the key international players, and with other partner countries?
4. What are the implications of this strategic dialogue for the external action of the EU, including the Common Foreign and Security Policy, trade policy, cooperation policy, and for the external projection of EU internal policies (on research, the environment, employment, education, and culture, among others).

---

the framework of the Lisbon Agenda, it must also improve the consistency between policies promoted by EU external action in partner countries. So far, there is an important gap between the internal and the external policies of the European Union.

And it is challenging its consistency because the action of the EU to reform the multilateral system and promote and improve basic rules for globalization requires much stronger coordination between the EU and its Member States in the multilateral arena.

BIBLIOGRAPHY

Bretherton, C. and J. Vogler (1999), *The European Union as a Global Actor*, Oxford and New York: Routledge.

Dicken, P. (1998), *Global Shift: Transforming the World Economy*, London: Paul Chapman Publishing.

European Commission (2005), *Joint Declaration by the Council, the European Parliament and the Commission on the European Union Development Policy 'The European Consensus'*, COM(2005) 311 final, 13.07.2005.

European Commission (2006), *Europe in the World: Some Practical Proposals for Greater Coherence, Effectiveness and Visibility*, COM(2006) 278 final, 08.06.2006.

Glenn, J.C. and T.J. Gordon (2007), *2007 State of the Future*, Millennium Project, Washington, DC: World Federation of UN Associations.

Gnesotto, N. and G. Grevi (2006), *The New Global Puzzle: What World for the EU in 2025?*, Institute for Security Studies, Paris: Corlet Imprimeur.

Held, D. and A. McGrew (eds) (2000), *The Global Transformations Reader: An Introduction to the Globalization Debate*, Cambridge, UK and Malden, MA, USA: Polity Press.

Montbrial, T. and P.M. Defarges (eds) (2006), *2007 L'Europe et le monde*, Institut Français des Relations Internationales, Paris: Dunod.

Rodrigues, M.J. (ed.), G. Arbix, I. Begg, J.C. Ferraz, M. Salerno, L. Soete and A. Valladão (2007a), *Dialogues for Sustainable Development: Brazil and the European Union*, Final Report, Instituto de Estudos Estratégicos e Internacionais.

Rodrigues, M.J. (ed.), G. Arbix, J.C. Ferraz, S. Fisher, F. Godement, G. Grevi, C. Huang, L. Soete, M. Telò, A. Valldão, A. Vasconcelos, C. Wagner and H. Zhou (2007b), *Developing the External Action of the European Union – New Instruments and New Global Players*, Portuguese Presidency of the European Union, Lisbon: Gabinete do Primeiro Ministro.

Rodrigues, M.J. (ed.), I. Begg, B. Dai, F. Godement, C. Huang, L. Soete, H. Zhou and Y. Zhou (2007c), *Dialogues for Sustainable Development: China and the European Union*, Final Report, Instituto de Estudos Estratégicos e Internacionais.

Rodrigues, M.J. and P. Courela (eds), G. Arbix, G. Joffé, C. Kobayashi, M.S. Neves, E. Ogawa, D. Redford, M. Salerno and H. Zhou (2007), 'The Lisbon Strategy: Reaching Beyond Europe' in *Estratégia*, no. 22–23, Instituto de Estudos Estratégicos e Internacionais, Lisbon: Bizâncio.

Rodrigues, M.J. and M. Telò (eds) (2004), 'Mission Report 1 on the International Mission to Beijing, China', in *Social Sciences in the European Research Area: For the Development of the Research Agenda*, European Commission's Advisory Group on Social Sciences, SSHERA Project, EU 6th Framework Programme RTD.

Sapir, A. (ed.) (2007), *Fragmented Power: Europe and the Global Economy*, Brussels: Bruegel Books.

Stiglitz, J. (2002), *Globalization and Its Discontents*, London: Penguin Books.

Telò, M. (2006), *Europe: A Civilian Power? European Union, Global Governance, World Order*, New York: Palgrave Macmillan.

Telò, M. (ed.) (2007), *The European Union and the New Regionalism: Regional Actors and Global Governance in a Post-Hegemonic Era*, Aldershot, UK and Burlington, VT, USA: Ashgate.

http://www.europa.eu/growthandjobs/.
http://www.mariajoaorodrigues.eu.

See further bibliography in Appendix 4 of this book.

14. The external implications of the Lisbon Agenda

Bengt-Åke Lundvall

14.1 INTRODUCTION

In this chapter, I argue that an external European strategy needs to be designed in such a way that it takes into account differences among Member States in terms of both economic structure and national political culture. At first glance, this suggests a minimalist foreign policy, but in fact the opposite is required. Taking the Lisbon Agenda as a platform and reference point helps us to understand why a comprehensive strategy of external strategic partnerships is not only a realistic but also a necessary option for Europe.

I also argue that while the most important and original element of the Lisbon Agenda was the new vision that sees knowledge as the most important source of growth, the full implications of that vision have yet to be worked out. A more balanced perspective, in which the importance of tacit and experience-based knowledge and the importance of transforming Europe into a learning economy are recognized, would both reinforce the Lisbon Agenda and make it a more adequate platform for external strategic alliances.

14.2 EUROPE'S ROLE IN THE GLOBAL ARENA

For several decades, Europe has been busy establishing the single market and its internal institutions. The original Lisbon Agenda paid little attention to external strategy. The relationship with the rest of the world was defined mainly through the goal of becoming 'the most competitive region of the world', and the original version of the Lisbon Agenda reflected a certain European envy of the flexible US economy and its apparent success in the context of the 'new economy'. It neglected the fact that the success of the US also reflected an ambitious strategy of global positioning leading to the inflow of both highly skilled top-level scientists and engineers, and illegal cheap labour at the bottom of the skills pyramid (Lundvall, 2003).

The recent change of focus, with greater attention paid to the external dimension, may be seen as a response to radical changes in the economic and political world order. The new role of China in the world economy, the energy crisis, global warming, terrorism and the Iraq War as well as the strong euro and the weak dollar have become major new items on Europe's political agenda. It is now more generally realized that it is fundamentally important for the European Union (EU) to succeed in developing a realistic and ambitious vision of what its global role should be. Given the unique nature of 'European construction', it is necessary to develop an external strategy that differs from the traditional approach pursued by nation-states (see Chapter 16 for more details).

One important implication of the limited capacity of the EU to raise taxes from its citizens is that it is not realistic to envisage the EU as a major military power. So it is not a viable option to develop traditional diplomacy with military intervention as a last-resort threat. The EU as a whole has, then, a strong vested interest in a world order with the lowest possible level of conflict, and it should support multilateral 'rules of the game'. As illustrated by the Iraq War and the crisis in the Balkans, it is important for the EU to develop institutions that make it harder and less attractive for Member States to become embroiled in foreign policy adventures. As argued by Maria Rodrigues in Chapter 13, the Lisbon Agenda constitutes a platform for developing strategic partnerships that may contribute to the formation of such a peaceful, sustainable and prosperous world order.

14.3　GLOBAL COMPETITION AND WIN–WIN STRATEGY: LESSONS FROM POST-WAR 'CATCHING UP'

The most successful growth period in modern history to date – the period between 1945 and 1973 – was propelled by a 'catching-up' phenomenon, whereby Europe and Japan emulated the US lead in technology and organization. It is important to note that this was a period of diffusion not only of technological knowledge but also of organizational practices and institutions emanating from the US. The Marshall Plan initiated a systematic exchange of people and ideas across the Atlantic, and many US practices were adopted in Europe. While the process was driven mainly by the logic of the Cold War and by fear of the spread of Communism, the net economic outcome was positive for both Europe and the US. Without the 'catch-up dynamo' it is quite possible that those who foresaw a post-World War depression for the world economy would have been proven right. There is little doubt that the unique leadership position of the US in the post-World War era was a result of its Cold War military leadership but also of the export of US institutions.

Europe cannot replicate this experience in its attempt to build strategic relations with challenger countries such as China, India, Russia, South Africa and Brazil. The conditions for post-World War growth were quite unique. The Second World War had destroyed both physical capital and old institutions, especially in Germany and Japan, and the existence of a political 'common enemy' strongly contributed to that unique setting. But some lessons may be drawn from that catch-up experience. In a world where globalization brings systems into closer interaction and more intense competition, systemic institutional features outside the realm of trade agreements become increasingly important for determining the degree of friction and synergy between systems. Better understanding of such systemic differences, and institutional learning among major competitors, reduce friction and increase synergy (Ostry and Nelson, 1995).

It therefore becomes increasingly important to stimulate challenger countries to develop further their labour market, social security, education and research institutions, as well as the regulatory systems for environment and energy using Europe as a model.[1] This implies a much more ambitious agenda than setting and enforcing social and environmental standards with the aim of increasing the costs of challenger producers.

14.4 THE EXTERNAL IMPLICATIONS OF THE LISBON AGENDA

'Globalization' is often referred to as an anonymous force that cannot be controlled. Today, it is obvious that specific bursts of industrial growth in certain parts of the world and stagnation in others shape the specificities of this process. Currently, the most obvious example is the rapid growth of export-oriented manufacturing production in China and India, and its secondary positive impact on the economic development in certain countries producing raw materials such as Brazil, South Africa and Russia. But Europe needs to take into account more than the development of growth economies. The impact on Member States of stagnation and crises in other parts of the world may be equally dramatic. As a result of stagnation, Africa suffers from underemployment, as reflected in the outflow of labour to Europe. Stagnation in parts of the Arab world feeds Muslim fundamentalism and, indirectly, cultural conflict and terrorism.

When designing an external strategy based on the Lisbon platform, it is necessary to distinguish between less developed countries in general and countries that may be seen as actual or potential challenger countries. In the case of challenger countries, strategic partnerships may aim to promote economic synergy to boost global economic growth; in the case of other poor countries (including most of Africa), the major objective may be the creation of job opportunities in these countries. Such efforts may be driven by humanitarian motives and moral obligations towards the countries that have suffered most from the deterioration of the climate through CO_2 contributions to global warming. A more reliable impetus may be self-interest. Creating jobs in Africa and in other stagnating parts of the world is the only way to weaken the pressure of emigration flows to Europe. To stimulate 'modernization' in the Arab world by supporting education and scientific progress may be the best way to counter the global threat of terrorism.

When specific 'challenger countries' can be identified, the external strategy can have a more or less ambitious aim, and can be more or less farsighted. Trade restrictions in the form of quotas for certain commodities (such as shoes) may be imposed to weaken the transformation pressure on specific sectors, regions and groups of workers. Bilateral agreements and global rules may be negotiated or imposed with the primary aim of making it more costly for external competitors to produce. This may take the form of 'decent work' or environmental protection principles and refer to the establishment of a 'level playing field'. But as argued above, such limited perspectives are insufficient in the era of the globalizing learning economy. A more sustainable way to combine competition with cooperation is to engage in institutional learning between Europe and challenger innovation systems. This lies at the heart of the idea of externalizing the Lisbon Agenda.

14.5   DEFINING EXTERNAL STRATEGIES BASED ON A RECOGNITION OF EU ECONOMIC AND POLITICAL DIVERSITY

The external dimension consists of a two-way relationship: the EU has an impact on the rest of the world through different mechanisms (see Chapter 16 in this volume); but, equally, what happens in the rest of the world has an impact on Europe. If the Lisbon Agenda is not implemented so as to address the concrete consequences of this process, including the destructive effects of growing regional and social inequality and insecurity, it is difficult to envisage a successful external strategy. Since the exposure of different regions and professions is very uneven (in the South of Europe, for instance, the proportion of workers in direct competition with workers in new emerging economies is much higher than in the North of Europe, as shown in Table 14.1) it would be difficult to agree on a common strategy of openness.

To agree on such a strategy is also difficult because of the substantial differences in political culture in different parts of Europe. To simplify, the British tend to see government as a necessary evil; the French tend to expect the state to intervene and solve all kinds of important societal problems; and the Nordic countries and Germany are in an intermediate position. Such differences are reflected in views of external relations, either as protecting domestic economies from or adjusting them to market processes. Different views of Europe's strategic relationship with the US are also fundamental. A process that aims to produce a coherent and effective external strategy must be based on transparent positions in these respects.

This might lead one to conclude that external strategy should be minimalist, restricted to areas where there is a common strategic interest. As argued above, though, a narrow version of national foreign policy would not be in the interest of the EU as a whole. And the Lisbon process has demonstrated that shifting the focus towards the knowledge-based economy makes it possible to build consensus over and above such differences. When knowledge is defined as a strategic resource, it generates opportunities for positive-sum games. The fact that, despite their different political cultures, the UK and France were able to back the Lisbon Agenda demonstrates the power of the new vision and its capacity to overcome the split between neoliberal and neo-protectionist ideas.

Beyond that, linking environmental and energy to innovation and innovation policies reinforces the 'bridging' character of the Lisbon Agenda.[2] This broadening of the agenda also makes it a more adequate and meaningful basis for building strategic relationships with emerging economies such as China, India, Russia, South Africa and Brazil.

14.6 A KNOWLEDGE-BASED OR LEARNING-BASED ECONOMY?

While the most radical new element in the Lisbon Strategy was its emphasis on knowledge as the most fundamental source of competitiveness and growth, the vision remained incomplete and we have yet to draw the full consequences it has for institution-building and policy-making. To develop this new vision further and fully work out its implications would turn the Lisbon Agenda into a more solid platform for building strategic external partnerships and for defining new global game rules.

More specifically, we need to understand the importance for economic performance of knowledge as competence, skills and know-how – forms of knowledge that are often tacit, embodied and difficult to measure. This is important when it comes both to understanding the implications of

Table 14.1   *National patterns in work organization**

	Discretionary learning	Lean production learning	Taylorist organization	Simple organization
North				
Netherlands	64.0	17.2	5.3	13.5
Denmark	60.0	21.9	6.8	11.3
Sweden	52.6	18.5	7.1	21.7
Finland	47.8	27.6	12.5	12.1
Austria	47.5	21.5	13.1	18.0
Centre				
Germany	44.3	19.6	14.3	21.9
Luxembourg	42.8	25.4	11.9	20.0
Belgium	38.9	25.1	13.9	22.1
France	38.0	33.3	11.1	17.7
West				
United Kingdom	34.8	40.6	10.9	13.7
Ireland	24.0	37.8	20.7	17.6
South				
Italy	30.0	23.6	20.9	25.4
Portugal	26.1	28.1	23.0	22.8
Spain	20.1	38.8	18.5	22.5
Greece	18.7	25.6	28.0	27.7
EU-15	39.1	28.2	13.6	19.1

Notes:
* The data originate from a survey of workers in 15 European countries about working conditions. They were gathered by the Dublin Institute for Working and Living Conditions. Discretionary learning refers to work situations where workers say that they learn a lot and that they have some freedom to organize their own work. Lean production-learning refers to work situations where workers learn but there is little discretion left for workers to organize their own activities. Taylorist organization offers little learning and very little freedom for the worker, while simple production gives more autonomy in solving simple tasks that offer few learning opportunities.

This table is based on a paper by Lorenz and Valeyre (2006). The four organizational models were constructed on the basis of factor analysis of responses to surveys addressed to employees in 15 European countries. The table shows that people working in different national systems of innovation and competence-building have very different levels of access to learning by doing. It also shows that, at lower income levels, the larger proportion of the workforce work in either simple or Taylorist organizations. The richer the country, the more workers are employed in discretionary learning contexts. But it is also important to note that countries at similar income levels (such as Germany and the UK), have quite different distributions of workers between the four forms. While the proportion of workers operating in lean production is more than 40 per cent in the UK, it is less than 20 per cent in Germany. The micro foundation of national systems of innovation differs not only because of levels of income but also because of other systemic features.

Table 14.1   (continued)

The table also helps us to see why globalization affects different economies differently, and why member countries have different external concerns. The higher the proportion of Taylorist jobs the bigger the potential for outsourcing jobs. The smaller this proportion, the more difficult it is to integrate low-skilled workers with a different cultural background into the labour market. The bigger the proportion of workers engaged in discretionary learning, the higher the capacity to innovate (Arundel et al., 2007).

Source: Lorenz and Valeyre (2006).

globalization and to developing realistic external strategies. As illustrated by the so-called European paradox, there is a risk that the currently narrow definition of knowledge leads to disappointment and confusion.

Knowledge is multidimensional and some dimensions are more easily recognized and measured than others. In the European discourse, most attention has been focused on science-based knowledge and learning through formal education; learning and skills formation through work experience has been largely neglected. This bias in the interpretation of the knowledge dimension is reflected in the public policies, that promote the 'structural reform' of labour markets with little attention to how they contribute to the learning economy.[3]

In Chapter 13, this bias is reflected in 'a knowledge triangle', in which research, education and innovation are nodes. Here it will be argued that there is a need to add a fourth node, in which workplaces are seen as 'learning sites'. The data presented in Table 14.1 indicate that differences among EU member countries in how (and how much) people learn at their place of work are dramatic – sometimes more so than differences in investment in research and education.

14.7   ECONOMIC GLOBALIZATION AND THE LEARNING ECONOMY

Globalization exposes European economies to more intensive competition and to stronger 'transformation pressure'. At the level of the single firm, more and more activities have to be reorganized, and new activities created, simply to survive. Old competences become obsolete more rapidly than before, and the capacity to build new ones becomes critical for long-term competitiveness. This is why a European strategy must focus on the design of policies, institutions, and organizational forms and skills that facilitate rapid learning. Table 14.1 indicates that the challenges will be different in the five major sub-regions of Europe (North, Continental, Anglo-Saxon, South and East).

Globalization affects different layers of the population differently. Workers with routine jobs, poor qualifications and limited access to learning and training are negatively affected. Well-educated workers receptive to career shifts with access to good learning and training opportunities have most to gain from the process. As demonstrated by the Organisation for Economic Co-operation and Development (OECD) Jobs Study, the last decades have witnessed a polarization in labour markets on the basis of skills and education (OECD, 1994). How far globalization should be allowed to shape socio-economic development and increase inequality without government intervention is therefore a major issue.

In the current era 'the Nordic model', which combines very limited industrial state ownership, certain forms of flexibility (not so much wage flexibility as functional flexibility), and lifelong learning with ambitious income redistribution policies, seems to be the most robust when it comes to promoting growth with social cohesion. In the Continental models and the Southern models, industrial transformation is hampered by certain rigidities, while with the Anglo-Saxon (and the Eastern) models industrial transformation tends to result in further polarization. The current strength of the Nordic model arises from social cohesion, and acceptance of and broad participation in processes of change and learning at both the societal and the workplace level.

Another dimension of globalization is the flow of people across regions and national borders. Future living standards and conditions in most regions outside Europe will be less attractive than those within Europe. In some regions (not least Africa) global warming, Aids and military conflict among other problems will make people desperate to enter Europe. With its ageing population, Europe may make efforts to recruit only the intellectual elite from poor countries. But it will be difficult (and morally unacceptable) to keep all those with low qualifications out. Again, it is workers in Southern and Eastern Europe and workers with routine jobs, poor qualifications and limited access to learning and training that will be most negatively affected by the immigration of low-skilled labour.

To build a capacity to upgrade the skills of low-skilled workers in Europe, to integrate citizens with different cultural backgrounds and different levels of qualifications, and to avoid a populist backlash against immigration are major challenges for Europe. This is where the Nordic model, so far, has been the least successful. The dimension of the challenge has been underestimated and, as a result, efforts have been too modest.

14.8 ON THE DIFFERENTIATED EXPOSURE OF WORKERS, COUNTRIES AND SECTORS

Different sectors and European countries at different levels of economic development experience intensified global competition and increased immigration differently.

Workplaces producing traditional industrial commodities for low-price segments of the market are especially exposed, and production may easily be outsourced to other parts of the world. Such workplaces are often characterized by a Taylorist type of work organization. But sectors offering many jobs of this kind may also be seen as entrance points for immigrant workers.

The least vulnerable sectors are parts of knowledge and learning-intensive clusters where manufacturing and service firms are interconnected to knowledge institutions and use skilled labour. In these clusters, a big proportion of employees work according to principles of 'discretionary learning'. Work is based upon advanced technical and social skills, and decisions are delegated to workers. To allow immigrants access to such jobs is highly demanding in terms of the upgrading of their social and cultural as well as technical skills.

Table 14.1 characterizes work organization based upon the empirical material and analysis from Lorenz and Valeyre (2006). The proportion of Taylorist jobs gives a good indication of how exposed a national economy is to the risk of job losses from outsourcing. The smaller this proportion, the more difficult and demanding it is to absorb low-skilled workers with a different cultural background.

In the long term, another indicator of exposure is the proportion of the workforce engaged in primary agriculture. Those working in agriculture have so far been protected from the full impact of globalization by the Common Agriculture Policy (CAP). An obvious option would be to transfer gradually resources from the CAP to support a catch-up strategy for regions depending strongly on the protection of agricultural products.

14.9 EUROPEAN INTEGRATION AND COHESION IN THE GLOBALIZING LEARNING ECONOMY

The reduction of income inequality between regions has been recognized as a legitimate EU objective. The regional funds have played an important role in raising the income level in Member States of Southern Europe. But at the level of regions, development remains uneven, reflecting that it is knowledge and learning-based.

When combined with intensified global competition, raising the income level, including the minimum wage, will contribute to a strong transformation pressure and to the need for rapid and deep industrial restructuring. Without major efforts in promoting learning and training opportunities, the outcome would be high rates of structural unemployment. So it is essential for the cohesion strategy to focus on learning capacity and on upgrading skills and work. Keynesian infrastructural investments aiming at creating low-skilled jobs are insufficient. Without such efforts, low-skilled workers in routine jobs would carry a major part of the negative consequences of globalization and European integration combined.

Investment in research and development (R&D), education and formal knowledge infrastructure is necessary but also insufficient. Without complementary changes in how management, labour market policy and education are practised, the transformation will be difficult. Broader participation by workers and students is a prerequisite to absorb radical change without major disruptive effects. Managers who establish workplaces as learning sites are more innovative than those who only invest in R&D (Jensen et al., 2007). Labour markets need to support the upgrading of skills. Education needs to teach students to learn. Currently, there is too much emphasis on formal qualifications and Programme for International Student Assessment (PISA) tests.

14.10   KNOWLEDGE PROTECTION AND KNOWLEDGE SHARING

In the context of a global knowledge and learning economy, access to different kinds of knowledge becomes a key issue. In a simpler world, it might be argued, all knowledge emanating from basic research should be public and shared while outcomes of 'strategic research' might be protected. At the level of the firm, core capabilities need to be protected while there might be an interest in supporting knowledge-sharing that relates to complementary capabilities.[4]

A basic principle for publicly financed knowledge production may be that all knowledge should be shared if there are no obvious counter-arguments. This seems to be the principle behind the Seventh Framework Programme. For private firms the situation is different. Firms operating on the basis of branding or specific technical knowledge in challenger countries with weak implementation of intellectual property rights will need to define carefully what knowledge may be shared and what needs to be protected formally, or through secrecy. But attempts to make such distinctions may be seen as fundamental for successful knowledge management, and they may pave the way for more generous knowledge-sharing than is possible at present.

When it comes to the protection of intellectual property rights and other regulations imposed through international agreements it is wise to have realistic ambitions and to put stronger emphasis on the implementation of rules. Overly ambitious rules that are weakly implemented generate constant friction and undermine the credibility of international rules. Goals may become more ambitious as mutual acceptance and understanding evolves and as the necessary institutional framework and competence base is built in emerging economies. Bilateral discussions between Europe and emerging economies may be useful to establish realistic goals.

Knowledge-sharing may take different forms, and people-embodied knowledge is as important as disembodied knowledge protected by property rights. The movement of people is especially important for the diffusion and distribution of knowledge. Students, scholars, policy-makers and business managers who operate in different regions of the world bring with them both theoretical and practical knowledge. But there is also a downside to the free and unregulated flow of competent people (and to what the Commission refers to as 'the fourth freedom'). Since strong, dynamic knowledge centres tend to attract people and stagnating regions tend to repel skilled workers, the spontaneous outcome is a growing knowledge divide both within Europe and globally.

Although the protection of (disembodied) intellectual property has been regulated through the World Trade Organization (WTO), there are no rules for protecting national investments in human competence (embodied) through international compensation mechanisms for the 'brain drain'. While the first set of rules tends to protect the interests of big multinational firms from rich countries, regulating the brain drain might help some of the poorest countries of the world by giving them resources and incentives to invest in human capital. When Europe builds strategic partnerships with major challenger countries, one aim should be the establishment of multilateral fair principles for the protection and sharing of knowledge.

14.11 HARMONIOUS DEVELOPMENT AND ENDOGENOUS INNOVATION IN CHINA

As discussed in Chapter 15 in this volume, the growth process in China is not sustainable in the long term. There is a need to change various dimensions of the growth trajectory. There are serious negative ecological consequences, and the use of energy is inefficient. Social problems related to health and old age as well as social and regional inequalities are growing. That the Chinese leadership has become aware of the need to shift direction is reflected in the current Five Year Plan, which refers to 'harmonious development' requiring change in the social and environmental dimensions.

The other major element in the next Five Year Plan (and the 15 Year Plan for science and technology as well) is the emphasis on endogenous innovation. The focus on innovation is very strong, and much of the literature on innovation systems is now being translated into Chinese. The idea of promoting independent innovation is to move away from strategies of imitation. The understanding in China is that the strategies followed by Japan and Korea are much less valid for China in the current era, and that it is fundamental for China to develop the capability to introduce 'home-spun innovations' (Gu and Lundvall, 2006).

Europe has broad experience with combining economic growth with environmentally sound, energy-saving technologies. Europe has also developed solid welfare states and institutions. A major market for such solutions is now opening up in China. But it is important to understand that the 'harmonious' intentions expressed in the Five Year Plans may not be easy to implement within the current system for public–private governance. The decentralization of power and the incentive system makes it difficult to enforce a new strategy. Therefore, it might be at least as important to support institutional as technological learning.

It is interesting to note that a major weakness of the plans for promoting innovation is a one-sided emphasis on science-driven technology, and that neither the demand side nor workplace learning is taken on board fully. This will reduce the impact on the economy and may lead to disappointments. To reform the education system and the management style in Chinese firms so that they become more creative and flexible may be more important than simply increasing R&D intensity in the economy.

There are good reasons to support such changes in China. One important reason is that it would generate pressure to make both schools and workplaces more open and democratic. So this could be seen as a gradual step towards a more democratic China. To link 'independent innovation' to 'harmonious development' echoes the most important concern with the further development of the Lisbon Agenda, and it could figure prominently when building strategic relationships with China.

14.12   SUMMING UP

The most radical new element in the Lisbon Strategy was the emphasis on knowledge as a source of economic growth. This perspective contributes to making the strategy a suitable platform for building strategic partnerships with major economies such as China and India. But the transformation of policy and institution-building in Europe is incomplete because of a too narrow focus on how knowledge is created, diffused and used. In order to cope with the uneven impact of globalization and thus to develop an adequate agenda for strategic partnership, it is crucial to take into account international differences in how Europe's economies learn (Lorenz and Lundvall, 2006).

It is important to make a distinction between coping with challenges arising from growth economies such as China and India, and challenges emerging from countries and macro-regions suffering from economic and cultural stagnation. In the first case, the Lisbon Agenda may be used to develop strategic partnership agreements aiming at a broad interaction, involving institutional as well as technological learning. In the second case, the Lisbon Agenda may be used to develop support programmes to build competence, and promote job creation and modernization.

In the case of China, the current willingness to promote simultaneously harmonious development and independent innovation should be seen as an opportunity to reinforce the link between innovation and sustainability as part of the renewal of the Lisbon Agenda. Another common challenge for China and Europe is to develop a growth strategy that pays more attention to the workplace as a learning site.

NOTES

1. The US has always been very aware of the diffusion of institutions and ideas to the rest of the world. In the 1930s, the Ford Foundation invited some of the most promising economists in China to study economics at the University of Chicago, and today US-trained Chinese economists are strong proponents of economic policies and institutional reforms close to US standards.
2. It is less clear whether bringing the 'social dimension' (and the regional and social 'learning divide') more strongly into play contributes to 'bridging'. As argued below, it is impossible to establish a sustainable internal and external strategy without taking into account the uneven distribution of the costs and benefits of transformation in the globalizing learning economy. But it is also obvious that the distributional issues are divisive both within the EU and between the EU and the rest of the world. It is not in the EU's long-term interest to neglect the issue or to refer only in a non-committal way to economic growth with 'social cohesion'. Jacques Delors was right to insist on the social dimension of the EU. Today, this social dimension needs to be external as well as internal. We need to transform Economic and Monetary Union (EMU) into EMSU, in which 'S' stands for 'Social'.
3. One reason for the incomplete and reluctant absorption of the new vision is the ideological power of standard economics. The Lisbon Agenda states that knowledge is the most crucial asset in the current economy. But standard economics, as practiced at US and European universities, is not equipped to understand and manage a knowledge-based economy. The assumption of the 'representative agent' in economic models is highly

problematic, leading to neglect of 'learning as competence-building' – the most funda-mental process in the knowledge-based economy. In order to strengthen the analytical base for the Lisbon Agenda there is an obvious need to establish a European institutional framework for a more relevant approach to the economy.

4. In real life, the borders between these categories are becoming increasingly blurred. In the area of biotechnology, it is difficult to distinguish basic research from commercial devel-opment. What are complementary capabilities of secondary importance today may become strategically important for firms tomorrow.

REFERENCES

Gu, S. and B.A. Lundvall (2006), 'China's Innovation System and the Move Toward Harmonious Growth and Endogenous Innovation', *Innovation: Management, Policy and Practice*, **8** (1–2): 1–26.

Jensen, M.B., B. Johnson, E. Lorenz and B.-Å. Lundvall (2007), 'Forms of Knowledge and Modes of Innovation', *Research Policy*, **36** (5) June: 680–93.

Lorenz, E. and B.-Å. Lundvall (eds) (2006), *How Europe's Economies Learn*, Oxford: Oxford University Press.

Lorenz, E. and A. Valeyre (2006), 'Organizational Forms and Innovation Performance: A Comparison of the EU-15', in E. Lorenz and B.-Å. Lundvall (eds), *How Europe's Economies Learn*, Oxford: Oxford University Press, pp. 140–60.

Lundvall, B.-Å. (2003), 'Why the New Economy is a Learning Economy', *Economia e Politica Industriale*, Rassegna trimestrale diretta da Sergio Vaccà, **117**: 173–85.

OECD (1994), *The OECD Jobs Study: Facts, Analysis, Strategies*, Paris: OECD.

Ostry, S. and R.R. Nelson (1995), *Techno-Nationalism and Techno-Globalism: Conflict and Cooperation*, Washington, DC: Brookings Institution Press.

15. Between China and the USA: which future and strategies for EU-based enterprises?

Benjamin Coriat

Over the last 25 years, the emergence of China as a new global player has put its international trading partners in a new position. To face the challenges posed by the new giant, they need to draw up and implement new strategies. This is especially true for the EU and its Member States, which occupy specific positions vis-à-vis China.

This chapter outlines what can be done to face this new giant. The argument is divided into two sections: in the first I provide some basic data regarding the relative position of the US and the European Union (EU) vis-à-vis China, highlighting some specificities of the European situation; the second, which is based largely on previous work in this field, provides a brief assessment of the competitiveness of EU-based firms. This is followed by some concluding remarks.

15.1 THE US AND THE EU VERSUS CHINA: SOME BASIC DATA

Chinese Macroeconomic Performance

Let us recall three aspects of recent Chinese economic growth. First, we must recognize, in light of the impressive performance of the Chinese economy – an average 9.5 per cent rate of gross domestic product (GDP) growth over the last 20 years – that this is an exceptional case, even among the 'tigers' and 'dragons' of Asia. Second, this performance has been achieved through a continuous reform process, which aims to promote a transition from a fully centrally planned economy to a so-called 'socialist market-based economy'. To promote this goal, a series of major economic reforms were undertaken each decade. The 1980s saw the first reforms in agriculture, followed by the development of the township and village enterprises (TVEs), and the establishment of the special economic zones (SEZs) for foreign investors. In the 1990s the stock exchange markets were established or consolidated, and some state-owned enterprises (SOEs) were privatized. In that period the price control systems, which were a pillar of the former system, were dismantled; and in the 2000s, China acceded to the World Trade Organization (WTO) regime, and amended its Constitution significantly to guarantee private property rights, among other elements. Most of these reforms were conducted in a very empirical way, through a process of trial and error. For this reason, most of them are somewhat 'incomplete' and/or partial. None can be regarded as completely implemented and enforced, and reforms are still an ongoing process. New regulations are continuously introduced, and they continuously influence the behaviour and performance of domestic and non-domestic (that is, foreign) actors.[1]

Nevertheless, a consequence of the changes introduced over the last decades is a growing and impressive opening-up to the world economy. Over the last 25 years, China has benefited from massive foreign direct investment (FDI) by foreign companies, be they Chinese, Japanese or Western firms. A key result is an increasingly high level of openness to the world economy, with external trade relations reaching 40 per cent of GDP (details in Figure 15.1).

Chinese Exports and International Trade

A first distinctive trait of Chinese foreign trade is the prominent role played by foreign-based companies: half of total exports come from foreign multi-nationals (FMNs) located in China, and it is easy to make clear correlations between FDI and export growth (see Figure 15.1 which is explicit on this point). Another major trait of Chinese international trade is that Chinese exports are concentrated in low-tech, low added value sectors and products. According to a recent detailed study by CEPII:

> Analysis of international trade by product range reveals that China is strongly specialized in the export of products at the lowest price segments. In 2004, 72 percent of its exports were of this kind, only 17 percent in the medium segments, and 12 percent in the high ones. In the exports of the Asian 'tigers', the corresponding proportions are 36 percent, 21 percent and 28 percent; in those of India: they are 49 percent, 28 percent and 23 percent. The structure of Chinese exports seems deformed downward, even for high-technology products exported mainly by subsidiaries of foreign firms. So at the beginning of the 2000s, three quarters of Chinese exports in the high-technology electronic product segment are in the lowest range, and only 8 percent in the high range, proportions which have not varied since the middle of the 1990s. By contrast, the exports of the Asian tigers in high-tech electronic products contain a stronger proportion of

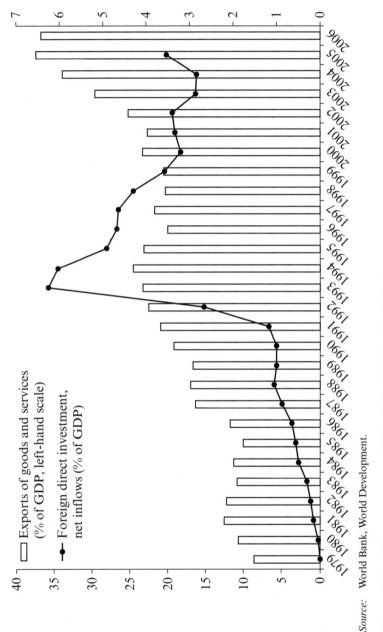

Source: World Bank, World Development.

Figure 15.1 China: exports and FDI, 1979–2006 (in % of GDP)

products with high unit added-value (42 percent), than of products with weak unit added-value (34 percent). (CEPII, 2006; Gaulier et al., 2006).

However, in many subsegments, Chinese firms have learnt how to climb up the learning curve and are now able to deliver to FMNs or to export by themselves a series of products (or sub-products) of medium and even high added value. It is likely that this upgrading of Chinese-based firms will continue and even accelerate in the coming years. A key strategic orientation of the Eleventh Five Year Plan (launched in 2005) is defined as aiming to 'further propel the fundamental of foreign capital utilization from "being quantity-oriented" to "being quality-oriented"'. The same document states that China will 'strive for the further expansion of foreign investments from simple assembly and production and production at a low level, to research, development, high-end design, modern circulation and other areas'.[2] Although such changes are not easy to achieve and time is needed for the benefits of such strategies to emerge, these new orientations in Chinese economic and industrial policy have to be taken seriously. They mark a shift in the vision of the Chinese authorities, which has already been enforced with some regulations passed in recent years. Further, encouraged by the authorities to 'go global', some national Chinese firms are now operating in the global mergers and acquisitions (M&A) market. As a consequence of the process of acquisition by Chinese-based firms of Western ones, we are witnessing the birth of the first global products with Chinese brand names (examples include Lenovo and Haier).

A final observation: if we consider the global division of labour, China is and remains primarily an Asian commercial and economic power. In 2005, Asian countries accounted for 51 per cent of total Chinese exports and 68 per cent of total Chinese imports.The flows of trade between the Asian partners are presented in Figure 15.2.

A closer look at the pattern of trade between Asian countries and its evolution suggests the following. First, the heart of the system is organized around a solid triangle of partners, each one playing a specific role. Thus, Japan is the provider of high-tech products, machines and equipment; Hong Kong, Taiwan and Singapore (the 'Chinese world') are key investors, particularly during the first phases of the take-off of the Chinese economy (with the remaining ten members of the Association of South East Asian Nations (ASEAN-10) playing a less strategic role for the time being); and South Korea appears to be a more and more important partner for Chinese firms, playing a growing role in the division of labour between the two countries (in recent years South Korea has acted as a principal in the electronic and semiconductor industry for Chinese subcontractors. Second, India, until now rather isolated, seems to be in the process of connecting

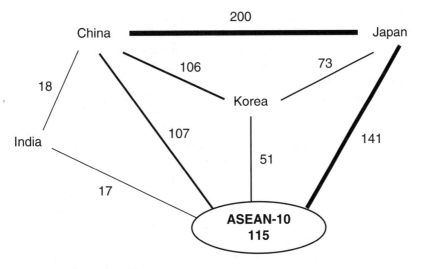

Source: Gaulier et al. (2006).

Figure 15.2 Exchange flux (exports and imports) between Asian countries in billions of dollars, 2005

itself to this core, with growing trade relations with China on the one hand, and with the ASEAN-10 on the other.

The EU and the US versus China: Two Very Different Patterns of Trade

If we concentrate first on the patterns of trade between China and the US, some key features should be noted.[3] The USA is the premier export partner for China (161.824 billion euros), and the fourth-ranking import partner (47.084 billion euros), accounting for 21.5 per cent and 8.4 per cent of Chinese exports and imports, respectively. The consequence of these very imbalanced terms of trade is a huge US deficit which peaked at around 120 000 million euros in 2006. Turning to EU–China patterns of trade, the picture looks different. The EU is the second-ranking Chinese partner both for imports and exports (respectively 71.716 and 144.791 million euros), which means that EU firms are exporting to China a much higher level of products than the US. As a consequence of this, and also because the volume of Chinese exports to the US is superior to the volume of exports to the EU, the EU deficit with China (even if rapidly growing) remains at a much lower level than that of the US (around 70 million euros).[4]

In practice, China occupies a very different position for the two players. EU-based firms are exporting mainly final and finished goods,[5] so that

China is seen by EU firms as above all a marketplace (a place to sell finished goods). By contrast, for large US corporations, China is a place for massive investment, so we can assume that US firms see China primarily as a production site (a place to manufacture components at a low cost, which are then assembled at home and re-exported).

This difference between the EU and the USA is largely explained by the fact that European firms, unlike US ones, are not (or are insignificantly) involved in the so-called 'trade processing' policy implemented by the Chinese authorities. This refers to 'certain government-approved transactions where a foreign party purchases Chinese manufactured goods, or has raw materials and components processed on a consignment basis in China, in both cases with the inputs imported free of duties and VAT'. This process, which involves the import of raw materials and components that the Chinese process into finished goods and then export, is favoured by the Chinese authorities. The regulations allow the processing company to enjoy special customs duty and VAT exemptions (Nicolas, 2008).[6]

In practice, under the heading of 'processing trade' China hosts a series of large, complex and integrated networks of contractors and subcontractors under the command of principals which are mostly large foreign multinationals. Most of these networks are formed by Asian partners. The data provided in Figure 15.2 illustrate the density of the relations among these partners. As is well documented, some large American firms have managed to penetrate these networks or to establish their own dedicated ones (Brandsetter et al., 2006). The evidence suggests that very few Europeans are active in the 'trade processing' business.

Although these observations must be mitigated, they are of crucial importance. They suggest that EU-based firms have yet to take full advantage of the opportunities opened by the emergence of the Chinese giant. Clearly, something can be done regarding the division of labour between European and Chinese firms. This is something that has yet to be exploited fully. I shall come back to this point at the end of this chapter.

Summing Up

Two provisional conclusions emerge from this brief introduction. First, we must take China seriously not only because of its impressive macroeconomic performance, but also because of its changing patterns of trade. As regards its enormous relative advantages in labour-intensive products and industries, China is moving along the learning curve, with some technological catching-up in many subsegments of advanced industries. At the same time, the first Chinese-based multinationals are emerging in the world market, selling their own brand name products for the first time. All these signs should be correctly interpreted to avoid losing the opportunity for partnership and before Chinese firms become rivals and competitors for European businesses, even in the high added value segments of the global value chain.

Second, we must keep in mind the serious imbalances and disequilibria affecting the Chinese transition process. We should not underestimate either the limits or threats to China's growth. EU players must take both into account when designing their strategies. Among them, the following deserve special mention: the lack of raw materials and energy; impressive social and spatial inequalities; fragile banking and financial systems; intellectual property rights (IPR) enforcement; and doubts about the sustainability of the political regime.

15.2 WHAT FUTURE AND WHICH STRATEGIES FOR EUROPEAN INDUSTRY?

As the above suggests, although European firms already have experience in China, the low level of exchange and the lack of sophistication of the division of labour between the two economic areas mean that the future of relations between the two partners is not set in stone. Consequently, the nature of the relations between the two giants is still a matter for strategic thinking and conjecture.

Assessing the competitiveness of European firms is a good way to contribute to a reflection on what might constitute desirable and realistic economic relations between the two economic areas. This assessment[7] is based on a methodology that was designed to be compatible with the goals of the Lisbon Agenda. The two basic questions it addresses are: how European firms are confronting the rise of the 'knowledge-based' economy; and how they are adjusting to the rise of new emerging activities and technologies. One key finding is that European firms face difficult challenges in new sectors and activities, where emerging disciplines open the door to new products and services (biotech, Internet, and some sub-segments of information and communication technologies, ICT). By contrast, Europe performs relatively well in sectors in which products derive from established disciplines (chemical and aeronautics), where user–supplier interaction is important (as for machine tools), and where 'non-price' elements of competitiveness are important (as with top-of-the-range and luxury cars). In fact, the picture is different depending on the perspective adopted. We chose to look at European firms from two different but complementary points of view. From the product life cycles and role of science point of view, EU firms clearly face real difficulties in most of the new science-based sectors; by contrast, the picture is quite different if we look at performance in terms of product differentiation and product range.

Product Life Cycles and the Role of Science: Difficulties in Science-based Sectors

Whilst Europe's performance is good or relatively good for mature industries and products (see below) it faces difficulties with the most sophisticated industries, emerging industries and fields of activities (biotechnology, Internet and important information technology segments). Various factors explain this situation. First, there is lack of investment in research and development (R&D) in the new emerging fields of science and basic research. This is obvious for the life sciences when one compares European to US investment. Some recent analyses show that in the case of the UK biotech sector, the main problem was not lack of venture capitalists ready to embark on new biotech start-ups, but the lack of good scientists able to promote firms of this type. When the scientific capacities exist, they seem to be too highly dispersed throughout European universities and territories. Thus, there is no network effect to structure the division of labour and efforts conducive to the promotion of these new activities. One should remember that around 80 per cent of venture capitalist investments from the US are concentrated in California around Silicon Valley and Route 128. In Europe, by contrast, no regional advantages have yet emerged in these fields.

Second, there is the problem of the type of educational systems and labour markets that prevail in Europe, particularly in the field of highly skilled engineers and researchers. Here, the relative advantage of European systems (largely based on internal labour markets) apparently becomes a series of relative disadvantages. Insufficient mobility and flexibility in these specialized labour markets make it difficult for firms engaged in the new emerging fields to find the right skills and to gather the necessary assets to launch new products or services. This is the case in the multimedia and Internet sectors, where innovative firms often face shortages in the supply side of the labour markets. This can be seen as an institutional failure, despite the obvious qualities of many European educational systems (see Coriat et al., 2006 for more details).

Product Differentiation and Range: Three Domains of 'European Excellence'

Turning to product range and differentiation, studies conducted at sectoral level have highlighted a series of domains in which the image and quality of

European products are recognized. Three groups of activities are emerging with particular clarity:[8] first, there is the group of diversified industrial products covered by strong brand names. This includes products and sectors like top-end luxury cars (Rolls-Royce, Bentley, BMW, Mercedes, Ferrari and Saab for instance) and machine tools (German, Italian and Swiss), as well as high-end products in various traditional subsegments such as haute couture and fashion clothing more generally, and jewellery, watch-making and cosmetics.

A second domain of 'European excellence' is various subsegments of short production runs of customized products, integrated complex systems, and prototypes. These types of products emerge from projects based on high-tech (often complex) product systems, where competitiveness depends less on price than on quality. These activities depend on high levels of technology and on a skilled labour force. They include aeronautics (Ariane-Espace and Airbus, for instance), key telecommunications segments (digital exchange equipment, for example); 'turn key' delivery of different types of complex product systems (including French, German or Italian networks of high-speed trains, as well as nuclear power stations, and water service management, among others).

More recently (and perhaps more unexpectedly) Europe has demonstrated a proven ability to assert itself in some markets of mass-produced products in high R&D-intensive industries. This is the case of mobile telephony. During the last few years, Ericsson and Nokia (the latter is now the world market leader) have demonstrated a European capacity to achieve a dominant share of the world market in small high-tech products. Also, after many failures, in the semiconductor industry SGS-Microelectronics has gained a significant presence in world markets for some customized products.

Notwithstanding the variety of sectors which they incorporate, the above activities share some common denominators. One shared characteristic is the relative advantage of products and services that are vertically differentiated and which involve a number of different partners and competencies. Be it seemingly 'simple' products (luxury perfumes) or more complex ones (aeroplanes), European competitiveness results from a capacity to combine different kinds of know-how along the chain, which converge in the delivery of the final product. The latter results from complex arrangements which combine institutional dimensions, large and complex organizational networks (between firms, and linking firms to different institutions and regulatory agencies, such as high-speed train systems, or the management of utility networks). In most of these domains, coordination between complementary activities is a key condition underlying the manufacture of quality products. Thus, specific networks of agents based on a highly skilled diversified labour force and competencies seem to be a crucial dimension of Europe's distinctive capabilities.

15.3   CONCLUSIONS AND POLICY IMPLICATIONS

The argument presented here is twofold. First, European firms do not suffer from a general weakness in science-based sectors; rather, difficulties are much more focused, and the problems are new disciplines, new emerging fields of knowledge, and the capabilities of new firms to exploit this type of knowledge in industry and commercially. It is to be noted that in some respects these difficulties worsened after European (or national) authorities failed to provide adequate and timely non-market resources and institutions to ease the entry into these new fields.[9] These deficiencies are clearly the source of difficult relations with the US, but they present no danger for EU–China relations. By contrast, the strengths of EU firms in products based on quality and non-price competitiveness have always been and remain nothing less than impressive.

The other question addressed here is the extent to which the emergence of the new Asian giant may undermine (or, on the contrary, contribute to) the competitiveness of the EU economies. The answer to this question is still in the making: much will depend on how firms and actors react and deploy their strategies. But what is emerging from the data and analyses cited here is the idea that if Europe plays its cards right, there are more complementarities than contradictions between the two economies.

In support of this argument, it can be said that the relative advantages of European firms (top-of-the-range products, and products presenting elements of non-price competitiveness) are precisely those where Chinese performance is poor and needs to be strengthened. Clearly, the recent move by the Chinese authorities to shift from 'quantity' to 'quality' opens up new avenues for European players. If the European firms acting as foreign investors and/or as principals with Chinese subcontractors are able to introduce themselves in the complex 'processing trade' system described above, they could at the same time contribute to upgrading the Chinese economy, and establish solid networks of industrial partners for themselves. No doubt such networks would also be of crucial importance to reach new consumers and build new markets in the very fast-growing Asian markets. It can be argued, therefore, that the idea of a 'strategic partnership' between the two economic areas is based on some solid shared interests.

NOTES

1. To give just one example, a series of new regulations were recently introduced regarding foreign direct investment (FDI). The changes introduced also relate to the classification

of activities (which are divided into three groups: 'encouraged', 'restricted' and 'prohibited') and to the fiscal status of the different types of enterprises in these activities. Obviously, this will have an impact on the behaviour of multinational firms, particularly on their future investments in China (Nicolas, 2008).

2. The complete English version of this document is available at http://www.fdi.gov.cn/pub/FDI_EN/Laws/law_en_info.jsp?do.cid=87372.
3. The data provided in this paragraph come from the DG Trade website of the EU, placed online on 7 August 2007, available at http://ec.europa.eu/trade.
4. Even if we consider only trade in services, there is a surplus to the benefit of the EU.
5. This point is convincingly argued in Gaulier et al. (2006).
6. The same author states that there are 'two types of processing trade: i) with imported materials (PTI) and ii) with materials supplied by clients (PTS). Under the PTS system local Chinese firms provide domestic firms with intermediate materials such as spare parts' (Nicolas, 2008).
7. In what follows, I present some key findings from two Targeted Socio-Economic Research (TSER) research projects, the Dynamic Competencies and Long-Term Growth of the Firms (DYNACOM) and European Sectoral Systems of Innovation (ESSY) projects sponsored by the European Commission, which combined research at the micro and sectoral levels, and involved 16 European research teams. For more details see Dosi et al. (2002) and Malerba (2004), particularly the last chapter by Coriat et al., 'The International Performance of European Sectoral Systems of Innovation'.
8. Not to mention a fourth group on agricultural products, characterized by the franchising of brand goods associated with a specific traditional knowledge, often covered by 'labels' and *appellations contrôlées*. This includes wines and spirits, from Irish whiskeys to French and Italian wines and Portuguese port, as well as high-quality foods such as Parma ham and Nordic salmon. Overall, some 2000 European products benefit from well-known labels, which serve to protect brand image and provide a guarantee of quality for exports.
9. For more details, see Coriat et al. (2006).

REFERENCES

Brandstetter, L. and F. Foley (2006), 'Facts and Fallacies about US FDI in China', NBER Working Paper 13470, August.

CEPII (2006), 'Chine: le prix de la compétitivité', *La lettre du CEPII*, no. 254, March.

Coriat, B., F. Malerba and F. Montobbio (2004), 'The International Performance of European Sectoral Systems of Innovation', in F. Malerba (ed.), *Sectoral Systems of Innovation in Europe: Concepts, Issues and Analyses of Six Major Sectors in Europe*, Oxford: Oxford University Press, pp. 388–421.

Coriat B., P. Petit and G. Schmeder (eds) (2006), *The Hardship of Nations: Exploring the Paths of Modern Capitalism*, Cheltenham, UK, and Northampton, MA, USA: Edward Elgar.

Dosi, G., B. Coriat and K. Pavitt (2002), 'Competencies, Capabilities and Firm Performances', Working Paper, Final Report of the DYANCOM Project, under the TSER Programme, DG12.

Gaulier, G., F. Lemoine and D. Unal-Kesenci (2006), 'China's Emergence and Reorganization of Trade Flows in Asia', CEPII Working Paper 2006-5, March.

Malerba, F. (ed.) (2004), *Sectoral Systems of Innovation in Europe: Concepts, Issues and Analyses of Six Major Sectors in Europe*, Oxford: Oxford University Press.

Nicolas, F. (2008), 'China and Foreign Investors: The End of a Beautiful Friendship?', *Asie Visions*, **4**, Paris: IFRI.

16. The Lisbon Strategy as a global EU strategy

Mario Telò

16.1 EXTERNAL DIMENSION OF THE LISBON STRATEGY: IMPLICATIONS, INFLUENCE AND POWER

There is a consensus among the authors of this volume that the Lisbon Strategy should be a European Union (EU) strategy to confront a partially globalized world, rather than an inward-looking strategy. So we must examine the external implications of the Lisbon Strategy, how its implementation can promote a global role for the EU, and how it can provide a vision to address the globalized world of the twenty-first century.

There are three definitions of Europe as a global actor that are useful for our discussion of the Lisbon Strategy. One is the idea that Europe is the 'world's Scandinavia' (Therborn, 2007). This suggests that European states can be an example to others of a sophisticated balance between social cohesion and economic competitiveness while building a knowledge society (see Chapter 14). Europe can take advantage of its internal diversity to deal with globalization more effectively (Schmidt, 2006). This view is about European influence, not power. A second view has been suggested by Susan Strange who says we should pay attention to how 'structural power' is changing, because knowledge accumulation and economic and trade matter increasingly for the 'wealth of nations', while power relations between states and macro-regions, and military power matter concomitantly less. This has obvious implications for the foreign dimension of the Lisbon Strategy.[1] A third view is that of Europe as a 'civilian power'. This one encompasses the latter but conveys the added sense of the EU as a united global actor pursuing its interests and offering solutions to global problems.

In fact, the EU is no longer just a simple 'set of regimes between member states' (Moravcsik, 1998), although, unlike classical state actors, its foreign and security policies were not the first but rather the last to be shared (in contrast with the US historically), and although the decentralized EU decision-making process is very far from replicating that of a state, even a federal one. But the EU is also no longer just an intergovernmental regime, or a simple regional entity, but rather an evolving actor, exercising external influence and power (as the association between 'low' and 'high' politics clearly shows. (See Keohane 1991; [1984] 2004.) The EU is an incipient civilian power to the extent that it can change the preferences of its Member States and the environment of other actors and their behaviour through peaceful means. It not only limits internal fragmentation and competition by increasing coordination and cooperation among Member States, but it also acts as a 'cooperative power' beyond its borders.

In sum, when we address the external dimension of the Lisbon Strategy, we must talk not only about its implications and influence, but also about a *sui generis* type of cooperative power that aims to limit conflicts through a multilevel institutionalization of international cooperation.

16.2 REGIONAL STRATEGIES AND MULTILEVEL GLOBAL GOVERNANCE

From the outset, the Lisbon Strategy fostered deep regional cooperation and integration, as confirmed by the idea of establishing a 'European model of a knowledge society' through common policies and new governance methods. But because of the climate in the 1990s, the Council and Commission were too optimistic about growth (hence the 3 per cent EU growth target, which was deemed easy to achieve at the time; hence, too, the idea of a harmonious relationship between EU regional development and globalization). Later, awareness that Europe was lagging behind the US set the stage for strategic regionalism, and led to calls for regulation, and for an assertion of the interests and competitiveness of Europe in the global economy. But the Commission remained focused on international liberalization (the Lamy-Bagwathi 1999–2006 trade agenda of global trade deregulation within the World Trade Organization, WTO), operating on the liberal assumption that globalization would benefit everybody.

The tension between supporters of a truly regional strategy (broadening and deepening the Lisbon Agenda) and the large and strong contingent of 'hyper-globalists' partly explains the controversies at each Spring European Council after 2000. The latter see the Lisbon Strategy as nothing more than 'negative integration' (Scharpf, 1997), a step towards global liberalization; the former, by contrast, see a European knowledge society as combining negative and positive integration and openness to global competition with a regionalist strategy. The hyper-globalist position sees global convergence merely as the global dissemination of the American 'new economy', while the 'regionalists' have a pluralistic understanding of the global economy (regional diversities matter). This cleavage has had clear consequences for international cooperation and relations with other regional entities (such as the Southern Common Market, Mercosur, and the Association of South East Asian Nations, ASEAN), and countries (including China, Brazil and South Africa), since the assertion that the US knowledge economy model is the only guiding model makes the EU an irrelevant partner.

If this ambiguity was a threat before 2006, thereafter it threatens to destroy any external appeal that the Lisbon Strategy may have. This is because of the implications of what has been called 'globalization malaise'. This malaise deepened because of the failure of the WTO Doha Round in the summer of 2006, the US mid-term elections of 2006, and the June 2007 end to the 'fast-track provision' allowing the US President to approve international trade agreements expeditiously. Its consequences for the EU and internationally will have a significant impact on the Lisbon Strategy.

The pre-existing balance between regionalism and globalization is definitely over, and a new one is necessary. In contrast with the past, the EU must call for a more regulated global governance with a clear awareness that globalization cannot be a win–win game if only the 'invisible hand' is at work; multilevel regulation and institutionalized cooperation are necessary. Since cosmopolitanism is not something we can aspire to in the near future, the best way to combat nationalism and fragmentation, and to counteract the 'competitor state' model, is to strengthen regionalism, inter-regionalism and, on this basis, global regulation. The question is what regional strategy is best suited to address an increasingly conflictive process of globalization. However, internal EU and global challenges are similar (sustainable development, protection of human rights, combating the proliferation of weapons of mass destruction – WMD), poverty, climate change and defensive protectionism), which justifies shared support for global regulation. Thus, as argued in Chapter 13 in this volume, the EU could play a vanguard role in strengthening coordination between the WTO, the International Labour Organization (ILO) and other global multilateral organizations like the Organisation for Economic Co-operation and Development (OECD) (and the Development Assistance Committee, DAC, the relevance of which I would like to stress), and possibly creating new ones, such as a global environmental agency. The EU can also contribute to improve the efficiency gap by using the open method of coordination (OMC) for global regulation. Only if regional associations play a more visible role in the UN system and other global organizations can they increase their legitimacy and efficiency.

What kind of regionalism and cooperation between neighbouring states do we need? As far as European regionalism and its relationship to globalization are concerned, there are three possibilities. The first possibility is protectionism, prompted by fears of globalization. But while globalization is less popular now than it was in the 1990s, and although some Europeans do not feel that they are protected enough from its negative effects, national or European protectionism is not a viable option. Post-referendum France, Italy and some other states have witnessed the rise of populist, anti-globalization movements and of a defensive understanding of social Europe; but other Member States, particularly Germany, would never accept such an inward-looking path, and not just because of its tremendous success as an exporting country. The divide between France and Germany could become deeper and broader. The view that regionalism is a protectionist shield against globalization is not new (see Gilpin, 2001). If some nations prove unable to adjust, the EU could react by strengthening its supranational regulating framework and combining negative and positive European integration more effectively. Ultimately, if protectionism wins the day, developing countries will be the first victims.

A second scenario is that the hyper-globalist position prevails. This would be suicidal for Europe, particularly as the US has shifted towards bilateralism and sidelined global multilateralism. It is not only the WTO with its failed Doha Round that is faltering; the Free Trade Area of the Americas (FTAA) and Asia-Pacific Economic Cooperation (APEC) are also on the rocks. There is a good reason for Europe to break with the hyper-global view (Gamble, 2007). Between 2001 and 2006, there were several examples of a linkage between the international civilian trade and security agendas. Thus, while a central tenet of the hyper-global view is that global economic convergence makes political cleavages marginal, in fact the EU was affected negatively by the US refusal to take on board some political international implications of the Lisbon Agenda (the open EU–US conflict about Chinese participation in the Galileo trust is an example). If the EU ignores the international political dimensions of the Lisbon Agenda, it will play the role of Voltaire's Candide rather than that of a new global cooperative power. The eventual return to office of the Democratic Party in the US in 2008 would certainly improve EU–US cooperation, but it would not fundamentally alter divergent transatlantic geopolitical interests and the *longue durée* 'division' of the West (Habermas, 2005).

A third scenario is the development of strategic regionalism, a middle way between hyper-globalism and defensive inward-looking regionalism. However, we need to answer the question of whether it is only the Lamy-Bagwathi vision that is failing, or whether the classic alternative view held by L. Summers (which has been revived by the 'new EU commercial policy' of Peter Mandelson that underpins ongoing bi-regional or bilateral trade negotiations with East-South Asia and Latin America), is a step towards the previous vision of the primacy of global convergence (with the Doha Round remaining a top priority). This view might suffer from the same illusions affecting the old 'open regionalism' that Bergsten referred to in the early 1990s, and that optimistic scenario could be challenged by an increasingly conflictive process of globalization. In other words, relaunching the Doha Round and globalization could take a while. We should be aware that both versions of strategic regionalism are possible. The weakness of the first alternative explains the transatlantic activism of Angela Merkel and the rhetoric of the 2007 EU–US Summit.

16.3   STRATEGIC REGIONALISM AND THE LISBON STRATEGY

Strategic regionalism seems to be the best way forward if the EU wants to evolve as a regional and global actor, as a distinctive knowledge society, and do more than just influence the behaviour of other players. Strategic regionalism is the best way to ensure the successful implementation of the Lisbon Strategy, and to engage in a productive dialogue and cooperation with external partners. But a new model of multilevel governance, which combines several levels and variants of multilateral and bilateral partnerships, will be necessary.[2] First, it will be necessary to support and disseminate regional cooperation to other continents. Most researchers agree that it is not just established regional entities that are structural and multidimensional features of the globalized world; rather, in 'the twenty-first century we will have more regionalism than in the twentieth century'.[3] Second, whether we like it or not, regionalism is spreading and deepening (encompassing trade, currency, policy cooperation, the political dimension, social cohesion and identity needs). Every macro-region is developing its own path to a regional knowledge society, within a pluralist understanding of globalization, respecting diversity and variations. Finally, interregionalism (bloc-to-bloc relations) is an 'identity marker' of EU external relations: not only does it include trade liberalization but it also includes cooperation for development, political dialogue, and cultural cooperation. One of its distinctive aims is to foster regional cooperation elsewhere, through distinctive conditionalities. However, the 2006 interregional summits (with Latin America in Vienna, and with East Asia in Helsinki) were seen as purely media events, or rhetorical forums. That is why interregional agendas should be more comprehensive and substantial, dealing with the issues included in the Lisbon Strategy.

It is necessary to support the evolution of individual strategic partnerships (including between the EU and several single big partners, such as

China, Russia, India, Canada, Japan and the US). Some of these countries (along with Brazil) are moving towards a strategic thinking that is comparable to the 'strategic regionalism' outlined here, albeit a state-centred version of it. With 'Brazil 3 Times', 'Japan Innovation 25', and the Indian Knowledge Commission, new agendas are being set that share many similarities with the EU Lisbon Agenda. This is already making dialogue and cooperation possible, not only to address common global challenges but also to activate areas of exchange and cooperation, including: comparing long-term and comprehensive reform agendas, including intermediary steps and monitoring; dealing with the knowledge society, growth, sustainable development, welfare reform, education, energy and other policies; and finally, major world entities may prove capable of providing an input to global governance in a challenging context, in which the US is often the third corner of an ideal triangle.

Bilateral dialogue must be enhanced with each of the members of the informal network of BRIC countries (Brazil, Russia, India and China) and IBSA countries (India, Brazil, South Africa). However, this bilateral dialogue should be improved, deepened and broadened. Thus, for instance, the EU has an interest in situating bilateral cooperation and partnership within a multilateral framework at the interregional level.

Latin America

The Lisbon Agenda must be included in the Rio process or the inter-regional dialogue between EU and Latin America started in 1999. Of course, despite the disappointments of the 2006 Vienna meeting, this framework must be organized into several narrower partnerships: between the EU and the Andean Community of Nations; the EU and Mercosur; the EU and the Caribbean countries, and so on. The challenge is that bilateralism seems more effective and easier to manage in the short term (the success of the EU–Chile and EU–Mexico agreements compared with the difficulties of the EU–Mercosur agreement, and the EU temptation to forge an EU–Brazil free trade agreement are examples), but it is essential that a new EU–Brazil strategic partnership is part of an EU–Mercosur agreement.

East Asia

It is urgent to react to US activism in East Asia (the free trade agreements with South Korea and with Singapore of 2006 and 2007 are examples of this) by supporting ASEAN and fledgling Chinese regional multilateralism. This means institutionalizing the six parties talks on the Korean peninsula, strengthening the Asia–Europe Meeting (ASEM) and cooperation with

ASEAN, which is already linked to China by a free trade agreement (scheduled for 2010), and the Shanghai Cooperation Organization, which includes the Central Asian countries and neighbouring Russia. The EU–Japanese partnership is suffering because of conflicts within the WTO, among other issues. Work needs to be done to engage in a comprehensive dialogue with Japan (including on the Lisbon Agenda), along with support for Japan as an active factor in East Asian regional cooperation (combating poverty and monetary coordination, specifically).

In sum, the EU must not neglect bilateral partnership with emerging giants, while providing consistent institutional resources for comprehensive interregional cooperation agendas in the Asian-Pacific region, Latin America and elsewhere.

India

The strategic partnership between the EU and India established in 2004 was the result of a long process,[4] which now has a multidimensional framework for enhanced cooperation. The September 2005 Action Plan laid out concrete measures, and both it and the strategic partnership have already been partially implemented, according to the Helsinki Summit of October 2006. It includes four chapters as follows. As regards political cooperation, the goal is to enhance cooperation within the UN framework and permit a dialogue on pluralism, social diversity, human rights, effective multilateralism, and strengthening the UN. There is also cooperation to train forces for peace-keeping missions and post-conflict reconstruction tasks. Combating terrorism, disarmament and non-proliferation are dealt with through a global and regional security dialogue. The EU was also an observer at the South Asian Association for Regional Cooperation (SAARC) Summit at New Delhi in April 2007, and India is a new member of the Asia–Europe Meeting (ASEM).

As regards trade relations, the bilateral partnership is becoming central, aiming to promote trade and investment. The question here is whether a bilateral free trade area can overcome past mistrust and the current limits of bilateral trade cooperation.[5] For the EU, free trade and capital investment negotiations should be accompanied by a dialogue on human rights, labour rules[6] and environmental standards. As regards economic cooperation, the EU will play an economic reform advisory role; there will be stronger cooperation on space research, and direct Indian participation in the Galileo satellite recognition project. There are already new joint working groups on science and technology, notably: biotechnologies, genomics, nanotechnologies, transport, energy policy (including alternative energies and issues pertaining to energy security), food, climate change, sustainable development and agricultural policy. Finally, as regards cultural cooperation, which is based on the EU–India Cultural Declaration of 2004, there is an interparliamentary and civil society dialogue. Within this framework, Indian migration flows may be an extraordinary opportunity for EU countries, making cultural dialogue a broader issue (this was recommended by the mixed high-level group established by the 2000 EU–India summit, which also called for an expedited visa policy). Another issue is student exchange programmes in the framework of Erasmus Mundus. Finally there is the issue of networking between EU and Indian universities; one way to do this would be to open the sixth and seventh EU Commission research framework programmes and adapt existing bilateral relations to the new European Research Area Net (ERA-Net) initiative.

Overall, the various bilateral strategic partnerships and action plans can constitute frameworks and road maps to foster broader and more inclusive interregional cooperation. They may lead to dramatic changes in EU external relations, although scepticism is justified by previous disappointments. Yearly summits should monitor progress with the implementation of action plans, while civil society involvement should complement high-level agreements and prevent failures. Much will depend on the coherence and consistency of EU external relations.

16.4   THE LISBON STRATEGY AND THE NEIGHBOURHOOD STRATEGIES: THE MEDITERRANEAN

The new Neighbourhood Policy, which features in the 2004 Treaty (Article 56), addresses states that border the EU (in Eastern Europe and the Mediterranean) that are not candidates for full membership. According to Treaty provisions, the policy paves the way for cooperation through specific agreements. These are based on the values of the Union, contain reciprocal rights and obligations, and make joint activities possible. Although the Ukraine, Belarus, the Caucasus and Moldova are beneficiaries of this policy, I focus here on the Europe–Mediterranean partnership.

The failure of the Barcelona process (1996–2006) could provoke a shift away from multilateralism towards bilateral conditionality within the framework of the neighbourhood policy. The Lisbon Strategy is not a part of that process (although it is notable that the Lisbon Agenda view that there is a link between socio-economic reform and stability can be seen as the cause of that failure). The consequences of failure are an increasing North–South divide and deepening social and territorial divisions within the Maghreb countries (only some cities of the southern rim of the

Mediterranean – from Agadir to Istanbul – actually benefit in any way from globalization). Disappointment and fear encourage mass migration flows to Europe, and the spread of populist radicalism and Islamic extremism. In this context, the EU cannot be a mere spectator. It must show that Europe can provide an alternative to the failed 'globalization for all' liberal view focusing only on foreign trade. This alternative model of globalization is based on a pluralistic understanding of the Lisbon Strategy, including eight issues that can underpin the EU model of democratization: sustainable growth and co-development; social cohesion and combating poverty; research and education; a spirit of enterprise; tourism; agriculture; infra-structure; and health. There should be an ambitious global, multilateral Euro-Mediterranean framework to renew the partnership agreements and put aside bilateral temptations. The inclusion of the French President Sarkozy's initiative in the new stage of the Barcelona process clearly shows the strength of the multilateral EU institutional framework.

16.5   A NEW DEVELOPMENT AGENDA AND EU COOPERATION POLICY

There should be a strategic framework for development to guard against further marginalization of Africa and the African, Caribbean and Pacific (ACP) countries in the post-Doha context. The idea of focusing on priori-ties complementing other sources, as proposed by Rodrigues in Chapter 13 of this volume, is correct. The agenda is very precise, including employ-ment, education, social cohesion, capacity-building and macroeconomic policy. As regards the crucial issue of governance, African regional org-anizations (the South African Development Community, SADC; the Economic Community of West African States, ECOWAS; and the Common Market for Eastern and Southern Africa, COMESA) could strengthen the social dimension of regional integration and help implement region-wide action plans, provide technical assistance, and monitor their impact supported by the EU.

In sum, it would be foolish to counter a US-centred global knowledge society with an EU-centred one. The comparative advantage of the EU is precisely its internal pluralism and concomitantly pluralist vision of global convergence, which respects diversity. The EU is not a universal model of a knowledge society; nor is it a counter-model. Given the existence of several paths to a knowledge society in Europe, the EU can assert itself as a pluralist regional knowledge society 'laboratory', one that is particularly well suited to manage national and subnational (regional) differences and promote increased convergence (rather than as a federal state in the making, according to one past vision). Its multilateral coordination of internal diversity may be a positive example for other regional groupings.

16.6   A 'NEW GENERATION OF EXTERNAL ACTION': THE CHALLENGE OF COHERENCE

For more than 50 years, the European Community (EC)/EU has sought to overcome or minimize the tremendous gap between its high international economic relevance and its limited international political role. In 2006, EU-25 gross domestic product (GDP) (12.000 billion euros) was comparable to that of the US, and the EU was the premier global trade power (20 per cent of global trade) and the second-ranked monetary power; however, in terms of its impact on global governance the EU remains a political dwarf. Creating a bridge between EU economic strength and its external political projection is urgent, particularly after the securitization of international agenda following 11 September 2001. The Maastricht Treaty provisions, which established a second pillar (the Common Foreign and Security Policy, CFSP), albeit 'within the common institutional framework of the EU' (TEU, Article 3), ended up aggravating problems of coherence and consistency in external relations, with external policies depending on the community pillar and political relations depending on unanimous inter-governmental agreement within the CFSP. We need a dramatic change in governance and institutional provisions (Treaty reform) to resolve this problem.

The 2006 Commission Communication on EU external relations is a step in the right direction; but it is no more than that. We need a 'new genera-tion of EU external action' to overcome two main inconsistencies. First, it is urgent to overcome the lack of coherence between the internal aspects of the Lisbon Strategy and its external implications. Second, the clear lack of horizontal coherence between the three pillars of the Treaty (namely between the second and third, and the first) and even between the various Commission directorates-general charged with external relations (we have the experience of the difficulties of balancing the trade and the Lisbon agendas, with the dominant trade agenda marginalizing the Lisbon Agenda), is a problem. Further, the lack of vertical coherence and solidar-ity between the foreign relations of states and the EU must be addressed.

The new Treaty is the best way forward; however legal provisions cannot make up for the absence of political will and know-how. There was an opportunity to move forward during the second semester of 2007, by preventing the divergences that arose in 2000 between governance reform (the Lisbon Strategy) and of the reform of institutions (the Nice

Inter-Governmental Conference, IGC), as the 2007 IGC added to the provisions proposed in the Constitutional Treaty of 2004 (legal personality, the creation of the post of EU Minister of Foreign Affairs, and a strengthened 'solidarity clause' among Member States (Article 42). It is also necessary to improve practical governance (Article 3 of the TEU charges both Commission and Council with ensuring the coherence of external relations).[7] In my view, the presidency of the Council and the EU Council can foster both horizontal and vertical coherence, at least at relevant events and international meetings. An OMC of sorts could improve the coordination of national foreign actions on shared goals.

NOTES

1. See, for instance, the external implications of the Galileo satellite system and its by-products for EU–China, EU–India and (negatively) EU–US relations.
2. Multilateral arrangements, regimes and organizations should 'trump' bilateralism. By multilateral I do not mean global or universal. Indeed, regional and interregional arrangements are multilateral to the extent that they include more than three partners, although they must involve the classical criteria of 'diffuse reciprocity' (strengthening reciprocal trust) and 'general principle of conduct' (as opposed to a 'coalition of willing', or 'ad hoc' multilateralism).
3. R. Higgott, (2007).
4. A positive step was taken at the Lisbon bilateral meeting in the spring of 2000 under the Portuguese presidency of the EU presidency, prepared by Commission experts (see the 2006 Commission Communication on India). However, there are major obstacles: the Indian and Pakistani goal to build nuclear military capacity, the coup in Pakistan, the anti-Pakistan evolution of the SAARC and, on the European side, protectionist effects of the Common Agricultural Policy (CAP) on trade.
5. There is the controversial EU–India Business Summit, and critical Indian statements, including that of Minister Kamal Nath in 2005. In 2005, EU exports of goods and services accounted for 25 billion euros (only 2 per cent of EU exports). EU foreign direct investment (FDI) in India accounted for 1 billion (1.4 per cent of total EU FDI) and focused on telecommunications, energy and transport. However, despite the modest numbers, the EU accounts for one-quarter of total FDI, higher than that of the US and Japan combined.
6. European trade unions are supporting the Stop Child Labour and the School is the Best Place to Work campaigns within this framework, which fosters a constructive dialogue with the Indian parliament (on the ratification of the relevant ILO conventions), and EU financial support.
7. The text of Article 3 states that: 'L'Union veille, en particulier, à la cohérence de l'ensemble de son action extérieure dans le cadre de ses politiques en matière de relations extérieures, de sécurité, d'économie et de développement. Le Conseil et la Commission ont la responsabilité de assurer cette cohérence et coopèrent à cet effet. Ils assurent, chacun selon ses compétences, la mise en oeuvre de ces politiques.'

REFERENCES

European Commission (2006), *The EU New Commercial Policy*, October.

Gamble, L.A. (2007), 'Regional Blocs, World Order and the New Medievalism', in M. Telò (ed.), *European Union and New Regionalism: Regional Actors and Global Governance in a Post-Hegemonic Era*, Aldershot: Ashgate, pp. 21–36.

Gilpin, R. (2001), *Global Political Economy: Understanding the International Economic Order*, Princeton, NJ: Princeton University Press.

Habermas, J. (2005), *Der gespaltene Westen*, Frankfurt: Suhrkamp.

Higgott, R. (2007), 'Alternative Models of Regional Cooperation', in M. Telò (ed.), *European Union and New Regionalism: Regional Actors and Global Governance in a Post-Hegemonic Era*, Aldershot: Ashgate, pp. 75–106.

Keohane, R.O. (1984/2004), *After Hegemony: Cooperation and Discord in the World Political Economy*, Princeton, MA: Princeton University Press.

Keohane, R.O. (2005), 'The Contingent Legitimacy of Multilateralism', paper presented at the Garnet PhD Seminar, 1 December.

Keohane, R.O., J.S. Nye and S. Hoffmann (eds) (1991), *After the Cold War: International Institutions and State Strategies in Europe, 1989–1991*, Cambridge, MA: Harvard University Press.

Moravcsik, A. (1998), *The Choice for Europe: Social Purpose and State Power from Messina to Maastricht*, Ithaca, NY: Cornell University Press.

Scharpf, F.W. (1997), *Governing the European Union*, Florence: IVE.

Schmidt, V. (2006), *Democracy in Europe: The EU and National Polities*, Oxford: Oxford University Press.

Therborn, G. (2007), 'Europe Trading Power, American Hunting Dog, or the World's Scandinavia or Watching Dog of the US?', in M. Telò (ed.), *European Union and New Regionalism: Regional Actors and Global Governance in a Post-Hegemonic Era*, Aldershot: Ashgate, pp. 277–94.

17. The Lisbon Agenda and the external action of the European Union: conclusions of the debate

Maria João Rodrigues

17.1 INTERNATIONAL CONVERGENCE AND THE EXTERNAL ACTION OF THE EUROPEAN UNION

The European Union has an ambitious economic, social and environmental agenda for sustainable development, but it cannot attain its goals in isolation. The implementation of this internal agenda needs to be supported by international convergence in the same direction, to generate a win–win game, avoid the risks of a race to the bottom, and strengthen cooperation to address shared global challenges.

These goals should be pursued by the new generation of external instruments of the European Union, when defining partnership and cooperation agreements with third countries. We need a new approach to strategic dialogue on development issues to enrich the agenda for these partnership agreements.

This concern should be integrated more systematically into the new generation of EU instruments for external action for 2007–13, which is now being redesigned within the framework of the Lisbon Treaty. First, the aim is that a broader approach should be developed for the external action of the Union, which combines the Common Foreign and Security Policy (CFSP), trade and cooperation policies with the external projection of the internal policies of the Union. This means that the external action of the EU should also integrate the external dimension of policies such as research, environment, education and employment. Second, a new generation of the EU cooperation programmes is being prepared, based on the new political orientations defined by the 'European Consensus'. Third, a new approach is being developed in trade policy in connection to the Lisbon Agenda, which aims at preparing Europe for globalization using trade combined with basic standards as a major lever for growth and more and better jobs.

17.2 THE NEED FOR A NEW KIND OF STRATEGIC DIALOGUE

A strategic dialogue on development issues should be organized between partner countries in a globalized world in order to ensure better use of all the instruments of external action. The method for this strategic dialogue will be more effective if it reverses the traditional sequence of many international dialogues, and organizes the discussion according to the following steps: first, there should be a general discussion on shared challenges we face as global partners; second, there should be a general discussion on development strategies and the implications of addressing these challenges for internal policies; third, there should be a discussion of new ways to cooperate to build capacity in order to disseminate better standards; finally, there should be a discussion about the implications of international relations and mutual opening of markets for global standards and governance.

This strategic dialogue should be developed at a high level, involving top representatives of the Council and the Commission, who should meet on a regular basis, define the agenda and discuss selected topics; and at the multi-stakeholder level, involving key civil society stakeholders, meeting in different contexts (workshops, conferences, or other fora).

There are some key goals that should underlie this dialogue: one is that the dilemma between globalization and protectionism should be overcome through effective multilateral action combined with strategic regionalism; another is that as a civilian power, Europe should use its external policies to project its internal policies; third, that access to knowledge and institutional learning should play an increasing role in the exchange with partner countries; and finally that a typical example of a win–win game can be generated by combining the mutual opening of the markets and access to knowledge, with higher environmental, social, intellectual property and political standards.

17.3 PREPARING A STRATEGIC DIALOGUE FOR SUSTAINABLE DEVELOPMENT

There are two main strands that should guide the organization of the strategic dialogue for sustainable development: first, promoting a more systematic identification of all the initiatives of international cooperation between the EU and its partner countries in the fields covered by the Lisbon Agenda (notably, science and technology; education and training; entrepreneurship and innovation; environment and energy; market integration; employment and social affairs; and regional development); second, developing a strategic dialogue for sustainable development.

We can draw the following conclusions from the European experience within the framework of the Lisbon Agenda, which can be used in a strategic dialogue with EU partner countries:

1. We need to design and implement a new comprehensive agenda for sustainable development with economic, social and environmental dimensions.
2. Synergies between these three dimensions should become more important than the trade-offs.
3. We should neither sacrifice social conditions to competitiveness nor vice versa. In order to resolve that tension, we should renew both.
4. The triangle of knowledge (research, innovation and education) plays a central role in this agenda. It is not enough to invest in research, and it is crucial to turn knowledge into added value through innovation.
5. Innovation provides a new approach to capacity-building, which gets past the protectionist approach to industrial policy. Innovation is not just about processes but also about products and services; it is not just about technology but also about organization, management, skills and culture; and it is not just for high-tech companies and high-skilled workers, but for all companies and people.
6. We need to encourage entrepreneurship, taking the initiative to mobilize new resources to address new problems, starting with schools and universities, to ensure one-stop shops and seed capital for start-ups, and support innovative companies to reach their markets.
7. Information and communication technologies (ICT) provide the basic infrastructures for a knowledge society. In order to overcome the risk of digital divide, ICT should provide better access for all citizens to schools, healthcare, leisure and public services in general.
8. Social policy can be a productive factor provided that it equips people for change, to move to new jobs by providing new skills and adequate social protection, and that it increases equal opportunities.
9. Sound basic and secondary education is a key factor to improve life chances. However, there should be learning opportunities throughout life cycles.
10. Social protection systems should be built and recalibrated to cope with demographic changes.
11. Respecting the environment is detrimental for investment and job creation; rather, it can generate new opportunities for investment and job creation.

12. Macroeconomic policies should ensure macroeconomic stability, but also a stronger focus on forward-looking investments in research, innovation, education, infrastructure and social conditions.
13. We need to reform multilevel governance to ensure that this agenda is well implemented at the local, national, regional and international levels. It is necessary to have more horizontal coordination of the relevant policies and a stronger involvement of the relevant stakeholders at all the levels.
14. Cultural openness, initiative, participation and partnership are key ingredients for the successful implementation of this agenda.

17.4 AGENDAS FOR EUROPEAN UNION EXTERNAL ACTION

This framework can be used to identify critical points in the various external action agendas to be developed by the European Union:

1. As regards the multilateral agenda, the goals are to achieve an agreement in Doha, to rebalance the international governance of Bretton Woods institutions, and to strengthen multilateral governance for the environment.
2. As regards the regional agenda (enlargement and neighbourhood), the aim is to foster convergence and catching-up.
3. Regarding the development agenda, the goals are to provide aid for trade, deepen the strategic dialogue for sustainable development, and improve policy coherence in development strategies.
4. For the transatlantic agenda, the aims are to make progress with regulatory convergence in Trade Related Aspects of Intellectual Property Rights (TRIPs), financial markets and energy.
5. More generally, as regards the agenda with strategic partners, the goals are to deepen strategic cooperation for sustainable development, encompassing climate change, the environment, energy, social inclusion, and generating a win–win game in trade.
6. Finally, as regards the agenda with the macro-regions, the above applies, along with a deepening of the dialogue on regional integration.

PART IV

The Lisbon Agenda and European
Governance

18. The Lisbon Agenda and European governance: key issues for policy-making

Maria João Rodrigues

In this chapter, I address the relationship between the Lisbon Agenda and European governance, by analysing the main features of the Lisbon process; the implications of the Lisbon Treaty; improvements in governance; and improvements in public administration. This will lead to the identification of some key issues to deepen the debate on a quite controversial but central theme.

18.1 THE MAIN FEATURES OF THE LISBON PROCESS

The development and implementation of Lisbon Agenda can be analysed as a political and social process which has involved, in a progressively organized way, the following institutions and actors: the European Council, in its several annual meetings, particularly its spring meeting; the seven formations of the Council (General Affairs, Ecofin, Competitiveness, Employment, Education, Environment, Energy and Telecommunications), and the Council committees and groups; the European Commission, involving 15 of the 27 commissioners and 17 directorates-general, with a smaller group of 'Lisbon' commissioners meeting on a more regular basis; the European Parliament, particularly six of its committees; the national parliaments, involving at least their European affairs committees, which also participate in a yearly Lisbon conference with the European Parliament; the European Economic and Social Committee and its Lisbon network of economic and social councils in the Member States where they exist; the Committee of Regions and its Lisbon platform, involving more than 100 regions; the European confederations of social partners, representing their national counterparts and meeting regularly with the other European institutions within the Tripartite Social Summit; and last, but not least, Member State governments, with the involvement of several ministries and the heads of state. A European network of Lisbon coordinators is also being developed, each of which is either a minister or a top-ranking official who reports to a minister or a head of state. In addition to these institutions, there is a vast network of civil society organizations working on various issue areas, which follow up and provide input in some way for the development of the Lisbon Agenda. Most such organizations, as well as other relevant political and media actors, are probably not aware of this European agenda, but work with or react to its national effects, which – differences between Member States notwithstanding – explains the generally low level of 'ownership' of the process. Nonetheless, there is a large network of civil society leaders across Europe who are explicitly linking up their work with the Lisbon Agenda.

Lisbon Agenda instruments are also quite diverse: there are directives, regulations, decisions, recommendations, guidelines, common objectives, community programmes and structural funds. However, the 'instrument mix' differs greatly according to the policy area in question (these are research, innovation, enterprise, the information society, the environment, energy, employment, education, social protection, and macroeconomic policies, as in Table I.1).

The integrated guidelines for growth and jobs provide the general orientation of the Lisbon Agenda, based on the so-called 'broad economic policy guidelines' and 'employment guidelines' Treaty provisions. These enable the Council and the Commission to coordinate the process, allow the Commission to issue 'country-specific recommendations', and permit the European Parliament to follow up the process (for the employment guidelines, this includes issuing a formal opinion). The integrated guidelines were defined in 2005, and build on the common objectives identified by Member States. This was done through the open method of coordination (OMC) launched with the Lisbon Strategy in 2000. The aim is to forge a new strategic consensus and promote broader involvement by the relevant actors. In operational terms, the integrated guidelines are translated into a Community Lisbon Programme, mobilizing the relevant above-mentioned European instruments, and into the national reform programmes, mobilizing the relevant national instruments. For each three-year cycle, it is possible to prioritize some actions over others, at both the EU and Member State levels.

All this adds up to what is certainly a complex edifice of institutions, actors and instruments. All these must be taken into account in an analysis of the development and the implementation of the Lisbon Agenda. Unfortunately, we also need to pose another question that further adds to that complexity, namely about the implications of the Lisbon Treaty for the Lisbon Agenda.

18.2   THE IMPLICATIONS OF THE LISBON TREATY

How can we assess the potential and the limits of the Lisbon Treaty when it comes to the implementation and the development of the Lisbon Agenda? Below I undertake a preliminary analysis of the Treaty from this perspective, focusing on EU aims and principles, EU institutions, and EU instruments and policies.

General References

The aims of the Union confirm the key elements of the Lisbon Agenda:

> The Union shall establish an internal market. It shall work for the sustainable development of Europe based on balanced economic growth and price stability, a highly competitive social market economy, aiming at full employment and social progress, and a high level of protection and improvement of the quality of the environment. It shall promote scientific and technological advance.

Nevertheless, there is no reference that highlights the central role of a knowledge economy as a response to globalization. The principles governing EU external action are also stated clearly in the Treaty, including support for democracy, the rule of law, human rights, peace, humanitarian assistance, sustainable development, the environment, and free trade.

The Charter of Fundamental Rights is supported implicitly by the goals of the Lisbon Agenda. It calls for a more ambitious development agenda to cover areas such as the right to education, placement services, social protection, health, environmental protection, and the freedom to choose an occupation, conduct a business, or to create in arts and sciences. The horizontal social clause and the protocol on services of general interest are also relevant provisions, which reveal the main EU concerns when it comes to the sustainability of its social model.

Institutions

The projected reform of EU political institutions also has implications for the Lisbon Agenda. According to the proposed reforms: the European Council is defined as a central guiding institution with a full-time and permanent president; and the Council is to extend qualified majority voting to 50 new areas, using a new double majority calculation rule after 2014–17. Further, the Council will have a new formation, a General Affairs Council, which is to be clearly distinct from the Foreign Affairs Council, and the purpose of which is to coordinate internal European policies and their interface with national policies; the presidency of the Council is to consist of a rotating team of three Member States, which can organize their tasks in various ways; the European Commission is to be chaired by a president with stronger democratic legitimacy and, after 2014, will be reorganized, with 20 posts rotated among the Member States; there will be a High Representative of the Union for foreign affairs and security policy, and a vice-president of the European Commission, who will coordinate EU foreign policy instruments; national parliaments are to be more systematically consulted on Union decisions and stronger interparliamentary cooperation is envisaged; the European Parliament will gain co-decision competences with the Council in 40 new areas. Finally, stronger interface between representative democracy and participatory democracy, building on the European Economic and Social Committee and the Committee of Regions, as well as the new tripartite summit for growth and jobs involving the social partners.

The expectation is that this system will evolve, producing a more legitimate and efficient decision-making process and stronger coordination mechanisms. Although some tensions and negative effects will remain, the expected positive effects are relevant for the Lisbon Agenda, which needs to be implemented quicker and with greater horizontal coordination. The new General Affairs Council should play a central role in this regard. Further, 'ownership' of the Lisbon process may be strengthened as the European and national parliaments as well as national and European participatory bodies are empowered.

The Instruments

The instruments of the Union are either compulsory (regulations, directives and decisions) or non-compulsory (recommendations and opinions), but the 'instrument mix' will vary greatly depending on which policy area is at stake, given the different ways that competences are assigned to the Union and Member States. For instance, the Union has exclusive competence over the customs union, competition policy, monetary policy, marine biological resources, and commercial policy, but it shares competences with the Member States in some areas regarding the internal market, economic, social and territorial cohesion, agriculture and fisheries, the environment, consumer protection, transport policy, energy policy, health and safety, and social policy, as stipulated in the Treaty. As regards research policy and development cooperation, the Union has competences to carry out activities without preventing Member States from undertaking their own. For other areas, the Union can only support, coordinate or supplement the actions of the Member States (this is the case of cultural, tourism, education, civil protection, and administrative cooperation policies). Finally, the coordination of economic and employment policies is undertaken according to common guidelines.

Lisbon Agenda policies are of all three types mentioned above and they are therefore Europeanized to different degrees. Thus, monetary, competition and commercial policies are of the first type; the internal market, the environment, research and some aspects of social policy are covered by the second type; and the third distribution of competences covers industrial and education policies, certain aspects of social policy and administrative cooperation.

In sum, as regards the strategic priorities of the Lisbon Agenda, this framework produces the following instrument mix: as regards the regulation of product and service markets and capital and labour, the predominant instruments are directives and regulations; when it comes to employment and social policies, the predominant instruments are guidelines, common objectives, common programmes and structural funds; for the environment, the predominant instruments are directives, decisions and structural funds; for knowledge policies, the predominant instruments are guidelines, programmes and structural funds; and as regards macroeconomic policies, with the exception of monetary policy, the predominant instruments are guidelines and regulations.

The scope for enforcing political reorientations varies quite significantly from one policy area to another, although progress can be made making full use of the available instruments: enforcing the implementation of the directives and regulations; identifying the need for new ones, to improve regulation of the process; monitoring the implementation of the guidelines with country-specific recommendations; improving the resources and the effectiveness of the common programmes; improving the effectiveness of the structural funds.

It is also important to mention that the external action of the Union will operate with quite different instruments: within the Common Foreign and Security Policy (CFSP), with guidelines and decisions; for commercial policy, with regulations and agreements; for development cooperation, with common programmes and guidelines; and for economic, financial and technical cooperation, with common measures.

Finally, it is also relevant to evaluate the level of Europeanization of these policies by identifying those that will be covered by the ordinary legislative procedure (which is to say, co-decision by the Council and the European Parliament on energy, education, intellectual property, industry, tourism, administrative capacity, structural funds (after 2013), cooperation, trade and social policy – except social protection, lay-offs, information and representation). By contrast, there will be unanimity for these fields, as well as for state aid, single market regulations, excessive deficits, tax policy for environment and energy, education, health and cultural services in trade policy, exchange rate, linguistic regime, own resources, common defence, and general European elections.

Relevant Changes in Specific Policies

In addition to the above, there are further, specific changes targeting policies that are relevant for the implementation of the Lisbon Agenda, namely: the introduction of co-decision for intellectual property rights and of the concept of a European research area; the inclusion of a European space policy; strengthening energy policy as it pertains to security issues, as well as environmental (the climate change dimension); co-decision and OMC instruments for research, industrial, health and social policies; the development of a European immigration policy; granting the Commission a stronger monitoring role over broad economic policy guidelines and the Stability and Growth Pact; a declaration emphasizing the need to ensure not only 'sound budgetary positions' but also to raise the 'growth potential' as the two pillars of the economic and fiscal policy of the Union; and a detailed organization of the functioning of the Eurogroup, including the external representation of the euro.

In addition to the changes to the Eurogroup, procedures to enhance cooperation in various areas have also been strengthened. It is too early to tell the extent to which they will foster the implementation of the Lisbon Agenda. Nevertheless, it is important to underline that even without these legal procedures, many initiatives with the framework of the Lisbon Agenda are closed to enhanced cooperation, such as the technology platforms and technology initiatives in research policy, or the lead markets in innovation policy.

The implementation of the Lisbon Agenda certainly requires an evolving combination of instruments to establish a level playing field with common rules; stronger instruments at European level; convergence between national priorities, although respecting national specificities; and to allow for differentiation, so that some goals are reached faster by the Member States that are willing to do so.

In spite of its limits, the Lisbon Treaty provides relevant opportunities to enrich and strengthen the toolbox of the Lisbon Agenda. Exploiting this potential will also depend on improving the governance of the political process that underpins the Lisbon Agenda.

18.3 IMPROVING GOVERNANCE IN THE LISBON AGENDA

We can identify some of the priorities to improve governance of the process. First, we need to identify clearly the European and national 'tool box' for each policy, and promote its better use in each instance (see Table I.1). Second, we can improve the implementation of existing instruments for each Council of Ministers formation and their respective committees and groups, to ensure better articulation at the European and national level (this means identifying the toolbox available for each Council formation; defining a general road map for its application; improving the support work that committees do for the Council, with permanent professional support necessary; and improving peer review methods for implementation at the national level). Third, we need to improve the implementation of the guidelines and the common objectives, taking advantage of OMC techniques (this would help to: improve the consistency between the reporting and the guidelines; define indicators and deadlines regarding the main objectives and invite the Member States to define specific ambitious, but realistic targets; develop more intelligent benchmarking, putting good practice in the right context, using progression indicators, and developing rankings on the capacity of each Member State to reach the targets set; improve the monitoring and evaluation process by focusing on the country-specific recommendations; and improve the learning process based on thematic workshops and databases on good practice).

Fourth, we need to improve articulation between the relevant Council formations, by developing the regular interfaces between its committees or trios to deal with concrete issues. Fifth, we must improve the action of and articulation between the national Lisbon Strategy coordinators (this will help to promote a more in-depth sharing of experiences between these coordinators; improve horizontal coordination at the level of national governments and the European Commission; and define clearer standardizing methods to assess national programmes and annual reports, to outline progress and responsibility for them). Sixth, we need to develop the role of the European Parliament and national parliaments in monitoring the process. Seventh, we should identify methods to improve the participation and mobilization of civil society and social partners (this would help to: improve the role of the tripartite summits and the macroeconomic dialogue; support the role of the European Economic and Social Committee and its network in the national economic and social councils; support the adaptation of the Lisbon Strategy to specific target groups; and develop various types of partnerships to implement projects). Eighth, we should improve communication instruments to promote a 'tailor-made' involvement of different types of actors in the Lisbon Strategy, including civil servants, opinion-makers, civil society partners and young people, as well as citizens in general. Ninth, we should develop methods to ensure better implementation at the territorial level and support the initiatives taken by the Committee of Regions. Finally, we must modernize public administration to ensure that the Lisbon Agenda is implemented more effectively.

18.4   IMPROVING PUBLIC ADMINISTRATION FOR THE LISBON AGENDA

Effective public administration is crucial for the implementation of the Lisbon Agenda and so deserves more in-depth analysis. The remainder of this chapter builds on recent experience, and puts forward proposals for a more systematic approach to strategic planning and management of a development agenda by public administration.

Strategic Planning and Management

Defining and implementing a development agenda means engaging in strategic planning. But is there any scope for planning today, given the complexity and speed of change in our complex societies? Is planning relevant, useful or even possible? My view is that it is relevant because change is driven not just by individual initiative and competition, but also by new forms of cooperation. Both require rules defining what the common good is, and the setting of long-term goals and priorities. The latter are useful because they can illuminate the path ahead. Indeed, the faster and more complex the 'train' we are conducting, the more useful such rules become. Strategic planning is indispensable when it comes to broad processes of change, such as the implementation of a new development agenda or stimulating processes of regional integration. And strategic planning is desirable when the goal is not to predict and define the future but rather to anticipate possible futures (there are always many) and seek to shape them through the strategic management of change.

In the 1980s and 1990s, criticism of past planning experiences dealt an apparent death blow to the concept of planning. But strategic planning was relaunched along different lines by large companies in the private sector and by the public sectors of various Asian and European countries, and more specifically by the European Union. It is also important to assess the different phases of Latin America's rich experience. This section focuses on this most recent view of and experience with strategic planning, systematically covering the seven stages of the strategic management cycle (preparation; strategic analysis; strategic prospective phase definition and development of the strategy; operational planning; implementation; and monitoring and evaluation).

Preparation

Preparation begins with a period of initial impetus which may arise as a result of various converging factors: the emergence of new challenges, changes in the composition of political power, stimulating foreign experiences, or new emerging perceptions and theoretical perspectives. The political will to define a new development agenda is a decisive factor, but it is not enough. For the process to take off properly, it is necessary to have: a core team that is familiar with state-of-the-art public policy-making; experts who can contribute new theoretical perspectives to solve the problems at hand, and can build the most relevant causal model; and coordinators who can organize systematic, creative and efficient interaction between civil servants and experts (who must be competent generalists as well as good specialists at this stage).

Strategic analysis

On the basis of existing reports (so as to avoid reinventing the wheel), strategic analysis should proceed as follows: the global context (the main economic, social, environmental and technological tendencies); the national situation (challenges and problems, strong and weak points, and threats and opportunities); the main factors structuring possible scenarios (to be selected on the basis of the causal model referred to above); testing, consolidating and deepening the causal model by constructing a matrix of cross-cutting impacts, perhaps resorting to a Delphi experts' consultation (although this is a lengthy process).

Strategic prospective phase

The strategic prospective phase should proceed as follows: the identification of possible scenarios, looking at the possible evolution of realistic and mixed structuring factors (see Table 18.1); ranking possible scenarios according to their degree of desirability, based on a definition of political values and priorities (which should be explicit), as this signals a shift from an analytical to a normative perspective; and finally, identifying a reference scenario among those deemed desirable and probable. This done, it is possible to define the development strategy to be adopted.

Defining and developing the strategy

Defining the development strategy involves: a clear enunciation of strategic objectives; the identification of broad strategic priorities, which should

Table 18.1   Structuring factors and building scenarios

Structuring factors and their possible evolution / Scenarios	Social context			Political system			National economic evolution			National social evolution		
	Hyp. A	Hyp. B	Hyp. C	Hyp. A	Hyp. B	Hyp. C	Hyp. A	Hyp. B	Hyp. C	Hyp. A	Hyp. B	Hyp. C
Scenario A	X			X			X			X		
Scenario B			X			X			X			X
Scenario C		X		X			X			X		
Scenario D		X		X			X			X		
Scenario E		X			X		X					X

Notes: Hyp. A = Hypothesis A and so on.

not be too many and should be articulated as causal factors that can help attain the sought-after strategic goal; and finally, transforming broad strategic goals into guidelines, on the basis of an 'objectives tree'.

Operational planning

To initiate the operational planning phase, it is necessary to use the guidelines to specify how the various sectoral policies should be reoriented, after which the programme of measures and the methodologies can be adopted and their translation into an agenda for development defined. To that end, it is also necessary to bring together officials familiar with the state of the art in different sectoral policies, and sectoral experts who can offer new perspectives; another fundamental step to ensure credibility is to provide the legal and financial instruments to implement the agenda, and define physical and financial indicators, and results and impact indicators; finally, it is necessary to organize services, clearly identify teams responsible for each programme and project, and create coordinating bodies that operate at the highest (government) level and can support the strategic management of the development agenda.

During this phase, and the implementation phases, it may be necessary to organize public services horizontally rather than according to a sectoral logic, mobilizing the relevant bodies independently of the ministry in charge of them. In such cases, horizontal coordination is managed by government central coordinating bodies or a coordinating ministry with a horizontal ministerial team, and a full-time programme manager. There must always be central government coordinators who systematically monitor all programmes and their articulation with the budgetary process.

Implementation

The implementation phase is obviously the key stage, and although it follows the planning phase, the latter must continue throughout the process of strategic management, and should be seen not just as a cycle but as a system of interacting stages. The first condition to ensure effective implementation is to gain the support of and mobilize society. There is another, more basic condition that is often underestimated: gaining the support of and mobilizing public servants who are charged with implementation (hence the importance of internal communication procedures and the mobilization of the teams responsible for each phase).

Whenever possible, implementation should follow pilot projects that test and refine solutions. Their extension must take local conditions into account, which means establishing context-friendly exchange mechanisms to discuss good practice (that is, workshops and reports elaborated with the help of experts, which explains the importance of monitoring and evaluation procedures). Pilot project methodologies cannot always be used: for instance, when equity criteria or issues of general access to incentives or benefits are involved, the methodology will depend above all on prior consulting procedures (discussed below).

The implementation of a development agenda happens in various ways: through state regulation, with the provision of public services, and with the management of processes of change. As regards the regulatory role of the state, there are ways to ensure 'good regulation' to undertake *ex ante* impact evaluations, so that undesirable effects and administrative burdens are minimized. As regards the improved delivery of public services, basic choices must be made in each area regarding the model to be adopted (decentralization/de-concentration), the design of the information technology and organizational systems adopted, and whether to outsource or forge public–private partnerships. Beyond the provision of services, the economic role of the state in the implementation of a development strategy is also very relevant because the state is a major source of jobs, investment and purchases. As regards the management of processes of change, this calls for project leadership and management, the ability to manage people, communication and relations with the various actors involved in the process, as well as much broader governance issues (dealt with below).

Monitoring and evaluation
Monitoring has become a lot more efficient with management control information technology (IT) systems, which permit ongoing assessments of physical and financial indicators, as well as the monitoring of results (the latter are harder to track because this often involves accessing less than perfect national statistical systems). As regards evaluation, the goal is to measure efficiency and effectiveness as well as programme impacts in light of broader strategic goals. Thus, there is much to be gained by placing evaluation within the broader context of the causal model and reference scenario adopted. Evaluation should have an internal aspect, conducted by the responsible agencies, and an external one, carried out by independent entities. It should be clarified that the central goal of evaluation is not to judge but rather to promote a collective learning process to improve performance. Depending on the evaluation, it may be necessary to update or revise the development strategy. This can initiate a new cycle, which should follow the stages outlined above.

Strategic Governance

The foregoing section outlined the cycle of strategic planning and management without reference to the institutional context. However, the latter is crucial throughout the cycle. In what follows, I assume that the institutional context is a representative democracy with mechanisms for participatory democracy.

Functions in strategic management and actors

To ensure efficiency, it is necessary to clarify the institutional functions of each actor as clearly as possible. In addition to each specific constitutional arrangement, governments must take the lead in proposing a development strategy, with legislative and financial instruments cascading down from the development agenda and programmes. However, in a democratic context counterproposals may be presented by political parties, civil society groups or citizens in general. Civil society organizations must then participate in processes of consultation and consensus-building proposed by government, according to previously agreed rules. Further, civil society can launch whatever initiatives it sees fit according to democratic norms. The government must then re-elaborate its proposals to take the results of consultation into account, and present them to parliaments. Parliaments must debate these proposals and adopt the relevant legislative and financial instruments. Governments may then further re-elaborate proposals to incorporate the results of parliamentary debate.

With the support of civil services, government must then initiate the implementation phase with the involvement of all the relevant actors. Civil society groups should participate in implementation through individual initiatives, projects undertaken by different organizations, or public–private partnerships. With the support of civil services, government should organize monitoring and evaluation processes, which also involve civil society and parliament. Finally, the media can disseminate information and views throughout the process.

Training actors for strategic management

Successful experiences prove that it is not enough to define the role of different actors; it is necessary to develop their capacities for them to perform their roles adequately. To give just some examples: government strategic management capabilities are reinforced by the personal characteristics of leaders, but also by the existence of a prospective and strategic management support team linked to counterpart teams in different ministries. Regular government workshops that permit free strategic debate are very useful. Civil service capabilities are reinforced when prospective and strategic management teams have an impact on the normal functioning of the relevant ministries for a more knowledge-intensive type of policy-making. This depends on internal communication, including the organization of workshops for high-level officials in the relevant

Table 18.2   Strategic management and governance

Strategic management	Strategic governance
Preparation	Political-strategic impetus
Strategic analysis	
Strategic prospective	Reference scenario selection
Strategic definition/development	Political-strategic options
	Political proposal
	Development of consultation process
Re-elaboration	Political proposal re-elaboration/
	parliamentary debate and adoption
Operational planning	
Implementation	Implementation
Monitoring/evaluation	Monitoring/evaluation

ministries. The management of projects and coordinating teams is also crucial for the development of new capabilities, as is the constant search for national and international best practice. The training of parliamentarians should not be forgotten either. Consulting experts, public consultations or new forms of organization such as horizontal articulation structures between various parliamentary commissions, can be particularly useful.

Training civil society groups depends on their degree of involvement in consultation processes, and on the development of specific technical capacities and workshops and conferences. When civil society organizations are involved in coordination as well as consultation activities, training becomes all the more important, as they must help to forge new common views. This is even more crucial when specific agreements or strategic pacts between unions and business associations are at stake. Finally, when implementation depends heavily on civil society groups, it may be important to transform their presentation into a format that is more intelligible to each actor involved. Governments elaborate so-called 'toolboxes' in order to reach each actor in the most appropriate way.

Based on the above, it is possible to present a global vision of the process of strategic governance and management to define and implement a development strategy (see Table 18.2).

Multilevel Strategic Governance

The above framework seeks to simplify something that is highly complex, given varied historical and political contexts, and because governance operates on various levels (local, regional, state, national, macro-regional and international). Although the national level is crucial, if governance is to be improved, it has to be articulated with all other levels. This is particularly true when a development agenda is at stake. In order to clarify the governance context at the various levels, it is useful to have a framework that specifies the competences of each level for each sectoral policy (Table 18.3).

It quickly becomes apparent that the degree of decentralization below the national level differs greatly depending on the policy at stake; the same is true for degrees of centralization above the national level, particularly when there is macro-regional integration. The question is not whether top-down or bottom-up management is best, since both are necessary: rather, what matters is how to combine those approaches for each sectoral policy. For instance, trade policy must be much more centralized than policies to combat poverty, but even the latter will involve highly centralized aspects, such as tax measures.

Whatever the case, when discussing the strategic governance of a development agenda, two conclusions seem inescapable: each above-mentioned governance level must use management procedures (see Table 18.2) for the domains over which it has institutional competences; and a certain level of strategic centralization is necessary in order to implement a broad policy of change. The central issue, then, is eminently political: the level that evinces the highest degree of centralization must have the necessary democratic legitimacy.

Strategic Governance in the Context of Regional Integration: Other Lessons from the European Experience

In most countries, the national level is still the relevant level of strategic centralization for the promotion of a development agenda. But, as was historically the case in Europe, in some areas, management can operate at the macro-regional level. In the EU, exchange rate, monetary, trade, agricultural and competition policy is macro-regional; in other instances competences are shared between the community and national levels, as in the case of the environment, transport, research and jobs; and in yet other cases, policies are national, as with industrial, social security, health or education policy. But even in these instances, the EU has some competences and develops a combination of diversified instruments. The EU has developed a process of strategic governance at the community level that involves all 25 Member States, which has increased the level of coordination between national policies. This process is based on the OMC, which applies to 12 sectoral policies in the EU, on the basis of more informal or 'soft' instruments.

The OMC aims to establish a certain level of strategic convergence among countries and regions while respecting specificities. It involves the

Table 18.3 *Sectoral policies and levels of governance*

Sectoral policies / Governance levels	Foreign trade	Macroeconomic	Industrial	Research	Jobs	Education	Social protection	Environment
Macro-regional	X		X	X	X			X
National	X	X	X	X	X	X		X
State/regional			X	X	X			X
Local					X	X	X	X

following steps: the identification of the main shared strategic challenges; the identification of and debate about good practice in response to these strategic challenges; the definition of goals or common public policy guidelines; the translation and adaptation of guidelines to establish national policies; the implementation of guidelines in a way that is adapted to each country and helps to mobilize civil society; monitoring implementation on the basis of common indicators and quantitative goals adapted to each case; and the evaluation of the process and the updating of guidelines.

There has been much theoretical and political debate about the OMC to which social science researchers have contributed. This ongoing debate and some recent theoretical contributions allow me to clarify key aspects of a method that has played a historical role in Europe: helping to build a new strategic consensus for a development strategy committing 27 different countries.

First, some general comments to shed light on the method itself. The goal of the OMC is not to rank countries in each policy arena, but rather to promote a regional learning process so as to stimulate exchange and the emulation of good practice, and to improve national policies. The method uses benchmarking but it transcends mere benchmarking. It establishes a regional dimension, enables political choices to be made through the definition of common guidelines, and encourages the management of goals through the adaptation of common guidelines to diverse national contexts. The method is a concrete way to develop modern governance based on the principle of subsidiarity; it can promote convergence around shared interests and priorities while respecting national and regional diversity. It is an inclusive method that serves to deepen cooperation and regional integration, and it can be used in conjunction with other methods depending on the problem being addressed, ranging from harmonization to cooperation.

The OMC occupies a middle position among the range of possible methods. It transcends intergovernmental cooperation and constitutes an instrument for integration that complements various other more general instruments. Political cooperation must play a crucial role to catalyse the different stages of open coordination, namely through the presentation of common guideline proposals, the organization of good-practice exchanges, the presentation of indicator proposals, and support for monitoring and peer review. The OMC can also become an important instrument to increase transparency and democratic participation.

The OMC is 'open' for various reasons: common guidelines and their ranking can be adapted to national contexts; good practice can be evaluated and adapted to the national context; it distinguishes between regional-level reference indicators and concrete national targets, taking national

---

BOX 18.1   THE LISBON AGENDA AND
           EUROPEAN GOVERNANCE: KEY
           QUESTIONS

How should we assess the implications of the Lisbon Treaty for the
Lisbon Agenda?
How can we improve the governance of the 'Lisbon process',
namely to pave the way for a comprehensive sustainable development strategy?
How can we improve the role of public administration in developing and implementing the Lisbon Agenda?

---

starting points into account (common indicators can be the ratio between investment in research and development and gross domestic product, or female participation in the labour market, for example, while the goal can vary from country to country; this means that monitoring and evaluation must be based on progress achieved regarding the national targets, as they must take into account the national context according to a systemic approach); and various civil society actors should participate at all stages, so as to propitiate new forms of partnership.

BIBLIOGRAPHY

Dony, M. (2008), *Après la réforme de Lisbonne. Les nouveaux traités européens*, Institut d'Etudes Européennes, Brussels: Editions de l'Université de Bruxelles.
Dror, Y. (2001), *The Capacity to Govern*, London and Portland, OR: Frank Cass Publishers.
Featherstone, K. and C.M. Radaelli (eds) (2003), *The Politics of Europeanization*, New York: Oxford University Press.
Määtä, S. (2004), 'The Lisbon Strategy and Strategy-Focused Public Administration', EPAN paper, http://www.eupan.net.
Piris, J.C. (2006), *The Constitution for Europe: Legal Analysis*, Cambridge and New York: Cambridge University Press.
Quermonne, J.L. (1994), *Le système politique de l'Union européene*, CLEFS Politique, Paris: Montchrestien.
Rodrigues, M.J. (2001), 'The Open Method of Coordination as a New Governance Tool', in M. Telò (eds), *L'Evoluzione della Governance Europea*, Rome: special issue of *Europa/Europe*, nos 2–3, pp. 96–107.
Wallace, H., W. Wallace and M.A. Pollack (2005), *Policy-Making in the European Union*, New European Union Series, New York: Oxford University Press.
Zeitlin J., P. Pochet and L. Magnusson (eds) (2005), *The Open Method of*

Coordination in Action: The European Employment and Social Inclusion Strategies, Brussels: Peter Lang.

http://www.europa.eu/growthandjobs/.
http://www.mariajoaorodrigues.eu.

See further bibliography in Appendix 4 of this book.

19. Assessing the implications of the Lisbon Treaty for the Lisbon Agenda

Mario Telò

19.1 AN INSTITUTIONAL FRAMEWORK

Does the 'Lisbon Strategy' need the support of a consistent institutional framework? In other words, do institutions matter? This is a rhetorical question, since from the outset nothing has existed in an institutional construction like the European Union (EU) without a consistent legal basis. Treaties provide values, allow competences to be shared between the constituent entities and the EU, and establish governance procedures.

However, there are two alternative views about the European public sphere: one, supported by Rodrigues and others, is that consistent new Treaty provisions should underpin the Lisbon Strategy; the other, functionalist view emphasizes EU policies as independent from EU polity reform. On this view, the Lisbon Agenda – a practical and pragmatic process that is part of a 'delivering Europe' – is rhetorically opposed to prioritizing EU Treaty reform. The functionalist understanding of the Lisbon Strategy has deep roots in the history of European cooperation, but also suffers from some internal contradictions. What are the arguments in favour of the so-called functionalist approach?

One argument can be called that of the 'original sin'. During the first semester of the year 2000, different people and ministers under the Portuguese presidency managed the Lisbon Strategy and the process of Treaty reform (notably, the Intergovernmental Conference in preparation of the Nice Treaty). The subsequent French presidency also failed to address both issues together, and entirely ignored the institutional implications of the Lisbon Strategy, so that the Treaty of Nice of December 2000 did not provide an institutional framework for it (when in fact the Lisbon Strategy was particularly adapted for inclusion in the new Treaty given its ambition of framing an inclusive enlarged EU). The Social Agenda of December 2000 was interesting in terms of content, but was very traditional and conservative in that it separated social from economic issues. It should be noted that two out of the three referred to in Declaration 23 annexed to the Treaty of Nice in view of a further Treaty revision (on sharing competences, the role of national parliaments, and status of the Charter of Fundamental Rights) are indirectly related to the institutional dimension of the Lisbon Strategy. At every Spring European Council the Lisbon Strategy proved to be highly controversial (and ambiguous) in the context of the missed 'Lisbon-friendly' Treaty revision of 2000, and the failed ratification of the Constitutional Treaty of 2004 (ratified by 18 Member States and rejected in two referenda in 2005). The Lisbon Agenda gradually came to include the main EU and Member State modernization agendas, but the technocratic and functionalist tendency led to a focus on 'negative integration' (getting rid of borders and barriers) rather than 'positive integration' (establishing a European regulating framework, according to Scharpf, 2002). Obviously, this unbalanced version of the Lisbon Strategy is less transparent, more unpopular and politically weaker, according to national and EU democratic criteria. Such unprecedented 'communication deficit' can also be seen as the most appropriate for the 'low profile' of the internal and international dimensions of the Lisbon Strategy.

The alternative view is that there should be a stronger and more regulating Lisbon Agenda. This view has always been present, but it was not pursued with any vigour for the seven years between 2000 and 2007. At the Santa Maria da Feira European Council in June 2000, it was proposed that governance of the Lisbon Agenda should be radically changed, with the open method of coordination (OMC) introduced as an innovative means to promote European integration, providing a 'third way' between the community method and intergovernmental cooperation. The OMC has strong multilevel implications for three EU institutions: with the help of the Commission, the Council sets European guidelines, encourages Member States to elaborate national plans (which often push to reform modes of national government), routinizes peer review, disseminates best practice, and benchmarks; the Commission ensures that the regular monitoring of national implementation is technically and politically possible. The Commission is charged with preparing the yearly report for the Spring European Council, and the latter is meant to lead, coordinate, relaunch and enrich the Lisbon process as a whole. However, the limited and controversial implementation record repeatedly raises doubts about soft coordination methods. The 2008 Treaty revision is showing the extent to which institutional revision and leadership were necessary for the Lisbon Strategy and how utopian and rhetorical were the Demosthenes-style pleas which opposed OMC soft law to the Community method.

How was it possible to revise the treaties in a more 'Lisbon-friendly' way in 2003–07? Strong opposition at the national and EU levels to the practical implementation of the Lisbon Strategy increased awareness of the urgency of placing the Lisbon Strategy within the EU legal framework. This became possible with the new Treaty revision, namely the European Convention (February 2002–July 2003).

The European Convention of 2002–03 discussed the Lisbon Strategy at various levels: within working groups, plenary sessions, the chairing committee and the four sectoral pillars (the European Parliament, national parliaments, the European Commission and national governments). First, the working group on shared EU and Member State competences eventually achieved positive results, as described in Chapter 18 in this book. Second, the working group on social Europe supported Treaty revisions concerning objectives, values and policies. The national parliament representations underpinned this 'Lisbon-friendly' evolution. Finally, the draft approved at the last plenary session (in July 2003) included four Treaty revisions mentioning, even if not explicitly, the OMC as relevant policy areas are concerned. They are included in the Treaty on the Functioning of the EU (formerly the Treaty of the European Community, TEC): in Articles 156 (on social policy), 168 (on public health policy), 173 (on industrial policy) and 181 (on research policy). For all these articles, the OMC is supported by the Commission, which has a leading role in coordinating Member State national policies. In all, whereas it was not possible to include the OMC in the first part of the Constitutional Treaty, the results were relevant and became possible thanks to intensive transnational networking and lobbying, coordinated by Rodrigues, at level of the national and European parliaments, among European unions (the European Trade Union Confederation – ETUC), European political parties, and with a leading role played by national ministers.

The inclusion of a narrower Lisbon Community Programme in the Lisbon Agenda in 2005 paradoxically supports the view that comprehensive Treaty reform is necessary: the EU (namely the Commission) considers that while it is short and partial, the existing legal basis is the only realistic framework for effective 'Lisbon' policy-making. The fact that it is currently limited to growth and job creation (the latter both have a legal basis: in the case of growth, the treaties of Maastricht, 1992 and Amsterdam, 1997; macroeconomic policy is covered by Article 99 TEC; and European Employment Strategy is covered by Articles 125–130 TEC) should have made the Commission the forerunner leading the Treaty reform process, which was not so evident in 2004–07. During the first semester of 2007, the German presidency was successful in reviving 90 per cent of the Constitutional Treaty (see the unprecedented detailed mandate of June 2007, including the provisions affecting the Lisbon Strategy). Thus, the 'Lisbon-friendly' Treaty provisions included in the Lisbon Treaty (December 2008) are consistent with the European Convention of July 2003 and the Constitutional Treaty of October 2004. These limited changes can be explained by the urgency of coping with new demands arising from practical EU policy-making (as with energy and environment policies, for example) and the French government's interpretation of the referendum of 2005 (see below for details).

At best, the Lisbon Reform Treaty will not enter into force before 1 January 2009. Thus, the absence of a consistent legal basis will have conditioned the implementation of the Lisbon Agenda for nine out of ten years (2000–2010), which largely explains its shortcomings and imbalances. Notwithstanding this gloomy context, the Lisbon Agenda will continue and share EU 'regulatory regionalism', whether because of a Hegelian 'astuteness of reason', or strong socio-economic interests in a globalized economy, or the relevance of the informal institutionalization process within multilevel governance in the EU system (see de la Rosa, 2007 and Zeitlin et al., 2005 for this view). However, internal policy achievements are still far from consistent with declared objectives and targets, and from being implemented across the board in the EU-27. The literature attributes the current implementation gap largely to the resistance and inconsistency of national governments which retain leverage over policy-making. Second, the Lisbon agenda gains by shifting from a merely internal to an internal–external agenda. That is why it is more urgent and necessary than ever to finalize the revision of the legal framework for informal governance and to ensure administrative implementation.

19.2   THE REFORM TREATY AS A 'LISBON STRATEGY-FRIENDLY' TREATY?

To what extent will the new Lisbon Treaty[1] legally frame the evolution of the internal and external dimensions of the Lisbon Strategy? And can the EU move from regulatory regionalism to 'strategic regionalism',[2] consciously and consistently acting as an international catalyst of a sustainable modernization agenda?

Objectives, Values, Conceptual Guidelines

The Reform Treaty revisions on values, goals, key concepts and decision-making procedures may have an impact on the normative context and the international identity of the EU. They do not address the creation of a

European knowledge society since lawmakers see this as a policy and not part of polity and identity of the EU. However, there are several elements that frame the Lisbon Strategy conceptually. I divide the provisions into three groups: those that revive the Constitutional Treaty (CT); those that change the Constitutional Treaty after the 2005–07 internal crisis; and those that renew the CT, while supporting the international openness of the Lisbon Strategy.

As regards the revival of the CT, the following is important: Article 3 of the Treaty of European Union (TEU) refers to the EU objective of building of 'a highly competitive social market economy', a balanced 'Lisbon-oriented' aim. It is originally of German origin (L. Erhard), but was proposed by the ETUC leadership at the Convention and backed by the two major political families (the European Socialist Party (ESP) and the European People's Party (EPP)) in the working group on social issues, and in the Plenary. The identity-marker concept of 'social market economy' is now being mainstreamed, and becoming a crucial part of the EU international identity (compared with the American, Japanese, Russian, Singaporean and Chinese models). It is also in line with the Declaration on Europe and Globalization approved by the European Council (13–14 December 2008). This is not just rhetoric: many observers underline the maintenance of the following *acquis* of the CT: the objectives of full employment, combating social exclusion, and territorial cohesion, which are innovative compared with the current Treaty of Nice and more coherent with the 'positive integration' version of the Lisbon Strategy.

As regards changes to the CT, there are some that are much more controversial and even inward-looking, which could work against regulatory regionalism and international openness (these are supported mainly by Sarkozy's France). Two of these changes regard the EU objectives: firstly, the duty of the EU to protect its citizens in a globalized economy (Article 3 TEU), as requested by France after the referendum of 2005.[3] President Barroso backed Sarkozy, but distinguished between 'protecting' and 'protectionism', consistently with the new fund for victims of globalization. The context of this rhetoric change suggested an almost generalized comment: it is an answer to internal pressures and lobbying, addressing the question of the external dimension of EU policies within the global economy in a mere defensive way. A second major change, also a result of the French referendum, is the deletion of 'non-distorted free competition' as an EU goal (Article 3 of the new TEU), although this concept is retained in Articles 119 and 127 of the second Treaty on EU policies (the Treaty on Functioning of the European Union – TFEU). The complementary Protocol on the Internal Market underlines that the EU has a 'system where the competition is not distorted'. No comment.

Finally, as regards the European Charter of Fundamental Rights, a huge problem for the EU as a promotion of human rights and norms both at home and abroad is the derogation requested and obtained by UK and Poland, which will discriminate EU citizens according to their nationality (including their social rights). Some of these derogations have been phased out (for example, the UK's 1992 derogation from the social protocol and several cases for Denmark), but the various derogations accepted for the UK (the euro, the Schenghen Treaty and the Charter mentioned above) may strengthen the tendency to establish a two-layered EU which is not consistent with an inclusive strategy like the Lisbon Strategy. How can we combine differentiation and inclusiveness? To what extent is a derogation not a provisional difference in the timing of integration but a permanent feature of the EU, dividing the EU polity into two layers?

There are also several new provisions improving the Constitutional Treaty that may support an open and updated Lisbon Agenda. There are the new Treaty provisions on the environment (Article 191 TFEU), energy policy (Article 194 TFEU) and on addressing climate change. Second, according to various observers, the CT is also improved by the Protocol on services of general interest: what was a mere reference is now part of 'EU common values', confirming the normative role of the EU in this policy area without weakening the competences of Member States when it comes to financing and implementing.

Institutional Leadership

The low level of institutionalized leadership, and concomitant discontinuity, implementation gaps and de facto hierarchies among EU bodies (in favour of the Economic and Financial Affairs Council, Ecofin) is the main Lisbon Strategy deficit in the view of many. As regards institutions and decision-making, the Lisbon Reform Treaty is a step forward in terms of the continuity and coherence of EU leadership. With the reform, the European Council (Articles 15 and 26 TEU), once outside the institutional system, becomes the leading European institution. The permanent and full time presidency could strengthen the continuity and consistency of the EU agenda and of the Spring Council in particular, thus solving one of the major problems of the Lisbon process (with its eight years of successive six-month rotating presidencies, each one with its own national priorities). The president has access to staff of the general secretariat once used by the rotating EC presidency. Of course, much remains vague, particularly the frontiers between the competences of the rotating Council presidencies (which will continue rotating among 27 Member States according to a calendar approved by the Council, including the troika working method in accordance with Seville European Council decisions). As regards the institutional setting for EU leadership, the major question is whether Brussels is strong enough to house three 'strong men' and a rotating fourth (namely, the president of the European Council, the president of the Commission elected by the European Parliament, the High Representative for foreign policy, and the rotating Council presidency).

As argued in Chapter 18, the specialized formations of the Council will be better coordinated when it comes to law-making and policy implementation. The new General Affairs Council (GAC, after the creation of the Foreign Affairs Council) will have the *de jure* role of coordinating the other specialized Council formations to coordinate internal domestic policies and their interface with national policies. For the first time, and in contrast with the asymmetric architecture of the Maastricht Treaty with its imbalance between negative and positive integration, it is provided that Ecofin will no longer be the de facto leader of the Lisbon process. However, it remains to be seen who will be a part of the new GAC. Deputy prime ministers or prime ministers would be the best solution to address the global nature of the Lisbon Agenda and the need for a central coordinating authority ensuring the consistent implementation of joint decisions. Whether we like it or not, deciding the level of national representation is up to national authorities and law. The four or six larger Member States could set a high standard of representation. The problem is that the largest states are those most opposed to policy coordination.

The Efficiency of the Decision-Making Process

The efficiency of the decision-making process has been improved in several ways. First, the Council will extend the qualified majority voting procedure to 50 new areas, including sensitive issues. The qualified majority voting (QMV) procedure is simplified to two criteria (the majority of 55 per cent of Member States and 65 per cent of the population), albeit only after 2014. Second, the end to the Maastricht three-pillar structure will have significant implications on the former third pillar, with an impact on immigration policy (less on the second pillar, for which unanimous voting remains the rule). Third, as regards EU economic governance, the euro is stated to be the EU currency and the eurozone is strengthened. A specific chapter on the eurozone enhances its internal cohesion (more so even than the CT). Fourth, as a last resort, Article 50 allows Member States to withdraw from EU membership. The negative implication is that this is a step towards a contractual understanding of the EU, although this can be very positive if there is a serious and prolonged internal crisis.

Shared Competences and Governance

There are two main points that arise from a reading of the competence-sharing provisions between the EU and Member States.

First, the Reform Treaty is reviving the legacy of clarification of the CT by distinguishing between three lists of competences, both in general and regarding the Lisbon Strategy (see Chapter 18 in this book). Shared competences are crucial for the Lisbon Strategy to succeed: the internal market, the environment, economic, social and territorial cohesion, agriculture, consumer protection, transport policy, energy policy, health and safety, research and (some aspects of) social policy. The OMC is particularly suited to address the low degree of Europeanization of Member State competences, when only supporting measures are allowed (as for industrial and research policies, certain aspects of social policies, and administrative cooperation).

Second, and on the other hand, the limits on any EU competence expansion and the subsidiarity principle are both much more underlined than in the Nice Treaty because of the 'red lines' established by UK and other Member States against the expansion of the community method (on fiscal policy, social policy and, of course, defence policy and foreign policy).

My view here is that the long and hard negotiation among EU Member States on competences between 2002 and 2007 clearly confirms how far-sighted the Lisbon Strategy is: the expansion of the EU agenda to the most sensitive issues on national agendas cannot realistically happen within the Community method legal framework (including four Treaty provisions: the Commission retaining a monopoly on initiatives; qualified majority voting, QMV in the Council; co-decision by the European Parliament, EP; and Court of Justice competence). What we need is a new method which allows the EU to enhance cooperation for policies that remain essentially national. This is why the strengthening of the OMC by the Treaty is so relevant (although it is not mentioned as such), giving the Commission a leading role in coordinating the MS national policy-making where four policy fields are concerned (as in the CT). Last but not least, including social dialogue as one of the main pillars of EU democratic life also opens the door for social partners to play an enhanced role with Commission initiative in policy-making.

The Lisbon Reform Treaty and External Policies

As suggested by the Declaration on Globalization approved by the European Council of December 2008, and by the documents included in *Presidency of the EU: Developing the External Action of the European Union* (Lisbon, Gabinete do Primeiro Ministro 2008), the Portuguese presidency successfully implemented the German presidency mandate, and strengthened coherence with the renewal of practical external policies. The Treaty clearly announces the goal of 'sustainable development' for internal (Article 3.3 TEU) and external (Article 3.5 TEU) policies. Also present are other objectives that are relevant for the external Lisbon Agenda (fair trade, solidarity, the fight against poverty, human rights, and international law).

The establishment of a legal personality for the EU (Article 47 TEU) is very positive, making international and interregional agreements possible for the EU as well as the European Community (EC); but there are limits in terms of coherence. There are different procedures depending on the pillar (unanimity for the second, and QMV for what were formerly the first and third pillars). For the first and third pillars, the new 'negotiator' for international agreements (designated by the Council) is the Commission, and the High Representative for the second pillar (the EP has no consulting role here). For trade policy, there was progress with goods, services and intellectual property rights. There are also new provisions that may increase foreign policy efficiency and improve on the CT (it will be easier to engage in enhanced cooperation whatever the future number of Member States after further enlargements, and the minimum number of countries – nine Member States – will remain the same).

The Treaty of Lisbon is increasing expectations of enhanced coherence and consistency between the Council and Commission, the two EU centres of international decision- and policy-making at the international level. Enhancing 'horizontal coherence' is essential, particularly for a non-state actor such as the EU. The High Representative could be the symbol of a new 'strategic regionalism' provided that: the border with the three other 'strong men' in Brussels (see above) is clear; the internal conflict of interest between the High Representative chairing the Foreign Affairs Council and the High Representative vice-president of the Commission is clear; the current capability–expectations gap is limited with coordination between the Council and Commission and among the many EU Commission directorates-general dealing with external policies; and that the vertical coherence of the EU, namely the loyalty of Member States, is better implemented (see the Treaty provisions). The commitment to enhanced cohesion and loyalty by Member States is mentioned in Articles 28, 32, 34 of the TEU among others. However, political conflicts require more than legal solutions.

19.3 CONCLUSIONS

The legal framework opens possibilities but it cannot determine the content and orientation of EU policies: for example, establishing more balance between negative and positive integration, or liberalization and regulation, depends on the political will of actors and evolving power relations (the political colours of the majority but also, very importantly, the national culture of the leading actors) within the Council, the EU Council, and increasingly the Parliament, even though it only has advisory powers in that policy area. What is new in the Reform Treaty is that the Commission is also more politicized because of the linkage between the choice of its president and members, and EP elections. Politics will matter more than before in the EU political sphere, which will affect the Lisbon Strategy. But the impact of the Reform Treaty on EU politics is quite ambiguous: politicization will increase, with the new Commission based on a political majority and the increasing application of QMV within the Council; however, the Reform Treaty strengthens the central governance system (Commission, EU Council president and General Affairs Council, GAC), whatever the national political majority, which supports continuity in national government policies and has centripetal effects in national political systems, while marginalizing extreme stances such as Thatcherite approaches or radical leftist national policies. In all, provided that it is ratified by the 27, the Lisbon Treaty is likely to provide the complex and long-term EU modernization agenda with more credibility and consistency by enhancing central soft and hard governance.

NOTES

1. The Reform Treaty (or Lisbon Treaty) is divided into two treaties (after the failed attempt with the Constitutional Treaty of 2004 to establish a single treaty): there is the Treaty of European Union (TEU) with 55 articles (corresponding mostly to the first part of the CT; and there is the Treaty on Functioning of the European Union (TFEU) with 358 articles, the updated version of the Treaty of the European Community (TEC) which overtook the Treaty of Rome, and the third part of the CT of 2004. The annexed declarations and protocols are also a relevant part of the Lisbon Treaty (see Dony, 2008). The Charter of Fundamental Rights used to be the second part of the CT, and the new Reform Treaty makes Charter provisions as effective as the Treaty provisions.
2. By 'strategic regionalism' I mean the EU as a regional actor and not just a regional entity, and an actor able to shape the global economy in a consistent way. See Telò (2007) and Chapter 16 in this volume.
3. See the famous speech of President Sarkozy at the EP (June 2008), supporting the *préférence communautaire* and 'reciprocity' through trade negotiations.

REFERENCES

de la Rosa, S. (2007), *La méthode ouverte de coordination dans le système juridique communautaire*, Brussels: Bruylant.

Dony, M. (2008), *Après la réforme de Lisbonne. Les nouveaux traités européens*, Institut d'Etudes Européennes, Brussels: Editions de l'Université de Bruxelles.

Scharpf, F. (2002), 'The European Social Model: Coping with the Challenges of Diversity', *Journal of Common Market Studies*, **40** (4): 665–70.

Telò, M. (ed.) (2007), *The EU and New Regionalism*, London: Ashgate.

Zeitlin J., P. Pochet and L. Magnusson (eds) (2005), *The Open Method of Coordination in Action: The European Employment and Social Inclusion Strategies*, Brussels: Peter Lang.

20. Paving the way for a strategy of sustainable development

Iain Begg

Any assessment of the governance of the Lisbon Strategy since it was relaunched in 2005 (Lisbon II) has to start from the shortcomings of Lisbon I, as revealed notably by the Kok Report (European Commission, 2004). The Strategy was criticized for a lack of focus, for having too many targets, while also lacking credible commitments by Member States, and for being devoid of real policy instruments, including a budget. The governance of the 'Lisbon process' also has to contend with the parallel development of other processes, notably the European Union (EU) Sustainable Development Strategy (SDS), which has certain objectives in common with Lisbon, but also differing priorities that are not always wholly consistent with Lisbon. With climate change, the EU response to globalization, concern about global trends in energy supply, financial stability and the recent surge in food prices all competing for the attention of policy-makers, it has not been easy to ensure that there is coherence in the economic governance agenda.

As Maria João Rodrigues notes in Chapter 18, governance has multiple dimensions in the context of the Lisbon Strategy (she lists ten distinct areas). In this chapter, the focus is on some of these areas, but also on aspects of governance that underpin or cut across some of these ten areas. In particular, the chapter discusses elements of the philosophy behind the Strategy and of the overall design of the strategic initiatives of the EU. It then discusses the merits of a Lisbon Strategy euro area dimension and suggests ways forward.

20.1 THE CHALLENGES

The Lisbon Strategy is, first and foremost, about structural reform of the EU economy. The weaknesses on the supply side of the EU economy have been documented and analysed extensively in numerous reports by the Organisation for Economic Co-operation and Development (OECD), the

European Commission and other bodies, and there is no need to review the diagnoses of what is needed. Instead, the principal challenge is to translate diagnosis and strategizing into effective implementation. In this regard, a primary governance imperative is how to relate the Lisbon Strategy to other major policy initiatives, especially those with strategic ambitions. They include, in addition to the SDS, the Energy Policy for Europe (EPE) and social protection and social inclusion (SPSI) strategies, in addition to policy initiatives that are more narrowly focused such as those on 'better regulation'.

To some extent, these 'mega-strategies' complement one another, but they also overlap and, on occasion, compete, engendering scope for confusion, which can result in a loss of commitment. An associated risk is that where the different 'mega-strategies' touch on the same objectives, goals will be given differing emphases that will not be easy to reconcile across different processes. For example, Lisbon II stresses growth and employment as the core objectives, implicitly diminishing the salience of social and environmental aims; yet the SDS appears to attach equal weight to competitive, social and environmental aims. To a degree, SPSI serves as the social dimension of the Lisbon Strategy, but is kept at a distance, despite the expectation that social reforms should – in the Brussels jargon – 'feed in' to Lisbon objectives, while Lisbon policies are expected to 'feed out' to facilitate the realization of social goals.

With processes competing for the attention of policy-makers and resources, overlapping channels for the formulation and implementation of policy, and the specification of diverse targets and indicators, there is a danger that the underlying strategic objectives become blurred. Is there a clear hierarchy of processes, or even a direct assignment of processes to goals? In some cases there is clarity, in others considerable ambiguity. Even a deceptively simple question about whether Lisbon is the competitive arm of SDS, or SDS the environmental arm of Lisbon, cannot so readily be answered.

What is clear, however, is that for the European Commission Lisbon has been the core project since 2005. Yet in devoting considerable attention during 2007 and 2008 to developing energy and climate change policies, the Commission has broadened the agenda, prompting the question of whether a coherent overarching goal can be articulated. The Lisbon Treaty reshuffles the fundamental objectives of the EU somewhat in the new wording of what used to be Article 2 in the TEU, but it cannot be said to make much difference to the overall economic governance structure established by the Maastricht Treaty. However, the reordering of objectives in the Lisbon Treaty arguably suggests that for analytic purposes it may be useful to highlight a dichotomy in economic objectives between what might be called wealth-creating objectives (such as the single market, monetary union and the promotion of scientific and technological advance) and wealth-distributing and quality-of-life goals (sustainable development, cohesion and quality of environment).

20.2 SUPPLY-SIDE POLICY COORDINATION

In practice, Lisbon, the SDS, EPE and SPSI are all variations on policy coordination, with differing blends of guidelines, resort to targets, and intensity of scrutiny. The merits of policy coordination have long been debated, with some protagonists seeing it as a second-best in the absence of true economic government of the sort canvassed by Boyer (1999), while others believe that it should be limited in scope. Coordination as a policy mode also places new demands on governance processes, especially in fostering the soft law methods and engagement of civil society that are at the heart of the open method of coordination (OMC). Research on the effectiveness of such processes in the macroeconomic and employment policy areas suggests that they have had a limited impact at best, not least because expectations that the deliberative element of OMC would contribute substantially to better policy-making have not been fulfilled (Linsenmann et al., 2007). There is some evidence that the need to produce coherent strategies has resulted in some policy innovation and, to borrow a phrase from the early years of the Blair government, more 'joined-up' government. Even so, Linsenmann et al. find that the impact on domestic policy-making processes within Member States has generally been disappointing.

The question, then, is whether the wave of process development in 2005–07 – when the Lisbon Strategy, the SDS, the Stability and Growth Pact (SGP), and the development of the EPE were relaunched – presages improvements. The main innovations of Lisbon II as a coordination process are the much greater integration of policy effort, the engagement of a wider circle of actors and, possibly most significantly, the determination of the Commission to lead the process rather than to be at the margins of an intergovernmental initiative. Integration is apparent in two dimensions: across policy areas, bringing the separate 'economic' and 'employment' guidelines together; and across levels of government, establishing the partnership between the Community level (the Community Lisbon Programme, CLP) and the Member States (the national reform programmes, NRP). Lisbon II entered its second three-year cycle and enough is now known about how the process has functioned to enable a critique to be made.

However, it would be wrong to describe Lisbon II as only coordination, insofar as it has become, especially through the Community Lisbon Programme and hard law initiatives relating to the single market, a hybrid between the OMC and more traditional *méthode communautaire* approaches. By contrast, SPSI relies almost exclusively on the open method, while it remains to be seen how extensive Community policies will become in the EPE or SDS. For effective governance, this notion of hybridity needs to be deepened and its implications for policy formulation and implementation clarified.

The Philosophy of Structural Policy Coordination

Although the imperative of structural reform is broadly supported by the economics profession, there are nevertheless widespread doubts among economists about the value of a coordinated process of reform such as Lisbon. The consensus seems to be that coordination is more valuable for product market reform and for initiatives to promote economic transformation (for example, innovation policies) than for restructuring of labour markets or welfare states (Tabellini and Wyplosz, 2006). This standpoint partly emanates from the fact that the latter facets of the supply side have much greater distributive content, which means that they have to be much more attuned to national political traditions and sensitivities.

At the same time, it has to be recognized that the nature of the policy coordination that falls under the various EU structural processes is distinctive in two specific ways. First, in contrast to the SGP which has preventive (encouraging 'good' policies) and dissuasive (penalizing 'bad' policies) arms, both of which are intended to exert a disciplining influence on fiscal policy, the underlying purpose of supply-side coordination is to push Member States to embrace reform, that is to innovate in policymaking. Second, much of the Lisbon methodology (and to some extent that of the SDS and SPSI) is geared towards the fostering of policy learning through the instruments listed in Chapter 18. The added value of organizing a process at EU level stems from diverse elements such as the strength of common goals, the salience of the policy issues in it and even the constitutional position.

This distinction suggests a way of conceptualizing policy coordination so as to shed light on its potential impact. Simplifying egregiously, a two-by-two matrix for classifying policy coordination can be put forward, comprising: first, the disciplining motivation as opposed to the learning motivation; and second, substantial added value from an EU process against the need to defer to national political constraints.

Motivation for coordination

	Disciplining	Learning
EU added value	SGP	Energy policy SDS Better regulation
National sensitivity	Wage formation	Labour market regulation Welfare policies

Figure 20.1   Scope for policy coordination

Figure 20.1 suggests some possible assignments within this crude framework. Thus, coordination of budgetary policies under the SGP has a demonstrable EU added value and is aimed at disciplining Member States by constraining discretionary policy. By contrast, welfare policies have to contend with entrenched national sensitivities and it is far from clear (other than in connection with certain aspects of freedom of movement) that there is an EU added value. Better regulation, parts of energy policy, and sustainable development and climate change are areas where value is added, but where the learning motivation, rather than the disciplinary one, is to the fore. However, for some elements of energy policy (such as targets for emissions reductions), a disciplinary motivation is evident.

Implementation

It can be difficult to show that a strategy such as Lisbon is delivering results, especially for the Member States that require the most extensive reforms. Most assessments tend to be ambivalent about its success, as exemplified by the successive scorecards produced by the Centre for European Reform. In the most recent of these, the overall grade is a disappointing 'C+' (Barysch et al., 2008), only a slight advance on the 'C' grades awarded in previous years. A possible explanation is that the structural reforms that are central to the strategy tend to be slow-acting and may result in dislocations while they are being implemented. Hence, the policies that Member States have written into their NRPs will only make a real difference to economic performance after a considerable lag. Yet after eight years of Lisbon, the lukewarm verdict is a concern for economic governance.

Nevertheless, a consensus has emerged that the 2005 relaunch has had positive effects in pushing recalcitrant Member States to accelerate reform, and encouraging countries to learn from one another. There is, too, some evidence that reforms undertaken between 2000 and 2005 are now bearing fruit, notably in Germany, improving EU growth potential. However, whether this is because of Lisbon or simply the result of domestic policies is an open question, although it could be argued that it is the fact of reforms that matters, not whether they conform to a particular model or process, or are explicitly credited to the Lisbon strategy (Begg, 2007). Moreover, for other policy strategies, even though it is early days, it is harder to trace a direct cause and effect from the existence of the strategy to new policy approaches.

Engaging Actors

The visibility of the Lisbon strategy within Member States remains disappointing, with only limited salience for national policy-making, and has been caricatured by one prominent commentator as 'Brussels talking to Brussels' (Pisani-Ferry, 2006: 836). There is some truth in this charge, but it is also something of a paradox that Member States have produced all the reports asked of them and shown a willingness to adapt policies to conform better to the Lisbon Agenda. The principle of reform, understanding options to ensure progress, and the political will to implement change have probably all been enhanced by pressures emanating from Brussels, even if the Lisbon strategy receives little credit in domestic politics.

That said, there remain governance problems. The contribution of Lisbon coordinators, perhaps rather optimistically envisaged as being at the heart of the responses of Member States to structural reform, has been rather disappointing. They only meet infrequently and differ substantially from one Member State to another in the authority they have in government. Some are political figures (this is the profile recommended by the Commission), others are officials of differing degrees of seniority, but the visibility of their role within Member States is generally quite limited. Nor do national parliaments, in most cases, exert much oversight over governments' structural policies that are germane to the EU strategies, and the general impression is that the media rarely put pressure on governments to improve their performance. The upshot is that the channels through which national ownership of commitments under Lisbon or the SDS ought to be held to account function only inadequately.

The Fatigue Phenomenon

The proliferation of processes can also lead to a form of 'reporting fatigue' with pernicious effects. On the one hand, this may mean that governments become more adept at presenting what they are doing than actually doing it; and, to cope with multiple reporting obligations, resort to 'cut and paste' rather than more creative thinking about policy-making. If, in addition, governments make little effort to take advantage of peer review, or to look for insights from the experience of other countries, the upshot may be that opportunities for innovative policy responses are simply missed. On the other hand, the EU-level processes risk being exiled to the sidelines of real policy-making and of having little effective influence, with the result that it becomes easier to neglect awkward reforms.

'One Size Fits All'

In all the policy processes, questions arise about the duration and content of common approaches. In some policy areas there are common targets (for example, for employment rates, R&D spending or poverty reduction), even if the very diverse starting-points mean that the timeline for countries to meet the targets is very different. A different approach has been adopted for the EPE with overall EU commitments (for CO_2 reductions and use of renewables), but national targets vary greatly because of different starting positions.

The integrated guidelines for Lisbon II are common to all Member States, but afford room for manoeuvre in two main ways. First, the functioning of the OMC allows Member States to tailor policies geared towards individual guidelines to their national circumstances, meaning that the common goals may be approached through quite diverse policy choices and methods. Second, in practice, governments put more effort into meeting some guidelines than others, and may give little or no attention to some of them – possibly attracting criticism from formal scrutiny procedures as a result. Yet at the heart of Lisbon there is nevertheless a presumption that there is a common model and set of goals. An alternative approach would be to argue (as the OECD does in its Going for Growth initiative – see OECD, 2008 for the most recent progress report) that a much more customized approach should be adopted. In this alternative, the key is to identify what it is about the economy that most needs reform. For Italy, the most pressing problem might be the productivity of public administration; for France, unblocking labour market reform; for Germany, rethinking aspects of social protection; and for the UK, dealing with transport infrastructure weaknesses, and so on. In the OECD model, five priorities are identified for each country, based partly on objective indicators and partly on judgements.

20.3   THE EURO AREA DIMENSION OF LISBON

The policies that are coordinated under the Lisbon Strategy do not stand alone, but an aspect that has been insufficiently developed in the architecture of the strategy is policy mix (Begg, 2008). In macroeconomic policy, there has been extensive – if unresolved – debate about the value of coordination between fiscal and monetary policies. Over the last two decades, the trend towards independent central banks and stability-orientated fiscal policy has militated against active demand management. However, within nation-states which have full control over both policies, there is still at least a regular dialogue between the two policy areas and, on occasion (as the recent US response to the sub-prime crisis signals) a willingness to coordinate policy actions. In the euro area, such coordination has tended to be rejected in favour of a 'keep your house in order' approach to each policy area and is, in any case, institutionally deterred because of the assignments of competences to different levels of government, although there are acknowledged problems of potential free-rider behaviour.

Coordination between macroeconomic policy and the structural policies which are the core of the Lisbon Strategy also warrants discussion, but receives only limited attention despite being subject to similar risks (see Leiner-Killinger et al., 2007). In this regard, an irony is that European Central Bank (ECB) board members regularly call for actions that link to the Lisbon Strategy. For governance, the question that arises is whether new approaches are needed to enable the euro area collectively to play a more extensive role in the Lisbon and sustainable development strategies. Although (for instance by addressing a 'fiche' to the euro area as well as to individual Member States as part of the annual reporting cycle of Lisbon II), the Commission has been trying to highlight the fact that there are common euro area challenges, it is far from clear how the relevant comments and recommendations should be dealt with or by whom. The problem here is the informality of euro area institutions, notably the Eurogroup, and the limited policy range of euro area actors (see Pisani-Ferry et al., 2008).

The Impact of the Lisbon Treaty

New provisions on the euro area in the Lisbon Treaty will, in effect, establish a remit for policy coordination similar to that under Article 99 of the

TEC and at least formally recognize the Eurogroup, albeit only in a Protocol. But there is no presumption that the Eurogroup membership will extend beyond finance ministers and central bankers, which means that it will not embrace ministries responsible for structural, social or environmental policies. As a result, euro area economic governance will tend to be orientated towards macroeconomic policy and will lack advocates of other aspects of sustainable development.

Hitherto, most of the debate has turned on whether the Eurogroup should or should not evolve into a form of *gouvernement économique*, rather than a sectoral focus in which other policy areas such as employment, science and technology or energy and transport, as well as cross-cutting themes such as competitiveness, are debated at euro area level. From a governance perspective, the Treaty does not appear to exclude the development of new bodies and there is always enhanced cooperation as a more formal mechanism, despite the fact that it has not yet been used. Given that the Eurogroup was able to constitute itself as an informal body, despite the strong reservations of other Member States, there is nothing in principle to stop other representative euro area bodies being established and this may be a way forward for the euro area. Moving in this direction would, however, prompt a need for 'coordination of coordination' as a form of institutional deepening.

Finding Ways Forward

If there is to be both better integration of the different processes and an enhancement of the prospects for structural reform, there are several governance changes that should be contemplated. First, greater clarity is needed about how the different processes are supposed to interact. Such clarity is needed in timetables, procedures and, above all, the 'division of labour' between the processes. Second, to achieve this aim, there should be a collective effort to define the overarching goals and objectives of structural policies in relation to Europe's citizens. Here, the SDS is the most credible starting point and the other strategies can be seen more as instruments to achieve the overarching goals. Third, the European Council should be made the guardian of policy coherence with a unified approach to economic and social governance, rather than being the recipient of different and competing policy initiatives. It is the European Council which is best placed to offer an integrated vision, not only of all the strategies, but also of how they connect to other governance procedures, including the SGP. Fourth, it would advance the overall aims of policy if there were a single point in the calendar – ideally the Spring European Council – at which the different economic governance processes were discussed at the highest level.

To lead up to this annual scrutiny, the overall European economic governance strategy should be subject to an annual review focusing on the most urgent issues, also ensuring that other policy areas do not 'fall between the cracks'. Fifth, enhancing the connections between the euro area as a collectivity and the major strategies – perhaps by envisaging a re-cast Eurogroup that encompasses inputs from ministries other than finance, or possibly the establishment of separate Eurogroup-style bodies for structural policy domains. Finally, when reworking the EU budget in the future, it will be important to place sustainable development priorities at the centre of discussion and, in so doing, to focus attention on the choices between regulatory and budgetary approaches to governance.

Other, more specific areas warrant discussion. First, it is necessary to look for ways to enhance the visibility of the 'processes' and link them more directly to citizen concerns. This should also address whether 'naming and shaming' ought to be more explicit, for example by tougher statements about Member States, in place of the rather gently worded recommendations that accompany Lisbon at present. Second, there is a case for reconfiguring the European Parliament's committee structures to focus more strongly and directly on sustainable development. It may, third, be worth fostering more productive ways of engaging national parliaments, the media and civil society, so as to exert political pressure on governments.

REFERENCES

Barysch, K., S. Tilford and P. Whyte (2008), *The Lisbon Scorecard VIII: Is Europe Ready for an Economic Storm?*, London: Centre for European Reform.

Begg, I. (2007), *Lisbon II Two Years on: An Assessment of the Partnership for Growth and Jobs*, Study commissioned by the European Parliament, Special CEPS Report, CEPS, Brussels, December.

Begg, I. (2008), 'Economic Governance in an Enlarged Euro Area', European Economy Economic Papers 311.

Boyer R. (ed.) (1999), *Le gouvernement économique de la zone euro*, Paris: La Documentation Française.

European Commission (2004), *Facing the Challenge: The Lisbon Strategy for Growth and Employment. Report from the High Level Group chaired by Wim Kok*, Luxembourg: OOPEC.

Leiner-Killinger, N., V. López Pérez, R. Stieger and G. Vitale (2007), 'Structural Reforms in EMU and the Role of Monetary Policy', ECB Occasional Paper 66.

Linsenmann, I., C. Meyer and W. Wessels (eds) (2007), *Economic Government of the EU: A Balance Sheet of New Modes of Policy Coordination*, Basingstoke: Palgrave Macmillan.

OECD (2008), *Going for Growth 2008*, Paris: OECD.

Pisani-Ferry, J. (2006) 'Only One Bed for Two Dreams: A Critical Retrospective on the Debate over the Economic Governance of the Euro Area', *Journal of Common Market Studies*, **44** (4): 823–44.

Pisani-Ferry, J., P. Aghion, M. Belka, J. von Hagen, L. Heikensten, A. Sapir and A. Ahearne (2008), *Coming of Age: Report on the Euro Area*, Blueprint No. 4, Brussels: Bruegel.

Tabellini, G. and C. Wyplosz (2006), 'Supply-Side Coordination in the European Union', *Swedish Economic Policy Review*, **13** (1): 101–56.

21. The Lisbon Agenda and public administration

Wolfgang Drechsler

21.1 PUBLIC ADMINISTRATION AND THE LISBON AGENDA, 2000–2007

The life-world of the Lisbon Agenda, today's Europe, can be described as a primarily administered environment. Despite all the criticisms of the public sector, the latter retains a significant and often dominant role in economy and society. So it is baffling that the original Lisbon Strategy did not address this topic until 2006, when documents about the Lisbon Agenda first started to mention public administration, particularly in relation to innovation (which is very different from 'innovative practices in public administration'). The 2006 *Implementation Report* states that the public sphere has a role to play in the innovation process (European Commission, 2006a: 17), which is also acknowledged in the Lahti conclusions (European Commission, 2006b: 6–7). All documents that mention the public sphere focus on e-government, public procurement and innovation (usually very loosely understood).

21.2 THE EUROPEAN PUBLIC ADMINISTRATION NETWORK

Virtually no attention has been paid to public administration in scholarly work on the Lisbon Agenda, with the notable exception of Seppo Määttä (2004, 2006), which is very strongly policy-oriented. This work was done in the context of the one institution that has addressed the topic fairly early on, EPAN (or EUPAN, the acronym seems to vary), 'an informal network of Directors General responsible for Public Administrations in EU Member States and European Commission' (http://www.eupan.org), which is in fact the main European-level institution that dealt with the issue at the European level, although it is only a voluntary organization without a staff or legal basis. In 2005, EPAN formed an ad hoc group on the Lisbon

Table 21.1   The significance of public administration for the Lisbon Agenda

Public administration: General	In the EU	For the Lisbon Agenda
as a central part of public governance	as the largest employer in the EU	as the main service provider especially in the key areas of the Lisbon Agenda (education, health care, social protection)
as context creator for citizens and businesses to act	as a large spender/ purchaser (more than 15% EU GDP overall)	. . . and governments as the designers of the Lisbon Agenda
as service provider (hindering role as well as positive one)	as the largest single industry in the EU (45% EU GDP overall)	

Sources: EPAN (2004), pp. 2–3; Määttä (2004), pp. 4–6; Määttä (2006), pp. 29, 58–9.

Strategy that worked for half a year under the chairmanship of the Luxembourg presidency, but the work of the group (EPAN, 2005) does not seem adequately reflected in later debates about public administration in the Lisbon Agenda.

The Wassenaar Memorandum of Understanding (November, 2004) established the Lisbon Agenda as a main point of reference, arguing for 'the importance of an excellent functioning public administration as a contributor to realising the Lisbon Strategy' (EPAN, 2005: 22). The final report of the ad hoc group stated that:

> implementing some of the key Lisbon priorities depends on a highly competent, professional and competitive public administration, being characterised by effective governance structures, innovative and effective policy-making practices and a performance oriented service delivery. In this sense the national public administrations are to be considered as important enablers for reaching the Lisbon targets. (EPAN, 2005: 5)

The EPAN study and the work by Määttä serve to highlight the significance of public administration for the various aspects of the Lisbon Agenda (see Table 21.1) (to which we will later add public administration's key role in innovation).

21.3   PUBLIC ADMINISTRATION IN THE LISBON AGENDA TODAY

Although public administration still plays a very minor role in the Lisbon Agenda today, it does so now largely as a result of the initiative of the Portuguese presidency. There have been specific meetings and policy papers (EPC, 2007), particularly as regards the Member States and national Lisbon programmes; and public administration was also an issue, if not a top priority, in the results report of the presidency (Presidency of the European Union, 2007). We can categorize public administration as it relates to the Lisbon Agenda into four basic categories, as in Table 21.2.

From the above, we can see that the current focus is almost exclusively on category 2, with some attention to category 1, and none to categories 3 or 4. Further, no Lisbon-related public administration documents address the structure and organization of public administration, except in very general terms; this may be partly because of the highly national nature of civil service structures, so that tools and methods have been the main focus. There seems to be no reflection of the current debate about the shifting public administration paradigm, especially in Europe. I attempt to fill this gap in this chapter.

A review of the various documents mentioned above from a public administration perspective shows that three elements are particularly salient: first, public administration and public policy are generally seen as synonymous; second, public administration is generally understood from within a (public) finance framework, focusing on (streamlining, customer-oriented) reform, which is seen to (indirectly) promote innovation; third, the aim is 'modernization', or a 'modern' and 'innovative' public administration. And in general, institutions are generally seen as barriers to, rather than promoters of, growth and innovation.

Policy

Even, perhaps especially, the very best documents connecting public administration and Lisbon Agenda do so from a policy perspective. Maria João Rodrigues's proposal to improve public administration for the Lisbon Agenda, as outlined in Chapter 18 in this volume, for instance, focuses exclusively on planning and strategic management. Even taking into account the many problems with strategic planning, this is undoubtedly important, but it does not address the main administration issues. This is also the case (albeit on a much more 'tool-based' level) with all other documents, such as in Määttä (2004, 2006). Obviously, there is a tacit conflagration of public administration and public policy, but while they

Table 21.2   Categories of public administration in the Lisbon Agenda context

Public administration	of the Lisbon Agenda	in general
on the Member States' level	1	2
on the EU level	3	4

overlap, we must recognize the specificity of public administration, its implementational nature, and the difference between administration and policy (Hegel, 1821, § 287 provides the classic statement on this) in order to maintain the focus on staff and organizational issues (the 'who' rather than the 'what', as there is no 'what' without a 'who') and the structure of the civil service structure. The focus on policy obscures the nature of and demands on administration itself, to the detriment of whatever project is at stake. So, in order to see who implements the Lisbon Agenda and how, it is necessary to look at public administration proper.

Finance

As regards the finance context, the main paper to prepare a meeting on these issues (EPC, 2007) states that public administration reforms must save money and lighten the bureaucratic burden. The final report of the Portuguese presidency on the Lisbon Agenda calls for 'stronger action', specifically for 'public administration modernization' (Presidency of the European Union, 2007, Main Outcomes: 1), but again the view is largely fiscal: 'The modernisation of *public administration* is key to improve efficiency and effectiveness of public finances' (ibid.: 3). Reported as a main result of the 2822nd Council meeting was:

> the reform and modernisation of public administration. The conclusions high-light the importance of such initiatives in enhancing competitiveness, delivering better services, achieving better value-for-money and ensuring the control of government expenditure, and thus meeting the objectives of both the Lisbon strategy for growth and jobs and the stability and growth pact. (ibid.: 2)

The following statement is typical: 'The Council discussed Member States' experiences of modernizing public administration in the context of the quality of public finances' (ibid.: 12). It addresses 'a re-organisation of public administrations' (ibid.: 12), but does not specify what this should look like, or why it should happen. It even recommends that the ministers of finance should play a key role in public administration reform (ibid.: 12), a move that has led historically and almost universally to disaster, because ministries of finance are, by definition, interested in cutting costs, not in value creation or in supporting innovation. Finally, the March 2008 *Presidency Conclusions* mention public administration only in the context of improving the quality of public finances (European Council, 2008: 3) (See also Appendix 2.). However, in financial terms, public administration can only be judged by the wealth it generates, so the question is not how much can be saved, but how great is the return on investments made (of course this is difficult to measure: the principle stands nonetheless). To save by cutting public administration may be foolish if this leads to lower productivity, entrepreneurship, innovation or economic development; and there are good reasons to think that it may.

'Modern' and 'Innovative' Public Administration

The key argument, one that appears in every document referring to public administration, is that public administration needs to be modernized. But what does 'modern' mean in this context? No document provides a working definition of the term apart from EPC (2007: 4), which states: 'In a broad sense, the modernization of public administration can be defined as reform measures aimed at improving the quality of governance and at raising the efficiency and effectiveness of public service provision.' This definition is both highly reductionist and vague, since it is not merely the quality of public administration that is the issue, and because public administration is not simply about the provision of services.

'Modern' in this context is not particularly meaningful, except when it refers simply to being 'up to date' or 'in line with the current situation'. But 'modern' in the sense of 'new' is not only ambiguous, but also highly ambivalent, especially after the experiences of the twentieth century – would a totalitarian shift away from democracy in the 1930s, say, have been better because it was new? What is wrong with workable traditional solutions? And although what is appropriate does indeed depend on the times and the situation, the vast majority of documents on public administration use the concept of 'modern' in a way that is, as we will see, not in line with the times.

The concept of innovation has also been used very loosely in the public discourse of the last couple of decades, and certainly within the public administration context, when it should be understood quite strictly in a Schumpeterian sense (albeit with some modifications and additions) if the effects, the reasons why innovation is so central, not least for the Lisbon Agenda, are going to be realized at all. The public sector, however, tends to use the term 'innovation' as a cliché referring to anything new or 'modern'. But, again, public administration does not have to be new or even genuinely innovative (if such a thing were possible) to work well. Clearly, the public sector has to go with the times, it is not immune to 'new best practice' organizational demands (Perez, 2002), but this is quite different from being innovative. Innovation is about profit, and in this regard the task of the state is neither to make money, nor to save it, but to see that money can be and is made.

In the context of public administration, this is no light matter, *a fortiori* as far as the Lisbon Agenda is concerned, with its emphasis on an innovation-based economy. The problem is that the paradigm in public administration has changed in the past few years, but the Lisbon Agenda discourse on public administration does not reflect that change. Instead, it is heavily retrospective and espouses the kind of public administration principles and structures that would have been adequate to solve the problems of the 1970s and 1980s (with some exceptions, such as e-governance), although these times are unlikely ever to come back.

21.4 THE NEW PUBLIC MANAGEMENT AND ITS DEMISE

The most important public administration reform movement of the last quarter of a century has been the new public management (NPM), which appears to be at the core of all Lisbon Agenda public administration initiatives. NPM is the transfer of private business and market principles and management techniques to the public sector, and is based on a neoliberal understanding of state and economy. The goal is a slimmed-down, minimal state with public activity run according to business principles of efficiency and pared down to a minimum. NPM uses concepts such as project management, flat hierarchies, customer orientation, the abolition of career civil service, de-politicization, total quality management and contracting-out. Transparency, citizen involvement and decentralization are not part of the original NPM model.

NPM is Anglo-American, and it was promoted vigorously by the key international finance institutions (IFIs) such as the World Bank and the International Monetary Fund (IMF). It originated in the 1980s when neoliberal governments were dominant and the welfare state was thought to be in crisis, although it came to full fruition in the early 1990s. NPM was a fashionable concept in public administration scholarship and practice, which explains much of its power; and it was also a genuine ideological concept.

Several NMP-inspired reforms were important and some even successful. However, when looking at the private and public sectors, what stand out are the differences, not the similarities. The state is denoted primarily by its monopoly on power, force and coercion, on the one hand, and an orientation to the public good, on the other; by contrast, the business world legitimately focuses on profit maximization. The use of business techniques within the public sphere thus mistakes the most basic requirements of any state, particularly those of a democracy, for liabilities: regularity, transparency and due process are, however, much more important than low costs and speed.

Genuine economic and particularly management-theory insights only took hold in public administration after the dominance of NPM came to an end, which as genuine ideology was not open even for counter-arguments stemming from its own avowedly leading method. For example, the NPM reforms established quasi-markets within administrative organizations to encourage market behaviour, but such behaviour can only develop in genuine and not in quasi- (or pseudo-) markets (König, 2001: 6–7). Also problematic is the concept of performance pay vis-à-vis the demands of multitasking and motivation through identification with the organization (Akerlof and Kranton, 2005, esp. 9–11, 27–9). As Lawrence Lynn, Jr, has recently pointed out (Bouckaert et al., forthcoming), if there is any social science concept that has been disproved it is that of performance pay, but it is promoted politically and implemented, including within the Lisbon Agenda, at least in theory.

In advanced public administration scholarship in Europe (but also elsewhere), NPM as a world view or ideology is very much on the defensive now, rather than being one of various useful perspectives for public administration reform (that is, a toolbox). It was an option a decade ago, but this is no longer the case. In 1995 it was still possible to believe in the NPM model, although the first substantial critiques had already emerged at this time; by 2000, the year of the launching of the Lisbon Agenda, the model was on the defensive, as empirical findings clearly condemned it; and by 2005, the year of the mid-term review, it was no longer a viable concept.

In other words, articles in top journals, essays and keynote addresses by leading public administration scholars in Europe and even in the United States no longer assume that the NPM model is a valid one, although the model is still alive and well, especially in policy-making. Nevertheless, in recent years, many communities at the local and regional levels have acted against NPM reforms, even in traditional NPM strongholds. The justification for stopping NPM reforms by the city of Dübendorf, Zürich, Switzerland, sums up the reasons for this very nicely: 'no improvements of efficiency, effectiveness nor quality could be attributed to NPM reforms' (Noordhoek and Saner, 2005: 38).

21.5   THE NEO-WEBERIAN STATE

The NPM counter-model, its 'bête noire', is what is called 'Weberian public administration'. This label is problematic, as NPM supporters make a caricature and paper tiger out of it. Weber's view was that the most efficient public administration consisted of a set of offices in which appointed civil servants operated under the principles of merit selection (impersonality), hierarchy, division of labour, exclusive employment, career advancement, the written form, and legality. 'Increased rationality' – his key term – would increase the speed, scope, predictability and cost-effectiveness that are necessary for an advanced mass-industrial society (Weber, 1922: 124–30). Despite its various problematic aspects, the Weberian model is still the best we have, and is certainly superior to NPM. To paraphrase Churchill, it is the worst form of public administration except all the others. Certainly, the connection between Weberianism and economic growth seems to be very close (Evans and Rauch, 1999).

Still, the optimal administrative structure for today cannot consist of a mere rehash of the organizational principles of the mass production paradigm, the weaknesses of which are well known: from excessive legalism via genuine bureaucratism to genuine antagonism to innovation and the economy. And some of the managerial elements and even broad principles of the NPM model are positive, as long as they do not become the basis of public administration, and as long as there are adaptations to current needs and varying challenges, and the specific socio-intellectual context.

Thus, the administrative paradigm that is most debated today, the post-NPM model, is not simply a return to the old one, but, in the words of Pollitt and Bouckaert (2004), a neo-Weberian state (NWS), a model that uses the positive elements of NPM, but on a Weberian foundation (both are asymmetrically *aufgehoben*) (Pollitt and Bouckaert, 2004: 96–102). The NWS was intended as an empirical-analytical rather than a normative model, and one of its creators, Pollitt, is quite self-critical about several of its aspects (Bouckaert et al., forthcoming). However, it is one explanatory model of what is happening in Europe, and it does not throw the managerial and participatory babies out with the NPM bathwater. It is still a research agenda, but in the absence of anything better, it does a lot to help us understand the development of contemporary public administration, especially in Europe.

21.6   THE NEO-WEBERIAN STATE AND INNOVATION

Why is the NWS (see Table 21.3) particularly appropriate for the Lisbon Agenda? Unlike NPM, it is the perfect match for an innovation-based society. When talking about the economics that are at the core of the Lisbon Agenda, the above-mentioned documents fail to mention the immense push–pull function of what is after all a state-based socio-economic development programme, the implementation of which requires a highly competent, long-term-oriented, dedicated and enabled civil service. In short, 'the Lisbon strategy does not happen by itself' (Määttä, 2006: 52, 59), it needs not only social actors but also, and above all, public administration. It is an understatement to say that empirical research 'indicates that modern and efficient public administrations have a positive impact on productivity and growth' (EPC, 2007: 3); rather, it is effective public administration that has this effect, and it is a *conditio sine qua non* rather than merely positive in its effects. If we aim at innovation in the general rather than the merely private interest, who should implement a successful innovation policy if not public administration? As Claude Rochet (2007) succinctly puts it: '*l'innovation, une affaire d'état*'.

Following Carlota Perez's great surges theory and techno-economic paradigm shifts model (2002), we are operating within the information and communication technologies (ICT) paradigm and heading towards a period of 'synergy', and this means that state and administration must rise to the challenge again and that the anti-state climate of the earlier ICT installation period is, or should be, history. And whatever the new leading technology that emerges after ICT (nanotechnological, biotechnological, convergence, or some other), setting it up calls for particularly capable state actors and science and technology policies implemented by civil services that can engage in long-term thinking, that are highly competent, and can tolerate errors – the opposite of NPM (Drechsler, forthcoming).

Finally, it should be emphasized that while they seem to share some features, e-governance and NPM are actually not related as is usually assumed (Dunleavy et al., 2005). ICT does not render obsolete almost any of the traditional Weberian categories, and some – such as the written principle and division of labour – are actually enforced. In the most prominent instance, hierarchy, there are mixed dynamics, as it is weakened by network models of organization but strongly enforced via the extreme control and coordination capabilities of ICT. Rather, it is e-governance and the NWS that can reinforce each other, and in fact empirically seem to do so rather well.

Table 21.3   The neo-Weberian state (summary)

Neo-	Weberian
Shift from an internal orientation towards bureaucratic rules to an external orientation towards meeting citizens' needs and wishes. The primary route to achieving this is not the employment of market mechanisms (although they may occasionally come in handy) but the creation of a professional culture of quality and service	[but:] Reaffirmation of the role of the state as the main facilitator of solutions to the new problems of globalization, technological change, shifting demographics, and environmental threat
Supplementation (not replacement) of the role of representative democracy by a range of devices for consultation with, and direct representation of, citizens' views	[but:] Reaffirmation of the role of representative democracy (central, regional, and local) as the legitimating element within the state apparatus
In the management of resources within government, a modernization of the relevant laws to encourage a greater orientation on the achievements of results rather than merely the correct following of procedure. This is expressed partly in a shift from *ex ante* to *ex post* controls, but not a complete abandonment of the former	[but:] Reaffirmation of administrative law – suitably modernized – in preserving the basic principles pertaining to the citizen–state relationship, including equality before the law, legal security, and the availability of specialized legal scrutiny of state actions
A professionalization of the public service, so that the 'bureaucrat' becomes not simply an expert in the law relevant to his or her sphere of activity, but also a professional manager, oriented to meeting the needs of his or her citizen/users	[but:] Preservation of the idea of a public service with a distinct status, culture, and terms and conditions

Source: Pollitt and Bouckaert (2004), pp. 99–100.

21.7   PUBLIC ADMINISTRATION AND THE LISBON AGENDA

Despite all this, the above-mentioned papers still present NPM as the basis of all public administration reform, albeit in an already weakened form (as in Määttä, 2006 and EPC, 2007). Thus, a reorientation towards the NWS, or towards any post-NPM paradigm, has yet to take place.

The Member States

What do public administration reform initiatives in the Member States look like? The *Initiatives* paper provides a narrative description of the measures (EPC, 2007: 4–10, 13–14), but a list that is more comparable would be helpful. Thomas Duve has researched this topic, and come up with the following results as illustrated in Figure 21.1.[1]

In terms of content, the dominant features are e-government initiatives (which nobody resists any more), one-stop shops (which are good, if obvious and simple NPM tools), and the reduction of bureaucracy. It is also apparent that countries with strong public administration reform activity also tend towards the NPM model. According to our study, the strongest NPM focus is found in Finland, Hungary and Italy. But it is interesting to observe how they differ: the Finnish model is largely *sui generis* and is built on such a solid basis that it can 'afford' NPM (it should be added that Finnish experts on public administration recognize that the NPM model is coming to an end, except at the municipal level). It is not for nothing that Finland is the most successful country in Europe, if not the world, according to most indicators.[2] As for Hungary and Italy, further studies are necessary, but it may not be too far off the mark to lump these initiatives under the heading of politics and rhetoric; both have very strong, classic systems (in the case of Hungary, until very recently consciously following Weberian models; and regarding Italy, rather pre-Weberian ones).

One should also generally consider that: (1) these are programmes and not actually implemented reforms, which tend to be very different in public administration; and (2) it is never clear which kind of public administration reforms had been pursued and were then written into the Lisbon Agenda reports in order to look good. But there is doubtless an influence – if only declarative and performative – of the EU, via the Commission, on national administrations on the basis of the Lisbon Agenda. The ample literature on the Europeanization of national administrations has not touched on this matter yet, but this is only a matter of time. If we look at our matrix in Table 21.2, we see that the focus was mostly on category 1, Member States' public administration; category 2, the issue of specific Lisbon Agenda administration, is not really considered yet, either.

European Union Administration

But if category 1 is neglected, we do not find anything about public administration reform on the EU level (the administration of the Lisbon Agenda by the Commission and the EU administration itself). From the perspective of the Commission, while categories 1 and 2 do not have a

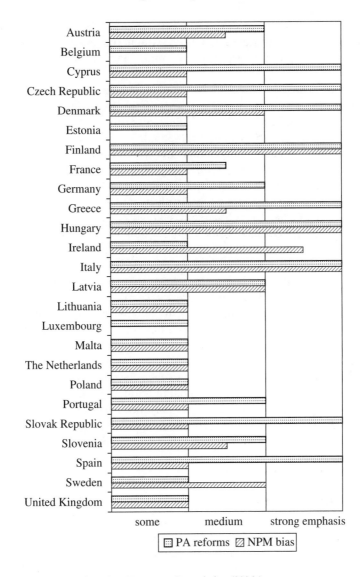

Source: Duve (2008), based on European Commission (2006c).

Figure 21.1   Public administration reforms and NPM bias in Member States' national Lisbon programmes, 2006

responsible directorate-general (DG); categories 3 – to a very small extent in practice – and 4 are located in the DG Admin, the DG for Personnel and Administration, and the responsible commissioner is Vice-President Siim Kallas.

As regards category 3, there is not much thinking about Lisbon Agenda administration within the Commission at all (at least none that is visible); but category 4 has been the focus of much attention, not least because it is a popular issue (to the extent that people dislike 'the bureaucrats in Brussels'). The general view is that EU staff constitute a Continental bureaucratic civil service system, along French lines. Partly for good reasons, in response to scandals, and partly because it is the fashion, there were serious managerial reforms, particularly under former Commissioner Neil Kinnock in 2000. EU scholarship is largely positive about the Kinnock reforms, judging them successful or at least well intentioned (Bauer, 2006). Currently, however, there has been an at least implicit shift towards the NWS model as well. Commissioner Kallas, who has been very sympathetic towards NPM reforms, recently underlined that the senior civil service of the EU at least should remain a career system and that there will more emphasis on career advancement, identity and motivation, rather than the recruitment from Member States which has produced so many problems, including in the area of cultural adaptation to the EU civil service (Kallas, 2008; Bauer, 2006 for the previous situation). Thus, despite the deployment of NPM tools, what we see is a return to even classically Weberian patterns (also echoing Akerlof) with a clear goal in mind, regardless of the specific tools that might be used to reach it. It may, however, take a while for this shift to percolate down to the Member States since some may see this not as a genuine progressive shift from NPM to the NWS, but rather as a return to bureaucratic rule.

21.8　PROSPECTS

To sum up, despite a positive change of focus, the public administration aspect of the Lisbon Agenda is still weak. What we need, then, is first to acknowledge the importance of public administration for the Lisbon Agenda: it cannot succeed without high-quality public administration. Second, we need to be clear that public administration is not policy, that it is not there to save money but, if anything, to promote wealth-creation; and that 'modern' should mean 'appropriate for the times'. Taking current scholarship into account, it is very clear that what the Lisbon Agenda needs is an NWS-based, or more or less NWS-like, public administration at the EU and Member State levels.

BOX 21.1   PUBLIC ADMINISTRATION CONCEPTS

Modern	→	Appropriate
Innovative public administration	→	Innovation-enabling public administration
Saving money	→	Return on investment

Such a claim alone will be contentious since public administration is seen to be a national issue that the EU should not interfere with. But it is also true that since the success of the Lisbon Agenda depends on high-quality public administration, then the issue concerns the EU as a whole, and there is a mandate for change, as suggested by references to the need for public administration reform to 'undergo regular analysis and exchange of best practices in particular in the context of the Lisbon National Reform Programmes' (see Presidency of the European Union, 2007, Main Outcomes: 3).

But there is a genuine ambivalence about whether the Lisbon Agenda should refer explicitly to public administration reform. Most documents show that even many of those supporting the Lisbon Agenda favour NPM, depicting the classic Weberian public administration (of which they are usually a part) as the enemy, partly because they lack information about public administration, but often with the best intentions. An open method of coordination type of process for Member States' public administration only makes sense if proper attention is paid to the specific features of public administration as such. It is therefore important to coordinate this at the top by an office that has the capacity to deal with and focus on public administration, that is, by the commissioner in charge of public administration. The Lisbon Agenda requires and supports (there is push and pull) the NWS and needs to move in this direction. It may be easier to do this now that the NPM model is no longer as fashionable, but there still needs to be an effort and a shift in emphasis and understanding. To that end, the following development of concepts is suggested, as laid out in Box 21.1

The key to the success of a strategy like the Lisbon Agenda is responsive and responsible state actors with the administrative capacity and competence to implement it. The best model is a genuine post-NPM, largely Weberian model which takes on board the lessons of NPM, and which – clichés notwithstanding – puts people at the heart of administrative decision-making, in line with the Lisbon Agenda and its goals, and the ultimate goal of promoting the good life in the good state (Drechsler, 2001). Such an administration is, both potentially and in reality, one of the great assets of the European Union as well as of many of its Member States. It is time to give this asset proper recognition and develop it in full, so that it can play a central role in the context of the Lisbon Agenda.

NOTES

1. Duve (2008). This is a quantitative-qualitative study, undertaken in the context of the Estonian Science Foundation project, Public Administration and Innovation Policy, at the Tallinn University of Technology, which measured the frequency of keywords, first, of general public administration reform, and second, of NPM, in the 2006 National Reform Programmes, using the most recent available data (European Commission, 2006c). The results for France are only estimates, since the French programme is not available in English.
2. For me personally, it became clear that the days of the NPM model were over when a leading civil servant in the Finnish Ministry of Finance emphasized to me that Finland would use NPM tools rather than follow the ideology of the model, and when a PhD student from the University of Helsinki referred to certain faculty members who supported NPM as holding 'traditional' views.

REFERENCES

Akerlof, G.A. and R.E. Kranton (2005), 'Identity and the Economics of Organizations', *Journal of Economic Perspectives*, **9** (1): 9–32.
Bauer, M.W. (2006), 'Die Reform der europäischen Kommission: Eine Studie zur Managementmodernisierung internationaler Organisationen', *Verwaltungsarchiv*, **97** (3): 270–92.
Bouckaert, G., C. Pollitt and T. Randma-Liiv (eds) (forthcoming), 'Towards the Neo-Weberian State? Europe and Beyond', *NISPAcee Journal of Public Administration and Policy*, **1** (2).
Drechsler, W. (2001), *Good and Bad Government: Ambrogio Lorenzetti's Frescoes in the Siena Town Hall as Mission Statement for Public Administration Today*, Budapest: Open Society Institute and Local Government Initiative.
Drechsler, W. (forthcoming), 'NanoGov: Nanotechnologie, Governance und Verwaltung', in A. Scherzberg and J. Wendorff (eds), *Nanotechnologie– Grundlagen, Anwendungsfelder, Regulierung*, Berlin and New York: de Gruyter.
Dunleavy, P., H. Margetts, S. Bastow and J. Tinkler (2005), 'New Public Management Is Dead: Long Live Digital-Era Governance', *Journal of Public Administration Research and Theory*, **16**: 467–94.
Duve, T. (2008), 'PA-Reformen im Rahmen der Lissabon-Strategie', Mimeo, Tallinn University of Technology.
Economic Policy Committee (EPC), European Commision (2007), *Initiatives to Improve the Efficiency and Effectiveness of Public Spending: Modernising Public Administration*, ECFIN/EPC(2007) REP/53684 rev. 2, available at: http// ec.europa.eu.
EPAN (2004), 'Innovating Public Administration and the Lisbon Strategy, Background Document for the Ministerial Troika on 4 November 2004', EPAN paper, available at http://www.eupan.eu/3/92/&for=show&tid=38.

EPAN (2005), 'The EPAN Contribution to the Success of the Lisbon Strategy, Final report', 'Présidence luxembourgeoise du Conseil de l'Union européenne/ European Public Administration Network, Lisbon ad hoc group, EPAN paper, Luxembourg, 10 May 2005, available at http://www.eupan.eu/3/92/&for= show&tid=63.

European Commission (2006a), *Community Lisbon Programme: Technical Implementation Report 2006*, SEC(2006) 1379, available at: http://ec.europa.eu.

European Commission (2006b), *An Innovation-Friendly, Modern Europe*, Communication from the Commission to the European Council (Informal Meeting in Lahti, Finland, 20 October), COM(2006) 589 final, available at: http://eu.europa.eu.

European Commission (2006c), Member States' Autumn 2006 Reports on the Implementation of their National Reform Programmes, http://ec.europa.eu/ growthandjobs/key/nrp2006_en.htm (individual country reports as pdf files).

European Council (2008), *Presidency Conclusions of the Brussels European Council* (13/14 March 2008), CONCL1(2008) 7652/08, available at: http://europa.eu/ european-council/index_eu.htm.

Evans, P. and J.E. Rauch (1999), 'Bureaucracy and Growth: A Cross-National Analysis of the Effectiveness of "Weberian" State Structures on Economic Growth', *American Sociological Review*, **64**: 748–65.

Hegel, G.W.F. (1821), *Grundlagen der Philosophie des Rechts*, Berlin: Nicolai.

Kallas, S. (2008), 'Leading Multicultural Organisations: Developing the Senior Managers of the European Commission', *Halduskultur*, **9**: 24–9.

König, K. (2001), 'Zum Governance-Begriff', in K. König and M. Adam (eds), *Governance als entwicklungspolitischer Ansatz*, Speyer: Forschungsinstitut für öffentliche Verwaltung, pp. 1–9.

Määttä, S. (2004), 'The Lisbon Strategy and Strategy-Focused Public Administration', EPAN paper, http://www.eupan.net.

Määttä, S. (2006), *Looking for a Deliverable Lisbon Strategy on Sustainable Growth and Jobs. Provisional Agenda for Strategy-Focused Public Governance*, Helsinki: Finnish Ministry of Finance.

Noordhoek, P. and R. Saner (2005), 'Beyond New Public Management: Answering the Claims of Both Politics and Society', *Public Organization Review*, **5**: 35–53.

Perez, C. (2002), *Technological Revolutions and Financial Capital: The Dynamics of Bubbles and Golden Ages*, Cheltenham, UK and Northampton, MA, USA: Edward Elgar.

Pollitt, C. and G. Bouckaert (2004), *Public Management Reform: A Comparative Analysis*, Oxford: Oxford University Press.

Presidency of the European Union (2007), *Preparing the New Cycle of the Lisbon Strategy*, Lisbon: Office of the Prime Minister.

Rochet, C. (2007), *L'innovation, une affaire d'état*, Paris: L'Harmattan.

Weber, M. (1922), *Grundriß der Sozialökonomie*, 3: *Wirtschaft und Gesellschaft*, Tübingen: Mohr Siebeck.

22. Improving governance of the Lisbon Agenda: conclusions of the debate

Maria João Rodrigues

The development and the implementation of the Lisbon Agenda have been influenced significantly by the governance of the process itself. The absence of coherence between policies, of consistency between the European and national levels, or simply a lack of implementation are signs that there are governance problems that need to be addressed. This chapter examines how governance can be improved, particularly to promote a comprehensive strategy for a knowledge economy with sustainable development; what approach to adopt to improve the role of public administration; and how to take full advantage of the potential of the Lisbon Treaty to improve governance.

22.1 IMPROVING GOVERNANCE

Governance can be improved, first of all, with the creation of a general framework to promote a knowledge economy with sustainable development, combining current strategies for growth and jobs with sustainable development and social policies. The European Council, the European Commission and the General Affairs Council should act as guardians of policy coherence. A first step in this direction is the synchronization of calendars and reporting procedures, with a particular role for the spring meeting of the European Council.

The toolbox for each policy should address the diversity of the mechanisms for coordination of national policies, ranging from those that aim to ensure a common discipline and those that focus more on fostering mutual learning about reforms. An appropriate mix should be defined for each policy.

The implementation of the guidelines at the national level calls for a focus on more accurate and country-specific recommendations, to strengthen the role of the Lisbon coordinators and involve all the relevant stakeholders more systematically.

At the current stage of involvement, a greater degree of politicisation of the process can be useful, as this can increase accountability vis-à-vis established commitments and provide a clearer identification of choices in a context of limited resources.

Parliamentary bodies can play a central role in this regard. More specifically, the European Parliament can shape general strategic priorities at the European level and the content of the Lisbon Community Programme; in turn, national parliaments can shape national strategic priorities, discussing the country-specific recommendations, and shaping some of the concrete measures.

This can also lead to livelier public debate, with greater involvement of the relevant media. So far, a lack of public communication limits the adaptation of European commitments to the national level to the technocratic sphere.

22.2   A NEW APPROACH ON THE ROLE OF PUBLIC ADMINISTRATION

The specific role of public administration in the implementation of the Lisbon Agenda has been underestimated and underanalysed, even though public administration plays a central role not only in the policy-making process, but also in creating a friendly environment for citizens and companies, providing services of general interest, and as a major employer. Many of the measures covered by the Lisbon Agenda have been translated into legal provisions and standards and in terms of the content of public services and procurement. This has been the case with information society, research, innovation, environment, single market, education, employment, social protection and social inclusion policies.

Public administration as a theme was finally introduced to the Lisbon Agenda in 2007, but the approach adopted was limited to promoting the efficiency and effectiveness of public finances. The implementation of the Lisbon Agenda requires a broader approach which should be based on a new synthesis and thus get beyond the traditional dichotomy found in the debate between the Weberian and the new public management schools of thought.

This means that the role of the state should be reaffirmed as the main facilitator of new solutions to the challenges posed by globalization, technological change, demographic trends and environmental threats, although there has to be a shift from the inward-looking orientation based on bureaucratic rules to an outward-looking user-friendly orientation. It also means reaffirming the role of representative democracy, as well as instituting new complementary forms of participatory democracy; reaffirming the rule of law and equality before the law among citizens, although focusing public action on achieving results; and it means preserving the idea of public service with a distinct status, culture and conditions, but one that is manned by professionalized public servants (and not just legal experts but also project managers who focus on responding to the needs of citizens).

22.3   EXPLOITING THE POTENTIAL OF THE LISBON TREATY

The potential of the Lisbon Treaty to improve the governance of the Lisbon Agenda can be exploited to various ends, namely: to enhance the leadership of the process; to strengthen European instruments; to improve the coordination of national policies; to develop the external policies of the Union; and to explore differentiation.

In the first instance, leadership depends on the capacity to develop a common vision and build a coalition of actors that can redirect the system. This requires a permanent combination of the relevant expertise and networks. In the framework of the Lisbon Treaty, leadership will depend on a complex interplay between the president of the European Commission, the president of the European Council and the rotating EU presidencies which will still preside over the internal policies of the Union. It is, so far, difficult to foresee the outcome of this interplay, the quality of which will depend greatly on the specific personalities involved. However, it is important to note that the Lisbon Treaty allows scope for some creativity within the rotating EU presidency, for consensus-building by the European Council president, and for an enhanced role of the European Commission by extending qualified majority voting and codifying how the open method of coordination is to be used. Last but not least, the European Parliament will have a broader say in strategic choices with the extension of the co-decision process. In all, this also means that leadership will depend increasingly not just on policies but also politics.

Strengthening the European instruments is important not only to ensure a level playing field and better implementation at the national level, but also to permit stronger European action to address globalization. The Lisbon Treaty reinforces the level playing field by extending qualified majority voting to many new areas, restating the overall European commitment to a highly competitive social market economy, adopting a Charter of Fundamental Rights, and with the general clauses on the social dimension and establishing services of public interest. Implementation can also be fostered by the extension of qualified majority voting and the co-decision procedure, and by strengthening the mechanism of the country-specific recommendations within the broad economic policy guidelines.

The instrument mix of each European policy covered by the Lisbon Agenda can also be improved in the framework of the Lisbon Treaty. For instance, as regards research policy, one step would be to develop a European Research Area (ERA) by combining co-decision with the open method of coordination; as regards industrial, innovation and environmental policies, co-decision and the OMC could also be combined; as regards immigration policy, the latter could move from the formerly second pillar of the Treaties to the Community method.

European instruments can also be strengthened with improved coordination of existing instruments. This may be the case of the research instruments (such as the research platforms), the instruments for innovation (the lead markets for instance), and education instruments (skills-needs expert panels, for example), which need to be coordinated better. However, it is well to remember that there are important limits on how strengthened European policies can be: there are the financial resources available, notably in the Community budget, and the political limits to the European regulation and coordination of national policies.

The possibility of coordinating national policies differs from policy area to policy area. Coordination is easier to justify when there are more visible spillover effects, as for macroeconomic, energy or immigration policies, which require a common discipline; conversely, it is harder to develop in sensitive, 'national sovereignty' areas, such as social protection or education, where redistributive effects are more directly visible. Moreover, national diversity can also be a European asset (as it is in the USA), provided that equal opportunities for a knowledge economy are enhanced, according to what can be called a 'New New Deal'. Cohesion policies, or more accurately, the cohesion dimension of European policies, should be designed with this purpose.

The external policies of the European Union should encourage international convergence towards a more balanced and sustainable development agenda, which is crucial to support the Lisbon Agenda. This concerns one of the most important 'added values' of the Lisbon Treaty: the creation of conditions for greater coherence between external policies by establishing the new post of High Representative for Foreign Affairs and Security, and the European diplomatic service. By establishing that this High Representative is also a vice-president of the Commission, the Lisbon Treaty also encourages stronger coherence between the external and internal dimensions of EU policies. As regards relations with international partners, the overall effect of these institutional innovations is reinforced by according the Union a legal personality.

Last, but not least, there are new possibilities of moving forward through differentiation. First, it is necessary to build on the clearer organization of the eurozone as defined by the Lisbon Treaty. The possibility of holding meetings of various Council formations in the eurozone could be considered. Moreover, as regards external policies, there are now improved conditions to organize enhanced cooperation. Whatever the case, even if the Lisbon Treaty does in fact open up greater scope for a better implemented Lisbon Agenda, the future remains very much an open book.

Conclusion

Maria João Rodrigues

The central purpose of the Lisbon Strategy should be that of preparing Europe for a global world through modernization in accordance with European values. Its strategic priorities remain relevant, and its governance mechanisms are delivering better results. But this is simply not enough: the new cycle of the Lisbon Agenda should go further, fully drawing upon the implications of the insufficient implementation and the scope of the new challenges.

As we take stock of the implementation of the Lisbon Strategy, it becomes clear that structural reforms have had visible effects in various policy fields – albeit unevenly from country to country. The growth rate appears to be increasing through a combination of a cyclical with a structural effect, which strengthens growth potential. But Europe needs to change faster and put a stronger focus on national and local implementation, since there is a gap compared with other partner countries. So the current governance structure should be maintained but improved to foster implementation: a special effort should be made by each Member State to address their specific critical points; the capacity to involve all the relevant actors should be improved; and horizontal coordination should be strengthened at all levels.

Moreover, the scope of the challenges for the next years is becoming larger: there is competition not only from the USA and Japan, but from many other poles as well, which calls for new developments in the multilateral framework; raising employment rates is important but not enough to offset the impact of the ageing trends on the sustainability of social protection systems; and the need to protect the environment and to change consumption and production patterns is becoming more acute due to the climate change trends. More fundamentally, a major change is under way towards a more multipolar global order, requiring new rules to ensure a more balanced and sustainable development at world level.

The strategic priorities and the political compromise of the Lisbon Strategy is still the right one (investing in knowledge, opening new markets and supporting entrepreneurship, modernizing the European social model, and improving the environment and gearing macroeconomic policies for sustainable growth). Still, the scope of the challenges must be taken into account fully: we need a more proactive approach regarding globalization to influence the trends and rules of globalization, and seize the opportunities it throws up; and we need to manage risks and open up new life prospects for European citizens. A bolder approach is required to develop the active population in Europe: to make full use of the potential of young people, generalizing equal opportunities for women and men, spreading active ageing, and attracting more people to Europe, and integrating them in Europe. Further, if we take into account climate change trends, the shift in the European and international consumption and production patterns should be more pronounced. In short, the main strategic priorities should remain the same, but they should be strengthened and complemented by external action that projects them at international level more effectively.

Against this background, the objectives for the next cycle of the Lisbon Strategy should be the following. First, to improve the implementation and the horizontal coordination focusing on the following strategic priorities: fighting climate change and ensuring a sustainable energy and environmental model; improving the framework conditions for enterprises and entrepreneurship, taking better advantage of the European single market and the external markets; strengthening the triangle of knowledge – innovation, research and education – as an engine for growth, employment and prosperity; improving social policies in order to support people moving to new jobs and to strengthen social inclusion and sustainable social protection; and improving the coordination of macroeconomic policies for sustainable growth. These strategic priorities should be used to improve horizontal coordination and the consistency of the integrated guidelines for growth and jobs. Second, we must strengthen the implementation at territorial level. Third, we must develop the implementation at international level and draw the implications for the external action of the European Union. Fourth, we must improve governance and the instruments for implementation.

C.1   SUSTAINABLE ENERGY AND ENVIRONMENT

Current climate trends are causing major changes in production and consumption patterns and a major redeployment of the industrial base. The central concern with sustainable development and growth can be turned into a major opportunity if Europe is able to strengthen its lead in the new industrial revolution towards high-knowledge and low-carbon economies that is currently under way. In this context, the key priorities of the European energy plan should be swiftly implemented, notably: to increase energy efficiency; to complete the single market for energy; to adopt the framework directive for renewable energies; to spread the new energy technologies; to promote greening tax incentives; and to prepare the new UN Framework Convention on climate change in order to create a level playing field at international level. What is at stake is to turn this new industrial revolution into new opportunities for growth and jobs. A new wave of innovation is required to address climate change.

C.2 IMPROVING THE FRAMEWORK CONDITIONS FOR ENTERPRISES AND ENTREPRENEURSHIP

Europe should focus more on the opportunities for growth and jobs that are generated by globalization. These opportunities are to be found in both internal and external markets. This means that the competitive challenge for Europe should have a double dimension: increasing attractiveness and global competitiveness. Europe's attractiveness is based on a set of comparative advantages which should be strengthened: the size of the European single market, the performance of infrastructure, the sophistication of consumers, the quality of public services and the dynamism of its regional structures. This requires the single market agenda to be updated in order to: complete the integration of the single market, notably in services and network industries, improving the quality of life of consumers and citizens; ensure better regulation; pursue the modernization of public services; use standards and public procurement as leverage for a high-knowledge and low-carbon economy; and promote regional development and regional attractiveness.

The comparative advantages for global competitiveness are also changing. The international division of labour is changing, differentiating nations not by products and services but mainly by the tasks they perform in emerging global production chains. The comparative advantages of Europe in these global chains are design expertise and product engineering, environmental technologies, the qualifications and creativity of European workers, and the strategic capacity to organize these global chains.

The review of industrial policy should aim to strengthen these comparative advantages, by improving the framework conditions and fostering cooperation involving big companies and small and medium-sized enterprises (SMEs). At the European level, the high-level group for each industry should be connected: downstream, to the lead markets and the general clusters which are required in this industry; and upstream, to the technology platforms and the human resources panels that identify the research and the skill needs of this industry. Better connections between all these instruments are necessary in order to improve the critical competitiveness factors.

Supporting the European companies in the globalized economy also requires external action by the Union that is more comprehensive. Thus: trade policy should address the issues of trade, investment, intellectual property rights (IPR), public procurement and competition to promote the mutual opening-up of markets within the multilateral and bilateral frameworks; a regulatory convergence should be promoted for better standards in the social, environmental and intellectual property fields; international cooperation should be more focused on capacity-building to raise these standards. The European single market can also be used as a powerful global standard-setter.

C.3   STRENGTHENING THE TRIANGLE OF KNOWLEDGE FOR GROWTH, EMPLOYMENT AND PROSPERITY

Regarding innovation, the comprehensive agenda recently adopted should be implemented at both European and national levels, putting a strong emphasis on a systemic and a demand-led approach. There should also be a stronger focus on new market opportunities mobilizing and connecting all the existing instruments, notably: the technology platforms, which identify the research agenda; the human resources panels, which identify skills needs; the high-level groups for industrial policy, which focus on the critical competitive factors; and the European network of clusters, which mobilize resources for innovation. The combination of all these instruments should provide a central engine for growth and jobs.

At the national level, it is crucial to develop innovation policy as a catalyst for the transition to a knowledge-intensive economy. There is a critical path: to use the European agenda as leverage to strengthen this strategic goal in the national agenda; to spread a richer concept of innovation, taking into account its different dimensions, technological and organizational, in processes or in products and services, based on science or in learning-by-doing, using or interacting; to highlight the implications of the innovation system approach for the coordination of policies; to define the priority areas of an innovation policy and prepare a toolbox of operational measures; to open the access to this toolbox in order to support innovating projects and companies whatever their sector; to focus on some clusters in order to illustrate the advantages of developing partnerships for innovation, as a good practice which can be followed by other clusters; to dynamize the national innovation system, by focusing on the missions and the interactions among its bodies, including the flexibility of labour markets; to reform public management with implications for innovation; to spread skills for innovation and to train innovation managers; and last but not least, to improve governance for innovation, by improving the internal coordination of governments and their relevant public departments, creating public awareness, and developing specific consultation and participation mechanisms with the civil society.

In the meantime, the effort to strengthen the scientific potential of Europe in forefront areas remains critical to renew the growth base and must be increased by: fostering the training of human resources for science and technology; creating a European labour market for researchers and attracting more people, from Europe and abroad, to research careers; and developing the European research area, opening up national programmes and infrastructure.

European competitiveness will also increasingly depend on creativity and on attracting talented people. Hence, a particular attention should also be given to the development of the creative industries for their direct contribution to growth and jobs and also for the competitiveness of many other sectors.

Developing lifelong learning with general access, quality and relevance should be envisaged as a central priority to achieve the Lisbon goals of a competitive knowledge economy with social inclusion. This means aiming to: generalize preschooling education as a main asset for the cognitive development of children; spread new key competences in primary education; reduce the drop-out rate in secondary education, allowing for the diversification of choice; raise access and excellence in higher education, which implies governance and funding reforms; encourage the choice of vocational and educational training, providing vocational guidance and keeping open pathways; develop adult learning, with learning organizations, interfaces with labour market policies, and new financial arrangements.

Moreover, the search for excellence in lifelong learning should be strongly encouraged: designing tailor-made learning environments for each learning project; involving education and training in clusters and technology platforms; simulating competition and diversification of universities; using the European Institute of Technologies (EIT) as leverage for the modernization of universities; and increasing the attractiveness of Europe for international mobility and developing a new model of brain circulation.

The framework conditions for lifelong learning should also be strengthened by: developing the infrastructure for e-learning; developing the European infrastructure for skills needs identification; broadening access to vocational guidance; spreading the standardization of qualifications by levels and competence modules (the Bologna Process; the European Qualifications Framework, EQF; and the European Qualifications for Vocational Education and Training, EQVET) to facilitate mobility; and encouraging working time management and family support services to facilitate access to lifelong learning.

Finally, much will depend on the capacity to develop new financial instruments for education and training, which involves: establishing more effective measures and projects using the structural funds; local arrangements for preschooling education and secondary drop-outs; fees, scholarships and private investment for higher education, including mobility; sectoral funds, labour contract provisions, learning accounts and vouchers for adult learning; European Investment Bank (EIB) and private investment for partnerships for innovation and skills; and a European credit system for lifelong learning.

C.4   IMPROVING SOCIAL POLICIES FOR JOB MOBILITY, SOCIAL INCLUSION AND SUSTAINABLE SOCIAL PROTECTION

The structure of employment is undergoing a major redeployment towards new activities, due to the new context created by the transition to a knowledge-intensive economy and a low-carbon economy, the process of integration in Europe, and as a result of faster globalization with emerging economies that are competing across the board. At the same time, the structure of the labour force is also undergoing a major recomposition due to ageing, immigration flows, education trends and the emergence of new family types.

According to the Lisbon goals, we need to improve our policy mix in order to create more and better jobs, combining stronger competitiveness with social cohesion. In this context, stronger priority should be given to the political orientations which can address these challenges by enhancing both competitiveness and social cohesion at the same time. Such is notably the case of the following orientations: developing skills by raising the education levels and spreading access to lifelong learning, with a particular focus on activities that create more and better jobs; developing family-friendly policies to harmonize working and family life over the life cycle; spreading active ageing with later and flexible retirement and ensuring adequate, adaptable and sustainable pensions; developing flexicurity labour markets for all, using internal and external flexibility and encouraging social dialogue; promoting active inclusion with active labour market policies, minimum income support, and better access to social services; and strengthening the external action of the Union to promote jobs, improve global social standards and managing migrations.

C.5 IMPROVING MACROECONOMIC POLICY COORDINATION FOR SUSTAINABLE GROWTH

The Lisbon Strategy and the Stability and Growth Pact (SGP) should be combined better to improve the prospects for growth and job creation in context of macroeconomic stability. It is possible to develop a more positive synergy: on the one hand, structural reforms are crucial to increase the growth potential and, if the growth rate increases, it will be easier to comply with the public deficit and public debt criteria. On the other hand, macroeconomic policies can contribute to sustainable growth in three different ways: first, by creating conditions of macroeconomic stability, which facilitate decisions about investment and consumption; second, by providing incentives to positive behaviours such as innovative investment in companies or lifelong learning in adult people; and third, by increasing productive factors accumulation and growth potential when redirecting public expenditure towards education and training, research and development (R&D) and important infrastructure.

In light of the above, there should be some fine-tuning of macroeconomic policies with a focus on three main points (already covered by the reviewed SGP), namely: more emphasis on the control of the long-term sustainability of the public debt, taking into account the central problem of the sustainability of the social protection systems; redirecting public expenditure towards key priorities of public investment that aim to increase growth potential (education and training, R&D, innovation and advanced infrastructure, for example); and complying with prior commitments to reduce the public deficit, defining trajectories which take into account the objectives of the two first areas. These objectives should be taken into account when assessing the public deficit and the public debt. The SGP should provide clearer incentives for the implementation of the Lisbon Agenda.

The fine-tuning of the macroeconomic policies should be underpinned by further technical developments in the definition of indicators concerning the sustainability and the quality of the public finances at both the national and European levels. Against this background, special attention should be paid to the modernization of public services and public expenditure in research, innovation and education. Moreover, the aggregate effect of these reorientations should be managed by the eurozone in order to raise the growth rate in Europe.

C.6 FOSTERING IMPLEMENTATION AT THE TERRITORIAL LEVEL

The implementation of the Lisbon Agenda should now be translated fully at territorial level by taking advantage of territorial specificities and ensuring the full use of the endogenous resources; developing stronger European and global territorial networks; enabling cities and metropolitan areas to become main hubs of innovation and creativity; and strongly linking the structural funds with the Lisbon goals.

C.7 DEVELOPING IMPLEMENTATION AT THE EXTERNAL LEVEL

The EU has an ambitious economic, social and environmental agenda for sustainable development, but it cannot achieve this alone. It needs the support of an international convergence in a similar direction to avoid a 'race to the bottom', to create win–win games, and cooperation to solve shared global challenges. This should be the one of the main goals of, and more systematically integrated into, the new generation of external policies of the European Union for 2009–12, when defining partnership agreements with third countries. As it redesigns that policy, Union external action should adopt a broader approach, combining the Common Foreign and Security Policy (CFSP), trade and cooperation policies and the external projection of the internal policies of the Union. This means that the external action of the EU should also take on board the external dimension of policies such as research, environment, education and employment. There is also a new generation of EU cooperation programmes being prepared, based on the new political orientations defined by the 'European Consensus'. And a new approach is being developed in trade policy in connection with the Lisbon Agenda, which aims to prepare Europe for globalization using trade combined with basic standards, as well as internal markets as a major lever for growth and more and better jobs.

A new approach should be developed for a strategic dialogue between partner countries in a globalized world in order to ensure better use of all these instruments of external action. We are assuming that the most effective method for this strategic dialogue includes a debate about: first, the common challenges we face as global partners; second, development strategies and some implications for internal policies to meet these challenges; third, new ways to cooperate to build capacity to spread better standards; fourth, the implications of the previous themes for external policies, and global standards and governance; and last, establishing win–win games to develop the strategic partnership.

This dialogue can also be supported by a more systematic identification of all the initiatives of international cooperation between the EU and its partner countries in the fields covered by the Lisbon Agenda, notably: science and technology, markets, entrepreneurship and innovation, environment and energy, education and training, and employment and social affairs.

C.8 IMPROVING GOVERNANCE AND INSTRUMENTS FOR IMPLEMENTATION

Improving governance will also be central for the development of the Lisbon Agenda. The following list presents ten key priorities in that context:

1. Identify clearly the European and national toolbox for each policy, and its better use by each policy.
2. Improve the implementation of existing instruments by each council of ministers formation and their respective committees and groups, for better European and national articulation; identify the toolbox available for each Council formation. In this context: define a general road map for the application of these tools; improve the committees' support work to the Council; and improve the peer review methods regarding the implementation at national level.
3. Improve the implementation of the guidelines and the common objectives taking advantage of the techniques used by the open method of coordination (OMC). Thus: improve the consistency between the reporting and the guidelines; define indicators and deadlines regarding the main objectives and invite the Member States to define specific ambitious, but realistic targets in their particular case; develop a more intelligent benchmarking, putting good practices in the right context, using progression indicators, developing rankings regarding each Member State capacity to evolve towards the targets set for each of them; improve the monitoring and evaluation process by focusing on the country-specific recommendations; and improve the learning process based on thematic workshops and databases on good practice.
4. Improve the articulation between the relevant Council formations by developing the regular interfaces between its committees or trios based on concrete issues.
5. Improve the action and articulation of the national Lisbon Strategy coordinators by promoting a more in-depth sharing of experiences

between these coordinators; by improving horizontal coordination at national government and at the European Commission level; and by defining a clearer standardization of national programmes and its annual reports in order to underline the progress obtained and the respective responsibilities.

6. Develop the role of the European Parliament and national parliaments.

7. Identify methods to improve the participation and mobilization of civil society and social partners: improve the role of the tripartite summits and of the macroeconomic dialogue; support the role of the European Economic and Social Committee and of its network with the national economic and social councils; support the adaptation of the Lisbon Strategy to the specific target groups; and develop various types of partnership to implement projects.

8. Improve communication instruments on the Lisbon Strategy in order to involve different types of actors (civil servants, opinion-makers, civil society partners, young people, and citizens in general).

9. Develop the methods for a better territorial implementation and support the initiatives adopted by the Committee of Regions.

10. Modernize public administration to enhance its proactive role in the coordination and implementation of this Agenda.

Last, but not least, the Lisbon Treaty can open new paths to improve governance by enhancing the leadership of the process, strengthening European instruments, improving the coordination of national policies, developing the external policies of the Union and exploring differentiation. But the future may always surprise us. At the time of writing, the ratification of the Lisbon Reform Treaty has still not been completed by all Member States.

Furthermore, the global financial crisis leading to a recession calls for urgent responses that should be harmonized within the broader and longer-term Lisbon Agenda framework. This is a matter for another book.

Appendix 1: Integrated Guidelines for Growth and Jobs (2008–2010), December 2007

 COMMISSION OF THE EUROPEAN COMMUNITIES

Brussels, 11.12.2007
COM(2007) 803 final
PART V

**COMMUNICATION FROM THE COMMISSION TO
THE SPRING EUROPEAN COUNCIL**

**INTEGRATED GUIDELINES FOR GROWTH AND JOBS
(2008-2010)**

including a

COMMISSION RECOMMENDATION

**on the broad guidelines for the economic policies of
the Member States and the Community
(under Article 99 of the EC Treaty)**

and a

Proposal for a

COUNCIL DECISION

**on guidelines for the employment policies of the Member States (under Article 128 of the
EC Treaty)**

(presented by the Commission)

TABLE OF CONTENTS

EXPLANATORY MEMORANDUM

In the Spring Council in 2005, Heads of State and Government renewed the Lisbon Strategy and placed its focus on growth and jobs. They organised the Lisbon Strategy around three-year cycles, whilst strengthening ownership and accountability by clearly distinguishing between reforms which should be undertaken by Member States and those for which the Community should take the lead. As one of the instruments to implement the Strategy, the Council approved a set of integrated guidelines and adopted the necessary legal instruments based on Articles 99 and 128 of the Treaty. These guidelines are meant to guide Member States, as they implement national reforms, through their National Reform Programmes (NRP). The integrated guidelines will expire at the end of the first three-year cycle, and will therefore need to be renewed for the next cycle. The re-launch of the Lisbon Strategy in Spring 2005 put Europe back on track to create sustainable growth and jobs.

During the first cycle of the renewed Lisbon Strategy (2005-2008) Member States have stepped up the implementation of structural reforms, although the pace and intensity differs between them. Whilst most of the upturn of the EU economy is due to cyclical factors, Lisbon-type reforms have helped increase the growth potential of Member States' economies. They have also helped to make the European economy more resilient in dealing with external shocks, such as higher energy and commodity prices and currency fluctuations. Further integration of Member States economies and alignment of business cycles, especially in the euro area, will allow for a monetary policy geared better to Member States needs.

Viewed as a whole, therefore, the strategy has helped to speed up the pace of reform, helping Member States to implement sometimes difficult but necessary change to address the challenges of globalisation. The new governance of the Lisbon Strategy, with its emphasis on partnership between the European and the Member States level, has proved its worth. An independent evaluation of the Integrated Guidelines concluded that they constitute a comprehensive and open framework which accommodates the essential policy developments related to growth and employment in Europe. The evaluation also concluded that stakeholders wish to focus on implementation, as the guidelines remain relevant. The integrated guidelines, hence, are fulfilling their role and thus do not require revision.

However, more remains to be done to prepare the EU and its Member States for globalisation and to strengthen the foundations for economic success in the medium- to longer term. At the same time they need to keep pace with fast changing social realities (longer working lives, increasingly diverse family structures, new patterns of mobility and diversity). The EU must better adapt its existing policies and instruments, but also build upon new policies such as the Globalisation Adjustment Fund, in order to better respond to the legitimate concerns of people adversely affected by changes in trade patterns and by economic and social change. The goal of making the EU a dynamic, competitive, knowledge based society remains essential. Within this framework, an even higher priority needs to be given to the social dimension, flexicurity policies, energy and climate change and to education and skills as elements to modernise European markets, promote innovation and ensure new opportunities for citizens in a knowledge society. The Lisbon toolbox is already bringing the different strands of policy together to offer a more comprehensive vision of how the EU and Member States can work in harness to tackle the complex issues facing Europe today. The common objective during the next cycle should be to use the Lisbon instruments, including the country-specific recommendations as adopted by Council in 2007 linked to the integrated guidelines, to full effect in order to speed up the effective delivery of outstanding reforms.

The integrated guidelines for the period 2008-2010 are presented in one comprehensive document with two parts:

Part 1 – The Broad Economic Policy Guidelines

Section A deals with the contribution that macroeconomic policies can make in this respect. Section B focuses on the measures and policies that the Union and the Member States must carry out in order to make Europe a more attractive place to invest and work and to boost knowledge and innovation for growth.

Part 2 – The Employment Guidelines

This part of the integrated guidelines includes the proposal for a Council decision on the Employment Guidelines, on which the European Parliament, the European Social and Economic Committee and the Committee of the Regions will be consulted, in accordance with Article 128 of the Treaty.

For Member States both economic, and employment policy, are a matter of common concern (Articles 99 and 126). For the purpose of multilateral surveillance and to ensure closer cooperation of economic and employment policies, Member States report on measures taken under these guidelines through National Reform Programmes (and Annual Implementation Reports). Based on these reports, where it is established that the economic or employment policies of a Member State are not consistent with the Integrated Guidelines, the Council may, using the possibilities under Articles 99 and 128, make recommendations to the Member State concerned.

THE STATE OF THE EU ECONOMY

Economic conditions have been favourable since 2005 when the Lisbon Growth and Jobs Strategy was re-launched, although recent months have witnessed growing downside risks. Growth picked up to almost 3% in 2007, increasingly driven by domestic demand and leaving Europe better placed to cope with adverse external shocks. However, recent financial turmoil and the slowdown of the US economy have substantially increased the risks to the downside, and the outlook for 2008-2009 indicates a deceleration in growth. Tighter financial conditions will take their toll on investment growth, in particular of construction investment, while the good performance of the labour market will support private consumption growth. While most of the recent upturn is cyclical in nature, there is some evidence of a structural component linked to past reforms enacted by EU Member States. Structural improvements have been most evident in labour markets, with the unemployment rate declining to below 7% and the employment rate approaching 65%, with particular strong increases recorded amongst women and older workers. Since mid-2005, productivity growth in the EU has picked up and while most of the acceleration in productivity growth can be attributed to cyclical factors, it does seem that the decade long decline in trend productivity growth has been interrupted. It is encouraging that job creation and productivity improvements have occurred simultaneously for the first time in a decade.

Notwithstanding the favourable developments over recent years, the recent international turbulences call for action to increase the resilience of the economy and to use the existing scope to improve both labour utilisation and labour productivity. In some countries, unfortunately, reform seems to be slowing down. The EU's employment rate has remained low relative to our competitors. Moreover, the rate of unemployment, especially of long-term nature and amongst young people, remains far too high. While many manufacturing enterprises have been sufficiently productive to withstand international competition, productivity growth in several service sectors has stalled. Looking forward the economic and budgetary impact of ageing populations is fast approaching, with the large baby boom cohorts coming towards retirement in many countries. This makes it imperative to reduce public debt at an accelerated pace and to modernise pension and health care systems. An emerging challenge is also to improve capacity of the financial system to respond to shocks in 2007.

Financial market transparency, effective competition rules and appropriate regulation and supervision will continue to be crucial for both confidence and performance. As will be social partner enabled wage developments compatible with employment growth and macroeconomic stability.

The EU now has an opportunity to pursue, even accelerate, structural reform efforts. The policy challenge is to avoid complacency and to continue addressing the structural weaknesses that are still holding back job creation, innovative activity, the adoption of technological progress, and limit the EU capacity to respond to international shocks. At the same time, there is a need to pursue macroeconomic policies that succeed in ensuring stability, containing inflationary pressures and reducing public budget deficits.

INTEGRATED GUIDELINES FOR GROWTH AND JOBS (2008-2010)

Macroeconomic guidelines

(1) To secure economic stability for sustainable growth.

(2) To safeguard economic and financial sustainability as a basis for increased employment.

(3) To promote a growth and employment orientated efficient allocation of resources.

(4) To ensure that wage developments contribute to macroeconomic stability and growth.

(5) To promote greater coherence between macroeconomic, structural and employment policies.

(6) To contribute to a dynamic and well-functioning EMU.

Microeconomic guidelines

(7) To increase and improve investment in R&D, in particular by private business.

(8) To facilitate all forms of innovation.

(9) To facilitate the spread and effective use of ICT and build a fully inclusive information society.

(10) To strengthen the competitive advantages of its industrial base.

(11) To encourage the sustainable use of resources and strengthen the synergies between environmental protection and growth.

(12) To extend and deepen the internal market.

(13) To ensure open and competitive markets inside and outside Europe and to reap the benefits of globalisation.

(14) To create a more competitive business environment and encourage private initiative through better regulation.

(15) To promote a more entrepreneurial culture and create a supportive environment for SMEs.

(16)   To expand, improve and link up European infrastructure and complete priority cross-border projects.

Employment guidelines

(17)   Implement employment policies aimed at achieving full employment, improving quality and productivity at work, and strengthening social and territorial cohesion.

(18)   Promote a lifecycle approach to work.

(19)   Ensure inclusive labour markets, enhance work attractiveness, and make work pay for job seekers, including disadvantaged people and the inactive.

(20)   Improve matching of labour market needs.

(21)   Promote flexibility combined with employment security and reduce labour market segmentation, having due regard to the role of the social partners.

(22)   Ensure employment-friendly labour cost developments and wage setting mechanisms.

(23)   Expand and improve investment in human capital.

(24)   Adapt education and training systems in response to new competence requirements.

*

*   *

Consequently, the Commission:

– recommends the following broad guidelines for the economic policies of the Member States and the Community, in accordance with Article 99(2) of the EC Treaty, and

– proposes the following Council Decision on guidelines for the employment policies of the Member States, in accordance with Article 128(2) of the EC Treaty.

Part 1

Commission Recommendation on the
Broad Economic Policy Guidelines (2005-2008)

COMMISSION RECOMMENDATION

on the broad guidelines for the economic policies of the Member States and the Community

Section A – Macroeconomic Policies for Growth and Jobs

A.1   Macroeconomic policies creating the conditions for more growth and jobs

Securing economic stability to raise employment and growth potential

As macroeconomic stability is secured by a sound mix of many economic policies, challenges to stabilisation should be addressed by macroeconomic measures as well as by implementing structural reforms in product, labour and capital markets. Monetary policies can contribute by pursuing price stability and, without prejudice to this objective, by supporting other general economic policies with regard to growth and employment. For new Member States, it will be important that monetary and exchange rate policies contribute towards achieving convergence. Exchange rate regimes constitute an important part of the overall economic and monetary policy framework and should be orientated towards achieving real and sustainable nominal convergence. Participation in ERM II, at an appropriate stage after accession, should help those endeavours.

Securing a sound budgetary position will allow the full and symmetric play of the automatic budgetary stabilisers over the cycle with a view to stabilising output around potential. For those Member States that have already achieved sound budgetary positions, the challenge is to retain that position. For the remaining Member States, it is vital to take all the necessary corrective measures to achieve their medium term budgetary objectives in particular if economic conditions improve, thus avoiding pro-cyclical policies and putting themselves in a position in which sufficient room for the full play of automatic stabilisers over the cycle is ensured prior to the next economic downturn. In particular, an annual fiscal adjustment of 0.5% of GDP as a benchmark (more under cyclically favourable conditions) should be achieved in euro area and ERM II Member States. In line with the 2005 reform of the Stability and Growth Pact, for individual Member States the medium-term budgetary objectives (MTO's) are differentiated according to the diversity of economic and budgetary positions and developments as well as of fiscal risk to the sustainability of public finances, also in the face of prospective demographic changes. Moreover, in accordance with the report on the SGP reform endorsed by the European Council on 22 March 2005, introducing or strengthening national fiscal rules and institutions, including monitoring mechanisms can usefully complement the Pact and support its objectives.

An additional macroeconomic policy challenge for some Member States is to operate in an environment of robust catching up, which is to varying degrees accompanied by external deficits, rapid credit expansion and financial deepening. Fiscal restraint, effective financial supervision and promoting competitiveness are essential in order to contain external and internal imbalances. A cautious fiscal stance is one important way to keep external deficits within the range where sound external financing can be secured. Fiscal restraint can also limit the risk of surging domestic demand causing persistently higher inflation and the occurrence of macro-financial risks which could cause swings in real exchange rates and a protracted loss of competitiveness.

Guideline 1. To secure economic stability for sustainable growth

1. In line with the Stability and Growth Pact, Member States should respect their medium-term budgetary objectives. As long as this objective has not yet been achieved, they should take all the necessary corrective measures to achieve it. Member States should avoid pro-

cyclical fiscal policies. Furthermore, it is necessary that those Member States having an excessive deficit take effective action in order to ensure a prompt correction of excessive deficits.

2. Member States posting current account deficits that risk being unsustainable should work towards correcting them by implementing structural reforms, boosting external competitiveness and, where appropriate, contributing to their correction via fiscal policies. See also integrated guideline 'To contribute to a dynamic and well-functioning EMU' (No 6).

To safeguard economic and fiscal sustainability as a basis for increased employment

Europe's ageing population poses serious risks to the long-term sustainability of the European Union economy in the form of an increased debt burden, lower potential output per capita, due to the reduction in the working age population, and difficulties in financing the pension, social insurance and health care systems. As documented in the Commission's Sustainability Report, a substantial sustainability gap for the EU in aggregate is likely to emerge. Several Member States are exposed to high sustainability risk, and a number of others to medium risk.

Member States should address the economic implications of ageing by, as part of the well established three pronged strategy for tackling the budgetary implications of ageing, pursuing a satisfactory pace of debt reduction and providing incentives to raise employment rates and increase labour supply so as to offset the impact of future declines in the number of persons of working age. In order to accomplish this further budgetary consolidation is necessary, going beyond recent progress, and resulting in the attainment of the MTO's by all Member States. It is also essential to modernise social protection systems so as to ensure that they are financially viable, providing incentives to the working age population to actively participate in the labour market, while at the same time ensuring that they fulfil their goals in terms of access and adequacy. Action on health prevention and promotion would help to increase healthy life years and ensure the sustainability of health care systems. In particular, improved interaction between social protection systems and labour markets can remove distortions and encourage the extension of working lives against a background of increased life expectancy.

Guideline 2. To safeguard economic and fiscal sustainability as a basis for increased employment

Member States should, in view of the projected costs of ageing populations,

1. undertake a satisfactory pace of government debt reduction to strengthen public finances;

2. reform and re-enforce pension, social insurance and health care systems to ensure that they are financially viable, socially adequate and accessible;

3. take measures to increase labour market participation and labour supply especially amongst women, young and older workers, and promote a lifecycle approach to work in order to increase hours worked in the economy.

See also integrated guideline 'Promote a lifecycle approach to work' (Nos 18, and 4, 19, 21).

Promote a growth, employment orientated and efficient allocation of resources

Well-designed tax and expenditure systems that promote an efficient allocation of resources are a necessity for the public sector to make a full contribution towards growth and employment, without jeopardising the goals of economic stability and sustainability. This can be achieved by redirecting expenditure towards growth-enhancing categories such as Research and Development (R&D), physical infrastructure, environmentally friendly technologies, human capital and knowledge. Member States can also help to control other expenditure categories through the use of expenditure rules and performance budgeting and by putting assessment mechanisms in place to ensure that individual reform measures and overall reform packages are well-designed. A key priority for the EU economy is to ensure that tax structures and their interaction with benefit systems promote higher growth through more employment and investment.

Guideline 3. To promote a growth- and employment-orientated and efficient allocation of resources

Member States should, without prejudice to guidelines on economic stability and sustainability, re-direct the composition of public expenditure towards growth-enhancing categories in line with the Lisbon strategy, adapt tax structures to strengthen growth potential, ensure that mechanisms are in place to assess the relationship between public spending and the achievement of policy objectives, and ensure the overall coherence of reform packages.

See also integrated guideline 'To encourage the sustainable use of resources and strengthen the synergies between environmental protection and growth' (No 11).

Ensure that wage developments contribute to growth and stability and complement structural reforms

Wage developments can contribute to stable macroeconomic conditions and an employment friendly policy mix. This requires that real wage increases are in line with the underlying rate of productivity growth over the medium term and are consistent with a rate of profitability that allows for productivity, capacity and employment-enhancing investment. This requires that temporary factors such as variation in productivity caused by cyclical factors or one off rises in the headline rate of inflation do not cause an unsustainable trend in wage growth and that wage developments reflect local labour market conditions. In countries with declining market shares, real wages would need to grow below productivity in order to restore competitiveness. These issues need to be taken into account in the continued dialogue and information exchange between monetary and fiscal authorities and the social partners via the Macroeconomic Dialogue.

Guideline 4. To ensure that wage developments contribute to macroeconomic stability and growth

And to increase adaptability, Member States should encourage the right framework conditions for wage-bargaining systems, while fully respecting the role of the social partners, with a view to promote nominal wage and labour cost developments consistent with price stability and the trend in productivity over the medium term, taking into account differences across skills and local labour market conditions.

See also integrated guideline 'Ensure employment-friendly labour cost developments and wage-setting mechanisms' (No 22).

Promote coherent macroeconomic, structural and employment policies

The role of sound macroeconomic policies is to provide conditions conducive to employment creation and growth. Structural reforms, consistent with sound fiscal positions in the short and medium term, are essential to increase productivity and employment in the medium-term, thus leading to the full realisation and strengthening of growth potential. They also contribute to fiscal sustainability, macroeconomic stability and resilience to shocks. At the same time, appropriate macro-economic policies are key for reaping the full growth and employment benefits of structural reforms. A key feature of Member States' overall economic strategy is to ensure that they have a consistent set of structural policies that support the macroeconomic framework and vice versa. In particular, market reforms need to improve the overall adaptability and adjustment capacity of economies in response to changes in both cyclical economic conditions and longer-term trends such as globalisation and technology. In this regard, reform of tax and benefit systems are important in order to make work pay and avoid any disincentive for labour market participation.

Guideline 5. To promote greater coherence between macroeconomic, structural and employment policies

Member States should pursue labour and product markets reforms that at the same time increases the growth potential and support the macroeconomic framework by increasing flexibility, factor mobility and adjustment capacity in labour and product markets in response to globalisation, technological advances, demand shift, and cyclical changes. In particular, Member States should: renew impetus in tax and benefit reforms to improve incentives and to make work pay; increase adaptability of labour markets combining employment flexibility and security; and improve employability by investing in human capital.

See also integrated guideline 'Promote flexibility combined with employment security and reduce labour market segmentation, having due regard to the role of the social partners' (No 21; No 19).

A.2   Ensuring a dynamic and well-functioning euro area

Since the creation of the euro area almost ten years ago, the euro has embedded economic stability in euro area countries, shielding them from exchange rate turbulence. Subdued growth performance and persistent divergences in growth and inflation raise questions as to whether internal adjustment in the euro area is working smoothly, suggesting that economic policies and governance structures may not yet have fully adjusted to draw the full benefit from the monetary union. Since euro-area countries can no longer make independent use of monetary or exchange rate policies, [further] reforms are key to develop alternative mechanisms to help their economies adjust to economic shocks and competitiveness challenges.

The policy mix in the euro area needs to support economic growth while safeguarding long-term sustainability and stability. At the current juncture, it is important that the policy mix underpins confidence among consumers and investors, which also implies commitment to medium-term stability. Budgetary policy has to ensure a fiscal position which can support price stability, and is consistent with the need to prepare for the impact of ageing populations on the one hand and to accomplish a composition of public expenditure and revenues that fosters economic growth on the other. Euro-area Member States committed accelerate adjustment towards the MTO so that most of them would achieve their MTOs in 2008 or 2009 and all of them should aim for 2010 at the latest. Due to the high share of the public sector in economic activity in the euro area, the quality of public finances has a considerable influence on economic performance. Therefore, it is crucial that resources are spent in a growth-supportive manner and distortions arising from the financing of public activity are minimised. Comprehensive structural reforms will allow the euro area to raise its growth potential over time and ensure that stronger growth does not build up potential for higher inflation. Reforms catering for more adaptable labour markets, more competition on product markets and deeper financial market integration accompanied by growth and stability-oriented macroeconomic policies are particularly salient for euro area Member States as they have an important impact on their capacity to adequately adjust to shocks.

To contribute to international economic stability and better represent its economic interests, it is critical for the euro area to play its full role in international monetary and economic policy cooperation. While the appointment of a Eurogroup President for a two-year term of office as of 2005 has brought greater stability to the external representation of the euro area, further steps are needed to improve the external representation of the euro area, so that the euro area can take a leading strategic role in the development of the global economic system that is commensurate with its economic weight.

Spill-over effects are most powerful and the need for a common agenda is strongest in the euro area. Sharing a common currency and a common monetary policy offers an extra dimension to coordination that could strengthen the role of the euro area in delivering growth and jobs for the whole EU. The Commission will present a comprehensive review of the functioning of EMU to mark its tenth anniversary, with ideas on how policies, coordination and governance can help the euro area to work to best effect.

Guideline 6. To contribute to a dynamic and well-functioning EMU, euro area Member States need to ensure better co-ordination of their economic and budgetary policies, in particular:

1. pay particular attention to fiscal sustainability of their public finances in full compliance with the Stability and Growth Pact;

2. contribute to a policy mix that supports economic recovery and is compatible with price stability, and thereby enhances confidence among business and consumers in the short run, while being compatible with long term sustainable growth;

3. press forward with structural reforms that will increase euro area long-term potential growth and will improve its productivity, competitiveness and economic adjustment to asymmetric shocks, paying particular attention to employment policies; and

4. ensure that the euro area's influence in the global economic system is commensurate with its economic weight.

Section B – Microeconomic reforms to raise Europe's growth potential

Structural reforms are essential to increase the EU's growth potential and support macroeconomic stability, because they increase the efficiency and adaptability of the European economy. Productivity gains are fuelled by competition, investment and innovation. Raising Europe's growth potential requires making progress in both job creation and productivity growth. After lagging US productivity growth for more than a decade, productivity growth in the EU has accelerated since mid-2005. Sustaining this improvement is a major challenge facing the Union, especially in the light of its ageing population. Population ageing alone is estimated to reduce by nearly half the current rate of potential growth. A continuation of the productivity upswing, and increasing the hours worked are thus indispensable to maintain and increase future living standards, and to ensure a high level of social protection.

B.1 Knowledge and innovation — engines of sustainable growth

Knowledge accumulated through investment in R&D, innovation, education and life long learning, is a key driver of long-run growth. Policies aimed at increasing investment in knowledge and strengthening the innovation capacity of the EU economy are at the heart of the Lisbon strategy for growth and employment. This is why national and regional programmes for the period 2007-2013 have been increasingly targeted on investments in these fields in accordance with the Lisbon objectives.

Increase and improve investment in R&D, with a view to establishing the European Knowledge Area

A high level of R&D is crucial for our future competitiveness. R&D affects economic growth through various channels: first, it can contribute to the creation of new markets or production processes; second, it can lead to incremental improvements in already existing products and production processes; and third, it increases the capacity of a country to absorb new technologies.

The EU is currently spending about 1.85% of GDP on R&D (although ranging from below 0.5% to nearly 4% of GDP across Member States). The level of R&D spending has remained slightly decreased since 2000. Moreover, only around 55% of research spending in the EU is financed by the business sector. Low levels of private R&D investments are identified as one of the main explanations for the EU/US innovation gap. More rapid progress towards establishing the European Research Area, including meeting the collective EU target of raising research investment to 3% of GDP is needed. Member States are invited to report on their R&D expenditure targets for 2010 and the measures to achieve these in their National Reform programmes and the annual Progress Reports paying attention in particular to integrating the European dimension within their national R&D policies. The main challenge is to put in place framework conditions, instruments and incentives for companies to invest more in research.

Public research expenditure must be made more effective and the links between public research and the private sector have to be improved. Poles and networks of excellence should be strengthened, better overall use should be made of public support mechanisms to boost private sector innovation, and a better leverage effect of public investments and a modernised management of research institutions and universities should be ensured. It is also essential to ensure that companies operate in a competitive environment since competition provides an important incentive to private spending on innovation. In addition, a determined effort must be made to increase the number and quality of researchers active in Europe, in particular by attracting more students into scientific, technical and engineering disciplines, and enhancing the career development and the transnational and intersectoral mobility of researchers, and reducing barriers to mobility of researchers and students. The international dimension of R&D should be strengthened in terms of joint financing, development of a more critical mass at the EU level in critical areas requiring large funds and through reducing barriers to mobility of researchers and students.

Guideline 7. To increase and improve investment in R&D, in particular by private business, the overall objective for 2010 of 3% of GDP is confirmed with an adequate split between private and public investment, Member States will define specific intermediate levels. Member States should further develop a mix of measures appropriate to foster R&D, in particular business R&D, through:

1. improved framework conditions and ensuring that companies operate in a sufficiently competitive and attractive environment;

2. more effective and efficient public expenditure on R&D and developing PPPs;

3. developing and strengthening centres of excellence of educational and research institutions in Member States, as well as creating new ones where appropriate, and improving the cooperation and transfer of technologies between public research institute and private enterprises;

4. developing and making better use of incentives to leverage private R&D;

5. modernising the management of research institutions and universities;

6. ensuring a sufficient supply of qualified researchers by attracting more students into scientific, technical and engineering disciplines and enhancing the career development and the European, international as well as inter-sectoral mobility of researchers and development personnel.

Facilitate innovation

The dynamism of the European economy is dependent on its innovative capacity. The economic framework conditions for innovation need to be in place. This implies well-functioning financial and product markets as well as efficient and affordable means to enforce intellectual property rights. Innovations are often introduced to the market by new enterprises, which may meet particular difficulties in obtaining finance. Measures to encourage the creation and growth of innovative enterprises, including improving access to finance, should therefore enhance innovative activity.[1] Technology diffusion, and policies to better integrate national innovation and education systems, can be fostered by the development of innovation

---

[1]   The EU's broad based innovation strategy therefore addresses intellectual property rights, standardisation, the use of public procurement to stimulate innovation, joint technology initiatives, boosting innovation in lead markets, such as cooperation between higher education, research and business, encouraging innovation in regions, innovation in services and non-technological innovation, and improving businesses' access to risk capital.

poles and networks as well as by innovation support services targeted at SMEs. Knowledge transfer via researcher mobility, foreign direct investment (FDI) or imported technology is particularly beneficial for lagging countries and regions. It is also crucial to strengthen further the integration of the knowledge triangle of R&D, education and innovation.

The EU's broad based innovation strategy therefore addresses intellectual property rights, standardisation, the use of public procurement to stimulate innovation, joint technology initiatives, boosting innovation in lead markets, cooperation between higher education, research and business, encouraging innovation in regions, innovation in services and non-technological innovation, and improving businesses' access to risk capital.

It is now imperative to deliver a unitary, affordable Community patent, set up an EU-wide jurisdictional system for patent litigation and facilitate the enforcement of intellectual property rights in the Internal Market.

Guideline 8. To facilitate all forms of innovation, Member States should focus on:

1. improvements in innovation support services, in particular for dissemination and technology transfer;

2. the creation and development of innovation poles, networks and incubators bringing together universities, research institutions and enterprises, including at regional and local level, helping to bridge the technology gap between regions;

3. the encouragement of cross-border knowledge transfer, including from foreign direct investment;

4. encouraging public procurement of innovative products and services;

5. better access to domestic and international finance;

6. efficient and affordable means to enforce intellectual property rights.

The diffusion of information and communication technologies (ICT), in line with the objectives and actions of the i2010 initiative, is also an important way to improve productivity and, consequently, economic growth. The EU has been unable to reap the full benefits of the information and communication technologies (ICT), due especially to the continuing under-investment in ICT, organisational innovation and in digital skills. Wider and more effective use of ICT and the establishment of seamless Single Market in electronic communication services are essential for the future competitiveness of European businesses. It is also important to reduce and prevent fragmentation of the 'e-Internal Market' by putting in place interoperable e-services between the Member States.

Guideline 9. To facilitate the spread and effective use of ICT and build a fully inclusive information society, Member States should:

1. encourage the widespread use of ICT in public services, SMEs and households;

2. fix the necessary framework for the related changes in the organisation of work in the economy;

3. promote a strong European industrial presence in the key segments of ICT;

4. encourage the development of strong ICT and content industries, and well-functioning markets;

5. ensure the security of networks and information, as well as convergence and interoperability in order to establish an information area without frontiers;

6. encourage the deployment of broad band networks, including for the poorly served regions, in order to develop the knowledge economy.

See also integrated guideline 'Promote flexibility combined with employment security and reduce labour market segmentation, having due regard to the role of the social partners' (No 21).

To strengthen the competitive advantages of the European industrial base

A strong industrial base is of key importance for Europe's economy. The competitiveness of the EU depends on the ability of the economy to reorient activities towards sectors with higher productivity. An approach where innovation, employment, regional and other policies are integrated, supports upgrading the EU industrial base.

In order to enhance and sustain economic and technological leadership, Europe must increase its capacity to develop and market new technologies, including ICT and environmental technologies. The synergies from jointly addressing research, regulatory and financing challenges at the European level, where for reasons of scale or scope individual Member States cannot successfully tackle market failures in isolation, should be analysed and exploited. The EU has still not managed to fully realise its technological potential. The pooling of European excellence and the development of public-private partnerships and cooperation between Member States where the benefits for society are larger than those for the private sector will help tap this potential.

Guideline 10. To strengthen the competitive advantages of its industrial base, Europe needs a solid industrial fabric throughout its territory. The necessary pursuit of a modern and active industrial policy means strengthening the competitive advantages of the industrial base, including by contributing to attractive framework conditions for both manufacturing and services, while ensuring the complementarity of the action at national, transnational and European level. Member States should:

1. start by identifying the added value and competitiveness factors in key industrial sectors, and addressing the challenges of globalisation;

2. also focus on the development of new technologies and markets:

(a) this implies in particular commitment to promote new technological initiatives based on public private partnerships and cooperation between Member States, that help tackle genuine market failures;

(b) this also implies the creation and development of networks of regional or local clusters across the EU with greater involvement of SMEs.

See also integrated guideline 'Improve matching of labour market needs' (No 20).

Encourage the sustainable use of resources

Lasting success for the Union also depends on addressing a range of resource and environmental challenges which, if left unchecked, will act as a brake on future growth. Recent developments have emphasised the importance of energy efficiency and reducing the vulnerability of the European economy to oil prices variations. An integrated approach to climate and energy policy is needed to increase the security of supply, ensure the competitiveness of the EU economy and the availability of affordable energy, and combat climate change. Member States and the Community must both contribute to achieving the EU targets of at least a 20% reduction in greenhouse gas emissions, a 20% share of renewable energies as well as a 20% improvement in energy efficiency by 2020. Member States should continue the fight against climate change in order that the global temperature increase does not exceed 2°C above pre-industrial levels, and implementing the Kyoto targets in a cost-effective way. Member States should halt the loss of biological diversity between now and 2010, in particular by incorporating this requirement into other policies, given the importance of biodiversity for certain economic sectors. The use of market-based instruments, so that prices better reflect environmental damage and social costs, plays a key role in this context. Encouraging the development and use of environment-friendly technologies, the greening of public procurement with particular attention to SMEs, and the removal of environmentally harmful subsidies alongside other policy instruments can improve innovative performance and enhance the contribution to sustainable development. For example, EU companies are amongst the world leaders in developing new renewable energy technologies. In a context of continued upward pressure on energy prices, and accumulating threats to the climate, it is important to push energy efficiency improvements as a contribution to both growth and sustainable development.

Guideline 11. To encourage the sustainable use of resources and strengthen the synergies between environmental protection and growth, Member States should:

1. give priority to energy efficiency and co-generation, the development of sustainable, including renewable, energies and the rapid spread of environmentally friendly and eco-efficient technologies, (a) inside the internal market on the one hand particularly in transport and energy, *inter alia*, in order to reduce the vulnerability of the European economy to oil price variations, and (b) towards the rest of the world on the other hand as a sector with a considerable export potential;

2. promote the development of means of internalisation of external environmental costs and decoupling of economic growth from environmental degradations. The implementation of these priorities should be in line with existing Community legislation and with the actions and instruments proposed in the Environmental Technologies Action Plan (ETAP), *inter alia,* through, (a) the use of market based instruments, (b) risk funds and R & D funding, (c) the promotion of sustainable production and consumption patterns including the greening of public procurement, (d) paying particular attention to SMEs, and (e) a reform of subsidies that have considerable negative effects on the environment and are incompatible with sustainable development, with a view to eliminating them gradually;

3. pursue the objective of halting the loss of biological diversity between now and 2010, in particular by incorporating this requirement into other policies, given the importance of biodiversity for certain economic sectors;

4. continue to fight against climate change, while implementing the Kyoto targets in a cost-effective way, particularly in regard to SMEs.

See also integrated guideline 'To promote a growth- and employment-orientated and efficient allocation of resources' (No 3).

B.2   Making Europe a more attractive place to invest and work

The attractiveness of the European Union as an investment location depends, *inter alia*, on the size and openness of its markets, its regulatory environment, the quality of its labour force and its infrastructure.

Extend and deepen the internal market

Whilst the internal market for goods is relatively well integrated, services markets remain, legally or *de facto,* rather fragmented. The complete and timely implementation of the Services Directive will be a significant step towards a fully operational Internal Market for services.The elimination of obstacles through administrative burden reduction to cross-border activities it [*sic*] will help unleash the untapped potential of the services sector in Europe. Finally, the full integration of financial markets would raise output and employment by allowing more efficient allocation of capital and creating better conditions for business finance.

The further improvement of the transposition of internal market directives should remain a priority in order to reap the benefits of a Single European market. Furthermore, directives are often not implemented or applied correctly, as illustrated by the high number of infringement proceedings launched by the Commission. Member States need to cooperate more positively with each other and with the Commission to ensure that they deliver the full benefits of internal market legislation to their citizens and businesses. For example, there is considerable scope for further improvements in public procurement practices. Such improvements would be reflected in an increase in the share of public procurement publicly advertised. Moreover, more open procurement would lead to significant budgetary savings for the Member States.

Guideline 12. To extend and deepen the internal market, Member States should:

1. speed up the transposition of internal market directives;

2. give priority to stricter and better enforcement of internal market legislation;

3. eliminate remaining obstacles to cross-border activity;

4. apply EU public procurement rules effectively;

5. promote a fully operational internal market of services, while preserving the European social model;

6. accelerate financial market integration by a consistent and coherent implementation and enforcement of the Financial Services Action Plan.

See also integrated guideline 'To improve matching of labour market needs' (No 20).

Ensure open and competitive markets inside and outside Europe

An open global trading system is of essential interest for the EU. As the world's leading trader and investor, our openness allows lower cost inputs for industry, lower prices for consumers, a competitive stimulus for business, and new investment. At the same time, it is important for the EU to use its influence in international negotiations to seek openness from others. Therefore the EU remains committed to further breaking down barriers to trade and investment, while it will stand firm against unfair practices in trade, investment and distorted competition.

Competition policy has played a key role in ensuring a level playing field for firms in the EU. It can also be beneficial to look at the wider regulatory framework around markets, in order to promote the conditions which allow firms to compete effectively. A further opening of European markets to competition can be achieved by a reduction in the general level of remaining State aid. This movement must be accompanied by a redeployment of remaining State aid in favour of support for certain horizontal objectives. The review of State aid rules has facilitated this.

Structural reforms that ease market entry are particularly effective for enhancing competition. These will be particularly important in markets that were previously sheltered from competition because of anticompetitive behaviour, the existence of monopolies, over-regulation (for example permits, licences, minimum capital requirements, legal barriers, shop opening hours, regulated prices, etc. may hinder the development of an effective competitive environment), or because of trade protection.

In addition, the implementation of agreed measures to open up the network industries to competition (in the areas of electricity and gas, transport, telecommunications and postal services) should help ensure lower overall prices and greater choice whilst guaranteeing the delivery of services of general economic interest to all citizens. Competition and regulatory authorities should ensure competition in liberalised markets. The satisfactory delivery of high quality Services of general economic interest at an affordable price must be guaranteed.

Empowered consumers who make informed choices will more quickly reward efficient operators. Further efforts are needed to improve the enforcement of consumer legislation which both empowers consumers and opens up the internal market to more intense competition at retail level.

External openness to trade and investment, by increasing both exports and imports, is an important spur to growth and employment and can reinforce structural reform. An open and strong system of global trade rules is of vital importance for the European economy. The successful completion of an ambitious and balanced agreement in the framework of the Doha-Round as well as the development of bilateral and regional free trade agreements, should further open up markets to trade and investment, thus contributing to raising potential growth.

Guideline 13. To ensure open and competitive markets inside and outside Europe and to reap the benefits of globalisation, Member States should give priority to:

1. the removal of regulatory, trade and other barriers that unduly hinder competition;

2. a more effective enforcement of competition policy;

3. selective screening of markets and regulations by competition and regulatory authorities in order to identify and remove obstacles to competition and market entry;

4. a reduction in State aid that distorts competition;

5. in line with the Community Framework, a redeployment of aid in favour of support for certain horizontal objectives such as research, innovation and the optimisation of human capital and for well-identified market failures;

6. the promotion of external openness, also in a multilateral context;

7. full implementation of the agreed measures to open up the network industries to competition in order to ensure effective competition in European wide integrated markets. At the same time, the delivery, at affordable prices, of effective services of general economic interest has an important role to play in a competitive and dynamic economy.

Improve European and national regulation

Market regulation is essential to create an environment in which commercial transactions can take place at a competitive price. It also serves to correct market failures or to protect market participants. Nevertheless, the cumulative impact of legislation and regulation may impose substantial economic costs. It is therefore important that legislation is well-designed, proportionate and regularly reviewed. The quality of the European and national regulatory environments is a matter of joint commitment and shared responsibility at both the EU and Member State level.

The better regulation culture has begun to take root in the EU. In the Commission's approach to better regulation, the economic, social and environmental impacts of new or revised legislation are carefully assessed to identify the potential trade-offs and synergies between different policy objectives. Moreover, existing regulation is screened for simplification potential, including of administrative burdens, and its impact on competitiveness is assessed. Finally, a common approach to measuring the administrative costs of new and existing legislation has been agreed, and an ambitious target has been set to achieve a 25% reduction in the burden arising from EU legislation and its national transposition by 2012.

Member States should set equally ambitious reduction targets for administrative burdens stemming from all levels of national legislation. More generally, Member States should adopt a comprehensive and explicit better regulation strategy, including appropriate institutional structures, monitoring tools and resources. Member States should systematically assess costs and benefits of legislative initiatives and revisions. They should improve the quality of regulation, while preserving their objectives, and simplify existing legislation. They should consult widely on the costs and benefits of regulatory initiatives; particularly where trade-offs between different policy objectives are implied. Member States should also ensure that appropriate alternatives to regulation are given full consideration. This is especially important for small and medium-sized enterprises (SMEs), which usually have only limited resources to deal with the regulatory requirements imposed by both Community and national legislation. Hence, special consideration should be given to whether SMEs could be exempted in total or in part from administrative requirements.

Guideline 14. To create a more competitive business environment and encourage private initiative through better regulation, Member States should:

1. reduce the administrative burden that bears upon enterprises, particularly on SMEs and startups;

2. improve the quality of existing and new regulations, while preserving their objectives, through a systematic and rigorous assessment of their economic, social (including health) and environmental impacts, while considering and making progress in measurement of the administrative burden associated with regulation, as well as the impact on competitiveness, including in relation to enforcement;

3. encourage enterprises in developing their corporate social responsibility.

Europe needs to foster its entrepreneurial drive more effectively and it needs more new firms willing to embark on creative or innovative ventures. Learning about entrepreneurship through all forms of education and training should be supported and relevant skills provided. The entrepreneurship dimension should be integrated in the life long learning process from school. Partnerships with companies should be encouraged. The creation and growth of businesses can be encouraged by improving access to finance and strengthening economic incentives. This can include adapting tax systems to reward success, reducing non-wage labour costs and reducing the administrative burdens for start-ups, notably through the provision of relevant business support services (especially for young entrepreneurs) and setting up of single contact points. Particular emphasis should be put on facilitating the transfer of ownership and improving rescue and restructuring proceedings in particular with more efficient bankruptcy laws. The implementation of the proposals which will be part of the upcoming 'Small Business Act' for the EU will contribute to unlocking the growth and jobs potential of SMEs.

Guideline 15. To promote a more entrepreneurial culture and create a supportive environment for SMEs, Member States should:

1. improve access to finance, in order to favour their creation and growth, in particular micro-loans and other forms of risk capital;

2. strengthen economic incentives, including by simplifying tax systems and reducing non-wage labour costs;

3. strengthen the innovative potential of SMEs;

4. provide relevant support services, like the creation of one-stop contact points and the stimulation of national support networks for enterprises, in order to favour their creation and growth in line with Small firms' Charter. In addition, Member States should reinforce entrepreneurship education and training for SMEs. They should also facilitate the transfer of ownership, modernise where necessary their bankruptcy laws, and improve their rescue and restructuring proceedings.

See also integrated guidelines 'To promote a growth- and employment-orientated and efficient allocation of resources' (No 3) and 'To facilitate all forms of innovation' (No 8, Nos 23 and 24).

Expand and improve European infrastructure

Modern infrastructure is an important factor affecting the attractiveness of locations. It facilitates mobility of persons, goods and services throughout the Union. Modern transport, energy and electronic communication infrastructure are an important factor element of the Lisbon strategy. By reducing transport costs and by widening markets, interconnected and interoperable trans-European networks help foster international trade and fuel internal market dynamics. Moreover, the ongoing liberalisation of European network industries fosters competition and drives efficiency gains in these sectors.

In terms of future investment in European infrastructure, the implementation of 30 priority transport projects identified by Parliament and Council in the trans-European network (TEN) transport guidelines, as well as the completion of the quick-start cross-border projects for transport, renewable energy and broadband communications and research (identified under the European Initiative for Growth and the implementation of the other transport projects, supported by the Cohesion Fund) should be a priority. Infrastructure bottlenecks within countries also need to be tackled. Appropriate infrastructure pricing systems can contribute to the efficient use of infrastructure and the development of a sustainable modal balance.

Guideline 16. To expand, improve and link up European infrastructure and complete priority cross-border projects with the particular aim of achieving a greater integration of national markets within the enlarged EU, Member States should:

1. develop adequate conditions for resource-efficient transport, energy and ICT infrastructures, in priority, those included in the TEN networks, by complementing Community mechanisms, notably including in cross-border sections and peripherical [*sic*] regions, as an essential condition to achieve a successful opening up of the network industries to competition;

2. consider the development of public-private partnerships;

3. consider the case for appropriate infrastructure pricing systems to ensure the efficient use of infrastructures and the development of a sustainable modal balance, emphasizing technology shift and innovation and taking due account of environmental costs and the impact on growth.

See also integrated guideline 'To facilitate the spread and effective use of ICT and build a fully inclusive information society' (No 9).

Part 2

The Employment Guidelines (2008-2010)

Proposal for a

COUNCIL DECISION

**on guidelines for the employment policies of the Member States
(under Article 128 of the EC Treaty)**

Appendix 1

Proposal for a

COUNCIL DECISION

on guidelines for the employment policies of the Member States

THE COUNCIL OF THE EUROPEAN UNION,

Having regard to the Treaty establishing the European Community, and in particular Article 128(2) thereof,

Having regard to the proposal from the Commission,[2]

Having regard to the Opinion of the European Parliament,[3]

Having regard to the Opinion of the European Economic and Social Committee,[4]

Having regard to the Opinion of the Committee of the Regions,[5]

Having regard to the Opinion of the Employment Committee,

Whereas:

1.   The reform of the Lisbon Strategy in 2005 has placed the emphasis on growth and jobs. The Employment Guidelines of the European Employment Strategy and the Broad Economic Policy Guidelines have been adopted as an integrated package,[6] whereby the European Employment Strategy has the leading role in the implementation of the employment and labour market objectives of the Lisbon Strategy.

2.   The examination of the Member States' National Reform Programmes contained in the Commission's Annual Progress Report and in the draft Joint Employment Report shows that Member States should continue to make every effort to address the priority areas of

    −   attracting and retaining more people in employment, increasing labour supply and modernising social protection systems,

    −   improving adaptability of workers and enterprises, and

    −   increasing investment in human capital through better education and skills.

---

[2]   OJ C ..., ..., p. .
[3]   OJ C ..., ..., p. .
[4]   OJ C ..., ..., p. .
[5]   OJ C ..., ..., p. .
[6]   OJ L 205, 6.8.2005, p. 21 (Employment Guidelines) and p. 28 (Broad Economic Policy Guidelines).

3. In the light of both the Commission's examination of the National Reform Programmes and the European Council conclusions, the focus should be on effective and timely implementation, paying special attention to the agreed quantitative targets and benchmarks, and in line with the conclusions of the European Council.

4. The Employment Guidelines are valid for three years, while in the intermediate years until 2010 their updating should remain strictly limited.

5. Member States should take the Employment Guidelines into account when implementing programmed Community funding, in particular of the European Social Fund.

6. In view of the integrated nature of the guideline package, Member States should fully implement the Broad Economic Policy Guidelines.

HAS ADOPTED THIS DECISION:

Article 1

The guidelines for Member States' employment policies as set out in the Annex are hereby adopted.

Article 2

The guidelines shall be taken into account in the employment policies of the Member States, which shall be reported upon in the National Reform Programmes.

Article 3

This decision is addressed to the Member States.

Done at Brussels,

For the Council
The President

ANNEX

Guidelines for the employment policies of the Member States:
promoting the European Social Model

Member States, in cooperation with the social partners, shall conduct their policies with a view to implementing the objectives and priorities for action specified below so that more and better jobs support an inclusive labour market. Reflecting the Lisbon strategy and taking into account the common social objectives, the Member States' policies shall foster in a balanced manner:

–   *Full employment:* Achieving full employment, and reducing unemployment and inactivity, by increasing the demand for and supply of labour through an integrated flexicurity approach is vital to sustain economic growth and reinforce social cohesion. This requires policies that address simultaneously the flexibility of labour markets, work organisation and labour relations, and employment security and social security.

–   *Improving quality and productivity at work:* Efforts to raise employment rates go hand in hand with improving the attractiveness of jobs, quality at work, labour productivity growth, reducing segmentation and the proportion of working poor. Synergies between quality at work, productivity and employment should be fully exploited.

–   *Strengthening social and territorial cohesion:* Determined action is needed to strengthen and reinforce social inclusion, fight poverty - especially child poverty-, prevent exclusion from the labour market, support integration in employment of people at a disadvantage, and to reduce regional disparities in terms of employment, unemployment and labour productivity, especially in regions lagging behind. Strengthened interaction is needed with the Open Method of Coordination in Social Protection and Social Inclusion.

Equal opportunities and combating discrimination are essential for progress. Gender mainstreaming and the promotion of gender equality should be ensured in all action taken. Particular attention must also be paid to significantly reducing all gender related gaps in the labour market in line with the European Pact for Gender Equality. This will assist Member States in addressing the demographic challenge. As part of a new intergenerational approach, particular attention should be paid to the situation of young people, implementing the European Youth Pact, and to promoting access to employment throughout working life. Particular attention must also be paid to significantly reducing employment gaps for people at a disadvantage, including disabled people, as well as between third-country nationals and EU citizens, in line with any national targets.

Member States should aim towards active social integration of all through promotion of labour force participation and fight poverty and exclusion of those and groups who are most marginalized in society.

In taking action, Member States should ensure good governance of employment and social policies and ensure that the positive developments in the fields of economics, labour and social affairs are mutually reinforcing. They should establish a broad partnership for change by fully involving parliamentary bodies and stakeholders, including those at regional and local levels and civil society organizations. European and national social partners should play a central role. A number of targets and benchmarks which have been set at EU level in the framework of the European Employment Strategy in the context of the 2003 guidelines should continue to be followed up with indicators and scoreboards. Member States are also encouraged to monitor the social impact of reforms and define their own commitments and targets, for which they should take these into account, as well as the country specific recommendations agreed at EU level.

Good governance also requires greater efficiency in the allocation of administrative and financial resources. In agreement with the Commission, Member States should target the resources of the Structural Funds, in particular the European Social Fund, on the implementation of the European Employment Strategy and the Union's social objectives and report on the action taken. Particular attention should be paid to strengthening institutional and administrative capacity in the Member States.

Guideline 17. Implement employment policies aiming at achieving full employment, improving quality and productivity at work, and strengthening social and territorial cohesion.

Policies should contribute to achieving an average employment rate for the European Union (EU) of 70% overall, of at least 60% for women and of 50% for older workers (55 to 64) by 2010, and to reduce unemployment and inactivity. Member States should consider setting national employment rate targets.

In addressing these objectives, action should concentrate on the following priorities:

–   attract and retain more people in employment, increase labour supply and modernise social protection systems,

–   improve adaptability of workers and enterprises,

–   increase investment in human capital through better education and skills.

1.   **Attract and retain more people in employment, increase labour supply and modernise social protection systems**

Raising employment levels is the most effective means of generating economic growth and promoting socially inclusive economies whilst ensuring a safety net for those unable to work. Promoting a lifecycle approach to work and modernising social protection systems to ensure their adequacy, financial sustainability and responsiveness to changing needs in society are all the more necessary because of the expected decline in the working-age population. Special attention should be paid to tackling the persistent employment gaps between women and men, further increasing the employment rates of older workers and young people, as part of new intergenerational approach, and the promoting active inclusion of those most excluded from the labour market. Intensified action is also required to improve the situation of young people in the labour market and to significantly reduce youth unemployment, which is on average double the overall unemployment rate.

The right conditions must be put in place to facilitate progress in employment, whether it is first time entry, a move back to employment after a break or the wish to prolong working lives. The quality of jobs, including pay and benefits, working conditions access to lifelong learning and career prospects, are crucial for a flexicurity approach, as are support and incentives stemming from social protection systems. To enhance a life cycle approach to work and to promote reconciliation between work and family life policies towards childcare provisions are necessary. Securing coverage of at least 90% of children between 3 years old and the mandatory school age and at least 33% of children under 3 years of age by 2010 is a useful benchmark. The increase in the average employment rate of parents, especially single parents, requires measures to support families. In particular, Member States should take account of the special needs of single parents and families with many children. Furthermore to prolong working lives, the effective average exit age from the labour market by 2010 would require a five year increase at EU level (compared to 59.9 in 2001). Member States should also enact measures for health protection, for prevention and for the promotion of healthy lifestyles with the goal of reducing sickness burdens, increasing labour productivity and prolonging working life.

The implementation of the European Youth Pact should also be a contribution to a lifecycle approach to work in particular by facilitating transition from education to the labour market.

Guideline 18. Promote a lifecycle approach to work through:

- a renewed endeavour to build employment pathways for young people and reduce youth unemployment, as called for in the European Youth Pact,

- resolute action to increase female participation and reduce gender gaps in employment, unemployment and pay,

- better reconciliation of work and private life and the provision of accessible and affordable childcare facilities and care for other dependants,

- support for active ageing, including appropriate working conditions, improved (occupational) health status and adequate incentives to work and discouragement of early retirement,

- modern social protection systems, including pensions and healthcare, ensuring their social adequacy, financial sustainability and responsiveness to changing needs, so as to support participation and better retention in employment and longer working lives.

See also integrated guideline 'To safeguard economic and fiscal sustainability as a basis for increased employment' (No 2).

Active inclusion policies can increase labour supply and strengthen society's cohesiveness and are a powerful means of promoting the social and labour market integration of the most disadvantaged. Every person becoming unemployed must be offered a new start in a reasonable period of time. In the case of young people this period should be short, e.g. at most 4 months by 2010; for adult people at most 12 months. Policies aiming at offering active labour market measures to the long-term unemployed should be pursued, taking into consideration the participation rate benchmark of 25% in 2010. Activation should be in the form of training, retraining, work practice, a job or other employability measure, combined where appropriate with on-going job search assistance. Facilitating access to employment for job seekers, preventing unemployment and ensuring that those who become unemployed remain closely connected to the labour market and employable are essential to increase participation, and combat social exclusion. This is also in line with a flexicurity approach. Attaining these objectives requires removing barriers to the labour market by assisting with effective job searching, facilitating access to training and other active labour market measures, ensuring affordable access to basic services and providing adequate levels of minimum resources to all. This approach should, at the same time, ensure that work pays for all workers, as well as remove unemployment, poverty and inactivity traps. Special attention should be paid to promoting the inclusion of disadvantaged people, including low-skilled workers, in the labour market, including through the expansion of social services and the social economy, as well as the development of new sources of jobs in response to collective needs. Combating discrimination, promoting access to employment for disabled people and integrating immigrants and minorities are particularly essential.

Guideline 19. Ensure inclusive labour markets, enhance work attractiveness, and make work pay for job-seekers, including disadvantaged people, and the inactive through:

- active and preventive labour market measures including early identification of needs, job search assistance, guidance and training as part of personalised action plans, provision of necessary social services to support the inclusion of those furthest away from the labour market and contribute to the eradication of poverty,

- continual review of the incentives and disincentives resulting from the tax and benefit systems, including the management and conditionality of benefits and a significant reduction of high marginal effective tax rates, notably for those with low incomes, whilst ensuring adequate levels of social protection,

- development of new sources of jobs in services for individuals and businesses, notably at local level.

To allow more people to find better employment, it is also necessary to strengthen the labour market infrastructure at national and EU level, including through the EURES network, so as to better anticipate and resolve possible mismatches. Better transitions between jobs and into employment are an essential part of a flexicurity concept and policies to enhance mobility and matching on the labour market should be promoted. Job-seekers throughout the EU should be able to consult all job vacancies advertised through Member States' employment services. Mobility of workers within the EU should be fully ensured within the context of the Treaties. Full consideration must also be given on the national labour markets to the additional labour supply resulting from immigration of third-country nationals.

Guideline 20. Improve matching of labour market needs through:

- the modernisation and strengthening of labour market institutions, notably employment services, also with a view to ensuring greater transparency of employment and training opportunities at national and European level,

- removing obstacles to mobility for workers across Europe within the framework of the Treaties,

- better anticipation of skill needs, labour market shortages and bottlenecks,

- appropriate management of economic migration.

2.   Improve adaptability of workers and enterprises

Europe needs to improve its capacity to anticipate, trigger and absorb economic and social change. This requires employment-friendly labour costs, modern forms of work organisation and well-functioning labour markets allowing more flexibility combined with employment security to meet the needs of companies and workers. This should also contribute to preventing the emergence of segmented labour markets and reducing undeclared work. To successfully meet these challenges an integrated flexicurity approach is needed, covering contractual arrangements; life long learning; active labour market policy; and social security systems (see also Guidelines 18, 19, 23).

In today's increasingly global economy with market opening and the continual introduction of new technologies, both enterprises and workers are confronted with the need, and indeed the opportunity, to adapt. While this process of structural changes is overall beneficial to growth and employment, it also brings about transformations which are disruptive to some workers and enterprises. Enterprises must become more flexible to respond to sudden changes in demand, adapt to new technologies and innovate constantly, in order to remain competitive. They must also respond to the increasing demand for job quality related to workers' personal preferences and family changes, and they will have to cope with an ageing workforce and fewer young recruits. For workers, working life is becoming more complex as working patterns become more diverse, irregular and an increasing number of transitions need to be managed successfully throughout the lifecycle. With rapidly changing economies, workers must be prepared for and furnished with lifelong learning opportunities, in order to cope with new ways of working, including enhanced exploitation of Information and Communication Technologies (ICT), and changes in their working status with associated risks of having to face temporary losses of income better accommodated through the provision of appropriate modernised social protection.

Member States should implement their own pathways, based on the common principles adopted by the Council. Flexicurity involves four key components that should be taken into account: flexible and reliable contractual arrangements through modern labour laws; collective agreements and work organisation; comprehensive lifelong learning (LLL) strategies to ensure the continual adaptability and employability of workers, particularly the most vulnerable; effective active labour market policies (ALMP) that help people cope with rapid change, reduce unemployment spells and ease transitions to new jobs; and modern social security systems that provide adequate income support, encourage employment and facilitate labour market mobility (this includes broad coverage of social protection provisions, unemployment benefits, pensions and healthcare, that help people combine work with private and family responsibilities such as childcare). Geographical mobility is also needed to access job opportunities more widely and in the EU at large.

Guideline 21. Promote flexibility combined with employment security and reduce labour market segmentation, having due regard to the role of the social partners, through:

- the adaptation of employment legislation, reviewing where necessary the different contractual and working time arrangements,

- addressing the issue of undeclared work,

- better anticipation and positive management of change, including economic restructuring, notably changes linked to trade opening, so as to minimise their social costs and facilitate adaptation,

- the promotion and dissemination of innovative and adaptable forms of work organisation, with a view to improving quality and productivity at work, including health and safety,

- support for transitions in occupational status, including training, self-employment, business creation and geographic mobility.

See also integrated guideline 'To promote greater coherence between macroeconomic, structural and employment policies' (No 5).

To maximise job creation, preserve competitiveness and contribute to the general economic framework, overall wage developments should be in line with productivity growth over the economic cycle and should reflect the labour market situation. The gender pay gap should be reduced. Particular attention should be given to the low level of wages in professions and sectors which tend to be dominated by women and to the reasons which lead to reduced earnings in professions and sectors in which women become more prominent. Efforts to reduce non-wage labour costs and to review the tax wedge may also be needed to facilitate job creation, especially for low-wage employment.

Guideline 22. Ensure employment-friendly labour cost developments and wage-setting mechanisms by:

- encouraging social partners within their own areas of responsibility to set the right framework for wage bargaining in order to reflect productivity and labour market challenges at all relevant levels and to avoid gender pay gaps,

- reviewing the impact on employment of non-wage labour costs and where appropriate adjust their structure and level, especially to reduce the tax burden on the low-paid.

See also integrated guideline 'To ensure that wage developments contribute to macroeconomic stability and growth' (No 4).

3.   Increase investment in human capital through better education and skills

Europe needs to invest more and more effectively in human capital. Too many people fail to enter, progress or remain in the labour market because of a lack of skills, or due to skills mismatches. To enhance access to employment for men and women of all ages, raise productivity levels, innovation and quality at work, the EU needs higher and more effective investment in human capital and lifelong learning in line with the flexicurity concept for the benefit of individuals, enterprises, the economy and society.

Knowledge-based and service-based economies require different skills from traditional industries; skills which also constantly need updating in the face of technological change and innovation. Workers, if they are to remain and progress in work and be prepared for transition and changing labour markets, need to accumulate and renew skills regularly. The productivity of enterprises is dependent on building and maintaining a workforce that can adapt to change. Governments need to ensure that educational attainment levels are improved and that young people are equipped with the necessary key competences, in line with the European Youth Pact. In order to improve labour market prospects for youth, the EU should aim at an average rate of no more than 10% early school leavers; and that at least 85% of 22-year olds should have completed upper secondary education by 2010. Policies should also aim at increasing the EU average level of participation in lifelong learning to at least 12.5% of the adult working-age population (25 to 64 age group). All stakeholders should be mobilised to develop and foster a true culture of lifelong learning from the earliest age. To achieve a substantial increase in public and private investment in human resources per capita and guarantee the quality and efficiency of these investments, it is important to ensure fair and transparent sharing of costs and responsibilities between all actors and to improve the evidence base of education and training policies. Member States should make better use of the Structural Funds and the European Investment Bank for investment in education and training. To achieve these aims, Member States must implement the coherent and comprehensive lifelong learning strategies to which they have committed themselves.

Guideline 23. Expand and improve investment in human capital through:

- inclusive education and training policies and action to facilitate significantly access to initial vocational, secondary and higher education, including apprenticeships and entrepreneurship training,

- significantly reducing the number of early school leavers,

- efficient lifelong learning strategies open to all in schools, businesses, public authorities and households according to European agreements, including appropriate incentives and cost-sharing mechanisms, with a view to enhancing participation in continuous and workplace training throughout the life-cycle, especially for the low-skilled and older workers.

See also integrated guideline 'To increase and improve investment in R&D, in particular by private business' (No 7).

Setting ambitious objectives and increasing the level of investment by all actors is not enough. To ensure that supply meets demand in practice, lifelong learning systems must be affordable, accessible and responsive to changing needs. Adaptation and capacity-building of education and training systems is necessary to improve their labour market relevance, their responsiveness to the needs of the knowledge-based economy and society and their efficiency and equity. ICT can be used to improve access to learning and better tailor it to the needs of employers and employees. Greater mobility for both work and learning purposes is also needed to access job opportunities more widely in the EU at large. The remaining obstacles to mobility within the European labour market should be lifted, in particular those relating to the recognition and transparency and use of qualifications and learning outcomes, notably through the implementation of the European Qualifications Framework. It will be important to make use of the agreed European instruments and references to support reforms of national education and training systems, as is laid down in the Education and Training 2010 Work Programme.

Guideline 24. Adapt education and training systems in response to new competence requirements by:

- raising and ensuring the attractiveness, openness and quality standards of education and training, broadening the supply of education and training opportunities and ensuring flexible learning pathways and enlarging possibilities for mobility for students and trainees,

- easing and diversifying access for all to education and training and to knowledge by means of working time organisation, family support services, vocational guidance and, if appropriate, new forms of cost sharing,

- responding to new occupational needs, key competences and future skill requirements by improving the definition and transparency of qualifications, their effective recognition and the validation of non-formal and informal learning.

Appendix 2: Conclusions of the Brussels European Council, March 2008

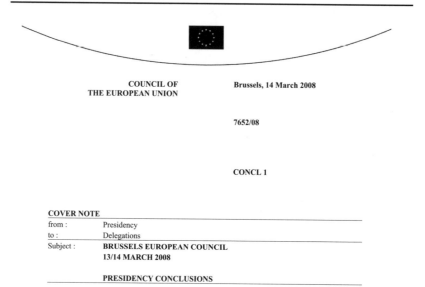

**COUNCIL OF
THE EUROPEAN UNION**

Brussels, 14 March 2008

7652/08

CONCL 1

COVER NOTE

from :	Presidency
to :	Delegations
Subject :	**BRUSSELS EUROPEAN COUNCIL** **13/14 MARCH 2008**
	PRESIDENCY CONCLUSIONS

Delegations will find attached the Presidency Conclusions of the Brussels European Council
(13/14 March 2008).

The meeting of the European Council was preceded by an exposé by the President of the European Parliament, Mr Hans-Gert Pöttering, followed by an exchange of views.

o

o   o

1. The fundamentals of the European Union economy remain sound: public deficits have been more than halved since 2005 and public debt has also declined to just under 60%. Economic growth has reached 2,9% in 2007, but is likely to be lower this year. 6,5 million jobs were created in the last two years. Although cyclical factors have played a role, these developments have been aided by the structural reforms undertaken over the last years within the framework of the Lisbon Strategy and the beneficial effects of the Euro and the single market.

2. However, the global economic outlook has deteriorated recently as a result of a slowdown of economic activity in the United States, higher oil and commodity prices, and ongoing turbulence on the financial markets. Excessive volatility and disorderly movements in exchange rates are undesirable for economic growth. In the present circumstances we are concerned about excessive exchange rate moves. This is why it is all the more essential for the Union to avoid complacency and sustain reform efforts through the full implementation of the National Reform Programmes and the Integrated Guidelines for Growth and Jobs. Efforts to complete and deepen the internal market must continue. Closely coordinated economic and financial policies must be geared towards ensuring macro-economic stability, taking up the opportunities of globalisation and addressing the challenges ahead including ageing populations, climate change and energy. In order to ensure greater stability of financial markets action is also required to strengthen their transparency and functioning and to further improve the supervisory and regulatory environment at national, EU and global level.

3. The European Council notes that recent significant increases in food and energy prices have contributed to inflationary pressures. In this regard, the European Council recalls the need to avoid distortionary policies that prevent the necessary adjustments by economic agents. It invites the Council to identify the driving forces behind developments in commodity and food prices and pursue EU and national policies which remove possible supply limitations.

LAUNCHING THE NEW CYCLE OF THE RENEWED LISBON STRATEGY FOR GROWTH AND JOBS (2008-2010)

4.   Further to the Commission's Strategic Report and in the light of work in the relevant Council formations the European Council launches the second three-year cycle of the Strategy by

–   confirming that the current Integrated Guidelines (BEPGs and Employment Guidelines) remain valid and should serve for the period 2008–2010. The Council (ECOFIN and EPSCO) is invited to formally adopt the Integrated Guidelines in accordance with the Treaty;

–   endorsing the country-specific recommendations for the economic and employment policies of the Member States and the Euro area as drawn up by the Council on the basis of the Commission's proposals. The Council is invited to formally adopt them. Member States should set out detailed and concrete actions addressing their specific policy response to the Integrated Guidelines, country-specific recommendations and 'points to watch' in their National Reform Programmes and the subsequent annual implementation reports. The Commission is invited to continue working with Member States to further develop a clear and transparent methodology for the monitoring and evaluation of Lisbon reforms;

–   taking into account the priorities identified by the Council and the concrete actions set out below, inviting the Commission, the European Parliament and the Council, within their spheres of competence, to take forward work on the 10 objectives identified in the Community Lisbon Programme, which provides a strategic reform agenda for the Community part of the renewed Lisbon Strategy; progress should be assessed annually.

5.   The focus of the new cycle will be on implementation. The European Council therefore:

–   reconfirms the four priority areas agreed at its Spring 2006 meeting as the cornerstones of the renewed Lisbon Strategy and at the same time calls for synergies among them to be exploited to a greater degree;

– invites the Commission and Member States in the context of multilateral surveillance to step up the exchange of best practices, in particular by making full use of existing methods of open coordination, efficient coordination within the euro area being of particular importance;

– invites the Commission and Member States to strengthen the involvement of relevant stakeholders in the Lisbon process;

– recognises the role of the local and regional level in delivering growth and jobs; increased ownership of the growth and jobs agenda at all levels of government will lead to more coherent and effective policymaking;

– emphasises that economic, social and territorial cohesion also contributes to fulfilling the objectives of the renewed Lisbon Strategy and welcomes the progress made in targeting cohesion funds in support of national reform programmes and implementation of the Integrated Guidelines. Now that the programming phase has been completed, the European Council calls on Member States to ensure that expenditure reflects the earmarking commitments made;

– underlines the importance of macro-economic stability in addressing longer-term challenges ahead. The EU budgetary framework, as defined by the revised Stability and Growth Pact, provides the appropriate tools in this regard. The improvement in the overall budgetary situation in the EU provides the necessary room for manoeuvre for automatic stabilisers to play if downside risks were to materialise. Countries that have reached their medium-term objective should maintain their structural position and all countries not yet at their medium-term objectives should speed up the pace of deficit and debt reduction, in line with the Council opinions on the Stability and Convergence programmes, and allocate possible higher-than-expected revenues to this objective. The quality of public finances needs to be improved by raising the efficiency and effectiveness of public expenditures and revenues, including continued efforts to combat cross-border tax evasion, modernising public administration and favouring measures in public budgets that promote productivity, employment and innovation;

Appendix 2

    – reconfirms the importance of the social dimension of the EU as an integral part of the Lisbon Strategy and in particular stresses the need to further integrate economic, employment and social policies;

    – agrees the concrete actions set out below. In this connection, the European Council endorses the key messages from the Council in its ECOFIN, Competitiveness, Employment and Social Policy, Environment and Education and Youth formations, as well as the Council conclusions on the Single Market Review.

6.   The European Council furthermore stresses that a continued EU-level commitment to structural reforms and sustainable development and social cohesion will be necessary after 2010 in order to lock in the progress achieved by the renewed Lisbon Strategy for growth and jobs. The European Council therefore invites the Commission, the Council and the National Lisbon coordinators to start reflecting on the future of the Lisbon strategy in the post-2010 period.

Investing in knowledge and innovation

7.   A key factor for future growth is the full development of the potential for innovation and creativity of European citizens built on European culture and excellence in science. Since the relaunch of the Lisbon Strategy in 2005, joint efforts have led to significant achievements in the areas of research, knowledge and innovation. The implementation of the broad-based innovation strategy is key to realising EU ambitions in the area. All the priorities of the strategy need to be taken forward rapidly. At the same time further efforts must be made, including in the private sector, with a view to investing more, and more effectively, in research, creativity, innovation and higher education and achieving the 3% R&D investment target. The European Council highlights the following actions on which the Member States and the Community are urged to make swift progress:

    • Member States are invited to set out in their National Reform Programmes how progress towards national R&D investment targets will be achieved and how their R&D strategies will contribute to the realising and better governance of the European Research Area;

- key projects, such as GALILEO, EIT, the European Research Council, the Risk-Sharing Finance Facility, the Joint Technology Initiatives must be swiftly implemented or further promoted; decisions on Article 169 initiatives and additional research initiatives should be taken as soon as possible;

- scientific e-infrastructure and high-speed internet usage must be significantly increased. Member States should aim to make high-speed internet available to all schools by 2010 and to set ambitious national targets for household access as part of their National Reform Programmes;

- an EU-wide market for venture capital for the most innovative companies must be promoted; in that respect the European Investment Fund must play a key role in the financing of innovative SMEs;

- efforts towards improving the framework conditions for innovation should be better coordinated, including through improved science–industry linkages and world-class innovation clusters and development of regional clusters and networks;

- particular attention should be given to further initiatives for joint programming of research, mutually complementary international S&T cooperation strategies and the strengthening of research infrastructure of pan-European interest;

- universities should be allowed to develop partnerships with the business community so as to benefit from complementary private sector funding.

8. In order to become a truly modern and competitive economy, and building on the work carried out on the future of science and technology and on the modernisation of universities, Member States and the EU must remove barriers to the free movement of knowledge by creating a **'fifth freedom'** based on:

    - enhancing the cross-border mobility of researchers, as well as students, scientists, and university teaching staff,

    - making the labour market for European researchers more open and competitive, providing better career structures, transparency and family-friendliness,

    - further implementing higher education reforms,

Appendix 2

- facilitating and promoting the optimal use of intellectual property created in public research organisations so as to increase knowledge transfer to industry, in particular through an 'IP Charter' to be adopted before the end of the year,
- encouraging open access to knowledge and open innovation,
- fostering scientific excellence,
- launching a new generation of world-class research facilities,
- promoting the mutual recognition of qualifications.

Unlocking the business potential, especially of SMEs

9. Decisions taken since the renewal of the Lisbon Strategy have started to improve conditions for market players. It has become easier to set up a business as all Member States have established one-stop shops or similar arrangements to facilitate registration and reduce paperwork. The European Council welcomes the progress made during 2007 on **better regulation** and considers that further efforts are needed in order to deliver crucial improvements to the competitiveness of EU business, in particular SMEs. Better regulation should be considered a high priority by each Council formation in its regulatory work. To ensure that the better regulation initiative delivers real and substantial economic benefits:

- efforts on reducing administrative burdens arising from EU legislation by 25% by 2012 should be stepped up, in line with the European Council Conclusions of March 2007; the appointment of an advisory group of independent stakeholders in the context of the Action Programme is welcomed; progress made will be evaluated at the 2009 Spring meeting on the basis of the Commission's 'Strategic Evaluation of Better Regulation';
- pending 'fast track' legislative proposals should be swiftly adopted and new ones identified, and the Commission should also continue to bring forward administrative burden reduction proposals on an ongoing basis; the simplification rolling programme should continue to be implemented;
- more should be done to develop the capacity of EU institutions on impact assessment, in line with the relevant key message from the Council (Competitiveness).

10. The **Single Market** remains a crucial driver for enhancing living standards of European citizens and Europe's competitiveness in the globalised economy. In order to further improve the functioning of the Single Market so as to allow business, in particular SMEs, and consumers to make full use of its potential the following measures and actions need to be taken forward as immediate priorities:

- ensure an effective follow-up to the Commission's Single Market Review on a yearly basis with a focus on actions needed to boost growth and jobs by removing remaining barriers to the four freedoms of the treaty, including, where appropriate, through harmonisation as well as mutual recognition. In this context market developments should be monitored in order to prioritise action in markets where there are genuine and significant barriers to market functioning and competition. Due attention must also be paid to the social dimension and services of general interest;

- reinforce efforts to strengthen competition in network industries (energy, electronic communications) and to adopt the adequate regulatory frameworks; in this context work on interconnections must be pursued and accelerated;

- ensure a complete, coherent, and timely transposition and implementation of the Services Directive which is an important step towards the creation of a genuine single market for services. In this context it is crucial to improve the functioning of 'e-Single Market' by putting in place cross-border interoperable solutions for electronic signature and e-authentication.

11. **Small and medium-sized enterprises** (SMEs) form the backbone of the European economy and have the potential to contribute significantly to creating more growth and jobs in the European Union. In order to reinforce the Union's SMEs policy and to allow them to operate more effectively in the Single Market, the following actions are of immediate importance:

- swift examination by the Council of the upcoming Small Business Act initiative setting out an integrated approach across the SMEs' life cycle in line with Better Regulation and Think Small First principles and intended to further strengthen SMEs' growth and competitiveness;

- the introduction, where justified and following screening of the acquis communautaire, of exemptions for SMEs from the administrative requirements of EU legislation;

Appendix 2

- strengthened support of research-performing and innovative SMEs with high growth potential, for example through a new European private company statute;
- further facilitation of access to finance, including through existing EU financial instruments;
- facilitation of increased participation of innovative SMEs in clusters and in public procurement.

12. Open markets and a sound international environment contribute to growth and jobs and should lead to reciprocal benefits. The EU should therefore continue its endeavours to shape globalisation by reinforcing the **external dimension of the renewed Lisbon strategy**. The European Council welcomes the Commission's intention to report annually on market access, identifying countries and sectors where significant barriers remain and believes that the EU should continue its endeavours to:

- promote free trade and openness as a means to foster growth, employment and development for itself and its trading partners and continue to take the lead in this domain;
- improve the multilateral trading system, in particular by continuing to strive for an ambitious, balanced and comprehensive agreement in the Doha Development Round;
- conclude ambitious bilateral agreements with important trading partners and further step up the efforts for integration with neighbouring countries and candidate countries through developing a common economic space;
- secure reliable access to energy and to strategic raw materials;
- strengthen existing economic relations and develop mutually beneficial strategic partnerships with emerging economic powers in a context of fair competition;
- foster regulatory cooperation, convergence of standards and equivalence of rules in the mutual interest of the EU and its partners, and improve the effectiveness of the Intellectual Property Rights enforcement system against counterfeiting.

Investing in people and modernising labour markets

13.   The education element of the knowledge triangle 'research-innovation-education' should be
       strengthened. Providing high-quality education and investing more and more effectively in
       human capital and creativity throughout people's lives are crucial conditions for Europe's
       success in a globalised world. This can bridge and facilitate the movement towards a
       'knowledge-based economy', create more and better jobs and contribute to sound fiscal
       positions. They are also effective ways of fighting inequality and poverty and can contribute
       to reducing youth unemployment.

14.   The European Council looks forward to the Commission's proposal for a renewed Social
       Agenda which should play a key role in strengthening the social dimension of the Lisbon
       Strategy by taking account of Europe's new social and labour realities and also covering
       issues such as youth, education, migration and demography as well as intercultural dialogue.
       In this context combating poverty and social exclusion, promoting active inclusion and
       increasing employment opportunities for those furthest from the labour market are all of
       major importance. To this end all the appropriate instruments and tools available at
       Community level should be used. In view of increasing skills shortages in a number of
       sectors, it invites the Commission to present a comprehensive assessment of the future skills
       requirements in Europe up to 2020, taking account of the impacts of technological change and
       ageing populations and to propose steps to anticipate future needs. Economic migration can
       play a role in meeting the needs of the labour market and can contribute to help reduce skills
       shortages. The European Council therefore considers that the employment and social impact
       of migration of third-country nationals needs to be addressed in the context of the
       Commission proposals for a common policy on migration.

Appendix 2

15. The European Council urges Member States to take concrete action to:

   - substantially reduce the number of young people who cannot read properly and the number of early school leavers, and improve the achievement levels of learners with a migrant background or from disadvantaged groups;

   - attract more adults, particularly low-skilled and older workers into education and training and further facilitate geographic and occupational mobility;

   - promote higher overall labour force participation and tackle segmentation in order to ensure active social inclusion;

   - improve policy consistency and coordination of economic, employment and social policies in order to enhance social cohesion.

16. Flexicurity strikes a balance between flexibility and security on the labour market and helps both employees and employers to seize the opportunities globalisation offers. In line with the recommendations of European social partners of October 2007 and recognizing that there is no single flexicurity model, the European Council calls on the Member States to implement the agreed common principles on flexicurity by outlining in their 2008 National Reform Programmes the national arrangements giving effect to those principles. Flexibility and security are mutually reinforcing throughout the life cycle. In this context, intergenerational solidarity should be considered within all four components of flexicurity. Continued attention needs to be given to youth employment, and in particular to the transition from education to employment in the context of the implementation of the European Youth Pact. Attention should also be given to the employment of disabled persons. The availability and affordability of quality child care should be increased in line with national and Community targets. Efforts should be pursued to reconcile work with private and family life for both women and men, substantially reduce gender pay gaps and implement the European Pact for Gender Equality. The European Alliance for Families can also contribute to achieving these aims.

CLIMATE CHANGE AND ENERGY

17. Last year the EU made firm and ambitious commitments on climate and energy policy; now, in 2008, the challenge is to deliver. In December of last year the Bali Climate Conference made an important breakthrough and launched an inclusive international negotiating process set out in full in the Bali roadmap. The EU is committed to maintaining international leadership on climate change and energy and to keeping up the momentum of negotiations on the United Nations Framework Convention on Climate Change and its Kyoto Protocol in particular at the next Conference of parties in Poznań. The objective is to secure an ambitious, global and comprehensive post-2012 agreement on climate change at Copenhagen in 2009 consistent with the EU's 2°C objective. By delivering on all the targets set by the 2007 Spring European Council, the EU will make a major contribution to this objective. A key challenge will be to ensure that this transition to a safe and sustainable low-carbon economy is handled in a way that is consistent with EU sustainable development, competitiveness, security of supply, food security, sound and sustainable public finance and economic and social cohesion. The EU proposes to contribute to an accelerated and concerted high level effort in support of the United Nations Framework Convention on Climate Change and the Bali Action Plan, to develop a coherent and consistent architecture for a post-2012 agreement that ensures scaled up finance and investment flows for both mitigation and adaptation. Taking into account that energy and climate is an integral part of the Lisbon Strategy it will also contribute positively to broader growth and jobs objectives.

Appendix 2

18. The ambitious package of proposals proposed by the Commission to implement the conclusions of the Spring European Council 2007 provides a good starting point and basis for agreement. The European Council invites the Commission to continue to support Member States' efforts to reduce their emissions of greenhouse gases through comprehensive and ambitious Community policies and measures. Comprehensive deliberations by the Council, working closely with the European Parliament, should result in an agreement on these proposals as a coherent package before the end of 2008 and consequently allow for their adoption within the current legislative term, at the latest early in 2009. In so doing, the Council should bear in mind the importance of maintaining the overall balance across the package as a whole and should base its work on the principles of transparency, economic efficiency and cost-effectiveness, and fairness and solidarity in the distribution of effort between Member States. It should also take into account Member States' different starting points, circumstances and potentials as well as achievements accomplished, and respect the need for sustainable economic growth across the Community with all sectors contributing. A cost-effective and flexible way should be followed as well when developing market-based instruments to reach energy and climate policy objectives, so as to avoid excessive costs for Member States. Stepping up to the more ambitious 30% reduction target as part of a global and comprehensive agreement needs to be built in explicitly and in a balanced, transparent and equitable way, taking into account work under the Kyoto Protocol first commitment period.

19. The European Council recognizes that in a global context of competitive markets, the risk of carbon leakage is a concern in certain sectors such as energy intensive industries particularly exposed to international competition that needs to be analysed and addressed urgently in the new ETS Directive so that if international negotiations fail, appropriate measures can be taken. An international agreement remains the best way of addressing this issue.

20.   The European Council underlines that the EU ETS forms an essential part of an integrated climate and energy policy and recognizes the importance of a single EU-wide ETS cap and an emissions reduction trajectory. The revised Directive should enhance the cost-effectiveness of the necessary emission reductions, enable the EU ETS to link to other mandatory emissions trading systems capping absolute emissions and strengthen the use of flexibility mechanisms resulting from projects implemented in third countries. The European Council also underlines the need for flexibility in achieving national non-ETS and renewable targets in line with the Action Plan adopted by the European Council in March 2007 and stresses the importance of effective national support schemes for renewable energies and an effective flexibility mechanism based on guarantees of origin as suggested by the Commission and stresses the need for Community and Member States' energy policy to increase energy efficiency and security of supply as key elements for achieving the EU's integrated climate and energy policy and sustainable economic development.

21.   The European Council recalls that the objective of proposing a regulatory framework on carbon capture and storage (CCS) is to ensure that this novel technology is deployed in an environmentally safe way, which will be demonstrated through projects, as agreed in spring 2007.

22.   In meeting the ambitious target for the use of biofuels it is essential to develop and fulfil effective sustainability criteria to ensure the commercial availability of second generation biofuels, which could in the future also be considered for the use of other forms of biomass for energy in line with the conclusions of the 2007 Spring European Council.

23.   It is necessary to achieve greater synergies between climate change and biodiversity policies as a way of securing co-benefits, in particular by strengthening mutually supportive activities and measures with regard to climate-change mitigation and adaptation and to the production, consumption of and trade in biofuels. The European Council encourages Member States and the Commission to strengthen efforts aimed at halting biodiversity loss by 2010 and beyond. The 9th Conference of the Parties to the CBD in May 2008 in Bonn and the full implementation of the NATURA 2000 network are essential steps towards achieving this objective.

24. An effective, fully-functioning and interconnected internal energy market is an essential condition for secure, sustainable and competitive supply of energy in Europe. The European Council therefore urges the Council to build on recent progress on the third internal market package for gas and electricity in order to reach political agreement by June 2008, taking full account of the Spring 2007 European Council conclusions. It invites the Commission to take account of the situation and needs of small or isolated energy markets in further developing these policies.

25. The European Council recalls the importance it attaches to enhancing the energy security of the EU and its Member States. Whereas action on climate change and energy, the internal energy market and new technologies all contribute to this objective, work must also be vigorously pursued on further developing the external dimension of the 2007-2009 Energy Policy for Europe. The European Council welcomes the progress achieved in this regard, as set out in the state of play report submitted to the Council (doc. 6778/08) and will undertake a more comprehensive assessment of progress on implementation and further actions needed in the light of the next Strategic Energy Review to be presented in November 2008 and endorsed by the Spring European Council 2009 and which will serve as the basis for the new Energy Action Plan from 2010 onwards to be adopted by the Spring 2010 European Council. This Strategic Energy Review will focus in particular on security of supply, including regarding interconnectors, and external energy policy. The European Council attaches particular importance to the EU and its Member States speaking with a common voice on energy issues with third parties.

26. The European Council welcomes the joint report from the High Representative and the Commission on the impact of climate change on international security. It underlines the importance of this issue, and invites the Council to examine the paper and to submit recommendations on appropriate follow-up action, in particular, on how to intensify cooperation with third countries and regions regarding the impact of climate change on international security by December 2008 at the latest.

27.   The transition to a safe and sustainable low carbon economy will have an impact on numerous policies and on the economic and daily life of citizens. Coherent policies exploiting the synergies relating to energy and climate change are also needed in the other three priority areas of the Lisbon Strategy as well as in other EU policy areas, including:

- developing coherent R&D and innovation policies at the European and national levels;
- unlocking the business potential of eco-industries and developing a sustainable industrial policy and sustainable and globally competitive lead markets, while taking into account the impact of Energy and Climate Change measures on competitiveness;
- promoting a sustainable transport system which allows Member States, in the framework of EU policies, to take the necessary measures to combat climate change effectively;
- considering a review of the Energy Taxation Directive to bring it more closely into line with the EU's energy and climate change objectives;
- improving energy and resource efficiency in all sectors;
- informing the consumer about the efficient use of energy in order to tackle social impacts and opportunities of Energy and Climate Change.

The European Council also invites the Commission, in bringing forward its legislative proposals on VAT rates, due in the summer of 2008, and working with the Member States, to examine areas where economic instruments, including VAT rates, can have a role to play to increase the use of energy-efficient goods and energy-saving materials.

28.   The European Council emphasises the need for sustained investment in research and development and an active take-up of new technologies in energy, as outlined recently in the European Strategic Energy Technology Plan put forward by the Commission.

29.   The European Council recognises that addressing energy and climate change is also a matter of shaping values and changing citizens' behaviour. It therefore urges national governments and European institutions to set an example by making substantial progress towards reducing energy use in their buildings and car fleets.

Appendix 2

THE STABILITY OF FINANCIAL MARKETS

30.   The European Council endorses the interim report by the Council (ECOFIN) on financial market stability. While conditions in the international financial system remain fragile, some adjustments in follow-up to the turmoil have already taken place in financial markets since last autumn as the European Central Bank, national and EU authorities and financial institutions have acted to stabilise the situation.

31.   Prompt and full disclosure of exposures to distressed assets and off-balance-sheet vehicles and/or of losses by banks and other financial institutions is essential. Improvements are needed to the prudential framework and the risk management of individual institutions, in an environment of constant financial innovation which has underscored new challenges for crisis prevention and financial supervision at national, EU and global level.

32.   In responding to the turmoil, the European Council agrees that while primary responsibility is with the private sector, authorities in the EU stand ready to take regulatory and supervisory actions where necessary. Policy action should focus on four areas:

   –   enhancing transparency for investors, markets and regulators, in particular on exposure to structured products and off-balance-sheet vehicles;

   –   improving valuation standards, in particular for illiquid assets;

   –   reinforcing the prudential framework and risk management in the financial sector, through reviewing a number of areas of the Capital Requirements Directive (CRD), and the enhancement of the management of liquidity risk. The Council encourages the Commission to proceed with consultations and to put forward its proposal by September 2008 and underlines the importance of striving for an agreement between the Council, the European Parliament and the Commission by April 2009 on the necessary regulatory changes; and

   –   improving market functioning and incentive structure, including the role of credit-rating agencies on which the EU stands ready to consider regulatory alternatives if market participants do not rapidly address these issues.

33. The current turmoil has highlighted the need for further strengthening of the financial stability framework, through enhanced prudential supervision and improved tools for financial crisis management. The European Council invites the Council (ECOFIN) to swiftly and completely implement the programme of work agreed in Autumn 2007; this encompasses further progress in Spring 2008 on:

    – financial supervision, where main issues include improvements to and convergence of key supervisory rules and standards; convergence of regulatory/financial reporting, with a view to supervision of cross-border groups; clarification of the relationship between home and host authorities appropriately reflecting their competences and responsibilities, including balanced exchange of information; the role of colleges of supervisors and improvement of the functioning of Supervisory Committees; and consideration of inclusion of an EU dimension in the mandates of national supervisors to facilitate convergence and cooperation;

    – the management of cross-border financial crisis situations, tools and procedures should be enhanced and, as a first step, a new Memorandum of Understanding on cross-border cooperation between the relevant authorities is expected to be signed in Spring 2008. On the basis of further work by mid-2008, the Council should also scrutinise the functioning of deposit guarantee schemes.

34. In addition, early warning systems at the EU and international level should be enhanced, including by strengthening the role of the IMF in oversight of macro-financial stability. On financial markets' stability issues, the EU should work in close cooperation with its international partners in the relevant fora.

35. The European Council invites the Council to continue to give high priority to these issues in the coming months, with a major review of progress in April 2008, and to monitor closely the situation so as to react swiftly to possible adverse developments. The European Council will come back to these issues as appropriate and at the latest in Autumn 2008.

Appendix 2

36. The European Council welcomes the Commission Communication on Sovereign Wealth Funds (SWFs). The European Union is committed to an open global investment environment based on the free movement of capital and the effective functioning of global capital markets. SWFs have so far played a very useful role as capital and liquidity providers with long-term investment perspective. However, the emergence of new players with a limited transparency regarding their investment strategy and objectives has raised some concerns relating to potential non-commercial practices. The demarcation between SWF and other entities is not always clear cut. The European Council agrees on the need for a common European approach taking into account national prerogatives, in line with the five principles proposed by the Commission, namely: commitment to an open investment environment; support for ongoing work in the IMF and the OECD; use of national and EU instruments if necessary; respect for EC Treaty obligations and international commitments; proportionality and transparency. The European Council supports the objective of agreeing at international level on a voluntary Code of Conduct for SWFs and defining principles for recipient countries at international level. The EU should aim to give coordinated input to this ongoing debate, and invites the Commission and the Council to continue work along these lines.

ANNEX I

STATEMENT ON 'BARCELONA PROCESS: UNION FOR THE MEDITERRANEAN'

The European Council approved the principle of a Union for the Mediterranean which will include the Member States of the EU and the non-EU Mediterranean coastal states. It invited the Commission to present to the Council the necessary proposals for defining the modalities of what will be called 'Barcelona Process: Union for the Mediterranean' with a view to the Summit which will take place in Paris on 13 July 2008.

Appendix 2

ANNEX II

LIST OF DOCUMENTS SUBMITTED TO THE EUROPEAN COUNCIL

LISBON STRATEGY FOR GROWTH AND EMPLOYMENT

Broad Economic Policy Guidelines
– Report from ECOFIN to European Council
7280/08

Country-Specific Integrated Recommendations
– Report from the Council to the European Council
7275/08

Key issues paper – contribution from Competitiveness Council
6933/08

Key messages to the Spring European Council in the fields of Education/Training and Youth
6445/08

Key messages from the EPSCO Council
7171/08

Joint Employment Report 2007/2008
7169/08

Guidelines for the Employment Policies of the Member States
7170/08

Joint report on Social Protection and Social Inclusion 2008
7274/08

Opinion of the EESC on the employment of priority categories (Lisbon Strategy)
SOC/251 – CESE 997/2007

Resolution of the CoR to be submitted to the European Spring Council 2008: The strategy for jobs and growth – handling the Lisbon paradox
CdR 331/2007

ENERGY AND CLIMATE CHANGE

Communication on a European Strategic Energy Technology Plan (SET-Plan)
– Council Conclusions
6326/1/08

Environment Council contribution to the European Council
7251/08

Climate change and international security
– Report from the Commission and the Secretary-General/High Representative
7249/08

STABILITY OF FINANCIAL MARKETS

Key issues paper – contribution from ECOFIN Council
6408/08

Stability of financial markets
– Report on the outcome of discussions in the Ecofin Council of 4 March 2008
7304/08

Sovereign Wealth Funds
– Report on the outcome of discussions in the Ecofin Council of 4 March 2008
7302/08

MISCELLANEOUS

Draft report on the progress of the European Union in 2007
7233/08

———————

Appendix 3: European Union Declaration on Globalisation, December 2007

EU DECLARATION ON GLOBALISATION

Adopted by the European Council
Brussels, 14 December 2007

Globalisation is increasingly shaping our lives by fostering the exchange of peoples, goods, services and ideas and by offering new **opportunities** to citizens and business. Greater trade flows and economic growth have increased prosperity, transforming the lifestyles of Europe's citizens and lifting millions worldwide out of poverty. But globalisation also confronts us with new economic, social, environmental, energy and security **challenges**.

We aim at **shaping globalisation** in the interests of all our citizens, based on our common values and principles. For this even the enlarged Union cannot act alone. We must engage our international partners in enhanced strategic cooperation and work together within stronger multilateral organizations. The Lisbon Treaty, in setting a reformed and lasting institutional framework improves our capacity to fulfil our responsibilities, respecting the core principles enshrined in the Berlin declaration. It will bring increased consistency to our external action.

The Union's internal and external policies need to be harnessed in order to respond to the opportunities and challenges of globalisation. We must deliver on the **Lisbon Strategy for Growth and Jobs** and further develop the four freedoms within the Internal Market while ensuring a strong social dimension and respect for the environment. This will both enhance Member States' capacity to compete in a globalised world and increase the Union's collective ability to pursue its interests and values in the world. Further reforms at national and Community levels remain the key to long-term economic success. Investment in research, innovation and education should be strengthened as a central driver for growth and jobs and to ensure that all will benefit from the opportunities of globalisation.

The EU agreed very ambitious commitments **on climate change and energy** at the Spring 2007 European Council. We will deliver on our promises and show global leadership in these fields. Yet we know that without major partners tackling with us the challenges of climate change, our efforts would remain incomplete. The Union insists on the need for a global and comprehensive post-2012 agreement involving most notably the US, Russia, China, India and Brazil, to be agreed at the latest in 2009. We will use our bilateral relations to promote joint research and technical co-operation. We should also seek ways of stepping up our development assistance in the environmental field and we will work towards increasing the role of International Financial Institutions in these issues.

Consistent macro-economic policies and stable **financial markets** are vital for sustained economic growth. The Euro already plays a major role for stability and growth in the global economy. The EU is a major global financial marketplace, benefiting from a single market for financial services and a sound supervisory framework. Work will have to be taken forward both within the EU and in the relevant international *fora* to improve prudential frameworks and transparency of financial markets.

The Union has always promoted free **trade** and openness as a means to foster growth, employment and development for itself and its trading partners and intends to continue taking the lead in this domain. We will continue striving for a balanced and global agreement in the Doha Development Agenda complemented by bilateral agreements. Dialogues with key trade partners, such as the one taking place in the context of the Transatlantic Economic Council, have started to help overcoming non tariff barriers to trade and investment. The European Union will press for increasingly open markets which should lead to reciprocal benefits. To this end, our partners must also demonstrate openness, on the basis of internationally agreed rules, in particular as concerns fair competition and the protection of intellectual property rights. With this in view the EU stands ready to assist its trade and investment partners in fostering global standards and in particular to support capacity-building in developing countries.

We will continue working with our partners to pursue vigorous and coherent **development strategies**. The European Union and its Member States are already by far the major Official Development Assistance and Humanitarian Aid donor in the world. We will deliver on our commitments in the framework of the Millennium Development Goals and expect others to do likewise. Promoting decent work and addressing the problem of communicable diseases and other global health issues also remains crucial. We recall that respect for democracy and human rights, including gender equality are fundamental for sustainable development.

The EU must be ready to share in the responsibility for **global security and stability**. Efficient use of instruments and development of capabilities of the Common Foreign and Security Policy and the European Security and Defence Policy will allow the Union to play a growing part in building a safer world. The Union is committed to effective multilateralism and strong international organizations, starting with the UN. Tackling security challenges, like terrorism, organised crime and fragile States, will benefit from our continued and principled promotion of rule of law. At the same time, we will pursue our common internal program for Freedom, Security and Justice meeting our citizens' expectations to see their security and rights safeguarded.

In the era of globalisation, **migration** is a challenge which is global in nature but mainly regional in its impact. We are further developing a comprehensive European migration policy in order to promote integration, manage legal migration and combat illegal immigration. By this we should be able to meet the challenges and reap the benefits that well-managed migration can bring for the EU and also for third countries.

The European Union is the largest market in the world and a major global player in promoting peace and prosperity. We are determined to remain so for the benefit of our citizens and people worldwide. Together, we will ensure that globalisation is a source of opportunity rather than a threat. For this, we will continue building **a stronger Union for a better world.**

Appendix 4: Official documents on the Lisbon Agenda: selected bibliography

A4.1 GENERAL DOCUMENTS

Council of the European Union (1999), *International Hearing for the Portuguese Presidency of the European Union: Employment, Economic Reforms and Social Cohesion – Towards a Europe based on Innovation and Knowledge*, Lisbon, 3–4 December 1999.

Council of the European Union (2000), Document from the Presidency, *Employment, Economic Reforms and Social Cohesion: Towards a Europe based on Innovation and Knowledge*, Ref. 5256/00, 12.01.2000.

Council of the European Union (2000), *Conclusions of the Lisbon European Council*, Ref. SN 100/00, 23–24 March 2000.

Council of the European Union (2000), Document from the Presidency, *Note on the Ongoing Experience of the Open Method of Co-ordination*, Ref. 9088/00, 14.06.2000.

Council of the European Union (2000), *Conclusions of the Santa Maria da Feira European Council*, Ref. SN 200/00, 19–20 June 2000.

Council of the European Union (2000), *Conclusions of the Nice European Council*, Ref. SN 400/00, 7–9 December 2000.

Council of the European Union (2001), *Conclusions of the Stockholm European Council*, Ref. SN 100/01, 23–24 March 2001.

Council of the European Union (2001), *Conclusions of the Gothenburg European Council*, Ref. SN 200/01, 15–16 June 2001.

Council of the European Union (2002), *Conclusions of the Barcelona European Council*, Ref. SN 100/02, 15–16 March 2002.

Council of the European Union (2002), *Conclusions of the Seville European Council*, Ref. SN 200/02, 21–22 June 2002.

Council of the European Union (2003), *Conclusions of the Brussels European Council*, Ref. SN 100/03, 20–21 March 2003.

Council of the European Union (2003), *Conclusions of the Brussels European Council*, Ref. SN 300/03, 16–17 October 2003.

Council of the European Union (2004), *Conclusions of the Brussels European Council*, Ref. SN 100/04, 25–26 March 2004.

Council of the European Union (2005), *Conclusions of the Brussels European Council*, Ref. 7619/05, 22–23 March 2005.

Council of the European Union (2005), *Conclusions of the Brussels European Council*, Ref. 10255/05, 16–17 June 2005.

Council of the European Union (2006), *Conclusions of the Brussels European Council*, Ref. 7775/1/06, 23–24 March 2006.

Council of the European Union (2007), *Conclusions of the Brussels European Council*, Ref. 7224/1/07, 8–9 March 2007.

European Commission (1993), *Growth, Competitiveness, Employment: The Challenges and Ways Forward into the 21st Century*, Luxembourg: Office for Official Publications of the European Communities.

European Commission (2000), *Contribution for the Lisbon Special European Council: An Agenda of Economic and Social Renewal for Europe*, Ref. CG1 (2000) 4, 22.02.2000.

European Commission (2001), *Realising the European Union's Potential: Consolidating and Extending the Lisbon Strategy*, COM(2001) 79, 08.02.2001.

European Commission (2001), *Sustaining the Commitments, Increasing the Pace*, COM(2001) 641 final, 08.11.2001.

European Commission (2002), *Contribution to the Barcelona Spring European Council: The Lisbon Strategy – Making Change Happen*, COM(2002) 14 final, 15.01.2002.

European Commission (2003), *Choosing to Grow: Knowledge, Innovation and Jobs in a Cohesive Society: Report to the Spring European Council, 21 March 2003 on the Lisbon Strategy of Economic, Social and Environmental Renewal*, COM(2003) 5 final, 14.01.2003.

European Commission (2004), *Report to the Spring European Council: Delivering Lisbon – Reforms for the Enlarged Union*, COM(2004) 29, 20.01.2004.

European Commission (2005), Communication to the Spring European Council, Working together for growth and jobs, *Integrated Guidelines for Growth and Jobs (2005–08)*, Luxembourg: Office for Official Publications of the European Communities.

European Commission (2005), *Working Together for Growth and Jobs: A New Start for the Lisbon Strategy*, COM(2005), 24 final, 02.02.2005.

European Commission (2005), *Delivering on Growth and Jobs: A New and Integrated Economic and Employment Co-ordination Cycle in the EU*, SEC(2005) 193, 03.02.2005.

European Commission (2005), Companion document to the Communication to the Spring European Council {COM(2005) 24}, *Working Together for Growth and Jobs, Lisbon Action Plan Incorporating EU Lisbon Programme and Recommendations for Actions to Member States for Inclusion in their National Lisbon Programmes*.

European Commission (2005), *Cohesion Policy in Support of Growth and Jobs: Community Strategic Guidelines 2007–2013*, SEC(2005) 0299, 05.07.2005.

European Commission (2005), *Common Actions for Growth and Employment: The Community Lisbon Programme*, COM(2005) 330 final, 20.07.2005.

European Commission (2006), Communication to the Spring European Council, *Time to Move up a Gear: The New Partnership for Growth and Jobs*, Luxembourg: Office for Official Publications of the European Communities.

European Commission (2007), *The European Interest: Succeeding in the Age of Globalisation*, COM(2007) 581 final, 03.10.2007.

European Commission (2008), Communication to the Spring European Council, *Strategic Report on the Renewed Lisbon Strategy for Growth and Jobs: Launching the New Cycle (2008–2010)*, Luxembourg: Office for Official Publications of the European Communities.

European Parliament (2000), *Resolution of the European Parliament on the Lisbon Special European Council*, Ref. B5–0236/0239 and 0240/2000.

European Parliament (2000), *Motion for a Resolution on the Preparation of the European Council Meeting in Feira on 19–20 June 2000*, Ref. B5–0529/2000.
European Parliament (2001), *Report on the Spring 2001 European Council: The Lisbon Process and the Path to be Followed*, A5–0034/2001, 30.01.2001.

A4.2   SPECIFIC POLICIES

Education

Council of the European Union (2001), Education, *Report on the Concrete Future Objectives of Education and Learning Systems*, Doc. 5680/01 EDUC23, 12 February 2001.
Council of the European Union (2002), *Detailed Work Programme on the Follow-up of the Objectives of Education and Training Systems in Europe*, Ref. 2002/C 142/01.
Council of the European Union (2002), *Resolution on Education and Lifelong Learning*, Ref. 8944/02, 30.05.2002.
Council of the European Union (2004), *Draft Council Resolution on Guidance throughout Life in Europe*, Ref. 8448/04, 16.04.2004.
European Commission (2000), *Amended Proposal for a Recommendation of the European Parliament and of the Council on Mobility within the Community for Students, Persons Undergoing Training, Young Volunteers, Teachers and Trainers*, COM(2000) 723 final, 09.11.2000.
European Commission (2001), *Report on the Future Objectives of Education Systems*, COM(2001) 59 final, 31.01.2001.
European Commission (2001), *eLearning Action Plan*, COM(2001) 172 final, 21.03.2001.
European Commission (2001), *Realizing the European Area of Lifelong Learning*, COM(2001) 678 final, 21.11.2001.
European Commission (2002), *Action Plan for Skills and Mobility*, COM(2002) 72 final, 13.02.2002.
European Commission (2002), *European Benchmarks for Education and Training: Follow-up to the Lisbon European Council*, COM(2002) 629 final, 20.11.2002.
European Commission (2003), *The Role of the Universities in the Europe of Knowledge*, COM(2003) 58, 05.02.2003.
European Commission (2003), *Education and Training 2010: The Success of the Lisbon Strategy Hinges on Urgent Reforms* (Draft joint interim report on the implementation of the work programme on the follow-up of the objectives of education and training systems in Europe), COM(2003) 685 final, 11.11.2003.
European Commission (2004), *The New Generation of Community Education and Training Programmes after 2006*, COM(2004) 156 final, 09.03.2004.
European Commission (2004), *Proposal for a Decision of the European Parliament and of the Council Establishing an Integrated Action Programme in the Field of Lifelong Learning*, COM(2004) 474 final, 14.07.2004.
European Commission (2006), *Implementing the Community Lisbon Programme: Fostering Entrepreneurial Mindsets through Education and Learning*, COM(2006) 33 final, 13.02.2006.

European Commission (2006), *Delivering on the Modernisation Agenda for Universities: Education, Research and Innovation*, COM(2006) 208 final, 10.05.2006.

European Commission (2006), *Implementing the Community Lisbon Programme: Proposal for a Recommendation on the Establishment of the European Qualifications Framework for Lifelong Learning*, COM(2006) 479 final, 05.09.2006.

European Commission (2006), *Efficiency and Equity in European Education and Training Systems*, COM(2006) 481 final, 08.09.2006.

European Commission (2007), *Key Competences for Lifelong Learning: European Reference Framework*, Luxembourg: Office for Official Publications of the European Communities.

European Commission (2007), *A Coherent Framework of Indicators and Benchmarks for Monitoring Progress towards the Lisbon Objectives in Education and Training*, COM(2007) 61 final, 21.02.2007.

European Commission (2007), *Promoting Young People's full Participation in Education, Employment and Society*, COM(2007) 498 final, 05.09.2007.

European Commission, Directorate-General for Education and Culture (2003), *Implementing Lifelong Learning Strategies in Europe: Progress Report on the Follow-up to the Council Resolution of 2002 – EU and EFTA/EEA Countries*, 17.12.2003.

European Ministers of Vocational Education and Training and European Commission (2002), *The Copenhagen Declaration on Enhanced Cooperation in Vocational Education and Training*, Copenhagen, 29 and 30 November 2002.

European Ministers of Vocational Education and Training and European Commission (2004), *Maastricht Communiqué on the Future Priorities of Enhanced European Cooperation in Vocational Education and Training (VET) (Review of the Copenhagen Declaration of 30 November 2002)*, 14.12.2004.

European Parliament and Council of the European Union (2006), *Recommendation no 2006/961 of 18 December on Transnational Mobility within the Community for Education and Training Purposes: European Quality Charter for Mobility*, Official Journal L 394, 30.12.2006.

Economy and Finance

Council of the European Union (2000), ECOFIN, *Report to the Nice European Council on Structural Indicators: An Instrument for Better Structural Policies*, Ref. 13217/00, 27.11.2000.

Council of the European Union (2002), *Key Issues Paper on the 2002 Broad Economic Policy Guidelines*, Ref. 6752/02, 01.03.2002.

Council of the European Union (2004), *Declaration on the Stability and Growth Pact*, CIG 83/04, 18.06.2004.

Council of the European Union (2005), *Integrated Guidelines: Broad Economic Policy Guidelines*, Ref. 10667/05, 28.06.2005.

Council of the European Union and European Commission (2001), Joint Report, *The Contribution of Public Finances to Growth and Employment: Improving Quality and Sustainability*, Ref. 6997/01.

Economic Policy Committee (2002), *Annual Report on Structural Reforms 2002*, ECFIN/EPC/171/02, 05.03.2002.

European Commission (2000), *Report on the Functioning of European Product and Capital Markets*, COM(2000) 26 final, 26.01.2000.

European Commission (2000), *Recommendation on the 2000 Broad Guidelines on the Economic Policies of the Member States and the Community*, COM(2000) 214 final, 11.04.2000.

European Commission (2000), *Financial Services Action Plan: Second Progress Report*, COM(2000) 336 final, 30.05.2000.

European Commission (2000), *Services of General Interest in Europe*, COM(2000) 580 final, 20.09.2000.

European Commission (2000), *Structural Indicators*, COM(2000) 594, 27.09.2000.

European Commission (2000), *Financial Services Priorities and Progress: Third Report*, COM(2000) 692 final, 08.11.00.

European Commission (2000), *The Contribution of Public Finances to Growth and Employment: Improving Quality and Sustainability*, COM(2000) 846 final, 21.12.2000.

European Commission (2001), *Strengthening Economic Policy Co-ordination within the Euro Area*, COM(2001) 82 final, 07.02.2001.

European Commission (2001), *Structural Indicators*, COM(2001) 619 final, 30.10.2001.

European Commission (2002), *Report on the Implementation of the Broad Economic Policy Guidelines for 2001*, COM(2002), ECFIN/16/02-EN, 21.02.2002.

European Commission (2002), *Recommendation for the Broad Economic Policy Guidelines for 2002*, COM(2002), ECFIN/210/02-EN, 24.04.2002.

European Commission (2002), *Public Finances in EMU*, COM(2002) 209 final, 14.05.2002.

European Commission (2002), *Communication on Streamlining the Annual Economic and Employment Policy Co-ordination Cycles*, COM(2002) 487 final, 03.09.2002.

European Commission (2002), *Strengthening the Coordination of Budgetary Policies*, COM(2002) 668 final, 27.11.2002.

European Commission (2003), *Structural Indicators*, COM(2003) 585 final, 08.10.2003.

European Commission (2003), *On Implementation of the Risk Capital Action Plan (RCAP)*, COM(2003) 654 final, 4.11.2003.

European Commission (2003), *The EU Economy: 2003 Review – Summary and Main Conclusions*, COM(2003) 729 final, 26.11.2003.

European Commission (2003), *Broad Guidelines of the Economic Policies of the Member States and the Community (for the 2003–2005 period)*, COM(2003) 170 final, 08.04.2003.

European Commission (2004), *Recommendation on the 2004 Update of the Broad Guidelines of the Economic Policies of the Member States and the Community (for the 2003–2005 Period)*, COM(2004) 238, 04.07.2004.

European Commission (2004), *Strengthening Economic Governance and Clarifying the Implementation of the Stability and Growth Pact*, COM(2004) 581 final, 03.09.2004.

European Commission (2006), *Public Finances in EMU – 2006:* the first year of the revised Stability and Growth Pact, COM(2007) 304 final, 13.06.2006.

European Commission (2006), *The Long-Term Sustainability of Public Finances in the EU*, COM(2006) 574 final, 12.10.2006.

European Commission (2006), *The EU Economy: 2006 Review. Strengthening the Euro Area: Key Policy Priorities,* COM(2006) 714 final, 22.11.2006.

Enterprise and Industry

European Commission (2000), *Challenges for Enterprise policy in the Knowledge-based Economy, Proposal for a Council Decision on a Multiannual Programme for Enterprise and Entrepreneurship (2001–2005)*, COM(2000)256 final, 26.04.2000.
European Commission (2000), *Benchmarking Enterprise Policy*, 05.05.2000.
European Commission (2000), *Towards Enterprise Europe: Work Programme for Enterprise Policy 2000–2005*, SEC(2000) 771, 08.05.2000.
European Commission, *European Charter for Small Enterprises*, Ref. Council of the European Union 9331/00, 09.06.2000.
European Commission (2001), *Report: Building an Entrepreneurial Europe – Activities of the Union in Favour of SMEs*, COM(2001) 98 final, 01.03.2001.
European Commission (2001), *Helping SMEs to 'Go Digital'*, COM(2001) 136 final, 13.03.2001.
European Commission (2001), *Productivity: The Key to Competitiveness of European Economies and Enterprises*, COM(2002) 262 final, 28.05.2002.
European Commission (2002), *Corporate Social Responsibility: A Business Contribution to Sustainable Development*, COM(2002) 347 final, 02.07.2002.
European Commission (2002), *Industrial Policy in an Enlarged Europe*, COM(2002) 714 final, 11.12.2002.
European Commission (2004), *Action Plan: The European Agenda for Entrepreneurship*, COM(2004) 70 final, 11.02.2004.
European Commission (2004), *Fostering Structural Change: An Industrial Policy for an Enlarged Europe*, COM(2004) 274 final, 20.4.2004.
European Commission (2006), *Global Europe: Competing in the World – a Contribution to the EU's Growth and Jobs Strategy*, COM(2006) 567 final, 04.10.2006.
European Commission (2007), *Overcoming the Stigma of Business Failure: For a Second Chance Policy – Implementing the Lisbon Partnership for Growth and Jobs*, COM(2007) 584 final, 05.10.2007.
European Commission (2007*), Strategic Energy Technology Plan (Set-plan): Towards a Low Carbon Future*, COM(2007) 723 final, 22.11.2007.

Employment

Council of the European Union (2000), Labour and Social Affairs, *Contribution for the Lisbon European Council*, Ref. 6966/00, 17.03.2000.
Council of the European Union (2000), Employment and Social Policy, *Conclusions on the Follow-up of the Lisbon European Council*, Ref. 9353/00, 09.06.2000.
Council of the European Union (2004), *Council Decision of 4 October on Guidelines for the Employment Policies of the Member States*, Ref. OJ 2004/740/EC.
Council of the European Union (2004), *Council recommendation of 14 October on the Implementation of Member States' Employment Policies*, Ref. 2004/741/EC, 29.10.2004.
Council of the European Union (2005), *Guidelines for the Employment Policies of the Member States*, Ref. 10205/05. 05.07.2005.

Employment and Labour Market Committee (2000), *Opinion with a View to the Lisbon Special European Council*, Ref. Council of the European Union 6557/00, 06.03.2000.

European Commission (2001), *New European Labour Markets, Open to All, with Access for All*, COM(2001) 116 final, 28.02.2001.

European Commission (2001), *Promoting Core Labour Standards and Improving Social Governance in the Context of Globalisation*, COM(2001) 416 final, 18.07.2001.

European Commission (2001), *Strengthening the Local Dimension of the European Employment Strategy*, COM(2001) 629 final, 06.11.2001.

European Commission (2002), *Taking Stock of Five Years of the European Employment Strategy*, COM (2002) 416 final, 17.07.2002.

European Commission (2002), *Streamlining the Annual Economic and Employment Policy Co-ordination Cycles*, COM(2002) 487 final, 03.09.2002.

European Commission (2002), *Joint Employment Report 2002*, COM(2002) 621 final, 13.11.2002.

European Commission (2003), *The Future of the European Employment Strategy (EES): A Strategy for Full Employment and Better Jobs for All*, COM(2003) 6 final, 14.01.2003.

European Commission (2003), *Employment in Europe 2003: Recent Trends and Prospects*, September 2003.

European Commission (2003), *Recommendation for a Council Recommendation on the Implementation of Member States' employment policies*.

European Commission (2003), *Proposal for a Council Decision on Guidelines for Member States' Employment Policies for the Year 2003*.

European Commission (2003), *Improving Quality in Work: A Review of Recent Progress*, COM(2003) 728 final, 26.11.2003.

European Commission (2004), *Jobs, Jobs, Jobs: Creating more Employment in Europe,* Report of the Employment Taskforce, Luxembourg: Office for Official Publications of the European Communities.

European Commission (2004), *Strengthening the Implementation of the European Employment Strategy; Proposal for a Council Decision on Guidelines for the Employment Policies of the Member States; Recommendation for a Council Recommendation on the Implementation of Member States' Employment Policies*, COM(2004) 239 final, 07.04.2004.

European Commission (2005), *Draft Joint Employment Report 2004/2005*, COM(2005) 13 final, 27.01.2005.

European Commission (2005), *Communication on the Social Agenda,* COM(2005) 33 final, 09.02.2005.

European Commission (2005), Green Paper, *Confronting Demographic Change: A New Solidarity between the Generations*, COM(2005) 94 final, 16.03.2005.

European Commission (2006), *Implementing the Partnership for Growth and Jobs: Making Europe a Pole of Excellence on Corporate Social Responsibility*, COM(2006) 136 final, 22.03.2006.

European Commission (2006), Green Paper, *Modernising Labour Law to Meet the Challenges of the 21st Century*, COM(2006) 708 final, 22.11.2006.

European Commission (2006), *Implementing the Renewed Lisbon Strategy for Growth and Jobs: A Year of Delivery*, COM(2006) 816 final, Part I, 12.12.2006.

European Commission (2007), *Improving Quality and Productivity at Work: Community Strategy 2007–2012 on Health and Safety at Work*, COM(2007) 62 final, 21.02.2007.

European Commission (2007), *Fourth Report on Economic and Social Cohesion*, COM(2007) 273 final, 30.5.2007.

European Commission (2007), *Towards Common Principles of Flexicurity: More and Better Jobs through Flexibility and Security*, COM(2007) 359 final, 27.06.2007.

Information Society

European Commission (2000), *eEurope: An Information Society for All, Progress Report*, COM(2000) 130 final, 08.05.2000.

European Commission (2000), *eEurope 2002: An Information Society for All, Action Plan Prepared for Feira European Council*, 14.06.2000.

European Commission (2000), *Amended Proposal for a Regulation of the European Parliament and of the Council on Unbundled Access to the Local Loop*, COM(2000) 761, 22.11.2000.

European Commission (2000), *eCommerce and Financial Services*, COM(2001) 66 final, 07.02.2001.

European Commission (2002), *eEurope 2002 Final Report*, COM(2003) 66 final, 11.02.2003.

European Commission (2003), *The Role of eGovernment for Europe's Future*, COM(2003) 567 final, 26.09.2003.

European Commission (2006), *Bridging the Broadband Gap*, COM(2006) 129 final, 20.03.2006.

European Commission (2006), *i2010 eGovernment Action Plan: Accelerating eGovernment in Europe for the Benefit of All*, COM(2006) 173 final, 25.04.2006.

European Commission (2006), *A Strategy for a Secure Information Society: Dialogue, Partnership and Empowerment*, COM(2006) 251 final, 31.05.2006.

European Commission (2006), *On the Review of the EU Regulatory Framework for Electronic Communications Networks and Services*, COM(2006) 334 final, 29.06.2006.

European Commission (2007), *Ageing Well in the Information Society: An i2010 Initiative – Action Plan on Information and Communication Technologies and Ageing*, COM(2007) 332 final, 14.06.2007.

European Commission (2007), *eSkills for the 21st Century: Fostering Competitiveness, Growth and Jobs*, COM(2007) 496 final, 07.09.2007.

European Parliament and Council of the European Union (2003), Decision No. 2318/2003/EC of 5 December, *Adopting a Multiannual Programme (2004 to 2006) for the Effective Integration of Information and Communication Technologies (ICT) in Education and Training Systems in Europe (eLearning Programme)*.

Innovation

European Commission (2000), *Innovation in a Knowledge-Driven Economy*, COM(2000) 567, 20.09.2000.

European Commission (2000), *Working Paper: Trends in European Innovation Policy and the Climate for Innovation in the Union*, SEC(2000) 1564.

European Commission (2001), Staff Working Paper, *2001 Innovation Scoreboard*, SEC(2001) 1414, 14.09.2001.

European Commission (2003), *Innovation Policy: Updating the Union's Approach in the Context of the Lisbon Strategy*, COM(2003) 112 final, 11.03.2003.

European Commission (2003), Staff Working Paper, *2003 European Innovation Scoreboard*, SEC(2003) 1255, 10.11.2003.

European Commission (2003), *European Competitiveness Report 2003*, SEC(2003) 1299, 12.11.2003.

European Commission (2003), *Some Key Issues in Europe's Competitiveness: Towards an Integrated Approach*, COM(2003) 704 final, 21.11.2003.

European Commission (2004), *Innovate for a Competitive Europe: A New Action Plan for Innovation*, 02.04.2004.

European Commission (2006), *Putting Knowledge into Practice: A Broad-Based Innovation Strategy for the EU*, COM(2006) 502 final, 13.09.2006.

European Commission (2006), *An Innovation-Friendly, Modern Europe*, COM(2006) 589 final, 12.10.2006.

European Investment Bank (2000), *Innovation 2000 Initiative*, Ref. Council of the European Union 6442/00, 15.03.2000.

Research and Development

Council of the European Union (2000), *Council Resolution on Establishing a European Area of Research and Innovation*, 15 June 2000.

Council of the European Union (2000), *Resolution on Making a Reality of the European Area of Research and Innovation*, 16 November 2000.

Council of the European Union (2003), *Resolution on Investing in Research for European Growth and Competitiveness*, 22 September 2003.

Council of the European Union (2003), *Resolution on the Profession and the Career of Researchers within the European Research Area (ERA)*, 10 November 2003.

Council of the European Union (2006), *Decision of 19 December Concerning the Specific Programme: People Implementing the Seventh Framework Programme of the European Community for Research, Technological Development and Demonstration Activities (2007 to 2013)*, Ref. 2006/973/EC.

Council of the European Union (2006), *Decision of 19 December Concerning the Specific Programme to be Carried Out by Means of Direct Actions by the Joint Research Centre under the Seventh Framework Programme of the European Community for Research, Technological Development and Demonstration Activities (2007 to 2013)*, Ref. 2006/975/EC.

European Commission (2000), *Towards a European Research Area*, COM(2000) 06, 18.01.2000.

European Commission (2000), *Making a Reality of the European Research Area: Guidelines for EU Research Activities (2002–2006)*, COM(2000) 612 final, 04.10.2000.

European Commission (2000), *Elaboration of an Open Method of Coordination for the Benchmarking of National Research Policies: Objectives, Methodology and Indicators*, SEC(2000) 1842, 31.10.2000.

European Commission (2001), *The International Dimension of the European Research Area*, COM(2001) 346 final, 25.06.2001.

European Commission (2001), *The Regional Dimension of the European Research Area*, COM(2001) 549 final, 03.10.2001.

European Commission (2002), *More Research for Europe: Towards 3% of GDP*, COM(2002) 499 final, 11.09.2002.

European Commission (2002), *The European Research Area: Providing New Momentum – Strengthening – Reorienting – Opening up New Perspectives*, COM(2002) 565 final, 16.10.2002.

European Commission (2003), *Investing in Research: An Action Plan for Europe*, COM(2003) 226 final, 30.04.2003.

European Commission (2003), *Researchers in the European Research Area: One Profession, Multiple Careers*, COM(2003) 436 final, 18.07.2003.

European Commission (2004), *Europe and Basic Research*, COM(2004) 9 final, 14.01.2004.

European Commission (2004), *Science and Technology, the Key to Europe's Future: Guidelines for Future European Union Policy to Support Research*, COM(2004) 353 final, 16.06.2004.

European Commission (2007), Green Paper, *The European Research Area: New Perspectives*, COM(2007) 161 final, 04.04.2007.

European Parliament, Council of the European Union (2002), *Decision Concerning the 6th Framework Programme of the European Community for Research, Technological Development and Demonstration Activities, Contributing to the Creation of the European Research Area and to Innovation (2002–2006)*, PE-CONS 3635/02, 27.06.2002.

Single Market

European Commission (2000), *Financial Services Action Plan: Second Progress Report*, COM(2000) 336 final, 30.05.2000.

European Commission (2001), *Completing the Internal Energy Market*, 13.03.2001.

European Commission (2001), *Internal Market Scoreboard*, May 2001.

European Commission (2002), *2002 Review of the Internal Market Strategy: Delivering the Promise*, COM(2002) 171 final, 11.04.2002.

European Commission (2003), *A European Initiative for Growth: Investing in Networks and Knowledge for Growth and Jobs, Final Report to the European Council*, COM(2003) 690 final, 21.11.2003.

European Commission (2007), *Action Programme for Reducing Administrative Burdens in the European Union*, COM(2007) 23 final, 24.01.2007.

European Commission (2007), *The Internal Market for Goods: A Cornerstone of Europe's Competitiveness*, COM(2007) 35 final, 14.02.2007.

European Commission (2007), *Accompanying the Communication on 'A Single Market for 21st Century Europe' Services of General Interest, Including Social Services of General Interest: A New European Commitment*, COM(2007) 725 final, 20.11.2007.

Social Dialogue

Council of the European Union (2003), *Council Decision of 6 March Establishing a Tripartite Social Summit for Growth and Employment*, 2003/174/EC.

ETUC, UNICE, CEEP (2000), *Joint Statement of Social Partners to the High Level Forum*, 15.06.2000.

ETUC, CEEP, UNICE, UEAPME (2002), *Multiannual Work Programme of the European Social Partners 2003–2005*, November 2002.

European Commission (2004), *Partnership for Change in an Enlarged Europe: Enhancing the Contribution of European Social Dialogue*, COM(2004) 557 final, 12.8.2004.

Presidency of the European Union (2000), *Presidency's Summing-Up of the Debate During the High Level Forum*, 15.06.2000.

Standing Committee on Employment (2000), *Presidency Conclusions*, Ref. ESC 501/1/00 REV 1, 13.03.2000.

UNICE/UEAPME, CEEP, ETUC (2005), *Joint Declaration on the Mid-Term Review of the Lisbon Strategy*, 15 March 2005.

UNICE/UEAPME, CEEP, ETUC (2005), *Report on Social Partner Actions on Employment in Member States*, 22 March 2005.

Social Protection and Social Inclusion

Council of the European Union (2000), COREPER, *Fight Against Poverty and Social Exclusion – Definition of Objectives for the Nice European Council: Political Agreement*, Ref. 12189/00, 10.10.2000.

Council of the European Union (2000), *EPC Progress Report on the Impact of Ageing Populations on Public Pensions Systems*, Ref. 12791/00, 30.10.2000.

Council of the European Union (2000), High-Level Working Party on Social Protection, *Progress Report on the Commission Communication on the Future Evolution of Social Protection from a Long-Term Point of View: Safe and Sustainable Pensions*, Ref. 12949/00, 06.11.2000.

Council of the European Union (2000), Employment and Social Policy, *Contribution to the Nice European Council with a View to the Adoption of a European Social Agenda*, Ref. 13880/1/00, 28.11.2000.

Council of the European Union (2001), *Joint Report on Social Inclusion, Part I: the European Union and Part II: the Member States*, Ref. 15223/01, 12.12.2001.

Council of the European Union (2002), *Fight against Poverty and Social Exclusion: Common Objectives for the Second Round of National Action Plans*, Ref. 14164/1/02, 25.11.2002.

European Commission (2000), *Building an Inclusive Europe*, COM(2000) 79 final, 01.03.2000.

European Commission (2000), *Social Trends, Prospects and Challenges*, COM(2000) 82 final, 01.03.2000.

European Commission (2000), *Proposal for a European Parliament and Council Decision Establishing a Community Action Plan to Encourage Co-operation between the Member States to Fight Social Exclusion*, COM(2000) 368 final, 16.06.2000.

European Commission (2000), *Social Policy Agenda*, COM(2000) 379 final, 28.06.2000.

European Commission (2000), *The Future Evolution of Social Protection from a Long-Term Point of View: Safe and Sustainable Pensions*, COM(2000) 622, 24.10.2000.

European Commission (2001), *Supporting National Strategies for Safe and Sustainable Pensions through an Integrated Approach*, COM(2001) 362 final, 03.07.2001.

European Commission (2002), *Scoreboard on Implementing the Social Policy Agenda*, COM(2002) 89 final, 19.02.2002.

European Commission (2002), *Joint report by the Commission and the Council on Adequate and Sustainable Pensions*.

European Commission (2003), *Strengthening the Social Dimension of the Lisbon Strategy: Streamlining Open Coordination in the Field of Social Protection*, COM(2003) 261 final, 27.05.2003.

European Commission (2003), *Proposal for a Council Decision Establishing a Social Protection Committee*, COM(2003) 305 final, 24.06.2003.

European Commission (2003), *Modernising Social Protection for More and Better Jobs: A Comprehensive Approach Contributing to Making Work Pay*, COM(2003) 842 final, 30.12.2003.

European Commission (2005), *Joint Report on Social Protection and Social Inclusion*, COM(2005)14 final, 27.01.2005.

European Commission (2005), *Communication on the Social Agenda*, COM(2005) 33 final, 09.02.2005.

European Commission (2006), *Joint Report on Social Protection and Social Inclusion*, COM(2006) 62 final, 13.02.2006.

European Commission (2006), *A Roadmap for Equality between Women and Men 2006–2010*, COM(2006) 92 final, 01.03.2006.

European Commission (2006), *Implementing the Community Lisbon Programme: Social Services of General Interest in the European Union*, COM(2006) 177 final, 26.04.2006.

European Commission (2007), *Gender Equality and Women Empowerment in Development Cooperation*, COM(2007) 100 final, 08.03.2007.

European Commission (2007), *Promoting Solidarity between the Generations*, COM(2007) 244 final, 10.05.2007.

European Parliament and Council (2001), *Decision Establishing a Programme of Community Action to Encourage Cooperation between Member States to Combat Social Exclusion*, Decision No. 50/2002/EC, 07.12.2001.

Sustainable Development

European Commission (2001), *A Sustainable Europe for a Better World: A European Union Strategy for Sustainable Development*, COM(2001) 264 final, 15.05.2001.

European Commission (2001), *Towards a Thematic Strategy on the Sustainable Use of Natural Resources*, COM(2003) 0572, 01.10.2003.

European Commission (2004), *Stimulating Technologies for Sustainable Development: An Environmental Technologies Action Plan for the European Union*, COM(2004) 38 final, 28.01.2004.

European Commission (2004), *The European Environment and Health Action Plan 2004–2010*, COM(2004) 416 final, 09.06.2004 (2 vols).

European Commission (2006), *External Action: Thematic Programme for Environment and Sustainable Management of Natural Resources Including Energy*, COM(2006) 20 final, 25.01.2006.

European Commission (2006), *Governance in the European Consensus on Development: Towards a Harmonised Approach within the European Union*, COM(2006) 421 final, 30.8.2006.

European Commission (2006), *Mobilising Public and Private finance towards Global Access to Climate-Friendly, Affordable and Secure Energy Services: The*

Global Energy Efficiency and Renewable Energy Fund, COM(2006) 583 final, 06.10.2006.

European Commission (2007), *Small, Clean and Competitive: A Programme to Help Small and Medium-Sized Enterprises Comply with Environmental Legislation*, COM(2007) 379 final, 08.10.2007.

European Parliament and Council of the European Union (2002), *Decision No. 1600/2002/EC Laying Down the Sixth Community Environment Action Programme*, 22.07.2002.

Index